THE CONTEMPORARY
UNIVERSITY: U. S. A.

THE DÆDALUS LIBRARY

Published by Houghton Mifflin Company and
The American Academy of Arts and Sciences

A New Europe? edited by Stephen R. Graubard

The Professions in America, edited by Kenneth S. Lynn

The Woman in America, edited by Robert Jay Lifton

Science and Culture, edited by Gerald Holton

Utopias and Utopian Thought, edited by Frank E. Manuel

The Contemporary University: U.S.A., edited by
    Robert S. Morison

The Negro American, edited by Talcott Parsons and
    Kenneth B. Clark

THE CONTEMPORARY
UNIVERSITY: U. S. A.

EDITED BY ROBERT S. MORISON

HOUGHTON MIFFLIN COMPANY BOSTON
THE RIVERSIDE PRESS CAMBRIDGE
1966

First Printing   R

The Introduction by Robert S. Morison, "On Judging Faculty" by
Stephen Orgel and Alex Zwerdling, "Styles of Teaching in Two New
Public Colleges" by David Riesman and Joseph Gusfield, "Rebellion in
Context" by David M. Gordon, and "The Faces in the Lecture Room" by
Kenneth Keniston are here published for the first time. Portions of
"The Arts" by W. McNeil Lowry have appeared in *Educational Theatre
Journal* (May 1962). "The Ethos of the American College Student"
by Martin Meyerson will also be found in *Higher Education in the
United States,* edited by Robert A. Goldwin (Chicago: Rand McNally,
1966). The other essays in the book appeared originally, some of them in
slightly different form, in the Fall 1964 issue of *Dædalus,*
the Journal of the American Academy of Arts and Sciences.

Printed in the United States of America

CONTENTS

CONTENTS

ROBERT S. MORISON

Introduction

MUCH HAS happened to the contemporary university during the three years since this volume was first conceived. Even more has happened to our conception of the university's nature and destiny. One sits down to summarize and to introduce with the uneasy suspicion that, almost as the words are uttered, the face being introduced is changing beyond all recognition. While our authors were thoughtfully reducing their observations and surmises to paper, events were writing even more penetrating, if not such graceful, essays on the state of the contemporary university. To illustrate how rapidly change occurs, we may note that several articles in this volume suggest a growing awareness of the concentration of talent and financial support in the two great coastal ranges which run from Boston to Norfolk and from San Francisco to San Diego. Since the essays were written, Congress has greatly increased the funds available for raising the level between these ranges and has made it clear to the established bureaucracy that it must redress the geographical balance "or else."

Perhaps we should pause for a moment to observe that the admitted geographical inequalities are not really the result of administrative whim, although administrative action can and indeed already has begun to effect a more even distribution of the funds generously supplied by the taxpayer. Of course, a good part of the geographical disparity described in Clark Kerr's scholarly paper and elaborated in still greater detail in several recent congressional hearings can be traced to what might be called in coroner's language "natural causes." Much of it is indeed due to the simple fact that there are more people in New York and California than in other places. Another aliquot can be traced to the even more interesting fact that the founders of the Massachusetts Bay Colony were more worried than were their cousins in Georgia and Alabama by the prospect of an "illiterate ministry"; but some of the unevenness is less easy to explain. Why, for example, do the great universities of the Middle West continue to produce a disproportionate share of the scholars and scientists of the country only to lose them to the mountain ranges on both coasts? This is far from a trivial question, for, when these men and women leave, they necessarily take with them the funds which increasingly supply the life blood of the American university system. Those familiar with the complicated business of recruiting the stars necessary to form a new academic constellation can think of a number of reasons for the migration; some may seem embarrassingly insignificant to those out of touch with the quirks and tastes of the academic world. Certainly the fact that Senator McCarthy represented Wisconsin at a critical period and the closely related fact that Colonel McCormick ran the most influential newspaper in the region didn't make it any easier to maintain the university standards set by Van Hise and Harper. Nor is it totally irrelevant that the home state of McKinley and Harding has found it difficult to establish a structure of taxation commensurate with the needs of a modern educational system.

In addition to these fundamental reasons, there is the possibly embarrassing admission that scientists and scholars are, after all, people—and so are their wives. The sunny beaches of California, the restaurants of San Francisco, the theaters of Broadway, the cold winds which sweep Michigan Boulevard all appear as parameters in the complex equations which determine where the brains go. As Secretary McNamara has pointed out, the money goes with them. In fairness to the dedicated civil servants in N.I.H., N.S.F., and the other responsible agencies (and it is hard to exaggerate the integrity and skill of these overworked and underappreciated officials), it must be pointed out that the figures do not support President Kerr's surmise that the concentration of effort "has probably widened the gap between those [institutions] of the first and those of the second and third ranks." Actually the evidence seems to show, if anything, that the gap has been somewhat narrowed.

Much of the highly publicized disparity consists of funds allocated to development rather than research and is a function of the concentration of industry rather than of scholarship. It is also possible to demonstrate that government funds for basic research have been distributed rather more widely than might have been expected on the basis of past research output, the availability of scientists with research training, and so on. Anyone with even casual acquaintance with the problem can think of a dozen instances in which an N.S.F. or N.I.H. grant has enabled an institution to establish an active research program essentially *de novo*.

The foregoing comment is "for the record only." Whatever the history of the situation and wherever the elusive quality of equity may lie, it is now clear that anything additional money can do to distribute scientific talent equally throughout the country will be done. The only remaining question is whether the effort will be confined to increasing the assistance to previously less supported institutions or whether aid will actually be taken from the better to improve the poorer ones. An event of last summer may indicate the direction, but it is difficult to interpret accurately. The bill for this year's appropriation to the N.S.F. was reported out of committee with the provision that not over 10 per cent of the foundation's fellowships should go to the residents of any one state. This would have reduced the aid available to New York students (a particularly hard-working and apparently gifted lot) by more than a third. The provision disappeared during consideration in the Senate. What is obscure at the present writing is how this particular dialogue will proceed in the future.

All this may seem an odd way to begin a volume on the contemporary university, but perhaps it will serve to document the contention made by many of the subsequent papers that the shape of the nation's most prominent institutions is crucially determined by the size and form of federal financial support.

Another equally striking feature of this collection of essays is the amount of space spent in discussing not the purposes of the university nor the values it embodies but its administrative form. To Presidents Kerr and Wallis and, to a somewhat less extent, Dean Heimberger, the university is first and foremost a process. It is not simply an institutional framework in which people learn, teach, investigate, and occasionally chat comfortably around the dinner table about the nature of the good life. No indeed—it is an organism in itself, and one which is rapidly evolving, if not exploding, before our very eyes. The question which runs uneasily, if not always explicitly, through the fabric of many of the articles is whether mere men can still manage the process. Here again, since the articles were originally prepared, events have written a more explicit essay which asks the same question with an insistence that cannot be ignored in spite of the obvious personal embarrassments.

The author of this introduction may be biased toward the "management" hypothesis; in the year since he wrote his article he has been swept by a quite different train of events from what he had thought of as the busy world of affairs in an office high over the corner of Sixth Avenue and 50th Street to "a secluded cloister, an ivory tower, remote from hustle and bustle, turbulent cross pressures, conflicting interests, and a sense of urgency." President Wallis was, of course, being ironic when he wrote the quoted words, but only one who returns after twenty years to an Ivy League campus way off in upstate New York can realize how ironic he really was.

It is not only that there are many more students pounding on the gates for admission; it is not even the astonishing amounts of money available almost for the asking for some purposes, and so difficult to find for others. The primary sources of stress are the great expectations under which one labors. The students not only expect to be instructed in what men have discovered about the nature of things; they positively demand to be endowed with a sense of direction and a conviction that life is worthwhile, all served up with an intimate personal friendliness rarely found even among blood relatives.

The faculty, in turn, expect salaries roughly comparable to those of middle management in large industry and a fringe benefit system that is the wonder of an increasingly paternalistic world. Not only must all these generosities be guaranteed for life by the time one reaches the age of thirty-five; in many cases they are overshadowed by the allocation of laboratory space and equipment running into the hundreds of thousands or even millions of dollars. At the same time, teaching responsibilities, or what are even more solemnly referred to as teaching "loads," have been progressively reduced so that many of the best men are in "contact" with students for as little as three hours a week.

Society at large has also developed great expectations that the knowledge industry will shortly solve most if not all of the problems which have arisen to plague the affluent society—as well as some persistent ones inherited from the scarcity society of the past. Not surprisingly, it turns out that the classical departmental structure of universities is not well adapted to devising new weapons systems, putting a man on the moon, cleaning up polluted rivers, planning for healthful and convenient cities, or learning everything one needs to know in order to deal sensibly with the emerging nations of Africa. Since these problems all require the cooperative use of several different types of knowledge, the university has found it necessary to develop interdisciplinary institutes or centers to deal with them. The least of the problems connected with their establishment is the acquisition of the necessary funds. Professor Rossi brings his personal experience with one type of affiliated institute and his sophisticated observation of other kinds to his thoughtful consideration of what is a growing problem for university administrators. Some of the historical background will be found in my own article on the influence foundations have had in tempting universities to adapt their medieval structure to the solution of modern problems. Clark Kerr reflects a relaxed acceptance of society's right to expect close collaboration from the universities it supports, while Allen Wallis represents the sturdy but now relatively small group of academic ascetics as he concludes his neatly written but still penetrating essay on this theme with Calvinist sternness: "That an activity is worth doing and involves scientists and science, or scholars and scholarship, is not . . . sufficient ground for concluding that the activity is not a menace to the university which accommodates it."

Another way of coupling the university more closely to society and one on which there is a large measure of agreement, at least in principle, is the development of continuing education for adult students already involved in careers. Mr. Ziegler gives us a brief history of this characteristic American contribution and brings his own experience to bear on a discussion of what might be done to help it achieve a fuller realization of its potential.

However one feels about the particularities involved, it is clear that the rising expectations of students, of faculty, and above all of society at large place enormous burdens on university administrators. Few even of the faculty avoid some of the resulting tension, the sense of involvement in an incompletely analyzed rush of external events. Only the vigorously idiosyncratic now find their way to the door of the Ivory Tower which still exists in some out-of-the-way corner of the campus.

In this rapidly whirling set of circumstances, how does the academic administrator determine whether or not he is doing a good job? In spite of all the worry and talk about the student and the importance of teaching, the truth is that there is simply no way of evaluating the overall results of a teaching program. Indeed, a recent attempt to explain the very diverse results of different kinds of colleges in the United States in producing graduates who go on to get a Ph.D. managed to account for all the variance by the difference in the quality of the entering students. In other words, the teaching in the best places had no more demonstrable effect than that in the most pitifully supported institutions in the rural South.

Evaluation of research output is somewhat less hopeless, but no one is very happy about weighing the number of reprints published by the faculty in a given year; and it is notoriously difficult to judge the quality or importance of new knowledge except with the aid of historical perspective.

In the absence of immediate objective criteria for appraising the output of the two most important sectors of his university, the administrator finds himself measuring his success on a more worldly scale. There are, of course, many factors that lead to victory in what Dean DeVane called "the fierce battle for prestige"—age, tradition, athletic prowess, participation of graduates in public affairs, a reputation for scholarship. Increasingly, the thing that counts, however, is the number of recognized scientists and scholars on the faculty; for it is very largely the number of prestigious scholars that determines the flow of capable graduate and post-graduate students (who do much of the actual work in the knowledge industry), and the equally important flow of funds to maintain the operation. Always in short supply, the number of top scholars appears to remain relatively constant as the needs of the university double every ten or fifteen years. As a result, much of the administrator's time and energy are spent in calculating how to attract this or that recognized scholar to his campus. The substantive issues involved in a satisfactory program of faculty recruitment are discussed with appropriate scholarly detachment by Professors Orgel and Zwerdling, but they tend to gloss over some of the more exotic features of what has now become a fascinating game. One of these is the fact that the game is played largely with other peoples' money. Most of the state universities and a very small* class of private universities expect to pay the scholar wholly out of their own pockets. Even they, however, plan to pay for most of his facilities and supporting personnel out of grants of one sort and another. Much, if not all, of the money and the supporting personnel will come with the prestigeful scientist himself, since the government agencies in effect regard most of their research grants as being tied to the "principal investigator" rather than to the institution which temporarily houses him. Thus what seems to the uninitiated like a substantial salary offer may bring in return an annual grant budget

* Possibly Harvard is the only member of this class.

of several, perhaps many times the now trivial investment. In fact, there exists the ultimate case in which the university need not even supply any of the salary for the principal investigator. A few of the special-purpose foundations grant career awards which provide generous salaries for life to prominent investigators who may work as faculty members in any institution they may choose. For a short time the National Institutes of Health conducted a similar program but found the implications for the game of university recruitment a little too rich for easy digestion.

Perhaps we have already said more than is necessary to explain why some of the classical concerns of university life have tended to become obscured in recent years and are somewhat underrepresented in this volume. Nevertheless Dean DeVane's article is a splendid statement of the values historically associated with that unique American invention: the four-year liberal-arts college. Reading it makes one realize what a serious loss collegiate education suffered last year when Professor DeVane died so soon after his retirement and at a time when his services as a consultant and guide were being sought by many developing institutions here and abroad. Although some will want to take issue with his flat statement that "only in the humanities does the old ideal of the productive scholar who is at the same time a devoted classroom teacher still flourish," no responsible person can afford to ignore his call for "some hard thinking about the future . . . [of] our most sought-after colleges . . . squeezed by two different pressures: from below by the improved instruction in the high school because of advanced credits; and from above by the strong trend towards early specialization that is demanded by the graduate and professional schools."

Concerned though we may be about the sense of urgency, the apparent confusion of purpose, the preoccupation with money and buildings, the worries about government intrusion, the gnawing uncertainty about the administrative feasibility of the multiversity, it would be a great mistake to sell the American university short. Most of its troubles come from the sudden recognition by virtually everybody of how important the university really is. It is simply much better than any other existing institution at determining not only the nature of things but the nature of man himself and of the social inventions necessary for his continued survival. If, for the moment, it seems somewhat inadequately prepared to explain to all its students and well-wishers what the purpose of its activity is, it can reasonably point out that only recently have such questions seriously been asked of the secular college. In the past the overwhelming majority of students came with a set of essentially dogmatic beliefs or "values" inculcated by home and church. The function of the college was to submit these beliefs to a certain amount of skeptical scrutiny. At its best, the classical tradition of the humanities managed to mellow the rigors of Bible-belt fundamentalism or Jansenist Catholicism with a gentlemanly understanding of literary Stoicism.

Now that many, perhaps the majority, of the students in name colleges come without much in the way of conventional religious equipment, the colleges and especially the humanities are being asked to carry a load for which they were scarcely designed. No longer can they content themselves with remodeling existing values. They are increasingly being asked to create values appropriate to radically changed circumstances. Several of the articles refer in one way or another to the need for help in defining values, and most of them look uneasily to the humanities in search of such assistance.

Almost all of the papers that refer to the humanities (and most of them do) express doubts about the present and worries over the future. The one dealing with this subject as its principal concern is frankly defensive. The following quotations from some of the articles illustrate the general lack of certainty.

DeVane: "The danger inherent in the older, and mainly verbal, liberal education is a loss of vitality and relevance, leading ultimately to stagnation."

Kerr: "Even philosophy, which once was the hub of the intellectual universe, is now itself fragmented into such diverse specialties as mathematics and semantics."

Heimberger: "Perhaps the greatest challenge of all in this day of crass materialism and self-seeking cynicism is that of finding ways to develop a new sense of personal and social values—of ethics, beauty, and humanity."

Morison: "One of the most challenging areas . . . lies precisely in the area of the humanities as the study of man in his moral relations with other men. . . . It will not be easy for many reasons."

Bush: ". . . no scientific problem is anywhere near so urgent as the preservation of individual man and his humane faculties and heritage."

There is astonishing unanimity on the nature and urgency of the task to be done. There is almost equal agreement that this is the peculiar responsibility of the humanities. In recent years, however, there seem to be few people either in or outside the humanities who are convinced that they are really up to the task.

In contrast with the uneasy state of the humanities, the sciences are booming. So rapid, in fact, is their growth and so great their prestige that their principal problem, as Professor Weiss shows, is to maintain an appropriate integration within the "educational continuum."

The challenging newcomers to the university scene are the performing and creative arts. Though they have long commanded the critical scrutiny and appreciation of university scholars, their living presence within the walls raises all kinds of problems that are as yet only dimly understood. Nevertheless, so many educators are now convinced of the desirability of encouraging student participation in artistic production and so many also feel that the arts themselves can be best provided for in a university designed to represent all man's highest achievements, that the attempt is already being made in many of the less traditional institutions. Success may well depend upon how much attention is paid to the obstacles and pitfalls pointed out in Mr. Lowry's concise and forthright paper which is based on his rich experiences as a twentieth-century patron of both art and education.

The admirable American determination to bring the benefits of higher education to as many young people as possible raises another series of questions, imaginatively analyzed by Martin Meyerson. His insights are doubly valuable, perhaps, since they come from a sympathetic observer who is not, as certain of our other authors are, a member of the "educational establishment."

If rapid growth raises problems, it also provides opportunities for experimentation. Professors Riesman and Gusfield demonstrate how clinico-sociological techniques may be used to record and interpret such educational experiments at the college level. Among other things, such an article reminds us how much has been written in the past about the purposes and processes of higher education, without telling us much of what actually takes place in the classroom.

And so at last we come to the student, for whom in large part the whole complex structure was designed. Two of our authors—Kenneth Keniston, a trained psychiatrist, and David Gordon, a student himself, a participant-observer, convincingly subjective in his approach—both agree almost in complete detail about the nature of the students' plight and the various ways in which different students attempt to escape or adjust.

The conclusion seems to be that for those who know what they want to do or to be, the universities are doing an excellent job, perhaps in fact the best in history. For those who don't yet know, or who come to college, as one once entered the church, in order to be saved, the universities still leave a good deal to be desired.

We have become so accustomed to expecting our universities to respond to every social and individual need that many institutions find themselves embarrassed by their apparent failure to provide a satisfactory major or minor in individual salvation. Before we allow the embarrassment to become general, it may be wise to remember that the modern university derives much of its essential character from encouraging doubts about the validity of any short-cut or bargain-basement approach to such large questions as the meaning of human existence.

It may be that the problem is one without a general solution. Indeed, if we accept what evidence we have, it would appear to be almost impossibly difficult to be a good man without first being a good doctor, lawyer, scholar, or tradesman, not to mention a good husband or wife and father or mother.

On the record, the university is well adapted to helping its students achieve all of these particulars. Not only do those who elect to follow this course remain "unalienated," to adapt Kenneth Keniston's conservative nomenclature; most of them by their own admission also have a wonderful time acquainting themselves with the richness and variety of the world and achieving a certain sense of mastery over a part of it. If this be "narrow vocationalism," maybe the university should make the most of it, without wasting too many tears over a generalization that never existed.

At the very least, this Editor finds it hard to believe that the university is not serving its students well if an appreciable number become equipped with the openness to experience, the intellectual cultivation, and the clarity of style revealed in the essay in this volume produced by a student of the alienated generation.

This volume benefited greatly from the guidance and counsel of Stephen R. Graubard, Editor of *Dædalus*, who organized the conference held at the American Academy of Arts and Sciences and from then on commissioned and cajoled until the volume was completed. Many of the authors included in this collection of essays attended the original conference; other participants who helped shape the original *Dædalus* issue are Daniel Bell, Peter Caws, Caryl P. Haskins, Gerald Holton, Harold C. Martin, Harold Orlans, Henri Peyre, Nathan M. Pusey, and Zeph Stewart. We are grateful to the Edgar Stern Family Fund for its generous support of this inquiry.

THE CONTEMPORARY
UNIVERSITY: U.S.A.

WILLIAM C. DEVANE

The College of Liberal Arts

WE HAVE lived so long and affectionately with our colleges of liberal arts that we seldom realize what a peculiarly native growth the college in America really is. The educational system of continental Europe has never seen the need of such an institution as the college as a separate entity between school and university, or has thought such a development too expensive. The student moved from the *lycée* or the *gymnasium* directly to the university and the professional phase of his training. Such broad and liberal education as the student received was crowded into the last years of the schools, and little time was allowed the student for the slow process of physical and emotional maturing. The British system, out of which our early colleges sprang, relied upon the great public schools, such as Eton and Harrow, to provide the basic liberal education for a small élite and allowed only a very limited group to go on to the university— though it must be said that Oxford and Cambridge in the seventeenth, eighteenth, and nineteenth centuries were rather more colleges than they were universities. The American college, born in colonial days and the early days of the Republic, lacked the strong foundations of English or continental schools and was little more than a high school. It is a curious fact that a college was often established in the sparsely populated country before there was any adequate secondary school in the area at all.

The characteristic institution of higher education in America in the first two-thirds of the nineteenth century was the independent college in the small town, in a few cases accompanied by a straggling collection of embryonic advanced schools. In the compactness of its studies and the limited number of its students, as well as in its isolation, such a college often developed a personality or character of its own—or rather, two personalities which had as little as

1

possible to do with each other. One reflected the robust, energetic, philistine world of the student with its own values and mores, rewards and punishments. The other personality was the reflection of the austere, learned, formal world of the faculty. At most the two worlds recognized the boundaries which should not be crossed, and occasionally they waved a greeting across the line. This kind of college lingered on in many places, even into the twentieth century, especially the denominational college in some remote part of the country, very little changed from the model of the earlier time.

But there were some very heavy blows in preparation for the nineteenth-century college. The college in colonial days and the early days of the nation had done surprisingly well in educating the leaders for church and state which the society required. But in the early nineteenth century a rigidity set in, and a great reluctance to make any change. But the old classical curriculum had little appeal for Jacksonian democracy, and as the country grew it could no longer meet the insistent needs of a changing society. As the agrarian and industrial revolutions caught up with the country the fact was recognized by Congress in 1862 when it authorized the land-grant colleges, stressing agriculture and mechanics. In the same decade, in answer to the new necessities of the nation, the idea of the university began to take visible form. The country was rapidly becoming industrialized and secularized, and it was keenly aware of the progress of science and technology; it demanded specialists of many kinds, and these the colleges were not capable of producing.

But Germany, the intellectual capital of the world at the time, *was* producing them, and thousands of young Americans flocked to the universities there for their training. When these men returned home they brought the idea of the German university with them as a model for our rising universities here. It is significant that the German models were primarily institutions for graduate work and research. In the United States the new universities grew out of the wealthiest and most advanced of our colleges, as at Harvard, Yale, Columbia, Pennsylvania and the state universities (which were up until that time little more than colleges) of the Middle and Far West. A more spectacular development was the creation *de novo* of new and complete universities, with a college as a base as at Johns Hopkins, Cornell, Stanford and Chicago. Perhaps the most devastating blow to the nineteenth-century college was the adoption of the elective system in the 1880's to let into the classical curriculum the developing scientific studies, and ultimately the full panoply of

2

social sciences also. As a final blow, in the midst of the twentieth century a still further development has had—and will have in the future—a far-reaching effect upon the shape and internal nature of American education. Since the end of the Second World War, and partly as a result of the war, the educational system of the country has felt profoundly the effects of a second great revolution in scientific and technological thinking. Many of our greatest universities are now being transformed into vast research institutions, sometimes to the neglect or damage to their educational function, with most serious effects on the liberal arts colleges.

Primarily because of our scientific and technological achievements, since the Second World War American education has come to be looked to for leadership by much of the world. At the same time our educational establishment has no clear idea of its direction and its goals; it has no unifying and ordering conception of itself or its purpose. The component parts of the system are each going separate ways. The high school is directed towards a mass egalitarian conception of a literate democracy; the college of liberal arts is torn between general education and early specialization; the graduate and professional schools are moving steadily towards complete specialization and vocationalism. There is little cooperation between the parts at present. Of the separate parts the college of liberal arts is in the most anomalous, perhaps even untenable, position. A strong case can be made for the idea that the designing of a curriculum and a structure for the liberal arts college which will make it an organic part of a total educational plan is our most urgent problem. Almost equally pressing is the necessity for considering the nature and quality of the training of teachers for the colleges. This is no time for the colleges to be complacent; and the public, too, should cultivate a sympathetic and intelligent understanding of the latent dangers to an institution it values.

The college of liberal arts today exists in two main types: first, there is the relatively small independent college in a semirural setting, which is the direct heir of the nineteenth-century prototype; and second, there is the college which is an integral part of a complex university, situated usually in a metropolitan center such as Boston, New York, Philadelphia, Chicago or San Francisco. The old ideal of the liberal college with its roughly common curriculum and its habits of discipline and order is better preserved, perhaps, in the small independent college than in the college in the university, where there are so many rival claims on the student's interest.

3

Both kinds of colleges, however, have yielded many positions to pressures which are exerted by an affluent, materialistic and egalitarian society. The university colleges set the pace, but the small colleges follow. The tangible results of our social development may be seen in the enormous proliferation of colleges throughout the country, their eager hospitality to all applicants, their often frivolous and scandalous award of scholarships, their vast and indiscriminate programs of study, their casual intellectual standards and their elaborate development of athletics and other side shows. The public, with its low appreciation of learning, thinks of the college as a place where a career in athletics may be begun, good connections may be made, and a glossy social patina may be acquired. For its graduates the college provides a home for a hearty loyalty which one may cherish with a clear conscience and even a sense of virtue. In a violently iconoclastic age one does not easily surrender such a pleasant idolatry.

Though the public mind retains a frivolous image of the college, it is a good deal out of touch with the reality in many places. A more critical attitude towards the college has risen among educational leaders in response to international events as well as domestic needs—the Cold War, Sputnik, and reports of a more strenuous, practical and successful system of education in the Soviet Union. Critics who greatly value the liberal tradition have recently asked again such penetrating and far-reaching questions as the following: Can an originally aristocratic conception of a liberal education be adapted and enlarged to serve well a huge society profoundly committed to an egalitarian idea of democracy? Can a liberal curriculum maintain its integrity and yet accommodate such necessities as early specialization and prevocational training? Can liberal education include and make use of the empirical and pragmatic methods now in the ascendancy and yet retain its largeness of view and its sense of pattern? How much of great value in the long run must be sacrificed to immediate necessity? These are all facets of one large question which must be answered if the liberal arts college is to be preserved in a new form to serve the country well, as it has done in the past.

The small, independent liberal arts college today has excellent representatives in every part of the nation. Such colleges are most numerous in the eastern part of the country where the first of such institutions were established and where the admirable additions of the women's colleges later were mainly made. These colleges have been relieved of their isolation by modern modes of communication and travel, and for the most part they have freed themselves from denominational ties. At their best they are no longer parochial, but have wedded with much success a free contemporary open-mindedness to the older ideal of a liberal education. They have emerged as modern institutions, providing ample curricula for their students, who are sometimes quite as able as any group of college students in the country. These colleges are especially valuable to the whole educational establishment in America because they have frequently set standards of teaching which the larger institutions have seldom been able to achieve. The chief danger to such colleges is that they may not be able to maintain themselves under modern conditions and costs.

In the large number of colleges, however, the small college of quality is distinctly in the minority. In some parts of the country small colleges that are completely undistinguished are far too numerous. Too frequently their libraries are meager and their laboratories ill-equipped, their curricula are patchy and lacking in design, their standards of teaching hardly existent. They are in fierce competition with each other for students, and usually the most energetic part of such institutions is the recruiting office. Such colleges frequently owe their survival to local, parochial and denominational pride, and one often wishes that several of them would pool their meager resources to make one reasonably adequate institution. But that is hardly in the cards. One trait both the excellent and the poor colleges have in common is that neither has often been willing to engage in bold educational experiments, the good college because of an inherent conservatism, often to the point of complacency; the poor college because of the lack of imaginative leadership, and material resources.

With the rise of the universities late in the nineteenth century there had come into existence a new kind of college, the college as an integral part of a larger educational organization, the university college. And this kind of college has, of course, advantages and problems peculiar to itself. At their best these colleges have more distinguished faculties, more adequate facilities, and far greater resources than the small colleges; but they also have more distractions and more divided aims. In general a few university colleges have provided the models to which the other colleges look. In the first four decades of the twentieth century the universities and their colleges overshadowed the small independent colleges in wealth and prestige and educated such specialists and professionally trained personnel as were demanded by the government and industry. They were the granaries of gifted personnel and ideas, but their mood was relaxed. Yet underneath a seemingly calm and assured exterior changes were taking place. In the second and third decades there began to be signs that the balance in the university had shifted in favor of the graduate school and the professional schools, and against the college. This trend was usually fiercely resented by the loyal but imperceptive alumni of the college with strong traditions, and the tension could be felt in any of the older institutions. Perhaps the strain was most severe at the University of Chicago, where President Hutchins called the existence of the typical American college into question and strove to make the college at his university different from anything else in the collegiate world. The abolition of football at Chicago shocked the nation at large; to the academic profession it was probably one of the least disturbing of Mr. Hutchins' reforms.

The growth of universities in answer to the needs of the country had inevitably begun a change of direction and purpose in our leading institutions. Instead of the old ideal of devotion to teaching, the new ideal of the advancement of knowledge became the prime obligation of the institution. The professor became a specialist to a degree hitherto unknown. There have always been specialists and gifted men of ideas and research in our educational institutions, but such men were formerly usually isolated and unappreciated individuals. Such a person was Willard Gibbs at Yale; he would be astonished if he could know now in this later time the honors that have been bestowed upon his name. Of course, no one now will challenge the immense importance of the specialist for the country's health, welfare and safety, nor the obligation of the university to train such men. As Abraham Flexner said in 1930, "It is fashionable to rail at specialization; but the truth is that specialization has brought us to the point we have reached, and more highly specialized intelligence will alone carry us further."[1] It is an ineluctable fact that without the academic specialist we would not have concluded so soon or so successfully the Second World War. But the result has been that now in our universities instead of the isolated scientist or scholar, we have whole departments of specialists serving as a faculty.

The Second World War and its consequences, then, have brought about the gradual conversion in large part of many of our eminent universities to research institutions. The specialists, drawn mainly from the university campuses, had created the atomic bomb and inaugurated a new phase in the history of science and technology at such great centers as Los Alamos, Argonne and Oak Ridge. As the usefulness of this activity for safety and health was clearly demonstrated, the government went on to establish and support lavishly such gigantic agencies as the Atomic Energy Commission, the National Science Foundation, the National Institutes of Health and many others for the encouragement of scientific research, and these agencies draw heavily upon the universities. Latterly the government has extended its interest to a number of the social sciences. Moreover, because of our newly won eminence among the nations and our programs of aid around the world, specialists and research teams have been sent, often from the universities and colleges, to all parts of the globe to assist in such diverse matters as agriculture, health, economics and politics. Our huge philanthropic foundations, too, have increased their awards for research and aid at home and abroad. The research professor has become an extremely busy and important person.

This is the expense of greatness, and it is vain to regret the cost. But there is a cost, and it is mainly being paid by the college, whether that college is a unit in the structure of the university or an independent college. In the swift developments since the war both kinds of colleges are suffering neglect. The new professor as a specialist in international economics or as a research scientist is frequently absent from his university on a mission abroad, or if he is at home he is in the laboratory, where his mind is diverted from the classroom. It is teaching in the college, and sometimes in the graduate school, that has suffered. Faculty neglect of its teaching duties may well be the cause in part of the present student unrest. Only in the humanities does the old ideal of the productive scholar who is at the same time a devoted classroom teacher still flourish. Almost equally unfortunate is the fact that there are fewer first-class persons of intelligence, character and personality concerned with the urgent problems of higher education in all its phases—the wise conduct of the universities and colleges, the health of the various parts, the ordering of the curriculum, the reconciliation of the traditional heritage which has been the substance of liberal education with the empirical and pragmatic methods and insights of a newer conception. These problems are not so imperiously insistent as those of our national safety and health, but in the long run they are matters of very great importance and they cannot be ignored without serious damage to the national welfare.

7

In the present circumstances it is inevitable that there has been a change in the attitude of the faculties of many institutions towards teaching. This trend was hastened by the greatly increased number of students, overtaxed facilities and inflated costs. The decline in teaching was most keenly felt in the university colleges, where many adjustments have been made to meet the new conditions. Large lecture courses have become more numerous, television and teaching machines have had to be resorted to, and a far greater number of graduate students have been employed for the purpose of instruction of undergraduates. Just two or three years ago one of the country's most distinguished universities, but by no means one of the largest, employed 887 graduate students for the instruction of its under-graduates. A common pattern of instruction consists of two lectures a week by a teacher of some experience, with the third hour of dis-cussion conducted by the graduate student. Such courses are by no means necessarily poor; that depends upon the quality and conscien-tiousness of the lecturer and the interest and skill of the hard-pressed graduate student. From the point of view of the university these arrangements have the advantage of providing stipends for great numbers of graduate students in lieu of fellowships and scholar-ships. But in this connection a difficulty has arisen: in some fields government agencies have provided so many and such handsome fellowships that in these areas the universities frequently have had to make do with fewer graduate assistants or hire inferior ones for the teaching.

Whatever the quality of the course, a program made up entirely of lectures is an extremely impersonal education, and one wonders if such programs are not substantially responsible for the large number of students who drop out of colleges where such con-ditions prevail. In most of our colleges, and especially in the larger ones, small courses of the discussion type for freshmen and sophomores have had to be abandoned and as a consequence the variety of programs and the careful personal and academic counsel-ing which such younger students need have not been provided. By the time the student has entered his major field, usually at the beginning of his junior year, he should have developed sufficient motivation, independence and familiarity with local procedures to enable him to manage his own education and personal affairs. And indeed this frequently happens today. One has only to see

8

the crowded library reading rooms to assure oneself of the earnestness and competence of the modern undergraduate. Independent study is unquestionably good for the student, but he deserves adequate preparation before being thrust into it.

The independent liberal arts colleges which do not engage in graduate training have not yet felt as heavily as the university colleges the changes in their faculties' attitude towards teaching, but they now are beginning to feel the new conditions in the recruitment of their faculties. These colleges have not escaped the pressures of greater numbers of students; nor have they been altogether immune to the demand by government and industry for highly educated experts. This has often made it difficult for such colleges to maintain adequate and competent faculties in all departments. The better of the independent colleges, too, have experienced from the students they admit the demand for more advanced work in the first years of college, and more complete and sophisticated specialization in their later years. One has the feeling that teaching in the independent college has held up reasonably well so far in most departments; but the many threatening pressures, including greatly increased costs in all phases of its operation, are not likely to be less in the future.

A primary task for all colleges of liberal arts at the present time is to rethink and reconstruct the curriculum generously in breadth and depth in the light of the vast expansion of knowledge in our times. The danger inherent in the older, and mainly verbal, liberal education is a loss of vitality and relevance, leading ultimately to stagnation. The danger in the new developments, mainly mathematical and scientific, is a degree of desiccation and the loss of any ordered pattern; for the new, held in check too long, has a habit of overwhelming the old and creating a new imbalance. It seems clear that the conventional form of education at the college level must be renovated and enlarged if the whole concept is to be saved. That a balanced curriculum, fair to both the old and the new, must be designed is the conviction of men and women of large minds and sympathies who are citizens of the modern world and who place a value upon their inner and personal as well as their external social freedom. Beyond such necessary bases of thought as English composition, mathematics and the languages, the older liberating studies in literature, history and philosophy must be amply represented.

WILLIAM C. DEVANE

These, taken in depth, are the maturing studies. But the new curriculum must also welcome the tough-minded sciences, which are so effective in encouraging curiosity and clear thinking. As a ticket of admission as liberal studies, however, the sciences themselves must recognize and willingly assume their responsibility as vital parts of a liberal education, and abandon their customary procedure of teaching their elementary courses as the first steps towards a professional degree. Rigorous thought is the essence of science and must not be lost; but neither must the purpose of the student's education at this stage in his career be forgotten, nor the fact that science has a history and a philosophy that give meaning and direction to the whole corpus of its learning. An important principle in an integrated program is that there are no second-class courses. A place must be kept, too, for a modest degree of specialization, for the specialist is here to stay; but that place need not be as all-consuming in the student's last two years as it often is today. With careful planning it could be made broader and at the same time more useful in itself or as a base for advanced work than it now is. Like Milton's prescription for a liberal education, all this is to ask a great deal of the student and of the college, and such a generous education is not often achieved today. But when such a functional and rational curriculum is designed, with flexibility to care for differing abilities, other matters such as the time required and the proper ordering of the component parts may be easily arranged. Such a curriculum can find a broad acceptance, however, only if there is present much academic statesmanship and a willingness in vested interests to yield some of their departmental sovereignty. As a first and fundamental task, then, it is necessary for the statesmen of the colleges to design a new curriculum which will do for our time what the *Trivium* and the *Quadrivium* did for an earlier age.

Knowledge is never static in a world so active in research as ours. Recent physiological studies, now in possession of long-term records, are confirming an impression upon which our high schools and colleges have already acted. In the last hundred years there has been a steady increase in the height and weight of young people in the Western countries, and an almost equally strong trend towards an earlier physical maturity. The educational world, like the public at large, has accepted the fact without being more than dimly aware of the recent studies which provide a strong undergirding for their belief.[2] It seems possible that there has been a comparable acceleration in the intellectual maturity of adolescents. At any rate, factual studies give reason to the recent admirable movement for granting college credits and advanced placement to high school students who have done well in advanced credit examinations. Courses roughly comparable to elementary college courses are now being given by secondary schools in all parts of the country. Such a development could hardly have taken place and made the progress it has made unless the students in the schools were emotionally and intellectually ready to take on the more difficult work which advanced credit demanded. The launching of Sputnik and the public concern at the achievements reported about Russian education provided the emotional stimulus that was necessary. The excoriating comments on secondary education by Bestor and the sober judgments of Conant have directed the attention of high schools to the more substantial and useful studies—at least for those students who are preparing for the better colleges. But the suspicion remains that the high schools have been lax in their demands upon their students; the reform did not come too soon, and it is still incomplete in its scope.

The implications of the advanced credit and placement movement are far-reaching for the college. It may well be some years before a true estimate of how effective in the intellectual and emotional development of gifted students such accelerated programs may be. In the meanwhile we must steadily ask how satisfactorily high schools can provide advanced courses, and in what areas. It is already clear, I think, that the more factual and exact subjects, such as the languages and some aspects of the physical sciences and mathematics, are more successfully taken in the early years than the more discursive and inexact studies, such as philosophy and literature. But the high schools aspire to give advanced courses in all fields. In the face of these facts, which bear also upon the curriculum of the colleges, and others that affect their structure, the better colleges, especially those with plentiful applicants, have welcomed advanced credit programs. Harvard College now admits more than 150 students to its sophomore class directly from secondary school, and many other colleges by one device or another permit the able student to graduate in three years. This is done in spite of the enormously expanded body of knowledge. There is no doubt, however, that the movement has quickened the spirit of learning in the colleges as well as in the high schools. Are we willing, then, to move to the educational system of France, Germany and the Soviet Union, where the liberal college does not exist?* In any case, the American college is now in a crucial phase of its development and some hard thinking about the future is called for. These problems are almost equally important for the independent college as for the university college.

In fact, it appears that our most sought-after colleges of both kinds are in the position of being squeezed by two different pressures: from below by the improved instruction in the high school because of advanced credits; and from above by the strong trend towards early specialization that is demanded by the graduate and professional schools. In the best colleges in the East, which are usually bellwethers for the nation, three-quarters of the graduating seniors now go on to advanced work in graduate and professional schools, and the bachelor's degree has largely ceased to be a terminal one. To an extent the squeeze has been alleviated by the fact that many graduate and professional schools have abandoned the combined programs in which the student took his last college year in law or medical school; but this is immediately countered by the demand for a greater degree of concentration during the student's last two years in the field to be studied further in the advanced school. What is lost from the student's education in this process of compression and concentration are the liberal and broadening studies which are not immediately useful for obtaining entrance to the advanced school or a well-paid job on graduation. It matters little to the student that the studies he forgoes at the moment are precisely those which will lead to wisdom as he takes his place in the social order, and for happiness

---

* After the close of the Second World War, France obviously underwent a reappraisal of many of its social institutions, among them its educational system. I was visited by at least two delegations from France enquiring into the nature and procedure of the American college. It was evident that these delegations felt that the American college provided something that the French system lacked and badly needed. I agreed and suggested that the unforced intellectual maturing that was allowed the American student had its practical advantages in matters of initiative and decision; that our team sports and our cooperative and competitive activities (which in their imbalance we so decry) might possess a hidden and instinctive wisdom. It should be added that the French system of education has not changed.

12

and wholeness in his private life. One reads in *The New York Times* that engineering students at Stanford concentrate upon their engineering subjects in the regular semesters and use the relaxed summer sessions for the liberal subjects which the college requires. In the minds of the students the nonprofessional courses are second-class studies. One may think that such students will be less wise and interesting persons than they might be, and possibly less good as engineers. Stanford is not alone in this trend. In many colleges the liberal studies, whose advantages are not immediately apparent, are resisted by students or regarded as secondary fields where the work may be hastily and slightingly done. In this the student is merely reflecting the prevailing temper of his culture and his time, and it avails little to tell him that a sustained study of a foreign language and literature, for example, may prove in after years the most profitable program he could have taken, even vocationally. Equally valuable in the future for him might be the liberal study of such a science as geology, or the understanding of man to be gained from a study of anthropology, history or philosophy. But a warning to the teacher may also be appropriate. It is not enough for him to be steeped in his subject and conscious of its great intrinsic value; he must know and show its integral place in the spectrum of knowledge, and be himself a persuasive exponent of its liberal virtues.

Most serious faculty people today prefer to be associated with a graduate school. This is partly because of the weakness of so many of the country's colleges of liberal arts, and the popular Hollywood image of their frivolity. Writing in 1936, President Robert M. Hutchins could say with a good deal of truth, "Collegiate life suggests that the choices [of colleges] of undergraduates are determined by other considerations than thought. Undoubtedly, fine associations, fine buildings, green grass, good food, and exercise are excellent things for anybody. You will note that they are exactly what is advertised by every resort hotel."[3] The reality has changed very considerably since that date, but the image lingers in the public mind. Therefore, status is achieved by appointment to the graduate faculty, and also a better salary. Yet nowadays in a first-rate college undergraduate teaching is often more interesting and important, for in the college the teacher will be engaged in instructing the brightest minds and the most daring and free spirits among our youth, the leaders of the nation tomorrow in all walks of life. They are not yet as knowledgeable as the graduate student;

13

but neither are they as docile. The graduate student is too often a disciple, an embryonic replica in ability, ideas and personality of the professor, and in teaching him there are few surprises. "It is hardly an exaggeration," says Hutchins, "to say that university departments exist to train people to teach in university departments."[4] Nevertheless, the problem of recruiting an adequate faculty is more difficult for the independent college, especially if it is weak or remote, than it is for the university college.

There is, of course, a genuine shortage of highly qualified teachers and scholars to man our institutions of higher education. As we have seen, this is partly because of the great demand upon the profession for research and public service of many kinds—activities that may not be questioned if they are honest. But the present status of the professor is concerned here, too. If he does not teach in the humanities his *amour propre* demands that he have a contract upon which he can spend most of his time; he must also have young men on stipend to help him on with the job. Moreover, if he is invited to join another faculty—a common occurrence as universities scramble for prestige—he often demands a position that requires few teaching duties and liberal sabbatical arrangements. The institution that supports such a professor is fortunate to have him at home and teaching one year in three. Few independent colleges can afford such luxuries.

In recruiting and maintaining young faculty members the university college has a number of advantages, the chief one being that the college is in a university setting. Better salaries for beginning teachers are not always on the side of the university college, but to the ambitious young man the prospects are more alluring. Prestige also is usually on the side of the college in the university. Moreover, the young scholars and scientists who have taken their advanced degrees at a university are easily persuaded to stay there to continue their research in the great libraries and laboratories with which they are familiar. Further, the university college is usually in a large city and offers such cultural attractions as concerts, plays and lectures more plentifully than the college in the country. As the competition among the younger faculty sharpens and the dreaded time for thinning the ranks to make room for even younger men approaches, tension is hard to bear; but at the beginning that is still three or four years away and dismissal may never happen. In any case, the university college is a better place from which to move.

14

Against these attractions the advantages of the small college seem to be few, and for the greater part intangible. But they are not entirely negligible. The wealthier independent colleges, such as Wesleyan or Amherst in New England, Bryn Mawr or Swarthmore in the Middle Atlantic district, and others like Oberlin, Carleton or Reed can often outbid the university college for younger men in salary and rank; nor are the students of these colleges less able and attractive. The young man or woman of a philosophical tempera- ment may prefer the relative quiet of the small college and shy away from the fierce competition of the university and the insistent demand for instant publication. The compact college community, though it may beget claustrophobia in some, will give others a sense of belonging and possession. It is probable, too, that the young man in the small college will rise faster, be able sooner to teach what he likes, and if he wishes may sooner have an active part in the councils and conduct of the college. Frequently, also, the living conditions in the small college are better for raising a family, and the automobile, airplane and television have relieved the college of much of its isolation. The less wealthy small college, however, especially if it is inhospitable to a generous intellectual freedom, has had to take for its faculty what it can get, and that is sometimes very poor.

Estimates of the quality of a faculty, however, are never grounded on a close inspection of its teaching effectiveness but rather on the well-publicized notion that the more Ph.D.'s a faculty has in its ranks the better it is. This notion is a large and easy assumption, and may be false in the matter of teaching as apart from research, but it is indubitably true that almost all small colleges are eager to have as many doctors of philosophy on their faculties as they can get. It is equally true that the number of Ph.D.'s in these colleges is small and is decreasing year by year. One sometimes wonders why the small college, whose interest is mainly in teaching, values so much the product of the graduate school whose training is so entirely devoted to research. The college has the right and duty to expect from its faculty depth and breadth of learning, power to communicate ideas, and in- terest in the development of youth. The doctor's degree does not guarantee these qualities. In any case, the less wealthy and less favored college often has a very difficult time in recruiting a com- petent faculty, and usually it has to settle for less.

A few further observations may be made in the matter of re-

cruiting a young or able faculty. First, as we have seen, the university college on the whole has the easier task, for the ambitious young scholar and scientist will usually choose the greater opportunity that he sees in the larger institution. The recruitment of older and well-established scholars and scientists is chiefly the concern of universities; the fierce battle for prestige which is prevalent today in the universities has not spread substantially to the colleges, for few of them are willing or able to offer salaries of $25,000 to professors who may be expected to do little teaching. Another point must be noted here. Though the competition for younger men and women is keen in many disciplines, the demand differs from field to field. It is greatest in those fields which are nowadays so needed in research and in public service. These are mathematics and the physical sciences, economics, psychology, anthropology and political science. In these areas it is usually necessary to offer the new Ph.D. the rank and salary of an assistant professor to attract him. But there are occasional shortages of available young teachers, although to a lesser degree, in fields which are new to the academic scene in America or in disciplines in which for some reason not many scholars have been trained in recent years. Examples of the first kind may be seen in Chinese literature or history; of the second kind, surprisingly enough, in the classics and Germanic languages and literatures. A final comment may be made: in the humanities and in some of the social sciences the quality and extent of the institution's library is a matter of much consequence in recruiting a faculty, old or young; the sciences and the more mathematical and newer disciplines depend naturally more on laboratories and computing machines and instruments, and this equipment is standard as the libraries are not. For this reason, as well as for others, the scientist is more mobile and changes his institution with less loss of time and less strain than the humanist.

Given, then, the present trends in higher education in the United States, it may be an interesting exercise to conjecture where we shall be a quarter of a century hence, and especially where the college of liberal arts will be, since its situation is the most dubious at the present time. I have reached the conclusion after much thought that we should not remain in the state of despondency about the American college of liberal arts and sciences that some of its most recent critics have assumed. For together with the fact of constant change there is also present in higher

education a strong principle of continuity and tradition. But first a few words are pertinent, I think, upon higher education as a whole.

At one extravagant extreme in the national development is the "multiversity" of President Clark Kerr's admiration. This gigantic "city" is a vast collection of heterogeneous communities huddled together under one name. Here there are separate, almost autonomous, schools and institutes with different purposes and qualities. The college of 1900, still the dominant part of higher education in spite of the emerging universities, was rank with personality though lacking in intellectual vitality. The multiversity is rife with intellect but has no personality at all. No doubt the country will have a few multiversities, but surely not many, and they will hardly engage the sympathy and understanding of the public, however useful they may be. A few institutions, too, may become purely research institutions for the federal government, and be smaller replicas of the vast research centers at Los Alamos, Livermore, Brookhaven, or Argonne. Their educational function will be sharply reduced in favor of necessary research. Still other universities no doubt will develop further as parts of a large, complex state system, such as we see in California, Michigan, Florida and elsewhere. Here, a further refinement may be introduced as the heavy pressure of student numbers forces such institutions to abandon or minimize the first two years of college and concentrate their energies upon the junior and senior years. This will require a strong and large system of junior colleges as feeders to the university centers. However useful such a system will undoubtedly be, I am not persuaded that it is suitable for the liberal studies in satisfactory depth, and it will hardly be conducive to the nonintellectual values of college life. Probably the most typical institution of higher education in 1990, as perhaps it is now, will be the state university of moderate size with a strong, active college, small but substantial graduate and professional schools, and a controlled and limited program in research for the government and for itself.

All the institutions that I have described above are already in embryonic existence, and they may be expected to develop along the lines they have set with ever increasing pace. The ideal for the college of liberal arts and sciences for the future, however, does not lie in any of them. The best hope, and it is not the last hope, lies rather in the strong private university colleges and independent colleges of long traditions that are profoundly loved. Here, protected from the fiercest pressures of numbers, these institutions may provide a time and a place for the liberal studies, and think in terms of an enriched experience for undergraduates carefully chosen for their significance to the nation in the future. Their students will be an élite, but an élite of an intellectual character rather than an economic or social kind. They shall be ancestors rather than descendants. The four-year term of college life has advantages, especially in the matter of a natural and full process of maturing in personality, intellect and wisdom. But there is nothing sacred about the four-year span, and in the past it has often been challenged. The present crisis in the college The general education that usually occupied much of the first years of college has been fractured by the advanced placement movement. The work in the major field which usually took place in the last two years has been largely captured by the graduate and professional schools. If the universities and colleges will put their minds to this task, as I am sure the best of them will do, the chances of creating an exciting and life-giving intellectual climate for the undergraduate in our colleges in the next twenty-five years seems to me excellent. What is needed is a model, or several of them, and if these are provided by the strong university colleges and the best independent colleges the whole establishment of higher education in America will benefit.

REFERENCES

1. Abraham Flexner, *Universities: American, English, German* (New York, 1930), pp. 17–18.

2. See J. M. Tanner, *Education and Physical Growth* (London, 1961), for an illuminating account of this phenomenon.

3. Robert Maynard Hutchins, *The Higher Learning in America* (New Haven, 1936), p. 29.

4. *Ibid.*, p. 36.

CLARK KERR

The Frantic Race to Remain Contemporary

"THE TRUE American University," David Starr Jordan once observed, "lies in the future." It still does; for American universities have not yet developed their full identity, their unique theory of purpose and function. They still look to older and to foreign models, although less and less; and the day is coming when these models will no longer serve at all.

The American university is currently undergoing its second great transformation. The first occurred during roughly the last quarter of the nineteenth century, when the land grant movement and German intellectualism were together bringing extraordinary change. The current transformation will cover roughly the quarter century after World War II. The university is being called upon to educate previously unimagined numbers of students; to respond to the expanding claims of government and industry and other segments of society as never before; to adapt to and channel new intellectual currents. By the end of this period, there will be a truly American university, an institution unique in world history, an institution not looking to other models but itself serving as a model for universities in other parts of the globe. This is not said in boast. It is simply that the imperatives that are molding the American university are also at work around the world.

Each nation, as it has become influential, has tended to develop the leading intellectual institutions of its world—Greece, the Italian cities, France, Spain, England, Germany, and now the United States. The great universities have developed in the great periods of the great political entities of history. Today, more than ever, education

This article is adapted in substantial part from the author's Godkin Lectures delivered at Harvard University in 1963, which were published by the Harvard University Press in 1963 under the title, *The Uses of the University*.

19

is inextricably involved in the quality of a nation. And the university, in particular, has become in America, and in other nations as well, a prime instrument of national purpose. This is new. This is the essence of the transformation now engulfing our universities.

American universities are currently facing four great areas of related adjustments: (1) growth, (2) shifting academic emphases, (3) involvement in the life of society, and (4) response to the new federal involvement. The direction of adjustment in each of these areas is reasonably clear; the detailed arrangements and the timing are not. There are several other areas where adjustments will be necessary but where the direction of adjustment is as yet by no means clear; and four such areas will also be noted below.

Growth

The number of university and college students in the United States will almost double during the 1960's. This addition of three million will duplicate in one decade the growth of the three centuries since Harvard was founded. The proportion of graduate students will rise considerably, and there are already 25,000 postdoctoral students.

Existing university campuses are being enlarged and many new ones founded. The University of California, for example, now has seven campuses and a total enrollment of 65,000 students. Four of those campuses will triple or more in size in the next decade. One campus admitting undergraduates for the first time this fall, and two entirely new campuses admitting students for the first time in 1965, are being planned to accommodate ultimate enrollments of 27,500 each.

But university expansion alone cannot begin to meet the demand for some kind of education beyond the high school level. In the years before World War II, post-high school study was the exception; it is rapidly becoming the norm. In California today four out of every five high school graduates seek further education; soon it will be even more. This great shift in the pattern of American education will call for many more four-year colleges, both public and private. And a particularly large number of junior colleges will be formed as the community college movement becomes nationwide. Problems of differentiation of function will arise among public sectors of higher education—junior colleges, four-year colleges, and universities—as they compete for state support. The State of California has already met that problem through legislative adoption of a Master Plan for Higher Education, and other states are working along similar lines. However the total demand for higher education may be parceled out among the public and private institutions of varying types, one fact is clear: this will be the most unprecedented period of campus development in American history, or indeed in the history of the entire world.

To accommodate the great increase in enrollments, many academic calendars are being rearranged, particularly in state-supported institutions, to permit more nearly year-round use of physical facilities. Students will be able to accelerate their work if they wish, and general students will come and go with less reference to their "class"; more of them will drop in and drop out as suits their particular schedules and needs.

There will be some further mechanization of instruction (television, language laboratories, programmed learning) to improve quality and to save faculty time for other endeavors, including more individual work with students. The sciences will almost eagerly embrace these aids to learning. The foreign language departments will be rather reluctant, because these devices can threaten their structure of faculty employment and the recruitment and utilization of graduate students.

Because of the competition for faculty members, salaries will continue to rise; fringe benefits of all sorts will be devised to tie professors to a particular campus. In addition to competition among universities, there is also intensified competition with industry and government. This competition has obvious advantages in raising faculty income, but it has its negative aspects. As the market becomes more active, internal equity will be injured, for some disciplines are much more in demand in the market than others. Teaching loads will be competitively reduced, sometimes to zero, although more teachers are needed and students are complaining about lack of attention. The identification of the professor with his university will be generally loosened—he will become more a member of a free-floating profession. The rules regarding how much time a professor can spend away from his university assignments, and those affecting the sources of his income within the university, will continue to be in great flux.

This current phenomenon of rising salaries and benefits, however, may be of relatively short duration, lasting, perhaps, for the remainder of this decade. Faculty salaries have been catching up with incomes in other professions after a historical lag. By 1970, also, the personnel deficit of today may be turning into the surplus of tomorrow as all the new Ph.D.'s roll into the market. A new plateau of compensation may be reached in the 1970's.

In addition to the great expansion of individual institutions of higher learning, there will be an increasing tendency for university centers to cooperate and even coalesce for added strength, particularly in their graduate and research programs. Allan Nevins has put it this way: "Observers of higher education can now foresee the inexorable emergence of an entirely new landscape. It will no longer show us a nation dotted by high academic peaks with lesser hills between; it will be a landscape dominated by mountain ranges." The highest peaks of the future will rise from the highest plateaus.

One such plateau runs from Boston to Washington. At the universities and laboratories situated along this range are found 46 per cent of the American Nobel Prize winners in the sciences and 40 per cent of the members of the National Academy of Sciences. A second range with its peaks runs along the California coast. C. P. Snow has written: "And now the scientific achievement of the United States is moving at a rate we all ought to marvel at. Think of the astonishing constellation of talent, particularly in the physical sciences, all down the California coast, from Berkeley and Stanford to Pasadena and Los Angeles. There is nothing like that concentration of talent anywhere in the world. It sometimes surprises Europeans to realize how much of the pure science of the entire West is being carried out in the United States. Curiously enough, it often surprises Americans too. At a guess, the figure is something like 80 percent, and might easily be higher."

The California mountain range has 36 per cent of the Nobel laureates in science and 20 per cent of the members of the National Academy of Sciences. The Big Ten and Chicago constitute a third range of academic peaks, with 10 per cent of the Nobel laureates and 14 per cent of the members of the National Academy of Sciences. These three groupings of universities—the East Coast, California, and the Big Ten and Chicago—currently produce over three quarters of the doctorates conferred in the United States. Another range may be in the process of development in the Texas-Louisiana area.

This concentration of talent partly follows history—the location of the older private and public universities. Partly it follows industrial strengths and population centers. But it also has its own logic.

No one university can cover all specialties, or cover them well enough so that there is a sufficient cluster of close intellectual colleagues. The scholar dislikes intellectual isolation, and good scholars tend to swarm together. These swarms are extraordinarily productive environments. No library can be complete, nor any graduate curriculum. Some laboratories, to be well used, must be used by more than one university. Thus the Big Ten and Chicago, through their Committee on Institutional Cooperation, are merging their library resources, creating a "common market" for graduate students, diversifying their research laboratories on a common-use basis, and parceling out foreign language specializations. Something similar is happening in the University of California system, and between Berkeley and Stanford. Harvard and M.I.T., Princeton and Pennsylvania, among others, run joint research enterprises. These clustering universities in turn have clustering around them scientifically oriented industrial and governmental enterprises. To match the drawing power of the great metropolis, there now arrives the Ideopolis. The isolated mountain can no longer dominate the landscape; the constellation is greater than the single star and adds to the brightness of the sky.

The rate of growth being forced upon American universities and colleges by the surging enrollment wave will present difficult problems. As President Johnson said in his 1964 Commencement address at the University of Michigan: ". . . more classrooms and more teachers are not enough. We must seek an educational system which grows in excellence as it grows in size." A period of rapid growth is necessarily a period of both flexibility and ingenuity. Institutions can readily adopt on new campuses ideas and programs that would require costly reorganization on older campuses. The University of California, for example, is building its new Santa Cruz campus as a series of small residential colleges, each with its own subject field orientation. The University's new Irvine campus will explore ways of involving organized research units in the formal process of instruction. The new San Diego campus of the university will subdivide its ultimate enrollment of 27,500 students into a series of smaller colleges, with groups of four such colleges constituting largely self-contained sub-campuses of varying academic emphases. The University of the Pacific, in Stockton, California, has established a new residential college in which the entire curriculum is conducted in Spanish. Thus the enrollment explosion may bring unusual opportunities for colleges and universities, along with the heavy burden of numbers.

The current surge in higher education is not, of course, unique to the United States. In Canada the proportion of eighteen- to twenty-one-year olds in higher education is expected to double in the decade from 1962 to 1972. In France the total enrollment in higher education is expected to soar from around 200,000 now to 500,000 by 1970. In Britain, the much-discussed Robbins Committee Report recommends doubling the number of universities by 1980. These figures reflect the rapidly growing pressures resulting from a vast increase in secondary enrollments throughout much of the world. The decade of the 1950's has seen a world increase of 81 per cent in secondary enrollments and an increase of 71 per cent in college enrollments.

The data both from this country and abroad clearly indicate that we are witnessing everywhere the demise of two long-held notions: that higher education ought to be restricted to a small elite minority, and that only a small percentage of a country's population is capable of benefiting from some kind of higher education. Growth is having quite uneven impacts on American universities. Some, and they are almost always private, are building walls around themselves as aristocratic enclaves protected from the swirling currents of the population explosion. Others, and they are mostly public, are engulfed with more than their share of accommodation to the new hordes, that do not wish to be barbarous, advancing through their gates. The aristocratic enclave offers refuge to the faculty member who wishes protection from the new invasion, and many do; but it will become a more and more isolated element within the society of the future. The university with the open door will suffer the pangs of adjustment, but it will become in the process a more central element in a dynamic society. The one will be a pleasant place to be but increasingly out of tune with the surrounding society. The other will be a less pleasant place to live but will provide a more challenging and exciting environment, and will be more a part of the evolving life around it. Each will have its place, but the places they occupy will grow farther and farther apart.

Shifting Academic Emphases

A second major factor in the changing scene for American higher education is that knowledge is exploding along with population. There is also an explosion in the need for certain skills. The university is responding to all these explosions.

The vastly increased needs for engineers, scientists, and physicians will draw great resources to these areas of the university. Also, some new professions are being born. Others are becoming more formally professional, for example, business administration and social work. The university becomes the chief port of entry for these professions. In fact a profession gains its identity by making the university the port of entry. This creates new roles for education; but it is also part of the process of freezing the structure of the occupational pyramid and assuring that the well-behaved do advance, even if the geniuses do not. The university is used as an egg-candling device; and it is, perhaps, a better one than any other that can be devised, but the process takes some of the adventure out of occupational survival, and does for some professions what the closed shop has done for some unions. The life of the universities for a thousand years has been tied into the recognized professions in the surrounding society, and the universities will continue to respond as new professions arise.

The fastest-growing intellectual field today is biology. Here there is a veritable revolution where the doctrine of evolution once reigned supreme. To the classifying efforts of the past are being added the new analytical methods of the present, often drawn from chemistry and physics. There are levels of complexity to be explored in all living structures. The "code of life" can now be read; soon it will be understood, and soon after that, used. It is an intellectual discovery of unique and staggering proportions. The secrets of the atom, much as they have changed and are changing human activity on this planet, may hold no greater significance than the secrets still hidden in the genetic code. If the first half of the twentieth century may be said to have belonged to the physical sciences, the second half may well belong to the biological. Resources within the universities will be poured into the new biology and into the resulting new medicine and agriculture, well supported though medicine and agriculture already are. Medical education and research may be, in particular, on the threshold of revolutionary change.

Another field ready to bloom is that of the creative arts, hitherto the ugly duckling or Cinderella of the academic world. America is bursting with creativity in painting, music, literature, the theater, with a vigor equaled in few other parts of the world today. Italy, France, Spain, Germany, Russia, England, the Low Countries have had great periods of cultural flowering. America is having one now. In the arts the universities have been more hospitable to the historian and the critic than to the creator; the latter has found his havens elsewhere. Yet it is the creativity of science that has given the sciences their prestige in the university. Perhaps creativity will do the same again for the humanities, though there may be less new to create than has recently been true in science, and though the tests of value are far less precise. A very important role remains for the historian of past ages of creativity and for the critic of the current productions. But the universities need to find ways also to accommodate pure creative effort if they are to have places on stage as well as in the wings and in the audience in the great drama of cultural growth now playing on the American stage.

These possibilities for expansion—in the training of engineers, scientists, physicians, and the newer professionals, in biology, and in the creative arts, among various others—raise the problem of balance. As James Bryant Conant has noted, the Western world has had for a thousand years a continuing problem of "keeping a balance between the advancement of knowledge, professional education, general education, and the demands of student life."

But the balance is always changing; this is the unbalancing reality. The balance is not equal treatment, the provision of equal time in some mechanical and eternal way between teaching and research, or between the humanities and science. The dynamics of balance did not give equal treatment to the available scientist in Padua in 1300 when Giotto was painting his chapel, or to the available artist in Padua in 1600 when Galileo was lecturing from his crude platform. Balance cannot be determined on the scales by blind justice, field versus field and activity versus activity.

The essence of balance is to match support with the intellectual creativity of subject fields; with the need for skills of the highest level; with the kinds of expert service that society currently most requires. None of these measures is constant. Balance requires, therefore, a shifting set of judgments which relates facilities and attention to the possibilities inherent in each field, each skill, each activity at that moment of time in that environment, yet preserves for all fields their essential integrity. To know balance is to know the potential creativity, the potential productivity, the potential contribution of each competing activity in an unfolding pattern of time and an evolving landscape of environment. To know balance is to know more than anyone can ever know in advance. But decisions must nevertheless be made, and time will tell how well. The only certainly wrong decision is that the balance of today must be preserved for tomorrow. Where will the world's work and the university's work best be done? The answer to that question is the true definition of balance.

Involvement in the Life of Society

The third great change affecting the contemporary university is its thorough-going involvement in the nation's daily life. At the heart of this involvement is the growth of the "knowledge industry," which is coming to permeate government and business and to draw into it more and more people raised to higher and higher levels of skill. The production, distribution, and consumption of "knowledge" in all its forms is said to account for 29 per cent of the gross national product, according to Fritz Machlup's calculations; and "knowledge production" is growing at about twice the rate of the rest of the economy. Knowledge has certainly never in history been so central to the conduct of an entire society. What the railroads did for the second half of the last century and the automobile for the first half of this century may be done for the second half of this century by the knowledge industry: that is, to serve as the focal point for national growth. And the university is at the center of the knowledge process.

So the campus and society are undergoing a somewhat reluctant and cautious merger, already well advanced in some fields. M.I.T. is at least as closely related to industry and government as Iowa State ever was to agriculture. Indeed, universities have become "bait" to be dangled in front of industry, with drawing power greater than low taxes or cheap labor. Route 128 around Boston and the great developing industrial complexes in the San Francisco Bay area and southern California reflect the universities in these areas. The Gilpatric report for the Department of Defense explained that 41 per cent of defense contracts for research in the fiscal year 1961 were concentrated in California, 12 per cent in New York, and 6 per cent in Massachusetts, for a total of nearly 60 per cent, in part because these were also "centers of learning." Sterling Forest outside New York City seeks to attract industry by location next to a new university campus. In California, new industrial laboratories were located next to two new university campuses before the first building was built on either of these campuses. Sometimes industry will reach into a university laboratory to extract the newest ideas almost before they are born. Instead of waiting outside the gates,

27

agents are working the corridors. They also work the placement offices. And the university, in turn, reaches into industry, as through the Stanford Research Institute.

The university and segments of industry are becoming more alike. As the university becomes tied into the world of work, the professor—at least in the natural and some of the social sciences—takes on the characteristics of an entrepreneur. Industry, with its scientists and technicians, learns an uncomfortable bit about academic freedom and the handling of intellectual personnel. The two worlds are merging physically and psychologically.

The rapid production of new knowledge has given new significance to university extension slogans about "life-long learning." Television makes it possible for extension to reach into literally every home; the boundaries of the university are stretched to embrace all of society. The student becomes alumnus and the alumnus continues as student; the graduate enters the outside world and the public enters the classroom and the laboratory. Knowledge has the terrifying potential of becoming popular, opening a Pandora's box.

Extension divisions are proving to be increasingly effective administrative devices for linking campus and community in the further pursuit of knowledge. Freer of traditions and rules than regular university academic departments, extension units can respond quickly and in a variety of patterns to meet society's needs for current information and training. Professional schools and colleges, in particular, are making widespread use of extension programs for "refresher" and "continuing education" courses for the active practitioners in their fields. University of California Extension, for example, now enrolls in its courses one of every three lawyers and one of every six physicians in the state. Its total enrollment now numbers some 200,000 students, and it sponsors a remarkably wide range of academic activities including workshops, resident seminars and conferences, theater groups, symposia attracting participants of world renown, and even, recently, a notable scientific expedition to the Galapagos Islands. During the summer of 1964, in response to the growing concern with problems of school integration, University Extension was able to present several short-term workshops and courses on this urgent subject. The new role for knowledge is bringing a new and potentially quite exciting role for extension divisions in American higher education.

The campus becomes a center for cultural life; it has a ready-made audience in its students and faculty and it has the physical facilities. Persons attracted by the performing and visual arts and the lectures come to live around the campus—also assorted crackpots. As the downtown area in some cities decays, the campus takes its place as the cultural center of the community. A new dimension has been added to the land grant idea of service.

The New Deal took professors to Washington from many campuses, the New Frontier from more than just one. In Wisconsin before World War I, the campus and the state house in Madison were exceptionally close. Today the campus is being drawn to the city hall and the state capitol as never before. The politicians need new ideas to meet the new problems; the agencies need expert advice on how to handle the old. The professor can supply both. Keynes concluded his *General Theory* as follows: ". . . the ideas of economists and political philosophers, both when they are right and when they are wrong, are more powerful than is commonly understood. Indeed the world is ruled by little else. Practical men, who believe themselves to be quite exempt from any intellectual influences, are usually the slaves of some defunct economist. Madmen in authority, who hear voices in the air, are distilling their frenzy from some academic scribbler of a few years back. I am sure that the power of vested interests is vastly exaggerated compared with the gradual encroachment of ideas." As, for example, the ideas of Keynes.

The university must range itself on the side of intelligent solutions to sometimes unintelligent questions. These questions more and more arise from abroad as well as at home; and the quality of the answers has been made all the more crucial in a world swept by Communist and nationalist revolutions.

There are those who fear the further involvement of the university in the life of society. They fear that the university will lose its objectivity and its freedom. But society is more desirous of objectivity and more tolerant of freedom than it used to be. The university can be further ahead of the times and further behind the times, further to the left of the public and further to the right of the public—and still keep its equilibrium—than was ever the case before, although problems in this regard are not yet entirely unknown. There are those who fear that the university will be drawn too far from basic to applied research and from applied research to application itself. But the lines dividing these never have been entirely clear, and much new knowledge has been generated at the borders of basic and applied research, and even of applied knowledge and its application. Whitehead once wrote of the creative margin when the "adventure of thought" met "the adventure of action."

Involvement with the Federal Government

Growth and shifting emphases and involvement in society all take money; and which universities get it in the largest quantities will help determine which of them excel a decade or two hence. Will federal support be spent according to merit or according to political power? Will private donors continue to do as well as they recently have done for those universities that have done well already? Will the states find new sources of revenue or will their expenditures be held under a lid of no new taxes? The answers to these questions will help predict the standings on the next rating scale of universities.

Of key importance to American universities is the role of the federal government, particularly through federal support of scientific research. This support, which received its great impetus during and after World War II, has already changed the face of the leading American universities almost as much as did the land grant program a century earlier. Federal support has today become a major factor in the total performance of many universities, and the sums involved are substantial. Higher education in 1960 received about $1.5 billion from the federal government—a hundredfold increase in twenty years. About one third of this $1.5 billion was for university-afflliated research centers; about one third for project research within universities; and about one third for other things, such as residence hall loans, scholarships, and teaching programs. This last third was expended at colleges as well as universities, but the first two thirds almost exclusively at universities, and at relatively few of them.

The $1 billion for research, though only 10 per cent of total federal support for research and development, accounted for 75 per cent of all university expenditures on research and 15 per cent of total university budgets. Clearly the shape and nature of university research are profoundly affected by federal monies. The effects of this extensive federal aid and the new problems that have arisen as a consequence are many and varied, but the more important of them might be grouped under the two general headings of "federal influence" and "balance."

(1). Federal control as a substantive issue is, as Sidney Hook has said, a "red herring." With a few exceptions—the generally necessary exception of secrecy in certain types of work, and the unnecessary exception of the disclaimer affidavit once required by the National Defense Education Act—there has been no control in any deleterious sense. The real problem is not one of federal control but of federal influence. A federal agency offers a project. A university need not accept—but, as a practical matter, it usually does. Out of this reality have followed many of the consequences of federal aid for the universities; and they have been substantial. That they are subtle, slowly cumulative and gentlemanly makes them all the more potent.

A university's control over its own destiny has thus been substantially reduced. University funds from tuition and fees, gifts and endowments, and state sources go through the usual budget-making procedures and their assignment is subject to review in accordance with internal policy. Federal research funds, however, are usually negotiated by the individual scholar with the particular agency, and so bypass the usual review process. Thus 20 to 50 to 80 per cent of a university's expenditures may be handled outside the normal channels. These funds in turn commit some of the university's own funds; they influence the assignment of space; they determine the distribution of time between teaching and research; to a large extent they establish the areas in which the university grows the fastest. Almost imperceptibly, a university is changed.

The authority of the department chairman, the dean, the president is thereby reduced; so also is the role of faculty government. This may have its advantages. The university's internal process of distributing funds would be generally less selective and less flexible than the federal research project approach. Within a university, the tendency is to give each faculty member about the same opportunity and once having given it to keep giving it thereafter; but the project method allows more attention to exceptional merit and has the advantage that all projects may end some time. Additionally, federal agencies are more responsive to particular national needs than the universities would be, given the same amount of money to spend according to their own priority system.

There are, however, clearly detrimental effects. Some faculty members come to use the pressure of their agency contacts against their university. They may try to force the establishment of a new administrative unit or the assignment of land for their own special

31

building, in defiance of general university policy or priorities. These pressures, of course, should be withstood; they speak well neither of the professor nor of the agency. Also, some faculty members tend to shift their identification and loyalty from their university to the agency in Washington. The agency becomes the new alma mater. There are especially acute problems when the agency insists on the tie-in sale (if we do this for you, then you must do that for us) or when it requires frequent and detailed progress reports. Then the university really is less than a free agent. It all becomes a kind of "putting-out" system with the agency taking the place of the merchant-capitalist of old.

(2). The question of "balance" in federal aid arises in relation both to support of specific fields within an institution and to distribution of support among institutions of higher learning. Among the totality of university functions, federal support has been heavily concentrated on research and on graduate and postdoctoral training in fields of national interest. Expenditures have been largely restricted to the physical and biomedical sciences, and to engineering, with only about 3 per cent for the social sciences and hardly any support for the humanities.

All this is said to have destroyed the "balance" among fields, and it is generally concluded that something should be done about it. The balance among fields, however, has never been a static thing. If it were, philosophy, theology, and the classics would still be the dominant areas of study, as they have not been for a long time. Assuming that the balance of 1942, say, was appropriate for 1942, this does not mean it would have been appropriate for 1962. It is not enough to say that the old "balance" has been destroyed. The real question is what should be the proper balance today. It is clear that the flowering of the Renaissance should have affected the "balance" in the sixteenth century. It would seem likely that the splitting of the atom and the deciphering of the genetic code should in their turn affect the balance of the twentieth century. We should expect the most money and the brightest students and the greatest prestige to follow the most exciting new ideas. By and large they have done so, and this is one way of defining the nature of balance.

The real question, it seems to me, is not one of balance in any historical or monetary sense, but rather what is most appropriate to each field in each period. "All fields are equal, only some are more equal than others." There should be no effort to do the same things in the same amounts for each field. Each should receive support in accordance with its current potentialities, and potentialities vary. There are no timeless priorities.

Federal research expenditures have also been heavily focused on relatively few institutions. If both project research and large research centers are included, six universities received 57 per cent of the funds in a recent fiscal year, and twenty universities received 79 per cent. If project research alone is considered, the figures are 28 and 54 per cent. As a percentage of total university expenditures for all purposes among the leading twenty recipients, federal funds have amounted to 20 to 50 per cent when project research alone is counted, and from 20 to over 80 per cent when the research centers are added. These twenty universities are only about one tenth of all universities in the United States. They constitute the primary "federal grant" universities.

The project approach almost automatically led to concentration of federal research effort in a relatively few universities. The universities best equipped to undertake the research were also those with the faculty and facilities to provide for the training of Ph.D.'s. It is no coincidence that the six universities with a little more than 25 per cent of project funds graduated about 25 per cent of the Ph.D.'s; and a similar situation prevails for the top twenty universities. If "only the best will do," this concentration of effort is inevitable. A different result would have been quite surprising.

The concentration of effort has undoubtedly strengthened the facilities and improved the quality of faculties of universities already in the front rank. It has probably widened the gap between those of the first and those of the second and third ranks. It may, in fact, have actually injured universities of the second and third ranks and some colleges by turning their potential faculty members into research personnel in the front-rank universities. The good are better; the poor may well be worse. And it has greatly accentuated the differences between colleges and universities.

The general policy of federal agencies in allocating research grants to universities for the last two decades has been one of "seeking excellence wherever it is." The period has been one of what I have called "intuitive imbalance." We are now clearly entering a new phase of federal support policy, one that might be called "bureaucratic balance."

The new balance calls for developing a larger number of outstanding centers of graduate instruction and research. The Seaborg report of 1960 suggested expansion from the present fifteen or twenty centers to thirty or forty over a fifteen-year period. The National Education Improvement Act of 1963 envisaged expansion from twenty to seventy. Teaching is being emphasized along with research. Summer refresher courses for teachers of science, improvement of science textbooks, and language laboratories are programs already established. The National Science Foundation has a large effort under way to improve and renovate equipment for undergraduate teaching in the physical sciences. Undergraduates, as well as graduate students, are being assisted by loans and scholarships. The social sciences are receiving increasing sums of money. More funds are being granted to colleges as well as to universities, and to universities of all ranks.

A particularly significant step in the direction of broadening institutional support is the new science development program announced in the spring of 1964 by the National Science Foundation. This program is specifically designed to raise the overall quality of science programs in good institutions to the level of excellent. Distinguished institutions are excluded: "institutions already recognized as being outstanding in science should continue to depend on existing programs for assistance."

Undergraduate as well as graduate institutions will be eligible, and the grants (up to $5 million per institution) may be used in any way the institution chooses to strengthen single departments or related departments, to create new departments, or to improve the entire science program. *Science* magazine, commenting on the NSF plan, said, "it is probably safe to say that the success or failure of this program is going to have a far-reaching influence on the evolution of higher education in the United States."

The approach to a university "as an institution" has interesting implications. If additional universities are to be selected to become centers of strength in research and graduate instruction, then it will be necessary for the federal government to be concerned with the "general health of the institution." This will be a notable departure from historical practice, except in agriculture. If we are to move toward federal orientation to the "total function of the university," then the University Grants Committee in Great Britain is the outstanding precedent, and one that has received some support in the United States. However, there are only about thirty universities in Great Britain, and it is clear what is and what is not a university. Additionally, the University Grants Committee has come to exercise more influence over the establishment of new programs, the cost and size and even the appearance of new buildings, the equalization of faculty salaries among institutions, and the determination of admission policies than would currently be acceptable if it came from the federal government in this country.

Some hard choices must be faced. The decentralized project approach of the last two decades has much to recommend it. It is selective on merit, flexible in accordance with quality of performance, and responsive to national goals. The universities and their scholars retain substantial freedom. But such dominant reliance on the project approach is no longer likely. It is said that support to institutions as such will "give a university the necessary autonomy" and will permit dispersion of effort and better balance in several directions. It is difficult, however, to assess the merit of a total institution as complex as a modern university. One alternative is to rely on a formula, as in the case of agriculture in the land grant institutions. Another is to be guided by political influence; and this is increasingly happening. Inter-university competition is being taken from the quasi-academic arena of the agency committee to the legislative halls.

The partnership of the federal government with higher education and particularly with the federal grant universities over the last two decades has been enormously productive in enlarging the pool of scientific ideas and skills. Now we are entering a new phase of widening and deepening relationships. This new phase can carry the American commitment to education to new heights of endeavor. It can also preserve the traditional freedom of higher education from excessive control. It can enlarge the horizons of equality of opportunity. It can maintain and even increase the margin for excellence. The challenge is to make certain it does all these things.

However this turns out, the scene of American higher education will continue to be marked by great variety, and this is one of its great strengths. The large and the small, the private and the public, the general and the specialized all add their share to overall excellence. The total system is extraordinarily flexible, decentralized, competitive—and productive. The new can be tried, the old tested with considerable skill and alacrity. Pluralism in higher education matches the pluralistic American society. The general test of higher education is not how much is done poorly, and some is; rather it is how much is done superbly, and a great deal is, to the nation's great benefit.

Changes Still to Come

But there are some problems still to be fully faced; and they are problems of consequence.

(1). One is the improvement of undergraduate instruction in the university. The much-advertised conflict between teaching and research puts the problem the wrong way. The teaching of graduate students is so closely tied to research that if research is improved, graduate instruction is almost bound to be improved also. And the almost universal experience seems to be that federal research support has improved graduate instruction. At the undergraduate level, however, a "subtle discounting of the teaching process" has been aided and abetted.

The reasons for the general deterioration of undergraduate teaching are several. Teaching loads and student contact hours have been reduced. Faculty members are more frequently on leave or temporarily away from the campus; some are never more than temporarily on campus. More of the instruction falls to teachers who are not members of the regular faculty. The best graduate students prefer fellowships and research assistantships to teaching assistantships. Postdoctoral fellows who might fill the gap usually do not teach. Average class size has been increasing.

There seems to be a "point of no return" after which research, consulting, graduate instruction become so absorbing that faculty efforts can no longer be concentrated on undergraduate instruction as they once were. This process has been going on for a long time; federal research funds have intensified it. As a consequence, undergraduate education in the large university is more likely to be acceptable than outstanding; educational policy from the undergraduate point of view is largely neglected.

Improvement of undergraduate instruction will require the solution of many sub-problems: how to give adequate recognition to the teaching skill as well as to the research performance of the faculty; how to create a curriculum that serves the needs of the student as well as the research interests of the teacher; how to prepare the generalist as well as the specialist in an age of specialization looking for better generalizations; how to treat the individual student as a unique human being in the mass student body; how to make the university seem smaller even as it grows larger; how to establish a range of contact between faculty and students broader than the one-way route across the lectern or through the television screen; how to raise educational policy again to the forefront of faculty concerns.

(2). Another major task is to create a more unified intellectual world. We need to make contact between the two, the three, the many cultures; to open channels of intelligent conversation across the disciplines and divisions; to close the gap between C. P. Snow's "Luddites" and scientists; to answer fragmentation with general theories and sensitivities. Even philosophy, which once was the hub of the intellectual universe, is now itself fragmented into such diverse specialities as mathematics and semantics. However, the physical sciences are drawing together as new discoveries create more basic general theories; the biological sciences may be pulled together in the process now going on; the social sciences might be unified around the study of organizations and the relations of individuals to and within them. Biochemistry and social psychology may come to be central focalizing fields. As knowledge is drawn together, if in fact it is, a faculty may again become a community of masters; but "a sense of the unity . . . of all knowledge" is still a very long way off.

(3). A third problem is to relate administration more directly to individual faculty and students in the massive institution. We need to decentralize below the campus level to the operating agencies; to make the collective faculty a more vital, dynamic, progressive force as it now is only at the departmental level; to bridge the growing chasm between the department that does the teaching and the institute that does the research, with the faculty member torn between; to make the old departments and divisions more compatible with the new divisions of knowledge; to make it possible for an institution to see itself in totality rather than just piecemeal and in the sweep of history rather than just at a moment of time; to bring an understanding of both internal and external realities to all those intimately related to the process, so that there may be greater understanding; to see to it that administration serves and stimulates rather than rules the institution, that it is expendable when necessary and flexible all the time; to assure that the university can do better what it does best; to solve the whole range of governmental problems within the university.

(4). Additionally, there is the urgent issue of how to preserve a margin for excellence in a populist society, when more and more of the money is being spent on behalf of all of the people. The great university is of necessity elitist—the elite of merit—but it operates in an environment dedicated to an egalitarian philosophy. How may the contribution of the elite be made clear to the egalitarians, and how may an aristocracy of intellect justify itself to a democracy of all men? It was equality of opportunity, not equality *per se,* that animated the founding fathers and the progress of the American system; but the forces of populist equality have never been silent, the battle between Jeffersonianism and Jacksonianism never finally settled.

George Beadle, president of the University of Chicago, once implied that the very large American university (but not his own) might be like the dinosaur which "became extinct because he grew larger and larger and then sacrificed the evolutionary flexibility he needed to meet changing conditions"; its body became too large for its brain. David Riesman has said that the leading American universities are "directionless . . . as far as major innovations are concerned"; they have run out of foreign models to imitate; they have lost their "ferment." The fact is that they are not directionless; they have been moving in clear directions and with considerable speed. These directions, however, have not been set as much by the university's visions of its destiny as by the external environment, including the federal government, the foundations, the surrounding and sometimes engulfing industry.

But the really new problems of today and tomorrow may lend themselves less to solutions by external authority; they may be inherently problems for internal resolution. And these solutions, if they are to come, are more likely to emerge on the campuses of those old, private universities which have prided themselves on control of their own destiny, and on the totally new campuses of the state universities in America (and the new public universities in Britain). The university for the twenty-first century is more likely to emerge from these environments than from any others. Out of the pride of the old and the vacuum of the new may come the means to make undergraduate life more exciting, intellectual discourse more meaningful, administration more human. And perhaps there will arise a more dynamic demonstration of how excellence makes democracy more vital and its survival more assured. Then the contemporary American university may indeed rise to "the heights of the times." Then it may demonstrate that it has a mind as well as a body.

W. ALLEN WALLIS

Centripetal and Centrifugal Forces in University Organization[1]

THE PEOPLE who constitute a university differ widely in knowledge, skill, wisdom, taste, culture, and purposes. This heterogeneity has been dramatized recently by C. P. Snow's phrase, "the two cultures," by Clark Kerr's discussion of the "multiversity," by Robert Hutchins's plaint, "Everybody specializes. There can be no academic community. . . ." The tasks carried out in universities range from profound consideration of the human condition to technical details about sewerage.

The work of all these dissimilar persons in unrelated tasks can be viewed as a matter of organization or communication. Some of the principles, or at least precepts, that apply to organization and communication in general are relevant, and even those that are not may nevertheless be illuminating, in considering universities.

Any organization must have some means of setting its goals: It must decide what to do, in what proportions, and with what priorities. It must appraise the degree to which primary purposes are advanced by alternative secondary goals.[2] Any organization must arrange to carry on the activities that will accomplish its purposes: It must find people, buildings, and equipment, combine them, and assign them to various tasks. Any organization must arrange to disseminate its product to people outside the organization: It must distribute its output among customers, clients, readers, students, and other beneficiaries.

These three functions—formulating objectives, directing activities, disseminating results—can be accomplished through a system of caste, status, and tradition, as in a beehive or a feudal society; or through a system of orders from an individual at the top by way of a hierarchy of ranks, as in an army or an authoritarian government; or through a network of directions and regulations, as in a bureaucracy or a mercantilist state; or through individuals following their own judgments, as in a traditional university or a laissez-faire economy.

Any of these types of organization can be looked on as a communication system. Indeed, the differences in the effectiveness with which organizations accomplish their functions are largely related to differences in various systems of communication.[3]

In any organization, two quite different kinds of information must be brought together. On the one hand, there must be broad, general information about the overall purposes of the organization and the degree to which any one purpose should be pursued at the expense of others—information, in short, about the organization's values and priorities. On the other hand, there must be highly specific, infinitely detailed information about the capacities and limitations of individuals, about interrelations among individuals, about materials and technology, about the extent to which some purposes are impeded by advancing others. From the combination of these two kinds of information, about institutional goals and individual capacities, the people and resources of the institution are organized to carry out the three functions: deciding what to do, arranging for it to be done, and distributing the results.

In a centralized organization—one that is authoritarian and hierarchical—information about individual capacities and details of time and place is transmitted toward the top or center. There the information is juxtaposed to the goals of the organization, which are established at the center. Decisions are made at the center, and instructions are transmitted from the center toward the individuals who will carry them out. Sanctions for individual compliance tend to be mainly in the form of penalties imposed from the center.

In a decentralized organization—one that is individualistic and laissez-faire—information on institutional goals is transmitted directly to individuals, often without ever having been formulated, or even collected, at a center. Individuals then decide what they will do in the light of this information, together with their direct knowledge of their own capacities, opportunities for coöperation, and access to materials and technology. Sanctions for advancing institutional goals tend to be mainly the incentive of rewards, not dispensed from the center but conferred by other individuals.

The great advantage of a centralized organization is that it is predictable and reliable. It can be controlled and directed. It can assume responsibility for bringing about a prescribed result. Correspondingly, however, a centralized organization has little ability to adapt (in the sense of developing novel responses to unprecedented conditions) and none to adapt quickly. The great advantage of a decentralized organization is its adaptability, both in the sense of speed and in the sense of making many simultaneous adjustments to details of infinite and unanticipated variety. Correspondingly, a decentralized organization is not well suited to accepting responsibility for prescribed performance.

The modern university finds itself increasingly betwixt and between. Traditionally, we think of the university as a sequestered cloister, an ivory tower, remote from hustle and bustle, turbulent cross-pressures, conflicting interests, and a sense of urgency. From this view of the university grows our traditional concept of total laissez-faire that we refer to as academic freedom. It is a freedom granted not as a special privilege to professors, but as the best instrument through which universities can obtain what they want from professors, namely, pursuit of truth wherever the pursuit may take them, and full disclosure of findings with no regard to the consequences. Traditionally, the university itself, not any outsider, sets its own goals, establishes its own standards, charts its own paths; and it does this most effectively by delegation to the professors— not even to the faculty as a group, but to the professors individually.

Today universities, besides trying to preserve their traditional role, have become important wheelers and dealers in affairs large and small. They accept, indeed seek, assignments (if accompanied by funds) from businesses, governments, foundations, or individuals to carry out specified missions on stated schedules. At times, they even agree to keep the results secret, for the exclusive benefit of the client. Only a little of the money they accept is for the narrowest purposes I have indicated, but comparatively little is offered to them for purposes as broad as those traditionally associated with universities.

Eric Ashby has described this dual nature of the contemporary university:

". . . the word university stands for something unique and precious in European society: a leisurely and urbane attitude to scholarship, exemption from the obligation to use knowledge for practical ends, a sense of perspective which accompanies the broad horizon and the distant view, and opportunity to give undivided loyalty to the kingdom of the mind. [At the same time] . . . the university is an institution with urgent

41

and essential obligations to modern society; a place to which society entrusts its most intelligent young people and from which it expects to receive its most highly trained citizens; a place which society regards as the pace-maker for scientific research and technological progress."[4]

Many of the organizational questions confronting the contemporary university grow out of this duality, out of the presence at the same time and same place of activities of both kinds: activities that are self-generated, problem-solving, exploratory, innovative, and scholarly, which are best organized atomistically, with a maximum of laissez-faire, individual responsibility, and academic freedom; and activities that are originated outside, undertake to accomplish specific tasks, and involve the kind of responsibility that a professional man owes his client, which must necessarily be organized with some degree of authority to see that obligations to the client are met.

The contrast can be illustrated by comparing a medical school with an academic department. In a medical school—indeed, in professional schools generally—it is usual for the head of a department to have some authority over the other professors in his department, for the professors to have some authority over the associate professors, and so on. This is especially clear in a clinical department, where the health and occasionally the very lives of patients or staff may be at stake. There is no trace of academic freedom or laissez-faire in an operating room, even if the surgery in progress has far-reaching implications for the advance of knowledge.

In a traditional academic department in the sciences or humanities, higher rank may bring a few minor and marginal perquisites, such as meeting classes at preferred hours and places, and it may even bring the right to discuss a little with lower-ranking men the contents of their courses. It does not, however, confer any authority over the research, and very little over the teaching, of department members of lower rank.

It is tempting to say that the dividing line runs between those parts of the university whose purpose is to advance knowledge and those parts whose purpose is to apply knowledge, with the humanities and sciences representing research and the professional schools representing application. Perhaps in the past the various parts of a university could be dichotomized on this basis. Medical schools at the beginning of the century, judging by Flexner's writings, were essentially "how-to-do-it" affairs, not only devoid of research but deficient in the scientific knowledge already in existence.

In engineering, Massachusetts Institute of Technology, California Institute of Technology, and Carnegie Institute of Technology, among others, all were originally schools for "mechanics"—skilled craftsmen and technologists. Schools of law, of business, of dentistry, of social service, of librarianship, still, with rare exceptions, carry on practically no research in the sense in which the term "research" is used by a good graduate faculty in the humanities and sciences.

The trend in all professional schools, however, is strongly away from exclusive reliance on a how-to-do-it approach, and toward the introduction into the curriculum of the basic sciences underlying the practice of the profession. Correspondingly there is a pronounced trend in professional schools towards research in these basic disciplines. With the introduction of basic research, methods of organization become appropriate that are different from those that were appropriate when the school was engaged solely in professional assignments on behalf of clients. Yet arrangements that may be effective for the new basic research programs may not be appropriate in the professional aspects of the school's work.

While the applied departments and professional schools have become more involved in basic research, the basic research departments have become more involved in undertakings for outside clients. Every important department of mathematics, physics, chemistry, biology, and psychology—and almost every unimportant one, too—now receives grants of a year's duration, or occasionally several years', from businesses, government agencies, or foundations. A few of these grants, including some from the government, are so broad as to be tantamount to general support of a department, unrestricted except for periodic review and consideration of renewal (not a negligible restriction!). Most grants, however, are for fairly definite purposes—for doctoral training in rather narrow specialties, for research on well-defined problems, for specific equipment. In accepting these grants the university assumes an obligation to the client which requires that responsibility, hence authority, be assigned to some one person for seeing that the obligations are fulfilled. Thus, outside support and its obligations produce subtle but steady pressures away from the complete, laissez-faire decentralization under which universities have functioned best.

Another pressure in the same direction results from the great mobility that characterizes faculties, particularly the staffs of programs supported from outside. In an important sense a university *is* its faculty, for they are the people in whose hands the ultimate power lies under a system of atomistic decentralization. But the ultimate power of an enduring institution cannot lie in a group that is here today, gone tomorrow. To the extent that a university is simply a resting place for birds of passage, who migrate with the climate of research interests and opportunities, it is forced to locate important decisions and controls more centrally than would otherwise be desirable.

Still another force tending to undermine the traditional decentralization that we refer to as academic freedom arises because today individual professors themselves participate in a wide variety of activities outside the university. Much of a modern professor's time is spent with people in business, professional associations, foundations, publishing houses, and "projects" of all kinds—not to mention public affairs and just plain politics. Indeed, the very fact that controlling influences over universities are passing to the center of the university has generated a growing interest on the part of faculties in the governance of universities—in faculty senates, in departmental voting on appointments and curricula, and in other collective or "democratic" apparatus. Similarly, the fact that, as I shall note later, universities are increasingly subject to control by outside sources of funds has generated a great interest by universities in placing their members on the boards, staffs, and advisory committees of agencies with funds to grant. Such outside commitments of the faculty raise questions of conflict of interest that undermine the basis for delegating the ultimate authority in a university to the faculty. The case for decentralization—for academic freedom, that is—rests heavily on the assumption that the faculty are governed by no interests other than their consciences: that "They are not out to make money or win political office, so that what they report should be disinterested."[5]

One more force threatening the traditional decentralization of universities is the rise of interdisciplinary work. In universities it is more nearly true than in any other institutions of modern life that evaluations of experts are made by other experts on the sole criterion of expertness. Other criteria do, of course, play some role: ability to teach, for example; a personality not so disruptive that a man's output is offset by his negative effects on the output of his colleagues; or abilities in obtaining and managing funds sufficient to outweigh deficiencies in expertness. By and large, however, the statement is true, provided appointments and promotions are based on the

44

judgment of faculty members who are indeed experts in the same field as the candidate.

The importance of this consideration makes it unwise to combine fields that are essentially different in a single department, as is often done with mathematics and statistics, economics and business, or anthropology and sociology. With the rise of deliberately interdisciplinary units—often a desirable development—the problem is accentuated. (Such units often result from focusing on a problem—urban studies, for example—rather than on a field of knowledge, and this in turn often results from trying to provide professional services to outside clients.) An interdisciplinary unit, if it encompasses several disciplines that are truly distinct, is ordinarily not competent to pass on its own appointments and promotions. If it is allowed to do so, in accordance with traditional decentralized procedures, it almost invariably declines in quality with the passage of time and the disappearance of the original enthusiasts who happened to represent an unusual combination of abilities. If the interdisciplinary unit is not allowed to make its own decisions, there occurs a further passing of authority toward the center. In addition there seems to be some tendency for interdisciplinary units to report higher in the administrative hierarchy than would otherwise be the case—to the provost where a comparable intradisciplinary unit would report to a dean, or to a dean instead of to a department chairman—thus moving authority toward the center.

(Interdisciplinary units should, of course, be distinguished from new disciplines. The field of statistics, to take an example with which I am personally familiar, has been organized into separate departments in most leading universities within the past fifteen years. This has meant bringing together people who formerly would have been in departments of mathematics, astronomy, economics, sociology, psychology, engineering, education, business, public health, and a dozen more. They are, however, people sharing a common discipline, including all the paraphernalia of national and international professional associations, technical journals, abstracting services, and so forth. Thus, they can be measured against the standards of their own field, by their publications and in other ways, and in fact the various departments in which they were formerly housed were usually not competent to evaluate them.)

The centripetal forces that are centralizing authority within the university are matched by centrifugal forces that are diffusing to outsiders the authority that formerly lay within the university. Universities are gradually losing control over the activities carried on within their walls. The role of the university in research is in danger of becoming something like that of hotel keeper for transient scholars and projects. Hotels provide rooms, staffs, and supporting services for travelers, conferences, parties, and banquets. What goes on in a hotel's rooms depends on outsiders—on the arrival of guests, conference organizers, and hosts inquiring about the availability of services. A hotel's only control over the quality of the activities carried on under its roof comes from its right to turn away business that is disreputable, shoddy, or immoral, and from its right to solicit business from those who control desirable activities.

Similarly, in today's university many of the staff are a little like transient roomers, in that they are connected solely with some project of research or application, transfer from one institution to another as their interests or opportunities change, and never develop the same attachment to the university as do the regular faculty, who, in a very real sense, are not just attached to the university— they *are* the university. Corresponding to the parties, conferences, conventions, and banquets of the hotel are the research projects and developmental grants decided upon by outside foundations, research institutes, government agencies, or corporations, who seek the home that will best suit their own needs. Even at the universities with the largest endowments, outside sources provide much of the support for research, scholarship, and graduate programs, since total expenditures on these advanced studies, by private and government agencies, now dwarf the amounts the universities can command for them from funds that they control.

As universities have lost some of the control over their own research and advanced teaching programs, they have lost correspondingly some of their individuality, and have tended to become more alike. As the fancy of some foundation is captured by a new development, the foundation pays for introducing the new development in many institutions. Still others, moving in the direction from which the winds seem to bring the scents of dollars, follow suit. When a government institute distributes funds for a certain type of purpose, it keeps an eye on the distribution of Congressional power and interest, and it is often advised by scientists who have their own systems of power and interest. Thus, the individuality of universities is being submerged by forces not unlike those that have made television into a "mass taste-land." This is happening to universities just when a similar transformation is taking place in individuals—when there are increasing pressures for accepting socially-determined values, for gradually subordinating the individual to the group and the group to the nation, and for making the nation coterminous with society. The change has crept up on universities almost unnoticed. It will in all probability continue to grow for some decades—indeed, at an accelerating pace.

Whether these centrifugal forces are dangerous depends largely on the degree to which the outsiders are themselves centralized or atomistic. If the outsiders are atomistic—that is, small and diverse—a university need not be dominated by outside sources of funds; for the possibility of shopping around for supporters whose interests are consilient with its own enables it to select its own course. With the role of the Federal government ever growing, sources of outside support are increasingly centralized. While the several Federal agencies have been reasonably independent so far, there have been steady pressures from Congress, the Bureau of the Budget, and the Comptroller General for uniformity. Similarly, some of the private foundations are too big for healthy diversity.

The forces that I have labelled centripetal tend to gather up the powers that in universities have traditionally been dispersed among individual faculty members and to concentrate them somewhat more than previously in the hands of administrators. The forces that I have labelled centrifugal then tend to disperse these powers outside the university. There are, as we saw in considering the circumstances in which centralization and decentralization are appropriate, profound and powerful reasons why universities have been, and should be, largely autonomous and organized along lines of laissez-faire decentralization. Yet the assumption by universities of responsibilities for performing prescribed tasks that are important to society inevitably works to reduce autonomy and decentralization. This raises the question whether these prescribed tasks, important though they may be, should be accepted by universities. The answer, to anticipate the argument, is that some should and some should not, and that the test should be the extent to which the tasks contribute to the central educational purposes of a university.

The heart of all the frantic, high-pressure, hurly-burly activity of today's professor is still the education of the young. This it is that ties all the activity together, gives it purpose, and provides a common focus to all the diverse activities of a university. Not only is teaching the central focus of all the activities of a university, but it is becoming almost the only activity that is not duplicated outside the universities. There are great independent libraries, such as the Library of Congress in Washington, the Morgan Library in New York, the Newberry Library in Chicago, and the Huntington Library in San Marino, which provide not only library resources but support for scholars. There are great research institutes, such as the Rockefeller in New York, the Brookings in Washington, and the Salk in La Jolla, that support not only research but doctoral study. There are havens, apart from the universities, for advanced scholars and scientists, such as the Institute for Advanced Study at Princeton and the Center for Advanced Study in the Behavioral Sciences in Palo Alto. There are other great research institutes that support post-doctoral study, for example, the National Bureau of Economic Research in New York or the national physical laboratories of Brookhaven, Oak Ridge, Argonne, Los Alamos, and Livermore. Whereas once the advance of knowledge in most fields depended on universities and on universities alone, now teaching is the only university activity that depends wholly on universities.

Teaching cannot be done effectively at a high level of quality except in conjunction with many other intellectual activities, especially research. The conflict between teaching and research which figures prominently in contemporary lay discussion of universities is mostly an illusion. Teaching and research are complementary, for the good teacher "must keep the machinery of his own mind hot with action if he would excite activity in the minds of his students";[6] so all leading universities, and most others, allow their faculty time for both teaching and research. Education of high quality can scarcely exist except as a joint activity with research, scholarship, advanced training, and applications of knowledge.

Hence the fact that education is almost the only activity that is unique to universities by no means implies that it should be the only activity, nor even that other activities are not equally important. But by remembering that a university has a special relation to teaching that it does not have to its other activities, we may occasionally help to clarify difficult questions about the proper scope of the university. Should a university include an institute of meteorology, or an institute for research on public opinion? A school of law, or a school of journalism, or a school of diplomacy, or a school of social work? Ought it to offer a doctoral program in operations research, or in political science, or in sociology, or in speleology, or in statistics? Such questions have innumerable ramifications, and to answer them will always be difficult at best. One test that we ought to apply is how contemplated innovations would relate to our educational programs and to other programs which relate directly to our educational programs. No proposal reasonable enough to be raised seriously is likely to be mortally wounded by such a test, but some may be slowed down enough to increase the orderliness of our growth.

To summarize: At the heart of the contemporary university is the traditional university, characterized by an extreme degree of individualism and decentralization, seeking knowledge for knowledge's sake, and seeking it in lieu of material goods and services rather than as a means of attaining them—indeed, seeking knowledge not even for its own sake so much as for the sake of the search. Superimposed on this traditional university are many socially-important functions which have burgeoned recently and could not have been provided for satisfactorily had not universities assumed responsibility for them. Organizational arrangements required to meet these responsibilities involve more concentration of authority within the university, and more delegation of authority to outsiders, than is compatible with the central, unique, and enduring purposes of a university. Other institutions now exist which are capable of handling most, perhaps all, of these responsibilities. That an activity is worth doing and involves scientists and science, or scholars and scholarship, is not sufficient grounds for pursuing it in a university. It is not even sufficient ground for concluding that the activity is not a menace to the university which accommodates it. Universities should, therefore, retain such responsibilities, or accept new ones, only if they are compatible with the decentralized decision-making that is essential to the basic purposes of universities, or if they contribute substantially to activities that are essential to these basic purposes.

REFERENCES

1. Several passages of this essay are taken from a commencement address by the author given at the University of Chicago on August 31, 1962 ("The Importance of Error," *University of Chicago Magazine,* November, 1962), and his inaugural address at the University of Rochester on May 17, 1963 (*Rochester Review,* June-July, 1963).

2. Frank H. Knight, *The Economic Organization,* (New York: Augustus M. Kelley, Inc., 1951).

3. F. A. Hayek, "The Use of Knowledge in Society," *American Economic Review*, XXXV (1945), pp. 519-530.

4. Eric Ashby, *Technology and the Academics*, (London: Macmillan & Co., Ltd., 1958), pp. 69-70.

5. Richard M. Weaver, *Academic Freedom: The Principle and the Problems*, (Philadelphia: Intercollegiate Society of Individualists, Inc., February, 1963).

6. Martin Brewer Anderson, first president of the University of Rochester, in an address in 1870. See William C. Morey, ed., *Papers and Addresses of Martin B. Anderson, LL.D.*, (Philadelphia: American Baptist Publication Society, 1895), Vol. I, pp. 83-84.

FREDERIC HEIMBERGER

The State Universities

THE NEAR future will bring changes of major consequence to all
segments of what is loosely called "higher education" in America.
No single part—whether it be a technical school, a community
college, or a true university—will escape the effects of a vast increase in what is factually known, or the urgent demands of a
social order that is being based more and more upon the uses of
the mind. Few if any of the separate parts which comprise the
collective whole will remain untouched by swiftly growing numbers
in the college-age population. But it is likely that among all of
the many and widely varied agencies for higher education that
now exist, the state universities will change the most.

Lest there be confusion now or later, let it be made clear that
the word "university" is here being given the descriptive meaning
which has long been accepted by educators. It is not being used
as an all-inclusive term describing a statewide system of which
the university proper is only a single, even though perhaps dominant, part. Neither is it being applied carelessly to almost any
school that gains the title of university by nothing more than the
fiat of its governing body. Furthermore, it is the writer's strong
opinion that it is very important just now to hold fast to the old
and highly respected concept of a true university. It still has
value and it is worth preserving, particularly at a time when huge
and all-inclusive educational systems are being planned and developed. There is something really distinctive about a university,
and the meaning and identification of that special quality should
not be lost in a welter of newly created or greatly expanded
agencies for post-secondary education or training.

The effects of change in our state universities will not be

limited to these institutions themselves. The forms and directions they take will have a powerful influence, for good or ill, upon all of the academic community. With wise and imaginative guidance, the state universities of tomorrow can attain new levels of excellence and contribute as never before to higher education in America. But there is also the frightening possibility that, lacking clear vision and intelligent leadership in the use of their size and power, they could become a blight upon the land—one perhaps not readily recognized but one still withering in its effects. The outcome ten years hence will depend upon certain major and even a good many seemingly minor choices that must be made in the time between.

Rapid growth in the numbers of students to be served is assured by the flooding tide of young people now moving through our elementary and secondary schools with no sign of an early ebb. Furthermore, the strength of that flow is being increased yearly by the rising percentage of high school graduates who either seek added opportunities for themselves or who are compelled by economic necessity to continue in some form of post-secondary education or training. The period of preparation for adult life and productive effort is being steadily lengthened to meet the new requirements of a swiftly changing, highly complex, and largely urban society. We are now at a time somewhat like that of the early twenties, when the need for more years of learning brought a great upsurge in high school enrollments. Today we see the beginnings of a fresh and powerful surge, this time breaking beyond the high school and calling for new or vastly expanded opportunities for almost countless thousands of young people. Due to increased emphasis upon graduate and professional studies, we also see a lengthening of the time devoted to formal education by many who are not so young.

It is true that much of what is newly needed is not in keeping with the nature and purposes of a university. But the needs are here, and without too much concern for the feelings of academicians the public will demand that they be met in one way or another. With a longer span of years, adequate opportunities might be provided in good time through the orderly expansion of existing colleges and universities, the building of new ones, and the development of a wider variety of limited-purpose schools. But time will not wait, and it is highly probable that our state universities will be held responsible for seeing that the major share of the job is done, either directly through sharply increased enrollments and a wide diversification of their teaching programs, or indirectly through enlarged or newly created ancillary schools. Some part of the need for added opportunities will be met, of course, by our private institutions. But the costs will be so great that in the absence of the kind of general and massive federal assistance which probably will not come in time to meet the immediate need, by far the greater share of responsibility must be assumed by the states and their agencies, old or new.

Many who are rightfully proud of the stature which their state universities have attained through years of effort will want no part of this new, distracting, and possibly debilitating responsibility. Some may be of the opinion that it would be better to create entirely new agencies to develop and operate separate systems of special-purpose colleges, schools, or institutes. Others may favor an extension of the public schools to cover at least one or two years of post-secondary work. There is little likelihood, however, that our existing state universities will be able to avoid the issue. They are generally looked upon as the principal public agencies for higher education. They also have a visible and impressive record of accomplishment in a wide variety of tasks. In fact, there is an almost frightening faith in their ability to do just about anything—and do it reasonably well. On the other hand, and perhaps for no valid reason, there is relatively little confidence in the ability of the public schools to go beyond the twelfth year in anything more than purely vocational training. Thus it appears that the solution to this dilemma must be sought and found by the state universities, either by doing the job themselves or by taking the lead in seeing that it is done—and done well—by others.

This whole question of what the state universities can do to meet mounting enrollments and rapidly changing needs will be easily answered by at least a few—chiefly administrators of the promoter-manager type rather than experienced educators. Having no deep understanding of the true nature of a university, they will simply accept the emerging situation as a welcome opportunity to increase the operational size, the diversity, and the public appeal of their own institutions. If there is a need for almost any form of post-secondary work they will offer to meet it through the "university" rather than see a chance for "growth" and power slip away to some upstart competitor. Hopefully, very few will be so lacking in vision and so personally ambitious. But there will probably be some, and these will surely promote at least a few sprawling monsters of mediocrity mistakenly called "universities."

It is often said by athletic coaches that a team rarely stays the same after mid-season. It gets either much better or much worse. Our state universities are now at mid-season and it remains to be seen which way they will go. The needs and opportunities of the next ten years will be used by some to good advantage, to gain new and much higher levels of academic excellence and effectiveness. In the process of helping to build a statewide pyramid of post-secondary training and education—one broad of base and high of apex—these institutions will seek first to define the forms and functions of a true university, and then try to find their proper places in the total structure. This will call for hard and sometimes unpopular decisions as to what to do and—of equal importance—what to leave for others to do. The state universities headed for greatness will be wise enough to assist in developing and giving direction to other institutions designed to meet other valid but different needs, thus freeing themselves to strive for education at its highest levels. Failing to take this longer view and to be more selective in their choices, some will no doubt attempt to be all things to all people and as a consequence end up as huge and physically impressive but still second-rate institutions ten years hence.

How well or poorly our state universities come through this period of rapid expansion and realignment must be a matter of great concern to the entire nation. To an increasing degree we shall all be dependent upon their quality and effectiveness as major sources of new knowledge, new ideas, and keenly whetted minds. While they may appear to be only local institutions, the actual fact is that collectively our state universities constitute a national resource of critical importance. The new forms and functions of these public institutions will also have very strong effects upon our many and richly diverse private colleges and universities. One effect will be felt through the uses made of their economic power to compete. It may be assumed that the state universities will not be expected to make bricks without straw—that when the pressures for providing expanded and improved programs of teaching and research are really felt by parents, businessmen, and other taxpayers, greatly increased public funds will be made available. This is what has actually happened as communities have faced the needs of their elementary and secondary schools, and there is little reason to think that the experience will not be repeated at a higher level.

This means that lacking the kind of immediate and very substantial federal or philanthropic assistance which seems improbable today, even the strongest of our private institutions may find themselves at an economic disadvantage in seeking to attract and hold those exceptionally able scholars and teachers who often make the difference between excellence and mediocrity. It will not be a question of salaries alone. The provision of immensely expensive laboratories, guaranteed research assistance, and other supporting elements is essential to the recruitment and retention of highly qualified faculty people in many important areas today. It is true that federal grants and contracts now help to provide support for certain fields of study in a relatively small number of our stronger private institutions. But there are literally hundreds of colleges and universities having little prospect for receiving really large-scale governmental assistance, at least in the near future. Moreover, it is not realistic to expect that private gifts will increase rapidly enough to keep pace.

The economic pulling power of the state universities may also have an effect upon the movement of students, particularly those at the graduate level. Relatively large numbers, many of whom might prefer to go elsewhere, will be attracted to these huge public institutions by opportunities for part-time employment, either in undergraduate instruction or as research assistants. In the latter case, the enticements will be quite strong in the applied fields which are now attracting increased attention and substantial support because of the current emphasis upon university research as a means to local or regional economic growth.

As a final example of the many ways in which a relative increase in the size and strength of the state universities may affect all of higher education, it is not fanciful to suggest that, through added numbers, their faculty members may gain greater power in guiding the affairs of professional societies and other associations that have much to do with determining the nature and quality of the entire academic enterprise. Thus our burgeoning state universities cannot be set apart, screened off by a curtain of disinterest, or perhaps even regarded with smiling condescension as peculiar but not too important American phenomena. The decisions they make and the paths they take must be of deep concern to all who cherish higher education at its best.

II

What, then, are some of the more important issues that will probably confront our state universities within the next few years? Who will decide them? Will these universities merely drift with the prevailing winds of public pressure? Will their faculties and administrations leave it to others who are far less able and experienced to decide their future? Or will they themselves take the lead in developing new and greatly improved centers and systems for learning and teaching? The first and probably most critical decision of all in this new era will be that of function or purpose. Are these state institutions to be true universities, ready to encompass any field of disciplined study and having no predetermined limits to either the range or the intensity of their work? Or are they constrained by their very nature to pursue only restricted interests—allowed to go all the way in some fields but forced to stop short of full accomplishment in others? Does the fact that they are state institutions, supported in large part by all who pay taxes, mean that they dare not make discriminating choices of either their educational programs or their student clienteles?

There was a time when, due principally to the early effects of the land-grant idea, a clear difference could be seen between most of our state universities and the more mature private ones. Heavy emphasis upon the most visible and practical problem of that time, full development and immediate use of the land and its riches, gave a strong agricultural and vocational cast to their interests and efforts. More than most of us realize today, the struggle to break beyond that limited concept has been a long and difficult one. It has claimed the time and attention of many far-sighted and courageous educational statesmen. In some cases, of course, that struggle continues even today, and what was undoubtedly necessary and valid in earlier years still has a perhaps hidden but still very real restrictive effect. But our better state universities are now moving far beyond any concept of restricted mission or purpose. They are claiming their right to range far and wide in subject matter and to seek the highest degrees of excellence in fields of their own choosing. A good many of them have already chosen goals and developed programs of teaching and research that are unsurpassed by those of even the most distinguished private schools. This does not deny the fact that certain special services, usually related to a particular vocation and often required by law, may still be found on the same campus with programs of high university quality in such fields as the humanities or the basic sciences. But these limited services are clearly recognized for what they are—added functions rather than programs growing out of restricted basic purposes.

The move toward higher quality and true university status is being hastened and facilitated by the development of more and more statewide plans and provisions for post-secondary education or training. Now, at last, we are beginning to see a full recognition of the fact that there are differing needs and differing clienteles, and that all must be served with dignity and effectiveness. This is leading toward a wider range of choices for the high school graduate, toward programs and agencies specifically designed and distinctly labeled for what they really are. It offers hope that our principal state institutions may be able to concern themselves as never before with the real business of education at the university level. It may be difficult, of course, to persuade legislators and others who control the purse strings, and thus strongly influence policy, that clear differences among needs and clienteles exist and must be taken into account. Many will probably continue to argue that "good old State" ought to be able to offer a program in mortuary science along with one in nuclear physics, or train typists as well as political theorists. And a good many university people will be tempted to agree rather than run the risk of losing much-needed appropriations. A few top administrators may even oppose the establishment or expansion of limited-purpose schools or institutes, fearing them as competitors for public funds. Those who take this latter position will do their universities no good in the long run. They would be far wiser to assist in finding other ways to meet those needs which cannot be properly met through the offerings of a major university. Then, and then only, can they insist that there really is a difference between a trade school and a university, and that each has its rightful place in a total system. Then, and then only, will they be able to win wide understanding and approval of selective, rather than restrictive, policies on admissions to public institutions.

It is true that there are still deep differences of opinion on questions of educational goals and standards within most of our state universities. Almost every campus has at least some members of the faculty or administration who vigorously oppose any tendency to emulate the Ivy League or, as they sometimes say, "to go high hat." Such fears of a possible violation of purpose and trust are often found among those who make much of "the land-grant idea" or the concept of "the people's university," without thinking too deeply about the true meaning of these oft-repeated words, which have been worked to death and which have now come perilously close to being mere clichés. Their error lies in assuming that these catch phrases can rightly be used to set limits to quality and standards of excellence, rather than to offer a constant challenge to make the best available to all. Among the many newly emerging provisions for post-secondary training or education, "the people" of a state are surely entitled to at least one public university that dares to match strides wherever it can with the best in America.

Holding to false or outdated notions about "the land-grant idea" can also have another somewhat different but still stultifying effect upon our state universities. One of the critical problems now facing these institutions is that of realigning their interests and efforts in order to meet the newer needs and broader opportunities of a swiftly changing social and economic order. Our society is no longer a predominantly local and agrarian one—or even the relatively simple one of the "mechanic arts," as they were known in earlier years. Yet the specific command of the Morrill Act, given more than a century ago, to teach agriculture and the mechanic arts still weighs heavily in the scales of what is most important, even in many schools that do not trace their origins to that particular bit of national legislation. As so often happens, the predominant interests and needs of one era have been fixed and institutionalized to such a degree that they strongly affect the next. It is difficult even today to progress beyond the notion that agriculture, engineering, and applied science have special importance and must therefore be given favored treatment. And since so many of our state universities either began as or were made into land-grant colleges, the effect has been widely spread.

Disproportionate representation in legislative bodies has contributed heavily to disproportionate interest in teaching and research related to agriculture. With one or even both houses of the legislature dominated by representatives from rural areas, leaders of our state universities have been tempted—sometimes virtually compelled—to give special attention to the needs and desires of the agricultural community, no matter how pressing other and newer problems may be. But the recent decision of the United States Supreme Court that both houses of a state legislature must be truly representative promises an early end to this situation. It will then be up to those who guide our state universities, freed from this dead hand of the past, to move boldly and quickly to achieve a balanced effort that is based upon things as they are today, not as they were yesterday.

The Association of Land-Grant Colleges and Universities, recently expanded to include all state universities, has long been a kind of focal point for strongly agricultural influences. One can only hope that before too long this powerful body will achieve a better balance of interests and control, thus catching up with the times and justifying its continued existence as the principal national association of state universities. This will not happen, however, unless the more alert and forward-looking educators in these institutions take increased interest and make their potentially strong influence felt, rather than abdicating to those habitual convention-goers who are often found to be among the less progressive and imaginative elements of the academic community. Like their national association, many of the individual state universities need to consider a basic realignment or a major extension of their educational interests and efforts. It is to their everlasting credit that in earlier years they led vigorously and effectively in developing programs of research and instruction suited admirably to the times. But times have changed and the areas needing most intensive study are no longer what they once were. We are now in a period of urbanization, of automated production, of radical reorganization of the working force, of shortened time and distance the world over, and of a host of other almost revolutionary developments that ought to be of great interest to our scholars and students. It is questionable, however, whether some of our state universities are as deeply concerned as they ought to be about these new and vitally important consequences of social and technological change.

This is not to propose that anything less be done in those programs of research and instruction which began in an earlier day and which still have meaning and importance. But it is to suggest a careful reappraisal and, if need be, a redeployment of resources better suited to the present and the future than to the past. For example, the problem of how to gain the advantages of automated production without doing unconscionable harm to mil-

59

lions of workers cries for attention and intensive effort on the part of our universities, particularly those which are constituted as public agencies, and likewise the many and critical problems of our great and still growing cities—problems of housing, public health, education, race relations, transportation, local government, and many others. Perhaps the greatest challenge of all in this day of crass materialism and self-seeking cynicism is that of finding ways to develop a new sense of personal and social values—of ethics, beauty, and humanity. Truly our changing society is producing an abundance of new needs and tasks, but at least some of our state universities are doing precious little about them. In one perhaps extreme case of which the writer has knowledge, the principal university of a major manufacturing state spends more each year on 4H clubs than it does for its entire program of research and teaching for literally millions of industrial workers and their highly important organizations. It is surely time to give fuller meaning to the concept of the people's university. Happily, quite a few of our better state universities are now beginning to cast off excessive and restrictive commitments to the past. Hopefully, others will soon follow.

There is danger, of course, in reacting too hastily and uncritically to demands brought about by changes in the social and economic order. At this moment the strongly competitive drive for new industries and products as means to local economic growth carries with it a very real threat that powerful persons and their associations may insist that the first and foremost responsibility of the state university is to serve prevailing economic needs and desires. Clear signs of this danger can be seen in the sudden burst of enthusiasm for higher learning now being displayed by many leaders in business, industry, and politics who had previously been much more concerned about holding down taxes than about providing adequate financial support for their state universities. Overnight it seems, gold has been discovered on the campus and there is a mad rush to turn it into usable profits. Through chambers of commerce, manufacturers' associations, and clever politicians not formerly noted for their generosity to state-assisted higher education, special appropriations and even bond issues for "research and development" purposes are now being sponsored and "sold" to the public largely in terms of promised economic gains to the local community.

This sudden and even startling discovery of the values of

higher education is indeed flattering, and no one is about to reject the added support which it is bringing to our state universities. But it is also a cause for concern. Will it lead to harmful distortions, diverting resources to those fields which produce a quick pay-off in dollars and cents? Will it create a new elite among faculties, giving special favor and dominant power to the scholars and teachers whose efforts promise to bring direct and tangible economic gains? What will it do to those whose lives are devoted to learning in the humanities, in the relationships of man to man, and even in pure science? Will it threaten freedom to investigate where the search might lead to conclusions that seem dangerous to powerful forces whose primary interest is in personal gain through the prevailing system? Will it cloud the true and eternal purpose of any university worthy of the name: the ceaseless search for truth wherever the interests, the curiosity, or the needs of men may lead? Comments much the same might be made about the effects of contract research financed in our state universities by agencies of the federal government, chiefly the Department of Defense. There is reason to worry lest the influence of millions of otherwise unavailable dollars may cause faculties to dance to tunes called by others whose special interests lie outside the university. The emphasis upon contract research and the amounts of money that can be pulled out of Washington has now reached the dangerous point where many who ought to know better are using these dollar volume figures as measures of comparative quality and greatness among state universities. All too little attention is being paid to what this money may do to the long-range goals of a university, and to the fruitfulness or sterility of its instructional programs as able scholars become so preoccupied with contract research that what was once the absorbing job of teaching their successors comes out second best.

The financial needs of today and tomorrow are so great that the leaders of our state universities have no choice but to seek support from every respectable source. But if they are wise and farsighted they will be constantly on guard against the danger that their institutions might be made captive by such support, thus losing their identity and freedom as true universities. This is not to suggest that either economic growth or national security is an unworthy goal, and that money provided for these purposes is tainted. But it is to remind those who speak for and guide our state institutions that they bear a heavy responsibility for insisting upon freedom and balance among all of the many and diverse values of learning, and upon full regard for that special quality of a university which requires that its goals must always be set a bit beyond the immediate, the practical, and the presently popular.

It is not within the purposes of this paper to go into a detailed exploration of the immense problem of financing our state universities. Furthermore, the writer is not competent to do so. But attention must be given to certain situations where financial problems and the methods proposed for their solution may strongly affect matters of educational policy or practice. Reference to one situation of this kind has just been made in connection with contract research, where dollars from the national government already exert a powerful influence. Moreover, it now seems certain that we are starting down the road of steadily increasing federal assistance. In spite of loud cries of alarm about the dangers of domination by Washington, national subsidies in one form or another will not only be accepted, they will be sought for and even demanded. There is nothing really new about this situation, since what is now happening is simply a vast expansion, in both volume and purposes, of a practice that has existed for a long time. Hopefully experience, even on a relatively minor scale, has helped to prepare most of our state universities to accept and use money from Washington to good advantage and with a minimum of danger.

Even with the greatly increased federal assistance which is likely to come in the near future, costs at the local level will still be very high. This means that tax-conscious citizens and legislators will almost certainly be looking for every possible way to ease or shift the heavy burden. One such way, laying more and more of the cost upon the student, is very attractive and is already being used so widely as to be cause for deep concern. In earlier years it was taken almost for granted that the provision of educational opportunities in our state universities was largely a social obligation, or investment if you will. As a matter of wise public policy, taxes were laid upon all in order to meet the major portion of the cost, leaving it to the individual student to pay only a minor and by no means prohibitive share. But we are now witnessing a broad retreat from what was once almost a basic principle in state-assisted higher education. There is real danger that a long-established and very important difference between public and private universities will be lost as legislators and budget officers, faced with the distasteful task of raising taxes, take the easy way out. This truly fundamental change attracts little attention and provokes few cries of protest. Fee increases come steadily but in relatively small amounts. Furthermore, they give the appearance of being only reasonable and fair, since the student who is afforded the opportunities of higher education is likely to profit personally. Nevertheless, this recent trend really marks an alarming departure from past principles and practices. It threatens the concept of public responsibility for equal opportunities in learning, and if it is allowed to continue unchecked it will ultimately deprive society of the immense benefits to be gained by making the most of intelligent and purposeful young people, no matter what their early economic levels may be.

Almost equally dangerous to the nature and quality of our state universities is the even swifter rise in nonresident fees. It is easy to understand the reluctance of the taxpayers of one state to subsidize the educations of young people from others. It seems only right to ask the outsider or his family to pay something like the full cost. But this seemingly sound and reasonable practice is penny wise and pound foolish in terms of education at its best. It is leading directly toward insularity and provincialism through the erection of what amount to prohibitive barriers against the free flow of learning and broadened intellectual experiences. Long ago this nation accepted and wrote into law the principle that all parts profit most when channels for interstate trade in material things are kept wide open. It rejected all thought that even what seem to be purely local interests can be permanently advanced by internal economic barriers. Our states may think that they are now saving money and serving their local interests by making it increasingly difficult for nonresidents to enroll in their subsidized universities. But what they are really doing is lowering the quality and limiting the breadth of the educational opportunities which they seek to provide for their own young people. Moreover, it goes almost without saying that any trend toward insularity and provincialism in higher education is unquestionably harmful to the national interest. In fact, it is not beyond possibility that questions might be raised in the future about the propriety of giving large federal subsidies, drawn from the taxpayers of the entire nation, to state universities which give a special and very substantial advantage to local residents.

There may be little or nothing that the state universities themselves can do to halt or reverse the present trend toward higher fees and almost prohibitive interstate barriers. But, of all people, their leaders and spokesmen must surely realize the danger to both the nature and quality of public higher education and do their level best to see that it is recognized and averted. Faculty members must also bear their share of this responsibility. All too often they remain silent and thus give their tacit approval to higher and higher student fees when legislative appropriations fail to meet pressing needs for salary improvements. The least that they can do is to be aware of what this easy way out is doing to the nature of their universities, and then speak up for all to hear.

Interestingly enough, there is a strong trend toward cooperation, often interstate in scope, among institutions of higher learning at the very moment that rising nonresident fees are reducing the mobility of students in our state universities. These cooperative ventures are taking two broad forms. The first is based upon concerted legal action by two or more states, while the second grows out of purely voluntary association on the part of universities and their faculties. Interstate compacts or agreements, entered into by the governments concerned, are being used principally to achieve economies and improved services through an apportionment of efforts, often accompanied by contractual arrangements calling for the home state to pay another for the costs of educating students in certain fields. Arrangements of this kind are proving to be very useful in preventing wasteful duplication and perhaps inferior education in those essential but costly programs which have relatively small enrollments. They are particularly useful in the professional fields and in highly specialized areas of graduate work. The second broad form of cooperation, that of purely voluntary association, has been in existence for a long time. But its use in the past was usually limited to the smaller schools which lacked the size, economic resources, and student enrollments which are necessary to achieve strength and quality over a broad range of educational endeavors. Such institutions have found much to be gained by sharing efforts in a common cause.

Voluntary association is now being given an entirely new dimension by some of our large and powerful universities. These are institutions of great size and diversity, of the kind which might seem to have the least need of all for seeking cooperative relationships with others. But their purpose is something far beyond simply gaining economies or acceptable levels of quality as they are recognized today. It is instead to exceed the best that now exists, even in our foremost institutions, achieving hitherto almost undreamed-of power and excellence in higher education. Their method is to bring together, to encourage, and to assist faculty members who are interested in using the combined resources of several universities to build programs of research or teaching that now lie beyond the reach of a single university in terms of highly competent people, special laboratories, costly instruments, or library collections which lose their value when spread too widely. It is also to reach agreements as to who will do what—and do it better than ever before—in certain highly specialized or so-called "exotic" fields where the resources of scholarship are sharply limited and cannot be scattered without a severe loss of quality and effectiveness.

The Committee on Institutional Cooperation (CIC), made up of the Big Ten universities and the University of Chicago, is a prime example of this type of voluntary association. Established only seven years ago with original support from the Carnegie Corporation, it has become an impressive example of what can be accomplished when even very large and seemingly self-sufficient universities, private as well as public, join forces for the advancement of learning. It now has more than a score of important ventures in actual operation, ranging from biometeorology to research in water pollution, from studies in economic growth to a "grand design" for the less familiar but still vitally important foreign languages and literatures. The CIC Summer Institute in Far Eastern Languages, assisted by the Ford Foundation, is but a single example of what can be done through voluntary cooperation among powerful universities. This institute moves from campus to campus, bringing together the best of scholars and students for two months of intensive work of scope and quality beyond what could be provided by any single one of the several members. Perhaps the most interesting development of all has been the recent establishment of the CIC Traveling Scholar Program. With the permission of the related graduate deans and faculty advisers in each case, this program allows a graduate student in any one of the member universities to move to any other for two quarters or one semester in order to study with a particular person, to work with instruments that do not exist elsewhere, or to have the benefit of unique library collections. The registration of the traveling scholar remains at his home university, and he pays no extra fees. Thus a way is opened for the individual student to add to his normal program of study the best that is available in several great universities. This plan also makes it possible for each university to select and develop certain specialties which might seem to be extravagant in terms of its own students but which could be fully justified when made available on a sharing basis to those of ten others. It remains to be seen whether the state universities and their faculties will make the most of the opportunity to gain unprecedented strength and quality through voluntary cooperation. One of the more attractive features of this approach is the fact that, unlike compacts based upon law, it can easily encompass private as well as public universities and thus bring great advantages to both. It is not idle dreaming to hope that the CIC and other associations of its kind may soon add an entirely new dimension to higher education in America.

The possibility of gaining some of the benefits of large numbers and wide diversity without losing identity or paying the price of monstrous expansion has at least some bearing upon one of the major problems now facing the state universities: the problem of optimum size, the question of when a limit is reached and it is better to create an entirely new institution or expand others. Many educators are now deeply concerned about rapidly increasing enrollments, wondering how long they can go unchecked without serious effects upon students and teachers as individual persons, fearing that they may become only faces in the crowd. They also worry about the mushrooming cloud of administrative offices and required procedures growing out of greater size and complexity and, as they view it, casting a deathly pall over the campus. There can be little doubt that, if kept within reasonable limits, size and diversity offer real and substantial advantages. The large multipurpose university needs and can usually support library resources of considerable breadth and depth; its laboratories are likely to be widely varied and equipped with the kinds of instrumentation which are beyond the reach of most smaller institutions; the special interests and abilities of its faculty members complement each other and provide a rich amalgam of differing experiences and points of view; and the cosmopolitan nature of its student body minimizes the danger of damaging insularity. The problem now facing the state universities is, of course, that of finding the point of diminishing returns, where sheer size becomes a monstrous hindrance rather than a helpful advantage. But as yet no one has come up with an easy and generally acceptable solution. In all probability there is no magic formula, one equally applicable throughout the land. Each state university will have to face this question in terms of its own goals, resources, and relationships with other institutions.

The problem of size and numbers is most acute as it affects great masses of undergraduate students, particularly in their general education rather than in their major fields of study, where relationships are likely to be more personal and intimate. A great deal of experimentation will be needed in order to determine how best to retain the advantages of size and variety without sacrificing the individuality of the student or of his teachers. In fact, such experimentation is now getting under way in several state universities. One approach is that of holding the student in a smaller branch during the first year or two of his university experience, a period usually devoted largely to general education and to preparation in courses that are basic to later work in a chosen major. It is obvious, however, that this approach sacrifices such advantages as the richness of library and other resources, the heterogeneity of student associations, and to a large degree the daily challenge of a faculty that is widely and actively engaged in research. The latter disadvantage is perhaps the most alarming of all. No matter now strong an effort may be made to hold to equivalent faculty standards, those who teach in "feeder" branches will be set apart by the nature of their teaching duties, by their daily associations, and by the kinds of opportunities which they have for research. By and large they will find it difficult to maintain for themselves and to nurture in their students the intellectual vigor and alertness ordinarily expected in a university setting. Another approach is that of establishing, relatively small colleges for undergraduate instruction clustered on or near the main campus and thus in close contact with the stimulating challenges and diversities of a major university. Coupled with counseling by carefully chosen faculty members, plus curricular requirements that are flexible within broadly established university limits, this approach appears to have real possibilities for retaining the advantages of both largeness and individuality while adjusting to numbers that seem to be inevitable.

It can be expected that in addition to the formal instruction of their regularly enrolled students, most of our state universities will be giving added attention and importance to continuing or extended education. Again, vision and careful planning will make a difference between massive but superficial and enervating engagement in busywork and the accomplishment of educational purposes of the highest order. Properly viewed and selectively chosen programs of continuing education can do much to develop and give real meaning to the concept that for the truly educated person there is no end to study and learning. The brief years of residence then fall into their proper place as an introduction to a lifetime of learning, and "commencement" begins to take on its proper meaning as an invitation to the future rather than a farewell to the past. But the attainment of this goal will call for discrimination and courage. Pressures for "short courses" teaching merely the tricks of a trade are very heavy, and a state university may easily fall into the error of courting public favor by transforming its campus into a huge county fair complete with bargains hawked by professors whose time and energies might be far better spent otherwise.

The first criterion for judging what or what not to do in continuing education should be that of the probable effect upon the individual student. Does the program simply pass on to him what others have learned, or is it designed primarily to develop his ability to find his own solutions to his own problems? Does it contribute to his continuing intellectual growth and acuity, or does it merely give him dulling answers to his questions of the moment? The second standard for measuring the worth and appropriateness of a program in continuing education is the use that it makes of faculty time and talents. Does it thoughtlessly waste them, or does it put them to their best possible use in a total approach to higher learning that lasts a lifetime? Probably the most difficult task now facing all American universities is that of building sufficient faculty strength to provide high quality instruction for students in unprecedented numbers. The state universities will be particularly hard pressed because they are less able to control enrollments and thus keep their teaching obligations within the limits of their faculty resources. It seems certain that the supply of adequately prepared scholars will fall far short of the need as measured by present teaching practices. Incoming freshmen will reflect the higher birthrates of seventeen to nineteen years before, while the potential instructors flowing out of graduate schools will come from those born in earlier years when the numbers were much smaller. Thus the most precious resource on any campus will be the talented faculty member. Ways must be found to use him well, to protect him from unbearably heavy teaching loads, to free him as much as possible from routine chores of doubtful value, and to keep him intellectually alive with time and energy enough to read and reflect, to study and travel.

Many self-appointed experts will probably expect to get much more mileage out of every available professor by means of such mechanical aids as TV and teaching machines for programmed instruction. Unfortunately, some university administrators, particularly those with little or no actual experience in the classroom or the laboratory, have helped to build false hopes as to what can be done, and done well, through a kind of automated speed-up. The result has often been undue and sometimes blind faculty resistance to even the proper use of what might prove to be valuable teaching aids and methods. This will not do. What is needed is a calm, honest, and open-minded appraisal of the very real possibilities for improved instruction and wider dissemination which may be afforded by at least some of the newer devices and fresh approaches to teaching. There is another approach to the problem of too few competent teachers that is also very much worth careful consideration and full exploration by the state universities. It lies in striking a new balance between the obligation to teach and the obligation to learn, in requiring students to assume greater responsibility for their self-education. On the whole, the state institutions have been more inclined than the private ones to concentrate teaching and learning in the classroom and in the closely supervised laboratory. This practice means a great number of face-to-face contact hours for the teacher, perhaps too many for the most profitable use of his time and for the kind of sound education which will last the student a lifetime. Through sheer necessity our state universities may be forced to demand more of their students, to do less "spoon-feeding," to rely more upon assignments that are carefully designed to develop lasting abilities for personal reading, reflection, and inquiry. Born of the necessity for conserving the time and talents of teachers, this new balance could turn out to be one of the major educational advances made by our state universities within the next decade.

Other aspects of instruction also merit careful consideration and, if need be, radical revision. It is likely that sharp and critical attention will soon be focused on teaching in our state universities. One reason for this will be their enormously increased operating costs and a corresponding public concern about how well and effectively the added dollars are spent. Another will be the extension of the widespread interest which has been centered upon our secondary schools over the past few years. This critical interest is bringing substantial improvement at the high school level, so much that many graduates of the better schools are now complaining openly about the content and quality of teaching on the campus. It is not inconceivable that the blasts of public criticism which have hitherto been directed against teaching in our secondary schools will soon be turned toward the state universities. In all honesty it must be admitted that there are enough wasteful and—what is worse—educationally unsound courses and curricula in most of our state universities to provide a field day for the critics, whether they be persons who are sincere in their desire for improvement or merely ambitious headline hunters. It will be up to the faculties concerned to put their academic houses in order if they are to retain their traditional right to control matters of educational policy and practice. This will call for serious concern and vigorous action with regard to such things as cheap and shoddy courses offered for full university credit, needless duplication of efforts, and the growing number of super-specialties that are both wasteful and educationally indefensible. Some faculties may shy away from the distasteful task of housecleaning and renovation, of building strength where weakness now prevails. But they must either be willing to do it themselves or have it forced upon them by outside amateurs, or even by the kinds of professional administrators who are sometimes a bit too sensitive to public criticism for the good of higher education.

This listing of problems and possiblilties, of choices to be made by or for the state universities, could be almost endless. It might well include such things as the difficult task of finding valid criteria for the selection of students; or the critical need for a re-examination of graduate curricula and degrees, particularly the doctorate, which in many cases is neither fish nor fowl, neither a truly research degree nor an openly professional one. Questions might be raised about the proper relationship between teaching and research in any worthwhile approach to higher education. There might be at least some reference to the increasingly important role of serious students and student government as they become more influential and even demanding in academic affairs. But there must be an end somewhere; furthermore, most issues such as those just mentioned need attention by our private universities as well as by the public ones. Let us turn now to a brief consideration of how choices will be made, of who will decide whether our burgeoning state universities will move strongly and confidently toward higher education at its best or, in any more than rare instances, will end up ten years hence as dull monsters of mediocrity.

III

The basic power to decide the future of a state university usually starts with the state legislature. In most cases these institutions were established and are still governed by legal enactments that are subject to change and that may thus be used to affect their structure, purposes, and management. Even when a state university has separate constitutional status and seems to be free to govern its own affairs, the legislature still has control over a substantial portion of the public assistance which it must have to survive, and this power of the purse strings can be used very effectively indeed. Thus, like any other agency founded in or dependent upon representative government, no state university can be entirely free from legislative authority. It is subject to public pressures exerted through the representative body, and it cannot afford to take them lightly. This makes it doubly important for those who plan and speak for the university to gain a long and clear view of direction, of purposes, and of methods—and then stand boldly and publicly for what is best in higher education. On the whole, leaders and spokesmen of this kind have had excellent records of bringing their institutions to strength and quality over a period of years. They will be more important than ever during the next few years of rapid change and greatly increased interest in our state universities.

The fear of direct legislative interference in the internal affairs of our state universities is often exaggerated by those who pay too much attention to frequent but usually short-lived flurries of excitement. It is true that scarcely a year goes by without one or two investigations or proposals for restrictive legislation. These attract wide publicity and the result may easily be a mistaken impression that legislatures are constantly meddling and thus making it impossible for the state universities to guide and manage their affairs in a highly professional way. Actually the situation is not nearly so serious as many may think. With rare exceptions it certainly is not beyond the control of wise and courageous educational leaders who know what their universities must be about and who are willing and able to rally powerful and intelligent opinion on their side. It may be assumed that such leadership will be equally effective as our state universities now re-examine their positions and search for new directions. There is at this moment, however, one threat of legislative intervention that is truly alarming—the threat of the proposed or actual enactment of laws placing special restrictions upon the freedom of scholars and students in the state universities to hear and consider opinions and exhortations that strongly organized pressure groups may regard as harmful to young minds, thus in effect barring from the campus expressions of views that are perfectly legal elsewhere. This danger, striking at the very heart of any true university, is now being countered boldly and publicly by our more enlightened and courageous presidents and governing boards. Somewhat paradoxically, the public universities may be saved from this peril, if need be, by the very fact that they are agencies of the state and thus subject to the Constitution of the United States and its amendments. Recent trends in judicial decisions suggest that there is at least a possibility that the federal courts, using the First and Fourteenth amendments, may have the last word to say about freedom of expression in state universities. It is intriguing even to imagine that there may come a day when the assurance of freedom will be stronger and more complete in the public universities than it is in the private ones.

In many states a relatively recent development has now inserted a kind of super-board or council into the line of control between the legislature and the governing boards of the separate public colleges and universities. These newer agencies are usually limited in both responsibility and authority, being designed largely to plan and facilitate the development of statewide systems of higher education, to achieve balance and effectiveness by deciding who does what, and to recommend a proper apportionment of funds to individual institutions. In most cases, they have no direct legal power to interfere with the university in the management of its own educational affairs, but there is danger that these new super-boards, armed as they are with the right and duty to make decisions in some important matters and recommendations in others, may become a bit too ambitious and thus threaten the educational autonomy and vital individuality of our state universities. Yet they offer promise of much good through the careful planning and balanced development of varied post-secondary opportunities. They can be of great assistance to the universities as they seek to find their rightful places and perform their expected functions within the total structure. What is needed now during the formative period of these relatively new super-boards is an earnest and sincere effort, joined in by all parties concerned, to sharpen the definition of their responsibilities and to depict the roles which they can properly and usefully play to the advantage of all.

Within the university itself, major responsibility for charting a course into the future will reside in three groups or centers of power. These are the governing board, the president and his principal administrative associates, and the university faculty. Each will play a very significant role, and for real success each must have reason to respect the others. The surest way to failure will be to confuse the corporate structure of business with the proper management of university affairs, ruling by authority wielded in successive superior and inferior relationships. For example, anyone who is at all familiar with university life knows that all the laws in the land cannot make a really vigorous and proud faculty recognize and meekly submit to the admittedly superior legal authority of its governing board in professional matters of educational policy and practice. Neither will any president who pretends to be an educator remain as a docile and obedient servant if either the board or the faculty seeks to assume unwarranted power. What is so often forgotten is the fact that even within a university based upon the full force of law, the power structure is closely akin to that of a professional association. It is not a relationship of master to servant, of employer to employee. Instead, it is essentially a working together by equals, each devoted to a common cause and each having a proper role to play.

Governing boards of state universities come in all shapes and sizes, the personal interests and backgrounds of their members vary widely, and there is little uniformity in the ways by which they are chosen. Among all of these variables, only two or three constants are likely to be found. In almost all cases the prevailing majority will be laymen, and persons with professional knowledge of higher education will be few and far between. It is also probable that in comparison with the private universities, the governing boards of state universities will include fewer men and women of scholarly pursuits and personal involvement, of those who are widely read and possessed by a love of learning for its own sake. This proportionate lack of direct interest and experience in academic affairs poses a delicate problem for the wise governing board, one of judiciously tempering its use of legal powers that appear to be absolute and all-inclusive. This does not means that the governing board of a state university is powerless in setting goals and shaping methods. It has great power to determine the broad future of the university in all of its aspects. But if wisdom prevails, that power is seldom exercised through direct and authoritative intervention. Instead, it is used slowly but effectively through the choice of those persons, beginning with the president, upon whom a lay board must depend for professional opinions and strong educational leadership. It is difficult to imagine a greater tragedy for a university than having a board that misuses its power and reaches beyond the limits of its knowledge in academic affairs, particularly if that body is largely controlled, as sometimes happens, by one or two dominant and aggressive individuals who expect and demand servility from the faculty, the president, and even from their fellow board members.

Within the next decade the nature of many a state university will be greatly affected by the choice of one man and, through him, a relatively small group of persons in important administrative positions. Countless bad jokes have been made about presidents, vice presidents, provosts, and deans, but the fact remains that these few, much as they may be ridiculed, have tremendous power for good or ill in the life of a university. Given a little time, their day-to-day decisions have a cumulative effect that weighs heavily upon any campus. Slowly but surely they can even shape the nature and fix the goals of a faculty that is lacking in vision, courage, and professional pride. Thus it is not fanciful to suggest that in the selection of a president and, subject to his strong influence, a few other important administrative officers lies the greatest power of any board to govern a state university. What then should be the nature of the office and the personal qualities of its occupant if a board really wants a president who will lead toward greatness? Not too long ago, when life was much simpler, the state university president was expected to be an experienced and respected leader in matters pertaining to the process of education itself. A handful of able associates could perform the necessary housekeeping chores, thus allowing him to give most of his time and attention to academic affairs. But times have changed. Most state universities today are very large and very complex establishments, so large and so complex that the major purpose of education sometimes seems to be only secondary. There are thousands of students to be housed and fed and their health and morals protected; millions of dollars to be gathered, spent, and accounted for; buildings to be built, cleaned, and kept in repair; alumni to be coaxed or cursed; an "image" to be created or preserved by using all the tricks of Madison Avenue—to say nothing of providing parking spaces for the faculty and seeing to it that the football team does not play like a bunch of amateurs.

It can be safely said that few business executives have more "publics" to please or tougher problems to face than does the president of a large state university today. Small wonder, then, that some governing boards tend to put too much emphasis upon purely administrative functions and skills, and correspondingly too little upon the role of the president as an experienced, respected, and courageous leader in higher education. As laymen, board members are understandably tempted to think of the office and the man in terms of their own experiences and desires. Longing for order, peace, and public acceptance in all things, they may overlook the hard facts that

74

there can be little peace and quiet in any university worthy of the name, and that not infrequently they must be prepared to listen calmly but confidently to public protests as they are shouted from the very housetops. A subservient president, provost, or dean may help to protect them from the terrors of true greatness, but over the long span of years the university and those it pretends to serve will be the tragic losers. The job of being president of a contemporary state university calls for a man who first and foremost understands the true nature of his mission and who is willing to accept all of its personal perils. He must stand ready to face strong public criticism as well as to accept honor and acclaim. Knowing the almost impossible complexity of his many tasks, the wise president will seek to surround himself with experienced and tough-minded university educators who are willing to differ sharply and sometimes stubbornly. He should be able to maintain a proper balance, being the captive of neither his board nor his faculty but, instead, respectful of the rights of both, giving each its due. Above all, he ought to be the principal defender of the faith—faith in the pursuit of learning wherever it may lead, faith in his faculty, faith in his students, and faith in the long future of his university.

The third center of power to determine the future of a state university, perhaps the most decisive of all in the long run, lies in the faculty itself. Boards and presidents come and go but the faculty lives on, and in its ever changing but never dying corporate being may best be found the true embodiment of a university. Those who come and go may leave a faculty stronger or weaker in quality and purpose, but they have neither the time nor the strength to transform it completely. Firmly grasped and fully asserted, its professional right and duty to point the way in educational affairs can make it the most potent and enduring force of all. But it must be realized that this inherent power will be as nothing unless it is recognized and used, unless its matching responsibilities are accepted and met. Weakness, disinterest, or even outright abdication on the part of a faculty may leave to far less competent persons the power to chart the course of a great state university in the critical years immediately ahead. On this matter and at this moment there is cause for deep concern. Perhaps because of sheer size and the diversity of specialized efforts, too many faculty members seem to be losing their feeling for the university as a whole and even for their oneness in what ought to be a proud, powerful, and responsible profession. All too often their attitude is one of live and let live, of lack of interest in what may happen elsewhere on the campus so long as personal or departmental endeavors are not directly affected. This will never do if a faculty is to accept and really use its full responsibility and traditional right to help shape the future of the university. There must be a rebirth of pride of membership in a distinguished profession and of determination not to let its power to govern affairs rightfully its own go by default.

One can only hope that the governing boards, administrative officers, and faculties of our state universities may be blessed with wisdom and courage over the next few years. They will be the principal architects of a vast structure of public higher education, and the effects of their vision and artistry will long be felt throughout America. At worst their designs may become a blight upon the land. At best they may help to infuse new quality, effectiveness, and even beauty into all of university life. One can also hope that their building, no matter how well done, will never overshadow our many and richly diverse private colleges and universities, for it is from these institutions with their high degree of individuality that we can confidently expect a continuing flow of fresh ideas, of new standards for academic excellence, of sharp challenges to stultifying sameness. In their well-being, along with that of our state universities, may be found two mighty forces for good, each complementing the other.

ROBERT S. MORISON

Foundations and Universities

AMERICAN foundations and American universities are both about a
hundred years old. Both are devoted to the same ends, and both
have in fact grown up together as members of the same family. Writing in 1930, Dr. Frederick P. Keppel, president of The Carnegie
Corporation and one of the most reflective and quotable of all foundation officers, outlined the kinship as follows: "What social instrument is the foundation's nearest relative? I think, without any question, it is the university. There are, of course, obvious differences.
Instead of a multitude of students the foundation may have only a
handful of research workers. The foundation is a spender only,
whereas the university both spends and earns. Instead of a central
location, the work of the foundation may be scattered over all the
world. . . . And yet to me, at any rate, the similarities seem more important than the differences. It is an interesting coincidence that the
aggregate endowment of our foundations and of our colleges and
universities is approximately the same—about one billion dollars,
though the property of the latter is, of course, much larger. The responsibilities of the trustees, both in the control of finances and in
the general direction of activities, are the same. In both, important
decisions are based on group rather than individual judgment and
derive their significance from this fact. Almost without exception
permanent foundation executives have had their training in universities. Dr. Pritchett was called to the Carnegie Foundation from the
Presidency of the Massachusetts Institute of Technology, and the
Rockefeller Foundation called successively President Vincent from
the University of Minnesota and President Mason from the University of Chicago. Furthermore, whenever a foundation needs temporary help, it turns uniformly to the university. It is only natural that
the relations between the two have always been close. The founda-

tions have learned by experience that one of the most satisfactory ways of disposing of their burdens of responsibility is to lay them upon the universities as operating agencies, sometimes in the form of general endowment, more often as time goes on, for specific purposes mutually agreed upon."[1]

A third of a century later the only modification one might wish to make in this account is in the matter of relative wealth. In spite of the rapid growth of foundations (total assets now estimated at about $12,000,000,000), the universities have grown even faster, and the endowment figure has become a less accurate index of financial strength. Many of our best universities depend quite happily on regular legislative appropriations. In addition, grants from the federal government and, to a lesser extent, from industry are increasingly acquiring a dignity and regularity which qualify them for the respect previously reserved for endowment income.

The foundation-university relationship, like all family relationships, has its tensions and hostilities as well as its satisfactions and rewards. Many of them, as we shall see, can be traced to the way foundations use universities to "dispose of their burdens of responsibility," to use Dr. Keppel's almost too well-chosen phrase. There is a very general feeling that the interest of the foundations in education has been growing closer in recent years and that their influence on universities has been increasing. Dr. Keppel's current successor began his address to the Association of American Colleges in 1956 with the words, "One of the most important trends in the work of the major foundations over the past thirty years has been their increasing commitment to education, and particularly to higher education."[2] However true this may be, it is not the same thing as saying that the relative impact of foundations is any greater than it used to be. Toward the end of this essay we shall try to gain a clearer view of this question, but first let us see what the foundation-university family looked like in the days of its childhood and early adolescence.

It may be a figure of speech to say that foundations and universities have both existed in the United States for approximately one hundred years. Rudimentary forms of both types of institution can be detected much earlier than this, and neither became fully developed until sometime later. The President and Fellows of Harvard College is over three hundred years old, and James Smithson left half a million dollars in 1829 "for the increase and diffusion of knowledge among men." A contemporary student of foundations feels that the

78

latter event marks the beginning of the modern foundation era.[3] In the face of these facts I choose, somewhat arbitrarily perhaps, to regard the appointment of President Eliot to Harvard in 1869 as the beginning of the university in America, and the establishment of the $2,000,000 Peabody Education Fund "to aid the stricken south" in 1867 as the beginning of the foundation as we know it.

The beginning of graduate study and research at Harvard was quickly followed by the establishment of Johns Hopkins and the development of several other existing colleges into full-fledged universities. Similarly, the Peabody Education Fund established principles and working procedures which, somewhat more slowly, were taken up by the spate of new foundations founded in the first two decades of the twentieth century. The clearest line of descent is traceable perhaps in the General Education Board, which also devoted a major part of its effort to the "stricken south." From the turn of the century to World War II the history of American foundations is essentially the history of the several benefactions established by Mr. Andrew Carnegie and Mr. John D. Rockefeller. Other substantial trusts were also founded at an increasing rate throughout the period, many of which have been conducted with enterprise and good judgment. The Milbank and Commonwealth funds and the Kellogg, Markle, and Macy foundations have all contributed importantly to public health and medical education. Other organizations, such as the Russell Sage Foundation and the Twentieth Century Fund, have pursued their specialized purposes with distinction and even elegance. But for overall impact on universities, there is only one major league and its members are (or in some cases, were) The Carnegie Foundation for the Advancement of Teaching, The Carnegie Corporation, the General Education Board, The Rockefeller Foundation, and The Laura Spelman Rockefeller Memorial. Since the war, of course, a new superleague has been formed which so far has only one member, but it is still a little early to say what its final impact on the universities will be.

In part the pre-eminence of the major league was due to mere size. Taken together the Carnegie and Rockefeller benefactions were simply very much larger than anything of the kind had ever been before. Walter A. Jessup, president of The Carnegie Corporation, in his annual report for 1944 estimated that the $6,000,000 per year spent by the Corporation in the "early years of its existence" was one-fifteenth of the total income of all institutions of higher learning in the country. During part of this period the General Education Board was spending even more, so that there were probably some years in which these two boards alone decided on an expenditure of funds equal to approximately one-fifth of the total income available to universities and colleges. When one realizes that toward the end of this period other members of the same league were also becoming prominent and that essentially all the funds available to the foundations were free for the encouragement of innovation while almost all the regular income of the university was tied to on-going commitments, it is easy to comprehend the overwhelming significance of the foundations' part.

Of almost equal importance was the matter of timing. The foundations happened on the scene at a time when higher education in the United States was almost unbelievably confused. There were several hundred institutions calling themselves colleges and universities. Admissions requirements were so vague that it was often impossible to differentiate colleges from high schools. The great mass of these institutions depended almost wholly on tuitions supplemented by periodic but uncertain gifts to meet running expenses. Only a few traditional institutions had significant endowments. The literature dealing with this period abounds with such terms as "confused," "unregulated," "substandard," "fresh water," and "fly-by-night." "Chaotic" is a particular favorite. The situation was clearly ripe for change; no modern nation could tolerate such a hodgepodge in its educational facilities. Change had indeed already begun when the Carnegie Foundation and, soon after, the General Education Board appeared with what seemed like infinite financial resources and what certainly were an extraordinary lot of officers and trustees.

The Carnegie Foundation for the Advancement of Teaching grew out of Mr. Carnegie's concern for the welfare of college and university teachers. Like most Scots he had a healthy admiration for education, and he was appalled to discover how poorly teachers were paid in the United States and how often their declining years were spent in abject poverty. After fifteen years of experience with the problem as a trustee of Cornell, he established The Carnegie Foundation for the Advancement of Teaching in 1905 with an endowment of $10,000,000.* Dr. Henry Pritchett, then president of the

* Increased to $15,000,000 a little later. In assessing Pritchett's influence it should be borne in mind that he was also Mr. Carnegie's primary adviser on philanthropic matters and in effect directed The Carnegie Corporation as well

Massachusetts Institute of Technology, agreed to be president and immediately embarked on what was in many ways the most spectacular and at the same time most controversial of foundation careers.

Incredible as it now seems, the original intention seems to have been to provide "free" (i.e. noncontributory) pensions to teachers in all the nondenominational, nonstate-supported colleges and universities in the United States. Equally surprising was the provision that eligibility began after twenty-five years of service. It rapidly became apparent that even Mr. Carnegie's generosity was not equal to the task of providing pensions for all who were eligible under these provisions. But the early difficulty was compounded by a failure to predict the rapid growth of the nation's educational apparatus. It is interesting to observe how some of the most farseeing men of that time—or of any other time for that matter—underestimated the needs and achievements of the years immediately ahead of them. At the same time that Henry Pritchett was assuming responsibility for the old age of most of the college teachers in the land, the General Education Board was estimating "that 100 colleges, each with an endowment of $1,000,000, would provide for the country's need in the field of higher education."[4] This is not the place to recount the several steps taken by the Carnegie Foundation to free itself from the embarrassing enlargement of its original commitments.[5] Ultimately, the path led to the establishment of the Teachers Insurance and Annuity Association of America, which has played such an essential role in stabilizing the financial future of American college teachers. We may note in passing that the development of this service organization is an excellent example of the indirect way in which foundations may help the whole educational world in solving a common problem.

More important for our present purpose is the direct role the Foundation played in changing the character and raising the standards of American colleges and universities and indirectly of American high schools. In the first place, Dr. Pritchett found that if his organization was to pay pensions to teachers in colleges and universities, he would have to have some definition of what such institutions were. As Abraham Flexner put it with a gravity which may sound faintly ironical to today's anxious parents, "After careful thought the Foundation decided that no institution could be consid-

as the Foundation until Mr. James Rowland Angell took over the presidency of the Corporation from Mr. Carnegie in 1921.

ered to be either a college or university unless the admission of students rested upon a definite basis,"[6] defined as a requirement of a four-year high school education. This step led in turn to the definition of a high school education in terms of "Carnegie units" which still underlie much of the digital determination of eligibility to enter the company of educated men in the United States. The resulting "regimentation" implied by this and other measures remains a subject of controversy even today, but there can be no doubt that higher and more uniform standards were badly needed by American education at the turn of the century, and equally that the Carnegie Foundation played an important role in establishing them.

Equally important perhaps, and a greater source of controversy and criticism, was Mr. Carnegie's restriction of his gift to non-denominational, nonstate-supported institutions. The latter requirement was removed in a few years, and the potential eligibility of state institutions to the approved list did a good deal to raise the standards in some of the more backward states and to encourage the healthy interchange of faculty between state and private universities which characterizes today's pattern. The nondenominational requirement persisted, although its rigors were somewhat mitigated by administrative procedure. After all, one could not avoid the uneasy memory that many if not most of the outstanding private colleges in the country had started under denominational auspices. Obviously some latitude must be allowed in the determination of just when a denominational college becomes a respectable secular one. On the whole, however, the rules were strict. For instance, one college was denied permission to require that "a majority of the faculty must be members of Protestant churches, but shall be so chosen that the members of no one church shall have a majority."[7] Clearly the Foundation was one of the strong influences which worked together to produce the largely secularized education characteristic of our country today. Another of the Foundation's regulations which seems less subject to dispute as a matter of principle nevertheless was a serious source of friction and resentment. In order to ensure a minimum of financial security and responsibility, the Foundation required that participating colleges have an endowment of at least $200,000. Furthermore, its officers seem to have been constantly inspecting the books to ensure that this fund was not eroded by the then common practice of borrowing from it to meet "emergency" expenses.

Some idea of the kind of feeling engendered by these reforms may be gained from the following paragraphs in President Pritchett's *Ninth Annual Report*: "When a man sets a lump sum of $15,000,000 rolling around the country there is no knowing what it will do. It was supposed that the endowment provided by Mr. Carnegie for the pensioning of superannuated college professors would simply serve to ease the declining years of a useful and underpaid class of public servants. Who anticipated that in less than five years it would effect profound changes in the constitution and management of our colleges, severing venerable denominational ties, tightening up requirements for admission, differentiating the college from the university, systematizing finances, raising salaries, and in more subtle ways modifying the life and work of thousands of educators. . . .

"Mr. Andrew Carnegie has been sharply attacked for inventing the 'Carnegie unit,' which with a diabolical ingenuity and a clever use of money he is urging upon the universities, with a special and particular design on religious colleges. A committee of the National Education Association on normal schools at its last meeting 'viewed with alarm' the efforts of the Foundation to 'control the educational standards of the country,' and a Methodist Bishop has solemnly warned the country of the same awful tendencies. The hardest blow has come from an eminent professor of Harvard in a pamphlet entitled 'A Plea for Independence in Provincial Education,' printed and circulated by Middlebury College. . . . He warns to beware of educational advice from the Carnegie Foundation, for its experts are 'professional standardizers.' Nothing so cruel as this has been said about the Foundation during all its short life."[8]

The Foundation did not confine itself to commenting on the affairs of institutions with which it was directly involved. W. S. P. Bryan in his monograph *The Church, Her Colleges, and the Carnegie Foundation* sardonically commented, "Some persons might suppose that denominational institutions, being excluded from the benefaction of the Foundation, would also be deprived of the benefits arising out of the scrutiny of the President of the Foundation. This, however, is a hopelessly narrow view. He seeks to elevate by his criticisms, institutions which the Foundation declines to assist with its money, and not institutions only, but denominations as well."[9] Sometimes these comments were elaborated into formal surveys and published as Foundation bulletins. By all odds the most influential of these was Bulletin No. 4 on medical education, which we will describe later. One of the last was published in 1929 on American college athletics. It certainly aroused a great deal of comment at the time and has at the very least served to imbue college administrators with feelings of guilt over the more blatant forms of campus professionalism. At best it may have contributed to the relative purity of the better college conferences and to the de-emphasis of athletics at certain institutions like the University of Chicago.

The General Education Board was the next great foundation to become involved directly and on a large scale with institutions of higher learning. Conceived in large part as a device for alleviating the backwardness of the southern states, it continued to give priority to southern problems throughout its existence. Its influence, nevertheless, was also very great on higher education throughout the country, especially perhaps in the revolution it inspired and financed in the realm of medical education. On the whole the General Education Board seems to have been more tactful than the Carnegie Foundation in its approach to colleges, and more willing to accept the existing situation as a starting point. On occasion, however, it was also found waving the admonitory finger and insisting on specific conditions in connection with its grants. Most significant perhaps was its frequent use of the "matching" principle whereby an institution was required to raise a certain sum from other sources in order to become eligible for a grant from the General Education Board. This device was apparently invented by the Peabody Fund and is still frequently used today, notably by the Ford Foundation in its current series of grants for the general development of colleges and universities. Even the federal government has adopted the practice, notably in the program of the National Institutes of Health for providing building funds for laboratories. It is interesting to note that early criticism of the procedure is echoed today in a concern that efforts to match a government building grant may draw funds from other equally worthy and more poverty-stricken fields, that is, the humanities and the social sciences.

The General Education Board also threw its weight behind efforts to raise and regularize admission standards, to reduce the number of inadequately administered institutions, to strengthen the most promising of them, and explicitly to encourage the growth of strong universities in centers of population. As an important part of its contribution to the overall strength of universities it initiated and carried on for many years a series of studies on the financial situation of academic institutions, and worked out detailed schemes for keeping account of university expenditures. This program, under the direction of an unusually capable and tactful officer—Trevor Arnett—culminated in a book on university finance which had wide influence during the 1920's and 1930's. In the words of the historian of the General Education Board, "It was brief, simple, and clear. It could be understood even by a college president unable to balance his own checkbook."[10]

By 1923 the General Education Board had contributed approximately $60,000,000 to the general support of education (exclusive of medicine), most of it in the form of endowment. Although in later years much has been made of the need to concentrate on a few leading institutions and to avoid what Mr. Frederick Gates called the dangers of "scatteration," it is interesting to note that no fewer than 291 institutions received endowment grants during this early period. Clearly the work of the Carnegie Foundation and the General Education Board during the early years of this century had a quantitative impact in raising educational standards "across the board" which would be quite out of the question today. A more or less final accounting in 1960 of the Board's work showed that it had appropriated a total of $208,204,883.52 to universities and colleges in the United States, plus $62,520,491.98 specifically earmarked for Negro education. (Some of the latter was for use below the college level.) In addition to these general efforts the Board conducted a large fellowship program and supported certain specialized developments in teaching method and curriculum content. Most notable perhaps was its interest in so-called progressive education and "general education" expressed by substantial grants to such institutions as Antioch, Reed, Sarah Lawrence, and Bennington, and to experimental and honors programs at Dartmouth, Swarthmore, and Minnesota.

As one reviews the relationship between institutions of higher learning and the major foundations during the critical first two decades of this century, one finds oneself wondering if it is too much to say that the foundations became in effect the American way of discharging many of the functions performed in other countries by the Ministry of Education. Certainly the United States has always tolerated and often encouraged a greater variety both in subject matter and in quality of higher education than is found in any other part of the world. But by the turn of this century this variety of growth had reached a luxuriance that was quite unmanageable. If academic standards showed somewhat less variation than other attributes, it was only because none were very high. Candidates were often admitted to college with less, sometimes far less, than the equivalent of a high school education. Even the best institutions admitted numerous people with one or more "conditions." The length of the academic year varied from place to place, and in 1920, 75 per cent of full-time faculty members were receiving between $600 and $2,500 annually, although as early as 1891 the University of Chicago was paying some full-time professors $7,000. There is of course no clearly constituted critical authority in the United States with the power to enforce reorganization and establish standards of higher education. In the early decades of this century the foundations, with varying degrees of consciousness about what they were doing, exercised the most significant coordinating influence in the education world. Part of their power, perhaps the largest part, was the power of the purse; but around this central force were deployed a number of other arms.

The early foundations were fortunate in possessing an outstanding group of officers and trustees, most of whom traveled a great deal and all of whom were constantly thinking about problems of education and human welfare. Perhaps fortunate is the wrong word; more likely the excellence of these staffs can be traced directly to the executive acumen and instinctive methods of personal selection that had made Mr. Rockefeller and Mr. Carnegie the two most successful entrepreneurs of their time. In any case, the combination of money, brains, accumulated experience, and organized information which grew up in the offices of foundations gave them a crucial role in bringing order and excellence to American higher education. Our current methods of differentiating one level of education from another, of selecting students for admission, of keeping academic books, of arranging pensions and insurance plans for teachers are all directly traceable to the activities of foundations. The foundations also played a very important role in raising teachers' salaries after the First World War and in fostering several important reforms in curriculum content and teaching methods.

By the decade of the twenties it had become obvious that the objectives of foundations had to be limited in some way, however, and the limitation by and large took the form of reserving foundation resources for experimenting with new educational methods, developing research programs, and demonstrating the value of new knowledge. A series of phrases and aphorisms was invented to describe and lend glamor to this reorientation. Foundations managed "risk capital" and sought out "germinal ideas." They pushed at the "growing edge of knowledge," and a little later they developed chemical as well as physical powers as they "catalyzed" interdisciplinary reactions. Since even these specialized activities could not be pursued everywhere, increasing emphasis was put on developing a few key institutions as models to inspire others. Mr. Wickliffe Rose of the General Education Board, perhaps one of the few real geniuses in the foundation world, spoke tellingly of "making the peaks higher." The influence of this era on the universities was perhaps as large as the previous one, but it was certainly different in character. To a far greater degree it raised questions about how the responsibility for university policy should be shared between the university administration and various outside bodies—questions which have become intensified as government has increasingly entered the field with larger and larger sums for special purposes. This is a problem to which we must return later. But first let us glance at one of the most significant chapters in the whole history of foundations and universities—the reform of American medical education. In addition to its intrinsic interest, it forms a bridge between the era of general developmental support for universities and the modern era of emphasis on special projects and limited demonstrations.

Foundations have given aid to graduate and professional education in a number of areas; the law, dentistry, the training of teachers—each has had some share of attention. But nothing compares with the effort in medical education in amount of money, in number of foundations involved, and in overall impact both on the universities and on society in general. The story of American medical education is a success story par excellence, and it has greatly influenced our thinking about what foundations can do. It has been told a number of times, and it is still unfolding. We can pause only long enough to note a few highlights. In the first place, there is the commanding presence of Mr. Frederick T. Gates, an ordained Baptist minister and Mr. Rockefeller's primary adviser in philanthropic matters. He had "an almost mystic belief in the promise and potency of medical research" and "that it would have as a by-product 'new moral and social laws and new definitions of what is right and wrong in our relations with each other.'"[11] Secondly there was Mr. Abraham Flexner, the teacher in a Kentucky private school, commissioned by Andrew Carnegie to survey American and then European medical education. His report descended on the academic world as Carnegie Bulletins Numbers 4 and 6, respectively in 1910 and 1912.

The findings were scandalous; of 155 schools then extant only 16 required two or more years of college for entrance, and 50 a high school education or its euphemistic "equivalent." Eighty-nine asked for little or nothing more than the rudiments or recollection of a common school education. Most of these were money-making ventures undertaken by groups of physicians whose major interest was in private practice. Further details may be sought by the curious in the original bulletins, where they are set forth with a vigor and color of expression rare in academic writing. Confronted by this exposition Mr. Carnegie is said to have commented as follows: "Dr. Flexner, you have proved that medical education is a business, and I have no interest in underwriting businesses."* Mr. Gates took a rather different tack and gave Flexner his opportunity with the General Education Board. By the time Flexner resigned in 1928 the Board had spent $90,000,000, the number of schools had been reduced from 155 to 80, the principle of full-time dedication to teaching and research had been established for teachers in the clinical arts as well as in the basic sciences, and Mr. Gates had broken permanently with the Board and especially with Mr. Flexner over the issue of making grants to state institutions (Gates was against it). American medical education had gone from almost the bottom of the list for civilized countries to a position from which it jumped to the very top during World War II.

Of course the trend was upward when Mr. Flexner started. Mr. Eliot had cleaned house at Harvard in the seventies and the Johns Hopkins Medical School had been started under excellent auspices in 1893. Washington University in St. Louis and several state institutions were doing their best to establish satisfactory standards and the American Medical Association played a progressive role which may strike those who have known it only in its later days as rather strange. Nevertheless, the impact of $90,000,000 and the peppery insistence of Flexner on the highest possible standards were of paramount importance. Furthermore, the mani-

* Charles Dollard in a private communication.

fest success of the operation firmly established medical education and research as a favorite object of private philanthropy. The Rockefeller Foundation, the Commonwealth Fund, the John and Mary R. Markle Foundation, the Josiah Macy Jr. Foundation, and many others have devoted a major part and often their entire resources to medicine and public health.

At first most of the financial support was concentrated on the development of a sound academic structure with emphasis on teaching. Toward the end of the twenties interest shifted to the support of research and gave rise to a trend which has spread from foundations to other agencies and which has become intensified in recent years as medical research has caught the attention of Congress. As foundation policy shifted from broad general support to more limited and more clearly defined objectives, relationships between universities and foundations became somewhat more delicate and from time to time frankly strained. Certain foundation officers and, less commonly, certain boards of trustees developed ideas of their own as to what university policy should be. Large sums of money were known to be available for the support of certain policies but not others. To the foundations this channeling of funds seemed merely the natural result of the sort of decision which anybody charged with the allocation of scarce resources for the advancement of human welfare must make. To some people in the universities it looked very much more like the arbitrary exercise of a power accidentally placed in the hands of a few self-willed and essentially irresponsible bureaucrats.

Almost all the things that can be said on this matter were actually said during the course of Mr. Flexner's campaign to establish full-time teaching and research for teachers of the clinical practice of medicine. Actually the idea was commonplace enough in Germany, where Flexner first saw it. Its introduction into Johns Hopkins was not first suggested by him but by a group of the faculty under the leadership of Professor Franklin P. Mall in the Department of Anatomy. Almost all the clinical teachers, however, wished to retain some of the responsibilities and privileges of private practice, and the very distinguished dean, W. H. Welch, would probably have preferred some moderate compromise. Flexner persuaded his board to hold out for the rigorous exclusion of private fees, and after two years of procrastination and debate, Welch finally asked for $1.5 million on Flexner's terms. The grant was made within forty-eight hours. Affairs moved much less smoothly elsewhere. President Eliot's repeated requests for help with a compromise plan at Harvard were brushed off brusquely enough to prompt a letter to Wallace Buttrick, the president of the Board, asking, "how could the insistence of the General Education Board on full time be reconciled with its theoretical hands-off policy? He had heard this policy 'stated with great distinctness by Mr. Gates when I first joined the Board, and have often heard it since. . . .' "[12]

Another member of the Board with less conflict of interest in the decision put the matter this way. "It is not a question of whether we are right or wrong in our opinions regarding the university or full-time basis of medical education. I think that where adequate funds are available we are absolutely right in favoring this policy, and I am very proud of what has been accomplished by the Board under Mr. Flexner's leadership in the field of medical education. But it is a question of whether or not we can psychologically and morally afford—in view of public opinion and our great wealth as a board—to be imposing, or at least requiring, detailed conditions regarding educational policy in medicine in elaborate contracts which can only be amended with our consent. . . . Personally, I think this policy unwise and fraught with serious dangers. . . ."[13] These and other complaints prompted the Board to liberalize in a series of steps the terms of its endowment grants, which at first had read almost like contracts in perpetuity. By 1937 recipients were under no legal obligation for more than ten years, although it was expected that they would spend the income for some "reasonably related purpose."

We have already seen how the various requirements of the Carnegie Foundation for admission to its pension plan aroused hostility, and how Henry Pritchett's sometimes gratuitous advice was even more intensely resented. In retrospect it is difficult to find serious fault with most of the conditions attached to foundation grants in this early period. Most, if not all, of these appear to have been directed at such general improvements in matters of basic policy and practice that any disinterested person must agree with them. Certainly no one today would seriously argue that private colleges do not need at least $200,000 of unencumbered endowment, that students should be admitted with less than a satisfactory high school record, that teachers and administrators should be required to profess the doctrines of a particular Protestant sect, or that professional schools should be conducted for the

90

private profit of their owner-teachers. More serious questions arose toward the end of the twenties, when as we have seen the foundations recognized that their resources were not up to assuming responsibility for the general welfare of universities. Foundation funds were from then on increasingly reserved for new and presumably venturesome undertakings which, once they had proved their worth, would be taken over by the universities' general funds. The universities have by and large been extremely ambivalent about this situation. On the one hand they wanted the money and prestige which come with foundation favor. On the other, they wanted to be masters in their own houses, and they were worried and resentful about being required to take over the ultimate financial responsibility for projects thought up by others.

In point of fact, university administrators are never quite sure of how much they want to be masters in their houses. A very famous president has been quoted as saying on some occasions that the real role of foundations is to give what may seem like disproportionate help to outstanding faculty members. In this view the university can and should take responsibility for appointing such people in the first place and for meeting their basic needs, but the realities of community life make it very difficult to provide much more for one man than for others. Foundations need not feel the same inhibitions since they do not have to live continuously in the same community. At least one of the large foundations discovered this truth for itself during the thirties. After experimenting for a while with so-called fluid research funds to be apportioned by a faculty committee, it decided that its own officers could make better selections much more easily because they need not engage in the logrolling which even the most dedicated intellectuals seem to find unavoidable as members of a faculty.

On other occasions, with a slightly different twist, this same president could take quite a different view. This correspondent remembers quite clearly discussing with him the possibility of taking over an enterprise which had been initiated with foundation help some twenty years before, and which had been continuously supported by it during all that time. It had been the first program of its kind in the country, and it was generally recognized as an outstanding success. To the foundation officer it was an almost classic example of the use of "risk capital" to demonstrate the validity of a new idea which should be taken up enthusiastically by the regular resources of the university. Mr. President felt quite differently. "Why, that is just one of those things worked out by Alan Gregg and Dean——and the university has no responsibility for it whatsoever!" (Incidentally, the program has continued to find support from the teaching hospital in which it was developed as well as from outside sources.)

There appear to be no general rules for deciding on who shall represent the universities' side in a negotiation with a foundation. In the early days, when grants were made largely for general purposes, the president and the board were the obvious principals. As foundations increasingly limited themselves to the support of research and the development of special programs—area studies for example—it became common to carry on the major substance of the negotiation with the people actually doing the work. This was especially true for organizations like The Rockefeller Foundation which rely heavily on a professionally trained staff. By and large a biologically trained foundation man found it more rewarding to talk with a biologist, or an economist with an economist, than to exchange formalities with administrators. On at least one embarrassing occasion things went so far that a foundation board actually voted a grant and the formal letter of notification brought the first news of the negotiation to the university president. His reply stated very clearly and with a certain nineteenth-century crustiness that the university had no intention of embarking on this one-half million dollar program and that the president and fellows would therefore not accept the grant. Nowadays few foundations would act without having received a written statement from the university administration expressing its knowledge of and interest in the proposal. Even today, however, some universities have no clearly established procedures for negotiating with outside agencies. In others, formal procedures respect at least the appearances of authority, but in practice many administrators find it difficult to withhold approval when one of their faculty members enters a negotiation for outside support. This is especially true if the faculty member is distinguished in his own field and a capable money raiser.

It is hard to demonstrate that central authority, at least in the stronger institutions, was ever systematically threatened in the days when private foundations were the principal source of outside funds. Here and there a university might have been encouraged to expand in a direction that later proved unwise or a foundation could seduce a willing faculty member to develop a stable for one of its hobbies. Speaking before the Central Society for Clinical Research in Chicago in 1952, for example, W. Barry Wood pointed to the error committed by foundations in insisting that psychosomatic medicine be set up in a separate department rather than being encouraged to diffuse throughout existing ones. But it would be equally difficult to show that administrative authority was seriously eroded by solvents applied from outside during this era. In recent times the problem posed in theory by foundation practices has become a practical reality, or perhaps even a clear and present danger, by the allocation of very large sums from government agencies. Opinions differ on the gravity of this problem, however, and as experienced a university official as McGeorge Bundy, seeing the situation from a different vantage point in 1963, expressed the view "that on balance the federal government makes its grants and signs its contracts with a better perception of the real needs of the higher learning than one can find, on the average, in the major private foundations."[14] If this is true, it is good news since the power wielded by government is obviously very much greater. Whether the quotient—amount of available money divided by perception—still favors government over foundation support may remain an open question.

If the foundations are guilty of using their power to persuade universities to do things they would not otherwise have done, how serious a crime is it? What are some of the things they have persuaded universities to do? One of the most obvious functions of foundations in the period which began in the 1920's and which is continuing even today has been to call attention to neglected areas of learning and to make it possible for universities to give them more attention. The Laura Spelman Rockefeller Memorial was one of the earliest to emphasize the importance, for example, of knowing more about what are now called the behavioral sciences. In one of its most spectacular moves, the Executive Committee voted funds in 1928 for the creation of the Institute of Human Relations at Yale, and this aid was continued by The Rockefeller Foundation after the two organizations merged the following year. The Institute enabled representatives of several fields—anthropology, psychology, physiology, psychiatry, among others—to work closely together on the overall problems of human behavior. The program attracted heavy financing from several foundations for over three decades and contributed much to the development of the individual departments involved, but for various reasons it failed in its basic "interdisciplinary" objective. Very probably the effort was too extensive, perhaps too spectacular for its time. Very little was known then about the difficulties of interdisciplinary research, and some observers have noted that the appointments to the principal positions in the program were all given to men of an uncommon degree of individuality. However that may be (and in spite of some other difficulties to be mentioned later) a large number of more modest grants from several foundations have helped to put the behavioral sciences in the firm position they occupy today. Perhaps deserving of special mention is the series of efforts by The Rockefeller Foundation which played a major role from 1932 until late in the 1950's in moving the focus of academic work in psychiatry from the state hospital to the laboratories and teaching wards of the medical school.

At least equally important, if somewhat less well known, has been the role of foundations in fostering work in the more exotic languages which led in several instances to the establishment of interdisciplinary groups devoted to the study of the entire culture of a nation or region. One of the earliest moves was that made by The Rockefeller Foundation in conjunction with the American Council of Learned Societies to establish summer institutes at several universities for the study of the languages and cultures of Japan, China, and Russia. The program developed rapidly and by 1941 provided the background for the intensive studies of a series of relatively unknown tongues to meet military needs. Immediately after the war the Carnegie and Rockefeller foundations took the lead in helping to establish comprehensive centers for the study of all aspects of Russian culture and the Soviet socio-political system at Harvard and Columbia. The importance for public enlightenment and the determination of national policy of the long series of papers and monographs produced by the eminent scholars in these two institutions can scarcely be overestimated. Somewhat similar organizations dealing with the Far East have been developed in the same way at Cornell, California, Washington, and others.

Many other special subjects or areas have been boosted into the university limelight—anthropology by the Viking Fund, psychosomatic and social medicine by the Commonwealth Fund and others, medical sociology by the Russell Sage Foundation, higher business management by the Alfred P. Sloan Foundation. The list of important developments of this kind growing out of foundation-university cooperation since the war far outruns our limitations of time and space and the investigative ability of this historian. Before leaving the subject, however, it is necessary to say a few words about the function of foundations in supporting projects of high risk. These risks may be due simply to the uncertainty that anything of consequence will emerge, or they may arise from the threatening nature of the subject under investigation. It is widely believed, or at least widely said, that a primary function of foundations is to help in the exploring of new areas of knowledge into which other investors are too timid to intrude. The very partial list of new university programs presented above as illustrative of foundation activity certainly supports the belief, but it is not easy to say whether it was an unwillingness to take risks, an inability to see the opportunity, or simply a lack of funds which kept other possible investors away. Now that government granting agencies are supporting research in the natural and social sciences, it appears that they are quite as prepared as the private foundations ever were to support projects which carry a fairly low probability of anything important emerging as a result.

The record in regard to projects of a "controversial" or threatening nature is considerably clearer. The foundations have a long record of contributing to research into problems of race relations, sex behavior, and even simple economics, many of which would still be considered too hot to handle by most, if not all, government agencies. At the present time, for example, several of the major foundations have active programs for the study of the dynamics of population growth and appropriate means for its control, most of which were started long before any government official was willing to admit that a problem even existed. Indeed, it must be remembered that federal support to education per se is still "controversial" and most of the general support to education given by foundations, let alone their strong interest in progressive education and other experiments, would have been impossible for government. Quite recently the Ford and Rockefeller foundations have developed multimillion-dollar programs to enable Negro colleges and selected integrated ones to give special attention to disadvantaged groups in our population. Certainly the foundations have been able to move faster than government has in this respect; and it is probable that even if it wished a government required to act in accord with the equal protection clause might encounter insuperable difficulties in designing similar programs.

It remains perhaps to comment on one of the more arguable

aspects of the relationship between foundations and universities. As we have seen, foundations have frequently been instrumental in encouraging the development of special purpose groups within or attached to universities. The problem is an important one especially since the government has encouraged the development of somewhat similar devices for the achievement of special, not always academic, purposes. Although it seems relatively easy to recognize the important contributions to knowledge of at least some interdisciplinary "institutes," it is a good deal less easy to be sure of their overall effect on university organization. In some cases they have served as little more than escape hatches for the sort of personalities which do not fit easily into conventional departmental structure. In almost all cases they have led to friction with the latter over appointments and promotions. The friction arises over the fact that in most institutions the senior tenure appointments are portioned out among the conventional disciplines. By and large the senior members of the institutes hold their appointments and draw at least part of their salaries from the departments, but they do their work in the institutes. As the years go by the prestige of their accomplishment becomes more and more identified with the institute rather than with their home department, while the department is left paying the bill. More serious problems concern the junior people. They are usually supported by outside funds and hold nontenure appointments as research fellows, associates, or lecturers. Their reputations are almost wholly "interdisciplinary"— they may be Russian experts but they are not historians, linguists, geographers, or political scientists. At least, none of these departments think that such people are sufficiently identified with a basic discipline to justify their obtaining one of the coveted tenure appointments.

There is no doubt that situations similar to the above have led to real trouble in several institutions, but there is much less certainty about how to assess the underlying cause. On the one hand there is the possibility that the existing departmental structure of our universities is indeed obsolescent and badly in need of reform. On the other is the horrid thought that the attempted reform is simply the misbegotten invention of an impatient foundation officer anxious to solve some immediate practical problem. Fortunately, as time goes by, univeristy administrators seem to be solving the problem by maintaining the traditional formal structure and encouraging informal interdisciplinary cooperation by carefully considering the specific interests of new appointees to traditional chairs, by judicious planning of libraries and other facilities for use on an interdepartmental basis, and by such devices as faculty clubs and dining rooms where interdepartmental barriers may be surmounted in conversation and if necessary dissolved in alcohol. The foundations have probably also become more cautious in recent years, and many of them have learned to inspect proposals for interdepartmental institutes for signs of foundation bait.

A particularly attractive instance of how foundations may exert important influences without hurting anyone's feelings is provided by the two very modest appropriations made by The Carnegie Corporation to send a few outstanding scholars and men of affairs to Africa before practically anyone had heard of the place except for Stanley and Livingstone and Theodore Roosevelt. Shortly after the war the Carnegie people foresaw that Africa was likely to be the scene of important political, social, and economic changes. They tried for some time to interest university groups in developing programs similar to the ones that had been so successful for other areas, but outside of the late Professor Melville J. Herskovits at Northwestern, nobody seemed much interested. They therefore fell back on the idea of sending prominent people out to Africa just to have a look. It is of course very difficult to assess the outcome of a program as unstructured as this, but it seems reasonable to suppose that the diaries, lectures, and luncheon conversations produced by these prominent men did have a significant effect in preparing the learned world for the deluge of requests for information and help which descended on it a few years later.

There are of course many other indirect ways of exerting influence on universities. Foundations have been the principal source of support for organizations like the National Research Council, the Social Science Research Council, the American Council of Learned Societies, the American Council on Education, the Institute of International Education, and numerous others which have been important in training teachers, providing research support, acting as "clearing houses" for information, and so forth. Incidentally, it is organizations like these that, useful though they may be, often give foundation officers bad dreams. By and large they tend to be expensive with high overhead costs, their output is intangible and hard to judge, and their officers are pleasant, conscientious people easily turned into personal friends of the foundation officers responsible for their future security. Only rarely do such organizations develop a constituency with sufficient financial resources to keep them going. Finally, they often conduct programs closely parallel to those of the sponsoring foundations themselves. These facts all combine to make it uniquely difficult to maintain a normal foundation posture toward them. Another related class of organizations, which has proved more capable of independent existence, is composed of those which perform specified services engaged by universities on a quasi-commercial basis. One of these is the Teachers Insurance and Annuity Association of America. Another is the Educational Testing Service, which grew out of several previous organizations all of which received heavy foundation support, especially from the General Education Board and The Carnegie Corporation. Here again, as suggested earlier, we find that foundations have played a role in providing centralized services to education that in other countries would stem from the government ministry.

What of the future?

Were it not for the advent of the Ford Foundation, it would be relatively easy to predict that the relation between foundations and universities would continue the trend which set in during the 1930's—away from general support for endowment, buildings, and overall running expenses, and toward specialized research projects, interdisciplinary "programs," "experiments" in education, and so on. For a while it looked as if the Ford Foundation might even try to outdo the pioneers in assuming across-the-board responsibility for financing broad areas of university work. The ninety millions distributed to all the medical schools in the country suggested this possibility, especially since this program was shortly followed by a number of large block grants for not very clearly specified purposes to other divisions of a number of universities. Recently a new program which might be thought of as a sophisticated version of the General Education Board's matching grants for endowment has been undertaken. Appropriations of up to $23,925,000 with the strong inference that more is to come have already been given to several carefully selected universities and colleges for general purposes on condition that matching funds be obtained from other sources at a ratio of 2 or 3 to 1. This program has already had a considerable impact not only on the institutions actually receiving grants but on many others which have been prompted to review programs and make plans which might attract future support. In a time when so much financial help comes to universities earmarked for special purposes, the emphasis of the Ford Foundation on broad general purposes and long-term institutional development is at least refreshing and probably highly significant.

For the more conventionally sized organizations the trend must probably continue to be toward special programs, with declining interest in medicine and the natural sciences and a cautious increase in the promotion of the social sciences, the creative arts, and humane scholarship in about that order. The natural sciences and medicine have of course long been a favorite object of foundation interest. The foundations were conceived by practical men, and they have always been more interested in practical results than is usual in the best university circles. The medical and natural sciences have had, of course, an astonishing practical success during our era, at least partly because of foundation support. It is thus inevitable that the foundations should be pleased and favorably inclined toward them. But foundation boards are coming to realize that there is not a great deal of point in playing in a game in which the government agencies hold just about all the chips. In any case, stronger arguments can be made for substantial private support for the still controversial areas of the social sciences and the arts.

Before going on to discuss possible future developments in these areas it may be necessary to step aside for a moment and deal with a general impression that the foundations have not only been more interested in the natural and medical sciences than in other branches of learning but also considerably more successful in developing them. It is a little difficult to know how these impressions arise, but the first at least may need some qualification. Over the years the major foundations have given much more for the general support of universities and for specific support of the social sciences than they have as grants earmarked for the natural sciences as such. The sciences never occupied an important place in the programs of the Carnegie Foundation, The Carnegie Corporation, or the Ford Foundation. Of the roughly $325,000,000 expended by the General Education Board, $94,000,000 was, it is true, devoted to medical schools, but only a fraction found its way to the support of science per se. Even The Rockefeller Foundation, with its heavy emphasis on public health and medicine, found over $160,-000,000 for the humanities and the social sciences. And even some of the nominally medical support has had an important bearing on

99

the development of the social sciences. For example, the famous Hawthorne experiments with small groups were carried out by a team of investigators which owed its existence to a Rockefeller Foundation grant recommended by its medical officers. What little we know in a quantitative "empirical" way about sex behavior owes much to the National Research Council's Committee for Research in Problems of Sex, supported for nearly thirty years by foundations interested primarily in medicine. Whatever sense of dissatisfaction there may be about the results of foundation aid for the social sciences can more easily be traced to the existing state of the art than to any special neglect or incompetence on the part of individuals either in the foundations or in the universities.

It cannot be too often remembered that the natural and medical sciences have spent the twentieth century reaping the luxuriant crops grown from seeds planted in the fertile soil of the Po Valley during the sixteenth and seventeenth centuries. The social sciences still cannot be sure that they have got hold of the right seeds. But this is not the only difficulty. The natural world is still pretty much what it was in the fifteenth century. What we knew about it then is still valid today. But the social and political world is very different. In a sense we have manufactured ever more problems for the social scientist to confront. Some of these problems are so severe as to threaten our very existence, and we naturally keep turning to the social scientists for help. When Galileo gave us two new sciences, we did not expect him to design a jet airplane or even a paddle-wheel steamer for us; but when Gunnar Myrdal tells us what our color problem is we at least hope that he will simultaneously provide the solution.

The sooner one abandons the production of practical results as a criterion for project selection in the social sciences the better. But what is then left as a guide? Here the investor in the social sciences has a more difficult time than do those of us who deal with the natural sciences. The natural sciences have developed a well-organized texture. At any one time there is a hierarchy of questions more or less waiting to be answered, and at the very top are some questions which have not been asked or even formulated. Most competent people concern themselves with the recognized questions. They gain their satisfactions and incidentally persuade their supporters by devising ingenious ways of finding the answers. Every informed person knows what the questions are and has an estimate of the difficulty of answering them. At the very top level, where one asks questions nobody has thought of before, there may be more difficulty in recognizing excellence; but in modern times even the great innovators are usually promptly recognized for what they are. The social sciences do not appear as yet to have the same agreed-upon texture. It has not proved easy to break social behavior down into a series of discrete steps each of which can be studied separately with each resulting bit of knowledge ready to fit into its place as an obvious part of an ever-growing edifice. The result is that it is difficult to tell what proposals are likely to give important results. Even when the results come to hand, one has difficulty in telling whether they really are important or trivial or, if important, whether they are not merely elaborations of the obvious.

Even when the foregoing difficulties are overcome, boards of trustees of both foundations and universities are likely to be uneasy about work in the social sciences. Even though the record seems to show that the application of the laws of motion and of thermodynamics have changed the socio-economic state of man to a far greater extent than anything the social sciences have ever done, it is the latter which disturb us more. For example, it seems hard to divest ourselves of the notion that it is dangerous to Anglo-Saxon justice to try to understand how juries make up their minds, and equally dangerous to something called morality to find out what college students do about sex. In one way or another, misgivings of this general type still manage to delay the progress which foundations and universities might make in understanding society. At an even deeper level, perhaps everybody feels threatened by the very idea that there can be such a thing as a science of social or individual behavior, for such sciences must ultimately be based on the assumption that behavioral output is a describable function of input. Even to people who are not much inclined to theological or philosophical speculation the idea that human behavior may be determined by outside "forces" raises painful questions about the nature of consciousness and human will. With all the listed handicaps, it is surprising that the quantitative social sciences have fared as well as they have. It is noteworthy, moreover, that they have been supported much more heavily and that they have produced more satisfactory results in this country than in Europe. Could it be that this superiority is in part due to the presence of several large foundations in the United States?

It is in their support of the humanities that the major foundations are most frequently criticized. They are said to be both timid[15] and inept. Above all, they fail to understand the importance of individual effort and achievement and to find appropriate ways of supporting it. Most critics omit the Guggenheim Foundation from this indictment, as well they might. In this unique setting Mr. Henry Allen Moe has used his innate good judgment, cultivated good taste, wide acquaintance with talented individuals, and a certain individual self-confidence which sometimes borders on puckishness to set a record which others might do well to emulate. He is, in fact, the only foundation officer of prominence who exercises those qualities which made the noble patrons of the arts so successful in an earlier period. Perhaps the creative artist and the humane scholar simply require more individualistic treatment than the universities or the foundations normally know how to provide.

In addition to simple ineptitude and lack of interest the foundations have other problems in their relation to universities when dealing with the humanities. The foundations, because of their dedication to "pioneering," new ideas, and the improvement of human welfare, are interested primarily in the creative aspects of the humanities, and they are apt to have some sort of utilitarian criterion at least in the backs of their minds. They realize, of course, that the humanities cannot currently be defended as contributing to greater production of food or even to better health (in spite of sporadic attempts to use music in treating the mentally ill), but they are prepared to think of a first-class drama or symphony or even a ballet as producing some sort of valuable increment in human enjoyment. The universities, on the other hand, are singularly uneasy in the presence of creative artists and have never really figured out what to do with them. A particularly striking illustration was provided at Harvard during the 1920's when Mr. Lowell decided that the 47 Workshop (drama) was beneath the dignity of gentlemen and scholars. A few state universities, and rather curiously the Carnegie Institute of Technology, have more recently found ways of integrating living rather than dead theatre into the university, but the Ivy League is still pretty uneasy about giving the mummers a free hand. The last couple of decades have also found the universities trying to rectify the situation by providing posts for artists-in-residence, but the very special handling given these packages only emphasizes the difference between them and proper university positions.

It has always struck the scientist as odd that the university has provided such an excellent environment for the creative scientist but has been so ambivalent in its relationship to the creative artist. Foundations also have come to expect creativity from the university scientists whom they support, and their officers and many of their board members continue to think up ways of helping the humanities to become more creative. But just when they think they may be succeeding, they find a distinguished humanist and academic administrator like Jacques Barzun asserting with his usual candor and perhaps somewhat unusual intensity that creativity of any kind (even apparently in the natural sciences) is out of place in the "House of Intellect." Considerably though not completely frustrated in their search for opportunities to support the creative arts in universities, the foundations have turned to those aspects of the humanities which at least *look* something like science. The greatest successes seem to have been in the theory of linguistics and its application to language teaching. In pursuing these objectives it has of course been particularly reassuring to find the use of computers in the development of theory and of tape recorders in the applied language laboratories.

There was a time when the humanities were fostered in universities primarily for the light they threw on problems of human conduct. In the essentially secular societies produced in the later days of Greece and Rome one naturally studied and discussed the lives of great men and the ideas of great philosophers for clues to the good life. The moralists of the religious era resurrected many of these ideas and incorporated them into natural law, which formed the backbone of instruction in the medieval university. As religion lost its force in the nineteenth century, Matthew Arnold eloquently set forth his devotion to humane letters as the principal guide to morals. The great bulk of the humanists in our universities follow this earlier tradition and regard themselves neither as creative artists nor as experts on the theory and practice of language, but primarily as curators of the "best that has been known and thought in the world." But there now seems to be a certain vagueness both in the minds of the humanists themselves and on the part of the foundations as to why it is worthwhile to study culture as Arnold defined it. Whether it is a becoming Christian humility or a basic lack of self-confidence is hard to say, but the humanists generally seem now to have a curiously difficult time in forcefully asserting their claim to support on the scale increasingly enjoyed by the social sciences—not to mention the luxurious life of the natural sciences.

Part of the problem of the humanities may stem from their very real difficulty in being sure that they really do have something important to say about some of the more spectacular contemporary moral questions deriving from the use of atomic energy, the uncontrolled growth of populations, or the possibility of directing human evolution. Conversely, the constant growth of science and its apparent capability for controlling many traditional evils has tended to change the direction while many men look for solutions to the problems of living. Much of the pain and tragedy of life has, in fact, been controlled or abolished by appropriate changes in the environment brought about by science. There therefore seems less need for the cultivation of those inward virtues which the humanities help to cultivate as protection against the onslaughts of an unkind fate. Finally, we come to a somewhat special explanation of the ambiguous position of morals in a modern university. For a variety of reasons which we cannot really go into here, all of the best and most of the better institutions of higher learning in the United States are aggressively secular in their orientation. On the other hand, morals and ethics continue to be closely identified in the public mind with organized religion.

Attempts at a serious intellectual approach to problems of morals thus tend to fall between two stools. The major universities have most of the best minds but feel inhibited from dealing explicitly with morals because of the common assumption that morals are a branch of religion. In part the intellectual's hesitancy comes from a reluctance to appear as a religious zealot, especially a sectarian one, and in part because he feels it wiser to avoid intruding on another domain. On the other hand, organized religion in the United States has only occasionally been intellectually oriented, and in recent years it has concentrated principally on social service and matters of administration. Theological speculation or any serious exploration of the basis of moral values is largely left to Europeans except for the occasional Niebuhr or Weigle. The foundations concerned with such problems have therefore had to content themselves with occasional forays into the field of secular philosophy, but few have found satisfaction in the modern trend toward more and more tidy ways of talking about talking. Rather more rewarding, perhaps, has been the series of small grants made by The Rockefeller Foundation for work in legal and political philosophy, but it would be too much to say that these have as yet served to change the universities' largely custodial and analytical attitude toward problems of value.

I go into these matters in some detail since it seems to me that one of the most challenging areas for the future development of the relationship between foundations and the colleges and universities lies precisely in the area of the humanities as the study of man in his moral relations with other men and with the pattern of the universe. It will not be easy for many reasons—the whole idea sounds pretentious, there are few obvious handles to take hold of, many of the issues are "controversial," the field is not easily divisible into projects or programs that form the usual grist of the foundation mill, and so on. But the arguments *for* such a policy are even more persuasive. In the first place, there clearly is a need—intellectuals everywhere worry about the drifting, meaningless quality of twentieth-century life, much of our most talented youth seems disoriented and wanders in and out of college without rhyme or reason, the less talented contribute to a rising tide of delinquency and crime, and the suicide rate is one of the best indices of "advanced" culture that we have.

In the second place, other branches of knowledge—physics and chemistry because of their bearing on war and industrial production, the biological sciences because of their relation to health and food production, and increasingly the social sciences because of the hope they offer of understanding and controlling some of the more disturbing aspects of human behavior—are all receiving heavy financial support and much public encouragement. It seems very unlikely and probably undesirable that similar heavy support should be provided to the humanities from government sources. This fact alone should give the field a higher priority in the eyes of private organizations. Thirdly, far from being opposed or at the least indifferent to humane learning and moral values, the sciences are providing more accurate ways of describing moral problems and are actually calling attention to types of moral problems which heretofore have not been recognized. As I shall try to show in a forthcoming article, one of the most challenging tasks for the arts might well be the translation of some of the cold objective conclusions of science into more immediately meaningful subjective terms. Such translation is needed if many of the findings of science are to be used effectively in changing human conduct, for it has been well said that "few men are moved by a statistic."

A concern with moral values might well be combined with a concern for another relatively neglected area—the liberal arts college. For various reasons—their largely religious origin, their somewhat isolated position, their relative lack of pressure or opportunity to produce new knowledge, their concentration on educating under-graduates rather than on training of graduate students—the liberal arts colleges have maintained at least a nominal interest in the humanities as essentials in the formation of good character. In theory at least and probably in practice it is easier for the faculty of a liberal arts college to live and function together as a "company of scholars" than it is in a great university with its emphasis on specialization, its unwieldly size, the overinvolvement of many of its ablest faculty in the world of affairs, and so on. At least it seems worthwhile to try to make the most of the apparent advantages of the small college in any effort which tries to combine the scientific and the humanistic modes of looking at man's predicament. The opportunity for the foundations lies, at least in part, in the fact that the liberal arts colleges are having a harder and harder time to recruit and hold first-class brains against the strong attractions of higher salaries, lighter teaching "loads," luxuriously equipped laboratories, and beautifully stacked libraries of the great universities.

These and other considerations like the sharp improvement in secondary education and the demand for advanced courses and specialized research by local industry have prompted many colleges to consider the development of graduate studies. It remains to be seen whether there is really a place for the "small university," but there well may be. Such an institution might continue to find it difficult to compete with its big sisters in specialized and expensive fields like high energy physics, but it might be just the place for the cultivation of what might be called "advanced general studies." Furthermore, the products of such a graduate school with judicious emphasis on synthesis as well as analysis might make better college teachers and much better guides to the good life than many who emerge from the conventional absorption in more and more about less and less. The opportunities should be particularly attractive to the host of small to medium sized foundations which have sprung up since the war. Even quite a modest sized foundation can play an important role in helping a college through the difficult transition to graduate work. Funds are needed to improve salaries, for release from the overheavy demands of the classroom, and for periodic leaves to consult with colleagues in other institutions or to work in specialized libraries or laboratories. It is frequently very difficult for the administration of a small college to provide what look like special privileges to selected faculty members. It is the natural business of a foundation to make such distinctions, and it is, of course, far easier for it to do so since it lives outside the circle of possible resentment.

Another area for expanded foundation effort may lie in the need for facilities which can be shared by several institutions. Some large-scale experiments with scientific laboratories, such as Brookhaven, or with regional deposit libraries already exist, but much more needs to be done to adapt the concept to the needs of smaller colleges and universities. The development of rapid storage recall and transmission systems on a regional basis might go far to meet the needs of scholars in small institutions for library facilities which cannot practically be provided locally. Indeed, it seems not impossible that the imaginative use of modern methods of information processing and communication can essentially erase the small college's handicaps of isolation and size while retaining most of their advantages.

While we are on the subject of the small college or university and the small to moderate sized foundation, we may observe that the small foundation has four alternatives before it. First, it can scatter its resources over a number of projects. Second, it can concentrate on a single subject as, for example, the Viking Fund has done so successfully in anthropology. Third, it can concentrate on a limited geographical area as the Hill (Louis W. and Maud) Family Foundation has done so helpfully in the northwest territory. Fourth, it can increase its impact by combining its efforts with a number of others. The second and third courses are the ones usually followed, but there would seem to be room for even further concentration and cooperation. For example, a foundation might select only one or two small colleges in its neighborhood for special help of the sort we have outlined. As the problem of developing more advanced work arises, a group of colleges and their sponsoring foundations could confer with one another about the construction of library and laboratory facilities to be used in common, rotating professorships, and other matters.

Another area which offers such obvious possibilities for foundation help that one wonders why it has never been exploited can be mentioned only briefly. Why has not some large foundation tried

107

to do for the law what the General Education Board and several other foundations already cited in this report have done for medicine? The corpus of laws developed over millenia for the regulation of community life is after all one of the great contributions to human welfare. Its effects are obvious enough to satisfy the most empirically minded foundation officer, and with all its excellencies it is still far from perfect. To the casual observer there seem to be many places where the law needs to catch up with modern knowledge of the nature of man, the reliability of various sorts of evidence, and so on. And there must be better ways of settling the liability cases growing out of automobile accidents which now encumber our courts to such a scandalous extent. The present writer is in no position to go into details as to how the foundations might effect reforms in legal education and practice similar in quality and extent to those they brought about so triumphantly in medicine, but there does seem to be a real opportunity here.

Emphasis on the expansion of foundation activity into relatively new areas does not mean, of course, that there is a diminishing role for the classical business of providing general funds, the support of specific research projects, the granting of fellowship aid, and the judicious encouragement of interdisciplinary institutes. The close family relationship between foundations and universities observed by Frederick P. Keppel, and mentioned in our opening paragraph, has been a most productive one in the past and should continue to be so in the future. Many of the characteristics of American universities owe their existence to the peculiar tendency of wealthy Americans to leave their capital in trust for the public welfare.

REFERENCES

1. Frederick P. Keppel, *The Foundation* (New York: The Macmillan Company, 1930), pp. 9, 10, 11.

2. John W. Gardner, "Foundation Operating Policies," address given at a meeting of the Association of American Colleges, 1956.

3. Ernest Victor Hollis, *Philanthropic Foundations and Higher Education* (New York: Columbia University Press, 1938), p. 21.

4. Abraham Flexner, *Henry S. Pritchett* (New York: Columbia University Press, 1943), p. 92.

5. "A Third of a Century of Teachers Retirement" (New York: Carnegie Foundation for the Advancement of Teaching, 1940).

6. Flexner, *Henry S. Pritchett*, p. 95.

7. "Rules for the Admission of Institutions" (New York: Carnegie Foundation for the Advancement of Teaching, 1929), pp. 28, 29.

8. Hollis, *Philanthropic Foundations and Higher Education*, pp. 51, 52.

9. *Ibid.*, p. 51.

10. Raymond B. Fosdick, *Adventures in Giving* (New York and Evanston: Harper and Row, 1962), p. 139.

11. *Ibid.*, pp. 228 and 233.

12. *Ibid.*, p. 164.

13. *Ibid.*, p. 164.

14. McGeorge Bundy, "The Blessing that is Federal Aid," *Princeton Alumni Weekly*, February 1, 1963, p. 7.

15. Edwin R. Embree, "Timid Billions: Are the Foundations Doing Their Job?" *Harper's Magazine*, 198 (March, 1949), 28–37.

PETER H. ROSSI

Researchers, Scholars and Policy Makers: The Politics of Large Scale Research

Introduction

THE CAMPUS of a major university was once marked by definite borders, on the one side of which were the distinctively academic buildings—dormitories, classrooms, libraries, laboratories and administrative buildings—and on the other side, the motley architecture of the town. Nowadays the physical boundaries of the university have blurred as academic activities have taken over the nearby town structures to house a proliferation of "centers," "institutes," "bureaus" and "laboratories." Some of the new organizations, like the Argonne National Laboratory or M.I.T.'s Lincoln Laboratories, are located at some distance from the campus; others cluster close by in old townhouses or in large Victorian homes; and some, such as Brookhaven, are located, like the theology of community churches, close to no particular position. The concept of a Campus on which all academic activities take place within the distance that can be spanned easily on foot by students and professors has given way to a more diffuse spatial pattern in which classrooms, dormitories and libraries are still at the center* but in which the periphery occupied by institutes and centers is vaguely defined and discontinuous. To walk from one end of the installation to the other is often a task beyond the capabilities of an academic procession.

The physical marginality of the new academic organizations reflects their academic marginality. Traditional university tables of

* Classrooms and dormitories also mark the center of the spatial distribution of prestige, with research centers and institutes making their importance to the university by how close they are to this center. When space is reallocated through the construction of new buildings, a fierce jockeying occurs with each striving to improve its prestige by minimizing its distance from the university center.

110

organization lose their branching symmetry in attempts to place them in their proper places in chains of command, and university officials sometimes ignore them in the planning of university expansion, perhaps in the hope that if ignored they will vanish. Academic departments or schools to which the research centers may be attached are somewhat at a loss to deal with them, for the personnel of the centers and institutes are hard to assimilate into the rank and privilege systems of academia. The personnel of the centers are not quite sure of their identity, for on the one hand they are members of the university community, while on the other their major commitments are not to the teaching and training functions which are at the center of the university's activities.

The first research center to evolve within the structure of the university was the library, occurring at a stage so deep in the beginnings of the institution that we usually do not classify the library as a center for research. In the modern sense of organizations devoted primarily to research and organized separately from departments, centers were first established by the natural sciences, with the astronomical observatories representing the first of the structures to be physically separated from the central campus.* In the empirical branches of the social sciences, which have only recently developed strong research programs, the precedents for research centers are now being established. Social science research centers are connected with almost every one of the major universities, the density varying from the proliferation on the Berkeley campus, on which it seems as if every full professor has his own center, to the sparser distribution at Johns Hopkins, where there are only one or two presently in existence.

The major concern of this paper will be with some of the organizational consequences of the development of research centers within the university environment. Properly to deal with this topic would require a breadth of knowledge which has yet to develop about how such centers are organized in a wide variety of fields.[1] I will be concerned primarily with the newer social science research centers, bringing in such information on other types of centers as is available in the very sparse literature on the organization of academic research, from direct knowledge of the few such research centers I

* As telescopes increased in size and power and as the atmosphere of urban centers became more and more an obstacle to good observation, the observatories changed from being a dome on one of the campus buildings to separate installations located where the atmosphere was clearer.

have been able to visit and from the excellent survey of social research centers conducted by P. F. Lazarsfeld.[2]

Because social science research centers have been established in any great numbers only in the last two decades, there has been a great deal of diversity in their organizational forms as universities and departments experimented with different arrangements. The experimentation, as I will indicate later, is an index of some tension between the research centers and the more traditional departments. To highlight this tension, I will deal with this topic as an analysis of political processes. More specifically, I will deal with the way in which the organization of research has affected the relationships among three roles—the *social researcher,* the *scholar* (or academic man) and the *policy maker* (officials of foundations and agencies which provide support for research). It should be clear that I will be using the term "politics" in a very broad sense to cover the processes by which power and resources are distributed in the system of relationships in which these three roles take part. Under this broadened definition, the study of politics then becomes the study of decision-making so that there is a politics of business enterprises or of university administration and, more relevant to our present case, a politics of research.

The essential nature of the American university* is being affected by these organizational developments, a topic to which the final section of this paper will be devoted. Universities may be more properly entitled "multiversities" as Clark Kerr claims: certainly the extraordinary diversity of activities which are now put within one large organizational framework must necessarily affect the nature of teaching, research and the administration of our foremost institutions.

---

* Most colleges and universities remain unaffected by these developments which are characteristic primarily of the larger and more prestigeful. But the total system of higher education must necessarily be affected by changes which are taking place at the head of the academic procession. It is extremely easy to lose sight of the fact that most American institutions of higher learning do not include research as a major goal. In 1963 there were close to 1,500 institutions which granted bachelor's degrees, of which about 1,000 were accredited institutions. But only 150 granted higher degrees, and the top 30 graduate schools turned out about two-thirds of the Ph.D.'s. The distribution of the production of academic knowledge follows the distribution of higher degrees granted, with the top 30 schools producing the greater part by far of scholarly books and articles. It is these 30 institutions to which I refer as the "major universities."

I. Why Research Centers Evolved

The major missions of the first-rank university include both training and research. Since the establishment of graduate study in America and its diffusion to the major centers during the early part of this century, training has come to include both undergraduate and graduate instruction, and research has included both scholarly and laboratory activities.

There is no doubt that the amalgamation of training and research in the professorial role is an alloy at the same time beneficial to both activities, while tension-producing. Professors are supposed to be both scholars and teachers, with the proper mix variously defined from department to department and from university to university. University officials measure the worth of their institutions by two major outputs—neophyte scholars and the end-products of scholarship: books, articles, monographs and patents. University business managers have to handle both instructional and, increasingly, research accounts, each type with its own peculiar logic. Even buildings and grounds departments are baffled by the different space and maintenance requirements of research and teaching activities.

The tensions between the somewhat contradictory activities of teaching and research have several sources. Within the professorial role the tensions are produced partly by the different phasings of the two activities: teaching demands that a set schedule of classes, seminars, etc., be met, while research has variable and unpredictable time demands. In addition, the two activities compete for time: the proper nurture of undergraduate and graduate students can absorb the full-time attention of an instructor, but so can his scholarly activities.

Within the organization of the university at the departmental level, the tensions are produced by other mechanisms. The allocation of authority within a department need only be extremely rudimentary as far as teaching goes. The basic unit of activity is the course, for which a professor is responsible and which is conducted essentially without supervision. The division of labor within a department centers around the curriculum in which responsibility for courses is allocated among department members. I venture that more friendships among colleagues in departments have floundered on the rock of curriculum revision than over any other cause. But once a curriculum has been fixed upon, instructors go their own way

113

PETER H. ROSSI

relatively unsupervised by their department chairmen or by other administrative officials.

In contrast, research activity which involves more than the minimum division of labor between a scholar and his acolyte graduate students produces continual organizational tensions. Decisions have to be made continually, responsibilities for particular activities have to be allocated to different persons, men have to pace their work to the paces of others. There are strong strains to produce a bureaucratic organization for research activities in which there is a much more clear line of authority than is necessary for the teaching activities of a department.

The evolution of research centers can be seen as one attempt to solve by segregation the tensions between teaching and research: research institutes were to be the proper place for research and the departments to remain the proper place for teaching. To be sure, there are other reasons for the establishment of research centers, some of which will be touched upon later in this paper. The important point to be made in this context is that the organizational needs of teaching and research are different and lead to different types of organization.

Not all research activities lead to the establishment of centers and institutes. Research and scholarship in the more humanistic fields typically have not led to the establishment of centers and institutes, and those established have not been very long-lived.* The major reason for this difference between the humanities and other fields lies in the fact that the humanist scholar evolved his research organization so long ago that we no longer recognize it as such but have incorporated it into the heart of the structure of the university. A central building on every campus is its library, and the division of labor into "library science" and scholarship constitutes the basic organizational structure of research in the humanities.** The scholar in the humanities is essentially a solitary worker using the facilities provided by a library surrounded by a few graduate students, each working with him but not with each other.† The division of labor

* When such "centers" have arisen (e.g., the Russian Research Center at Harvard), they have often taken the form of *ad hoc* departments designed to cover an area of study common to several disciplines.

** This is not true of many European universities, where professors are expected to acquire and maintain private collections of works in their fields, and where university libraries are poorly supported and have sparse collections.

† Indeed, when collaboration of an enduring sort does occur, it is hard to assimilate. I know of the case of two young historians who had worked as a

114

involved in research in the humanities is a primitive one in which each scholar has at best one or two persons of considerably lesser skills working with him, and in which there is a relatively minor amount of direct collaboration among colleagues.

The example of the humanities underscores the organizational imperatives that give rise to research centers in other fields. Research centers arose when research activities demanded collaboration among colleagues that went beyond the traditional organizational pattern of scholarship as presently exemplified in the humanities.

II. Research Centers in the Social Sciences

In the social sciences a good illustration of the organizational impetus toward the establishment of research centers is provided by the development of sample surveys in the last two decades. One of the major research developments in the empirical social sciences has been the set of techniques which has enabled social scientists to gather their own data on a broad enough scale to make statements about significant segments of large scale societies at relatively reasonable costs. Sample surveys have become a basic research tool in sociology and social psychology,* are a major tool in psychology, and are increasingly important in political science and economics.

Properly accomplished, a sample survey is a large scale enterprise involving a fairly elaborate division of labor and using a considerable amount of resources. This is best exemplified in the two major academic survey centers, the Survey Research Center at the University of Michigan and the National Opinion Research Center at the University of Chicago, as well as the survey activities of the Bureau of the Census or some of the better commercial firms. It takes a combination of skills, ordinarily not residing in a single person, to conduct a large sample survey properly. Even smaller surveys

---

team as graduate students and obtained, with great difficulty, appointments to the same department. Their historian colleagues developed so strong an antipathy to the pair that neither was reappointed even though their scholarly production was considerably greater than the average, and either alone would have been (and eventually was) a proud acquisition for separate major departments of history.

* For example, about one-third of the articles in the most recent two years of the major professional journals in sociology were based on surveys, outstripping by a good deal the employment of other methods.

(involving perhaps the sampling of a small city or neighborhood) can be carried out by a single person only in an inefficient manner.

Not all survey research is carried out within the context of large research centers. Each year scores of surveys are conducted by single individuals or by small groups of researchers: a sample of articles in professional journals or of Ph.D. theses would provide ample evidence that it is possible for individuals and small research groups to conduct such surveys by themselves. However, there is a severe limitation to such research. In the light of current technical standards, one can discern that such surveys are often rather poorly designed and executed, and, at best, severely limited in their coverage.*

Properly to conduct a survey, one needs to assemble at a minimum the following skills: (1) sampling; (2) questionnaire construction (an art perhaps rather than a skill); (3) interviewing; (4) data processing; and (5) statistical analysis. All of these would be needed to conduct a survey of an area larger than a small city or neighborhood.** To sample survey a population to which one ordinarily wants to generalize implies skills at a high enough level to require specialization. Furthermore, a large scale sample survey is expensive. Properly conducted national surveys (or for that matter, regional, state, or metropolitan surveys) collecting about 2,500 interviews of about an hour's length can cost anywhere between $50,000 and $125,000.† Surveys of special populations (for example, chiropodists or college students) can cost more or less depending on the exist-

---

* The limitation of coverage gives rise to bewilderingly contradictory findings in some areas of knowledge. Thus, the score or more of studies of child rearing conducted over the last two decades have produced results which can lead to no firm conclusions concerning what are the *facts* concerning how children are reared in this country.

** Institutionalized populations (e.g., students or soldiers) can be reached more easily, and hence surveys of such populations are favored by the social scientist working on his own.

† Of course, there are commercial firms who will collect data from a national "sample" and present you with a report for less than $10,000. But if you examine their procedures, it is evident that the sampling plan is either non-existent or highly deficient, the quality of interviewing haphazard and suspect, the number of interviews small (perhaps less than 500), and the analysis sketchy. While I am convinced that for many purposes such an operation may be all that is necessary (for example, to prove that most housewives are women or that people do not look kindly on foods that smell of sulphur dioxide), where the precision of data to be gathered is critical, such surveys do a considerable disservice.

ence of reliable sampling frames for the populations in question.

Survey research did not develop initially within universities but was grafted onto them after it had passed through the critical periods of infancy. The National Opinion Research Center is still an independent corporation affiliated with the University of Chicago. Michigan's Survey Research Center was set up initially by a group of researchers who had worked together in a survey organization run by the Department of Agriculture during the forties. This is not to deny the contributions that academic men have made to survey research, but merely to state the historical fact that surveys were being made long before survey research centers became accepted parts of university organization. There are undoubtedly many reasons why survey research did not develop inside the groves of academe, but among the most important reasons is the organizational setup of academic departments. Essentially, an academic department is a collection of scholars whose work is only minimally integrated in a division of labor sense. Professors are required to teach courses, and these courses are supposed to be organized in some sort of rational way. In American universities, departments do not engage in common scholarly enterprises in which a research task is broken down into components, each member of a department taking one component as his contribution.* Indeed, when an academician refers to the independence of the academic life,** he is usually referring to the fact that once he has met his teaching obligations (over which he has often a great deal of control) he is free to pursue his own intellectual interests within the limits set by local production standards and the amount of research funds he is able to obtain. Indeed, so pleasurable is the lack of a defined division of labor that any attempt to engage in large scale research

---

* In contrast many European universities have maintained a different internal rank system in which there is usually only one professor for each major field and under him (and at his disposal) a number of assistants whose research activities can be directed by him. In adopting the German model of universities, American universities introduced a fundamental modification by allowing the appointment of many professors within each field, a development perhaps fostered by the larger number of American universities and the competition among them for personnel.

** I recall many incidents in which men from the industrial and commercial world have been baffled by their inability to locate the lines of authority within a department. Neophyte book salesmen have been floored by the discovery that a department chairman has little to say about adoption of textbooks, and irate conservatives railing against the imprudent radicalism of a press statement have been unable to find a "boss" to complain to.

enterprises has led to the grafting onto university structures of organizational entities in which such a division of labor is possible rather than imposing such a division of labor upon existing departmental structures.

Large scale research in the social sciences is no exception to this generalization. Large scale survey research in the universities is conducted by institutes and centers whose organizational principles involve a hierarchy of command and a distinct division of labor. Indeed, the larger the scale of research, the steeper the hierarchy and the more elaborate the division of labor. Thus the two university-affiliated centers which conduct national surveys (Michigan's Survey Research Center and Chicago's National Opinion Research Center) have more complex structures than that of the Bureau of Applied Social Research at Columbia or the Institute for Social Research at North Carolina, the scope of whose work is more restricted in scale.

Characteristically, institutes and centers have "directors" while departments have "chairmen," expressing in the titles of their chief administrative officers the greater authority of the one as compared with the other. Because of his greater authority the director's role is more critical to the proper functioning of a research center than a chairman's role is to the prosperity of a department. A research center functions best when its director provides both intellectual and administrative leadership.* It may have been the pious hope of university administrators as they allowed and in some cases fostered the establishment of research centers that the departmental organization and the institute organization could be integrated very closely. Indeed, the ideal pattern in some ideal sense might be one in which the personnel of a department and the personnel of an institute would be one and the same, and that while teaching courses, sociologists, for example, would run themselves along departmental organizational lines, and while doing research they would run themselves according to institute lines. In fact, this has never occurred. Rather, either the department has restructured itself along the hierarchial lines of the center (as was the case for Columbia's department of sociology) or the center never developed a good division of labor (as was the case for North Carolina's institute) or the two structures remained side by side with some overlap

* Paradoxically, this means that a man makes the best director when he is in the prime of his intellectual powers, but academic statesmanship favors the mature older man past his intellectual prime.

of personnel (as in the case of the Survey Research Center and the National Opinion Research Center) but with considerable tension between the two.

The strains against the amalgamation of these two types of organization arise out of the relatively greater demands for precise timing and phasing of activities that result from an elaborate division of labor. As long as he meets his classes and writes books and articles, a professor has fulfilled the demands of his job. In contrast, a researcher working in the context of a research center has to pace his total activities so that they gear into the work of the sampling section, coding section, tabulating section, etc. Were the academic department organized along the lines of research centers, professors would soon chafe under their apparent loss of freedom. Even where professors have attempted to work within the context of a hierarchically organized research center, the collaboration has been short-lived, for the demands of directors to maintain the flow of work among the specialized components of the center have been viewed by the academician as an infringement on his prerogatives. Furthermore, a director must oversee the quality of research as it is being performed, while the individual scholar has the end product of his work judged by his colleagues located usually at some distance. In response to the difficulty of integrating departments and research institutes, the latter have developed separate staffs to the extent that their operations are on a large scale. Thus, within the institutes has developed a set of persons whose primary task is research, whose position within the academic community is ambiguous because they have only "courtesy" rank within the instructor-to-full-professor hierarchial order, and whose freedom to control their own activities is considerably less than those of departmental members.

However, not all social science research centers have taken the direction indicated above. Others have more or less deliberately remained paper organizations without a significant division of labor (except between clerical and professorial personnel) providing convenient sally ports from which the professors can emerge to gather funds from foundations and government agencies. Most university social research centers are of this sort, collections of individual professors surrounded by their project staffs (composed of advanced graduate students), providing secretarial services, but mainly serving as administrative rubrics for the purpose of obtaining research support. Other research centers have developed organizational struc-

PETER H. ROSSI

tures analogous to libraries, with their functions mainly to provide services to the professors.* Some of the newer survey research centers—for example, that established at Berkeley—have developed as their mission the expediting of research initiated by faculty members. Computer centers are also constructed on the same lines, manned by technicians and designed to serve the faculty.

Where research centers have accommodated themselves to the traditional academic organizational scheme by becoming primarily administrative subunits of departments or service arms of departments, tensions between centers and departments are minimized. In either case there is little infringement on traditional academic prerogatives, and no challenge to the freedom of the professor. But, as in the case of research centers which have engaged in research on a large scale, an attempt has been made to develop an elaborate division of labor, and tensions have arisen. The ability to embark on research on a greater scale has been bought at the price of coming into conflict with traditional organizational principles of academic departments.

There is little doubt that being a professor is more prestigeful than being a researcher. Tenure—that mysterious state of grace into which a professor is elected by his colleagues and from which he can fall only by committing crimes of the most revolting character—has not generally been extended to the institute personnel except on the highest level. Researchers' salaries have been generally higher for persons of the same age and academic accomplishments, but professors can and often do supplement their salaries from outside sources. Drawing a balance, it appears as if the professor has the edge; he has the higher prestige, the greater security, the greater freedom, and sometimes, through his outside activities, the greater income.

In fact, it now appears that there have grown up two distinct career lines—that of researcher and that of professor—with relatively little interchange between the two occupations. If one follows the researcher line, one ends up a second-class citizen in the university community; if one follows the professor line, one ends up a first-class citizen but restricted in the scope of the research in which one can engage. This accounts for much of the low quality

* Amitai Etzioni has pointed out that hospitals are also service organizations in the same sense as are libraries. Doctors have not organized themselves along elaborate organizational lines but use their hospitals primarily as service units.

120

of research reported in the professional social science journals. The individual scholar working on his own cannot command the kinds of skill that make for a first-rate piece of research. This also accounts for the oft-noted tendency on the part of academicians to start up their own research centers to increase their scope and power while looking upon the similar activities of their colleagues as academic imperialism.

Although the full-time personnel of a research center may not have the same psychic and sometimes monetary rewards of the members of the professoriat, there are advantages to full-time membership which in time may outweigh disadvantages. At its best functioning, the research center can multiply by some factor the efforts of a researcher, raising his work productivity as well as its quality. More than one better-than-average social scientist has been raised to the level of first-rank social scientist because he has had at his command the facilities and organization that a large scale research center represents. The efficiency of a division of labor cannot be gainsaid. But there are more subtle advantages as well that stem from close contact with colleagues of varying interests and accomplishments on a day-to-day basis. When a social research center is working well, it is indeed an exciting locale for one's work. One can feel the excitement in the snatches of conversation at lunch or in the visits made by colleagues to each other's offices.

Although the community of social scientists does not yet have the extensive character reported by Holton in which collaboration in the writing of an article may be the joint work of as many as ten different individuals from several institutions and two or three countries,[3] social science research is beginning to take on more and more of a cooperative slant. I surmise that the advantages of collaboration and close contact will become more obvious when the social scientists have more in the way of specialization in knowledge. At the present time, there is hardly a subfield of sociology and social psychology in which a good social scientist could not pick up as much detailed knowledge as the prime experts in that subfield to write an acceptable proposal to a grant-giving agency. When almost everybody knows as much as everyone else (or could know it easily) the benefits of collaboration are not as obvious as in the case when knowledge from one subfield could materially advance the progress of work in another.

III. The Financing of Large Scale Research

Large scale research in any field is expensive whenever it requires an extensive division of labor (as is the case for most social science research) and/or large capital investments in equipment. Unlike research in the humanities, in which continuing support is provided by the capital investment represented by a library collection and by regular allocation provided in the university budgets, other types of research tend to be financed on a project-by-project basis.

In empirical social research the *ad hoc* nature of financial support has important implications for the kinds of research that can be conducted and the kinds of personnel who can be attracted to research centers. Surveys on any appreciable scale are quite expensive. Furthermore, such research has grown increasingly expensive as its technology becomes more complex and as survey researchers demand more and more precision from their data. In some lugubrious sense, it is a shame that probability sampling was developed to a degree that it could be applied to the sampling of human populations, for the greatest increase in cost of surveys stems from the adoption of this technique. To draw a probability sample is expensive, and to administer personal interviews to the sample once drawn is also quite costly, particularly relative to the costs of surveys conducted under the now largely abandoned quota sampling technique. For example, the best known of the National Opinion Research Center's studies, the 1947 study of the prestige of occupations, cost a little more than $9,000 to conduct. We are presently conducting another study on this topic for which we have received a grant of more than $150,000. While the prices of many things have gone up since 1947, few have increased as much as large scale surveys.[4]

What are the implications of such high costs for surveys? One of the important consequences is that few individual researchers can command enough in the way of resources to mount an extensive survey operation. The limited scope of researches reported in the professional journals in sociology and social psychology are one of the consequences. Incidentally, this further exacerbates the tensions between the research institutes and the departments. In departmental research courses, graduate students are being taught how to do research in ways which their teachers themselves are unable to follow. Professors eye with some envy the large project budgets of the research centers, which are put at the disposal of persons often junior to them in status.

The most important implication of the high cost of surveys is that there are only a limited number of sources from which sums on this scale can be obtained, and the purposes for which such funds are given are limited in a peculiar sense. Few of the sources from which funds flow into social research give grants of one hundred to two hundred thousand dollars lightly. The major foundations and government agencies from whom funds on this scale are usually obtained are reluctant to part with this much money without being quite convinced of the practical importance of the survey in question. Hence large scale survey research is generally "applied" social research; that is to say, the grantor is convinced that the results will have some immediate bearing on policy formation. The high cost of social research has meant a close tie with the machinery of policy making.*

Some specific examples may help to illustrate dramatically what this implies for large scale research. At NORC we have developed a fairly strong program of research into the related areas of manpower and higher education, support for which comes primarily from the National Science Foundation and the National Institutes of Health. One of our studies involves a longitudinal study of the June, 1961 graduating classes of American universities and colleges. In 1961 we sampled that year's crop of new Bachelors for the purpose of studying how this group found their niches in the occupational world. The interest of the sponsoring agencies, in this case the National Institutes of Health, the National Science Foundation and the Office of Education,** was quite clear and direct: they

* Recently, NORC was visited by Mr. Louis Moss, who is director of the Government Social Survey in Great Britain. The Government Social Survey is a survey research organization within the British government which conducts surveys at the request of other government agencies. I was not surprised to find a great similarity between the structures of our two organizations, but I was very much surprised to discover that we had conducted so many parallel studies, his organization on behalf of Her Majesty's government, and NORC on behalf of federal agencies and private foundations. We could find parallel studies on about two-thirds of ours and about one-half of his projects. This means that together with other survey research organizations connected with universities or functioning as commercial enterprises, NORC is serving the same function for the American policy maker as the Government Social Survey functions in England.

** Coordinating three federal agencies is an administrative feat so massively delicate that it is surprising that our federal government manages to exist at all.

were concerned about the impact of federal scholarship and fellowship policies on postgraduate training and how such policies might
be changed to channel more of the talented into postgraduate training leading into critical scientific and professional niches. Spread
over a period of five years, the total sum allocated to this project
is half a million dollars. Two of these agencies are supporting a
replication of this study on June, 1964 graduates, and I predict
that we may be conducting such studies on a periodic basis in
the future. Another of our researches is concerned with the educational activities of adults, particularly measuring participation in
such adult educational activities as formal courses, and on-the-job
training. The sponsor in this case is the Carnegie Corporation, which
has a strong interest in supporting adult education and whose staff
feels that there is a definite lack of information on how much
adult education is going on, who participates, and what is being
learned.

These two cases are typical in the sense that the surveys in
question are supposed to yield information of value to the sponsoring organizations. They are also typical in that the initiative for the
studies came from the sponsors and they have taken a strong interest in their outcomes.* The consequence of this pattern of research support is that if one wants to study a particular subject, one
has to find some foundation, agency or person with a direct interest
in the outcome of the study and with some understanding of and
concern with social research. Consider the following hypothetical
example: Suppose one were interested in recruitment to the humanities, such as history, English literature, and the fine arts. Support probably could not be found for a study of recruitment into
these fields because there is no source of funds which has a direct
interest in this problem and which is *at the same time* appreciative
of the value of research.

These remarks should not lead to the erroneous impression that
all of the work of the large scale survey centers is applied. This
is not the case. Each manages to get some projects sponsored which
are of no particular applied interest whatsoever, although it must
be admitted that this happens infrequently and usually involves
research on a lesser scale.** At least as important is the process of

* Indeed, in one case we had difficulty keeping the client out of our hair,
so eager was he to receive the results.

** In recent years, the establishment of a Social Science Division within the
National Science Foundation and behavioral research study sections within the

broadening applied interests to cover research topics of considerable intensive interest but only indirectly related to each applied interest. For example, there are probably no funds available to study directly the supply of humanists mentioned earlier. NORC did get a considerable amount of money to study recruitment to the physical, biological and social sciences, engineering, medicine and education. However, we are *also* studying recruitment to the humanities because we were able to convince the clients that it was more expensive for technical reasons to restrict the research only to those who might go into the "hard science" fields. Similarly, although Carnegie is primarily interested in adult education, NORC was able to broaden the study out to include other uses of leisure time because it is more fruitful to study adult education in the context of a study of leisure time activities than by itself.

What I have just described might be called passive "robinhooding"—as some researcher facetiously named the broadening of objectives of a policy-oriented sponsor to include concerns which are of intrinsic interest but for which no funded (or vested) interest is likely to be found to supply support. There is also the active type of robinhooding, in which one starts out with an objective of some intrinsic interest and then fits it to the applied interest of some agency or foundation. NORC's study of the career plans and aspirations of the June, 1961 graduates grew in part out of a long standing interest in measuring the productivity of colleges and universities as affected by their organizational characteristics. Robinhooding in both its passive and active forms leads to considerable tension between the policy maker and the researcher. On the one hand it looks as if the researcher is hoodwinking the policy maker; on the other hand it can be viewed as a process of bargaining in which the research center agrees to do something in return for support to do something else in addition. Incidentally, it often turns out that in the end the policy maker is quite pleased with the results of the extended study, perhaps more than he would be if he were given only that which he wanted originally.

In the negotiations between the researcher and the policy maker, there is an important weapon in the hands of the researcher—his technical expertise often puts the policy maker at a disadvantage. In the end, technical considerations must override other considera-

---

National Institute of Mental Health has increased considerably the amount of funds available for basic social research.

tions if research of any great scientific stature is to appear. Indeed, one of the major reasons why government agencies come to the universities rather than to the commercial firms is that we are more concerned with technical purity than are the latter. Incidentally, when the market researchers and the advertising agencies want to have something that literally will stand up in court, they also come to the academic research organizations.

Of course, this pattern of financing large scale social research means that there may be projects of considerable intrinsic merit which are not supported at some particular point in time because there are no sources of support committed to research in the areas in question. For example, when the first draft of this paper was written in 1963 there were apparently no sources of support for research on the impact of the Negro protest movement on both whites and Negroes, even though this was (and is) one of the most salient features of the public life of our nation in this decade. We had an unparalleled opportunity to study a social movement in the making, but government agencies are understandably reluctant to support such research; and private foundations, for reasons I cannot fathom, also showed little interest. It is my impression that this is an unusual case. Ordinarily, given the diversity of interests represented by the large foundations and government agencies, there are usually some sources whose interests are close enough to a project to consider supporting it.

The financing of large scale social research has put a distinct advantage into the hands of those social scientists who have affiliated themselves to the social research institutes. Foundations and government agencies properly conceive of such organizations as having better capabilities to carry through such research, and more of a sense of responsibility to carry them through. But there are disadvantages as well. Large scale social research is likely to have an applied emphasis, and worthy research endeavors may go unsponsored because none of the sources of large funds have an interest in the topic to be studied.

IV. Implications for the Contemporary University

The basic structure of American universities scarcely has had a chance to react and accommodate to the great development of research activities within the university in the past forty years, and virtually no time at all to adjust to the growth of social science research in the two decades since World War II. The final pattern of accommodation has probably not yet appeared, to judge at least by the fact that few university officials, researchers and professors in any institution are sure that they have found a proper pattern in the organizational arrangements worked out on their campuses.

Partly because the solutions are not yet in sight, the problems resulting from the broadening of the goals of universities to include research as well as teaching are very much visible. There can be little doubt that the teaching function of universities, especially of undergraduates, is carried out differently today than when research was carried out by professors primarily as an extracurricular activity. In the major universities fewer and fewer faculty members are much less frequently exclusively teachers. In my own department of fourteen members, only two members are entirely on the departmental budget. The "teaching load" is becoming an item over which bargains are made in order to entice new faculty members.*
Only in the small liberal arts college is teaching considered an activity through which a faculty member can make his major contribution to the university community.

It is hard to judge whether research activities unduly intrude upon the teaching function or whether it enriches teaching.** Certainly the faculty member who is wrapped up in his research may not be able to spend the time necessary to prepare lectures which are of the highest quality, but his lectures may have the benefit of being more up to date and alive because his research is on the frontiers of the field in which he is teaching. Perhaps the most serious inroad upon the university arises out of the rise of research as an alternative to entering upon a career of academic statesmanship. Departmental chairmanships appear to be going begging and

* In a joint NORC-Bureau of the Census study of persons in critical occupations and professions, the probabilities of scientists in all fields designating teaching as their primary duty declines drastically with age. For example, nine out of ten biologists over 55 with the Ph.D. list teaching as a primary duty while only one out of every ten under 35 make the same claim. Similar although not as dramatic contrasts can be made for other scientific fields.

** Harold Orlans makes the point that the best graduate students are assigned duties as research assistants while the poorer quality students are given jobs as teaching assistants, thereby laying the groundwork for sorting out the best into research and the poorest into teaching. There is no evidence to support his argument in NORC's study of graduate students (Seymour Warkov's "Subsidies for Graduate Study," NORC Report #97 [1964]). Teaching assistants and research assistants are roughly of the same quality.

on occasion few candidates have appeared as contenders for dean-ships. The rewards arising out of research are greater and lead to national recognition, while the rewards for chairing a department are restricted in the usually highly egalitarian department and arise out of local rather than national acclaim.

The teaching of graduate students appears to me to have bene-fited considerably from the development of research in the univer-sity. No longer is the dissertation the sole research experience of the new Ph.D. Ordinarily he has participated as an apprentice on per-haps several research projects of his major mentors. He has also probably had some practice teaching as a teaching assistant under the general supervision of an experienced lecturer. Since graduate study is more and more the goal of new B.A.'s,* the experiences of new entrants into the scientific and technical occupations more and more include some period of close and intimate contact with a mem-ber of the faculty. The intimacy of contact between faculty and stu-dents has disappeared in this era of mass higher education, to be re-placed by intimacy centered around research on the graduate level.

It is more difficult to discern the trends concerning the roles of professor and of researcher. On the one hand there are strong trends toward the amalgamation of the two roles, with research institutes becoming more intimately parts of the university community. On the other hand, the trend toward research activities on larger scales and involving larger sums produces a strain toward the develop-ment of quite separate research organizations. Professors are doing more research, and greater demand exists for persons who will do only research. Right now the researcher and his institute are located at the periphery of the campus in both geographical and social structural senses, while the traditional departments are located at the heart of the university. The converted buildings in which the institutes are housed will give way to more permanent structures built with their use specifically in mind, and second-class citizenship for the researcher will probably give way to some kind of status equal to that of the professor.

It is hard to predict the specific form that the status of researcher will take in the evolving university structure. Perhaps the recent rashes of appointments of persons to "research professorships" pre-

* A NORC study of the June, 1961 graduating classes of American universi-ties and colleges indicates that one out of three seniors enter upon postgraduate studies immediately after completing the B.A. See James A. Davis, *Great Aspirations* (Chicago: The Aldine Press, 1964).

sages the future position.* Or it may be the case that research institutes will develop into entities like departments, with complements of tenure positions to bestow. Whatever specific organizational forms will arise in the future in response to tensions I have described in this paper, one expectation will certainly be upheld: the American university will be profoundly affected by massive changes in the definition of the professorial role and perhaps even in the definition of the goals of the university community. Scientific activity apparently flourishes in the academic climate. I hope that the ecology of the academic community can support without radical alteration the rise to dominance of the species of scientific researcher.

* The University of Chicago has evolved a new status—Professorial Lecturer—to be held by persons with primarily research appointments who are so senior in accomplishment that they cannot be left out of the academic rank system. However, this new status does not involve the critical issue of assimilation of researchers into the university, their participation as voting members in departmental decisions.

REFERENCES

1. A literature concerning research centers has just started to develop, stemming in part from the needs of foundations, government agencies and universities to understand the intellectual implications of this organization of scientific activity. See, for example, H. M. Vollmer, "A Preliminary Investigation and Analysis of the Role of Scientists in Research Organizations," Stanford Research Institute (1962).

2. P. F. Lazarsfeld, "Observations on the Organization of Empirical Social Research in the U. S.," *Information,* Bulletin of the International Social Science Council, XXIX (December, 1961).

3. Gerald Holton, "Scientific Research and Scholarship," *Dædalus,* Spring, 1962.

4. Derek de Solla Price, *Big Science: Little Science* (New York: Columbia University Press, 1963), shows that the costs of research have been increasing exponentially in a wide variety of fields in response to a corresponding increase in the complexity of research endeavors.

JEROME M. ZIEGLER

Continuing Education in the University

The Tradition of University Adult Education

HISTORICALLY, the purposes of the university in the United States have been teaching and research: informing the younger generations of the intellectual traditions and achievements of the past, helping students to understand the world they were about to enter as adults, preparing them for employment and civic responsibility, and pursuing new knowledge through research. To these tasks most universities in this century have added two others: developing educational courses and programs for adults, and providing a wide range of services to local, state and federal government and to other institutions and agencies in society. While the university is old, adult education has been largely a twentieth-century development. The trickle of adult students in the earliest decade of the 1900's has grown to many millions by 1964,* a change which parallels the growth in public school and university undergraduate education and which to a great extent is the result of the recognition our society increasingly has given to the uses and value of education in general. Adult education differs, however, from the public school and college and university institutions in the ways by which it has become established, in the purposes it serves and in the degree of public and governmental financial support it enjoys.

At the outset, we must make clear that one cannot speak of "adult education" as one can speak of the public elementary and high school program, and expect a common understanding of what

* The most recent and reliable estimate of the number of adults in some form of educational activity is that of the National Opinion Research Center of the University of Chicago. In a 1961–1962 survey, the NORC found that 28,770,000 persons were engaged in some kind of adult educational course or activity. See John W. C. Johnstone, *Volunteers for Learning: A Study of the Educational Pursuits of American Adults* (Chicago: National Opinion Research Center, University of Chicago, 1963).

130

is meant by the term. For in addition to the variety of course content presented at many different intellectual levels and the range of activities which comprise adult education, this branch of education has been and continues to be conducted by a multitude of contrasting institutions and agencies, each proceeding according to its own plan or method. Adult education has not occurred in this country, as it has in some others, according to some overall purpose or special need,* nor has it developed functionally, as have the public schools, because of society's insistence that the populace must possess common understanding of a particular body of knowledge. A child can get his education in half a dozen public schools in as many different cities and the body of knowledge which is taught him remains much the same, whatever the differences in competence of teaching or method of presentation. Not so with adult education.

Consider what the term adult education now includes: the credit and non-credit or "informal" courses at all institutions of higher education open to adults; programs of the public schools, evening high schools and junior colleges; the secretarial and vocational work offered at commercial schools; the technical and management courses given by technical institutes and professional graduate schools as well as by business and industry themselves; the recreational and educational programs of social, civic, religious, fraternal, professional and public affairs organizations, associations and clubs; the religious education, public affairs forums and creative arts courses to be found in many churches and synagogues; the lectures, films, discussion groups, art fairs and music festivals offered by public libraries, museums and other civic institutions; the home demonstration and technical-agricultural work provided by the Cooperative (Agricultural) Extension Service; the courses offered by government agencies and the armed forces to government employees (and others); the field of community development; education by television; the commercial correspondence schools and home-study departments of many universities; and finally, the enormous and

---

* In Denmark, the Folk Highschool conceived by Bishop Grundtwig in the nineteenth century served a special purpose, which was early recognized by the state, of providing civic and cultural education for all those who had not completed earlier schooling, as well as for many adults who wished to improve their general educational background. The Danish State supported the Folk Highschool and gave it institutional form and status. Similar institutions for this kind of adult education developed in the other Scandinavian countries as the Folk Highschool's success was demonstrated in Denmark.

increasing amount of independent self-study or self-education.

The variety, scope and magnitude of this enormous enterprise which we term adult education, including millions of adult students, hundreds of thousands of teachers and many thousands of sponsoring agencies or institutions makes almost impossible any attempt to discover order in this branch of our educational system. Adult education as a whole has grown in the six and one-half decades of this century without a comprehensive plan or theory, with very little articulation among its separate parts or divisions, and chiefly in response to individual or group needs made known at different times in different places. No doubt this was inevitable, given the pluralism of American society and the sheer size of our country. Nevertheless, we must take account of this general condition in describing what university adult education in particular has been, what it is today and what it may become.

Considerably more clarity can be found in the philosophy, purposes and programs of university adult education today than can be discerned in the field of adult education overall. This is not to say that university adult education is or is becoming a unitary system, but tendencies and trends of earlier years appear to be causing university evening colleges and university extension divisions to formulate common answers to common problems. The contemporary evening college and the university extension division are closer in purpose and educational program to each other than to other levels of adult education, and closer to each other today than they were in the years of their origins, the decades between 1890 and 1910. Until those years, adult education in any formal institutional sense was rather haphazard. Just before the turn of the century, educational opportunities for adults were scarce and rudimentary but beginning to be institutionalized in a manner that foretold the future.

In the nineteenth century, if adults wanted further education they had to get it by attending evening high schools for youth (and these only in the larger cities) or by enrolling in Farmers' Institutes or courses presented by the Chautauqua circuit or in institutions like the Cooper Union in New York or the Junto in Philadelphia. Churches, fraternal societies and labor organizations offered occasional lectures, and the high schools in eastern seacoast cities provided English lessons and "Americanization" for the foreign born. A few liberal arts colleges organized public lectures for adults to acquaint them with advances in science or to discuss religious or political topics of current interest. Colleges which offered vocational instruction to undergraduates in the form of agriculture or the mechanic arts occasionally permitted adults to participate. The passage of the Morrill Act in 1862, establishing the land-grant colleges, provided increased opportunities for undergraduates to enroll in technical or agricultural courses which much later were extended to adults. When the Cooperative Extension Service was established in 1914, working through the County Agricultural Agents in cooperation with the land-grant colleges, agricultural and technical education became available to adults in rural or semi-rural communities on a wide scale. It was not, however, until the development of the university extension system and the university evening college that adults in significant numbers began to use the resources of the institutions of higher education.[1]

The modern era of adult education may be said to have commenced during the final two decades of the nineteenth century and the first decade of the twentieth, when the idea of extension, conceived in England at Oxford and Cambridge, was adopted by American educators at Johns Hopkins, the University of Chicago, Harvard, Columbia and such land-grant institutions as the University of Wisconsin and the University of Minnesota.[2] President William Rainey Harper, the first president of the newly established University of Chicago, organized that university's extension division simultaneously with the founding of the university itself. The purpose of the University Extension Division was, in his words:

To provide instruction for those who for social or economic reasons cannot attend in its classes is a legitimate and necessary part of the work of every university. To make no effort in this direction is to neglect a promising opportunity for building up the university itself, and at the same time to fall short of performing a duty which from the very necessities of the case is incumbent upon the University. It is conceded by all that certain intellectual work among the people at large is desirable; those who believe in the wide diffusion of knowledge regard it as necessary; all are pleased to see that it is demanded. This work, while it must be in a good sense popular, must also be systematic in form and scientific in spirit; and to be such it must be done under the direction of a university, that thus (1) there may be a proper guarantee of its quality; (2) character may be given it; (3) continuity may be assured; (4) suitable credit may be accorded.[3]

President Harper's Extension Division became the University College within a decade, to be followed by the establishment of similar university colleges or evening divisions within the growing number of municipal universities in the last decade of the nineteenth century and the first of the twentieth.

In 1906, President Charles Van Hise organized General Extension at the University of Wisconsin, commenting, in his now famous statement, that he wished to make "the boundaries of the University campus coterminous with the boundaries of the state." The central idea of this division was to serve all the people of the state with university level courses, not just those persons who, because of financial resources or geographic proximity, were able to enroll on the Madison campus. With the establishment in Wisconsin of classes off campus, which later developed into full-time extension centers, the concept of extension as a regular responsibility of the university took root and spread. Between 1906 and 1913, twenty-eight extension divisions were organized in other land-grant and private universities.[4] In 1915, the National University Extension Association was founded with twenty-two members; by 1960 the NUEA had one hundred and five members; and the Association of University Evening Colleges had one hundred and sixty members (many institutions belonging to both organizations).*[5]

Between the first and second world wars, three mechanisms of adult education through the universities reached mature form, each with a somewhat different philosophy and methodology: the university (general) extension system, the cooperative (agricultural) extension system, and the evening college. University extension took the university into far corners of the states and organized classes for adults or groups in an enormous variety of subjects, including credit and non-credit work. Cooperative extension, through the system of county agents, offered advice and technical assistance to farmers on the latest research and knowledge in agriculture, and instruction in home economics through home demonstration to rural families. The evening colleges, located in urban communities, provided for adults who were fully employed the opportunity to get an undergraduate or graduate degree at night and thus to complete a higher education which might have been interrupted or never

* In 1915, the Association of Urban Universities was organized as a result of a conference called by the Commissioner of Education in Washington the previous year to consider the problems of universities located in urban communities. Attended mainly by evening college deans and directors because adult education was an important and constant concern, these men formed their own organization, the Association of University Evening Colleges, in 1939.

started. The evening college also offered adults who were not interested in acquiring a degree the chance to fulfill their intellectual interests by enrolling in various liberal arts courses. In more recent years, the evening college and the extension system have approached one another in basing their courses on the concept of service to an entire community, utilizing every device of instruction from the standard lecture and seminar for credit to the organization of "informal," meaning non-credit, conferences, workshops, special institutes and educational television. In the great urban communities such as New York City, Chicago, Cleveland, St. Louis and Los Angeles, the evening or extension divisions of New York University, the University of Chicago, Western Reserve, Washington University and UCLA respectively have organized classes throughout their entire metropolitan areas, including suburbs or separate towns and cities many miles distant from the downtown campus. In many other cities, such as Atlanta, Dayton, Toledo, Kansas City, Omaha, Oklahoma City, Denver and Portland to name but a small sample, the local institution or institutions of higher education have similarly extended their reach to the outskirts of their communities. Indeed, so rapid has been the development of adult education opportunities since the end of World War II that one could say almost no city of any appreciable size which possesses a city university (whether municipal or private) lacks a higher adult education facility. Many of the larger state universities, such as Rutgers, Wisconsin and California, in addition to operating a state-wide extension, have established evening colleges or centers either on campus or in other major cities of the state as in Newark, Milwaukee and San Francisco. Thus the evening colleges and the extension divisions often resemble each other in geographic area and in the kind of population served. This would appear to be inevitable as America's rural and semi-rural population diminishes. Nevertheless, the state-wide extension systems still preserve their state-wide function of serving citizens in all parts of the state, and institutions such as Pennsylvania State University and the universities of North Carolina, Oklahoma and California continue to organize classes in countless smaller cities and towns far removed from the central campus.

The Change from Adult to Continuing Education

Until about ten years ago, the education of mature persons or of persons who had at least finished high school was termed adult education. Educators and administrators by the use of this term meant to distinguish the education of adults from the formal schooling of earlier years. The term has been used to include the widest range of educational, recreational and hobby activities for anyone not in day-time public school. Arts and crafts, motor boating, bridge clubs, Bible discussion groups, chorus singing and orchestra playing, home nursing, vocational, technical and secretarial courses, evening high school or YM and YWCA courses and regular evening college and university extension degree work were and are all subsumed under adult education. With the enormous growth in the adult student body and the consequent expansion of facilities and opportunities, it was natural that college and university educators should seek for some definition of education for adults that would separate in the public mind what the university offered from what a fraternal, civic or community organization or association offered. But far more important than a wish for distinguishing phraseology was the change in concept of the education of adults which had been developing and maturing for many years and which gained common acceptance among college and university administrators by the middle 1950's.

The change in concept was from "adult education" to "continuing education." The new term expressed an understanding of education as a process—something different from the former notion of education compartmentalized into elementary school, high school, undergraduate and then graduate studies, with most people ending at high school or less, some people ending at the bachelor's degree and a few finishing with a graduate degree. The YM and YWCA's used the phrase "Lifelong Learning," which was also used in some evening college catalogues. Today many institutions of higher education have to use the phrase continuing education to describe their departments or divisions for adults; and with the establishment of Centers of Continuing Education at major universities such as Michigan State, Georgia, Oklahoma and Chicago, under grants from the Kellogg Foundation, and with the organization of Colleges of Continuing Education at the central campuses within state-wide extension systems, the students and the faculty, as well as the administrators, are beginning to think of education in a new and different way. It is recognized that adults, at different periods of their lives possessing different interests and different needs, require distinctive educational programs. There is a difference between the goals of undergraduate and graduate students and the goals of young adults in the years when they are securing their first jobs, getting married and becoming established. There is a difference between the educational needs of young adulthood and middle adulthood, the first being characterized by a concern for vocational and technical training which will assist in professional competency and job advancement, the second being characterized more perhaps by a desire to fulfill one's intellectual interests and creative impulses. There is also a difference between the educational needs of middle adulthood and old age, and between the ways men and women regard their own further education. The growing awareness of these differences by administrators and faculties has led to new types of courses, to a greater range of subject matter, to specialized approaches and to a new emphasis upon individual counseling and guidance for adult students.

The general concept that education should be a continuing process was understood in the nineteenth and early twentieth centuries as a part of broad educational philosophy—witness the views of Presidents Van Hise and Harper in this country, and Sir Richard Livingstone in England, or of Henry Adams and Bernard Berenson, who, although writing about education in entirely different contexts, gave us a fresh view of the unity between education and human existence. Such insights but rarely informed the practice of many university administrations until very recent years, when the influx of students, such changes in American society as greater mobility and leisure and the work of certain new national organizations concerned with the continuing liberal education of adults combined to change the traditional views of adult educators.* Large numbers of

* In the 1950's, the Fund for Adult Education was established as a separate, independent entity by the Ford Foundation. The Fund for Adult Education defined its task as one of stimulating and supporting liberal education and education in public affairs and public responsibility at all levels of the adult education movement, utilizing educational television—which was largely brought into existence by the Fund—the public school systems, colleges and universities, public libraries and a number of national organizations. See The Fund for Adult Education, *Advancing the Idea and Practice of Continuing Liberal Education, 1951–1961* (White Plains, 1962). During this period, several national organizations, which predated the Fund, such as the American Library Association, the American Foundation for Continuing Education and the Great Books Foundation, were supported by the Fund for the purpose of expanding their liberal education programs. In 1951, with financial assistance from the Fund, the Center for the Study of Liberal Education for Adults was established by the Committee on Liberal Education of the Association of University Evening Colleges. The Center has worked cooperatively for over a decade with both the

new adult students demanding new courses in politics, the social sciences, philosophy and the arts and in natural and physical science, and not content with established teaching methods, gave educators the opportunity to experiment, to innovate, to develop new materials and new approaches. National organizations such as the Fund for Adult Education, the Center for the Study of Liberal Education for Adults and the American Foundation for Continuing Education brought new influences to bear upon the adult higher education structure. Study-discussion programs for small groups of mature students were organized on hundreds of college campuses through the country. Several hundreds of thousands of adults took advantage of these new opportunities to study world politics, American government, modern poetry, drama, literature, science, the Great Books and a host of other liberal subjects either on campus or in the extension and community centers, in public libraries or in their own homes. These adults, who were not interested in formal credit or working toward degrees, became a large new audience for the evening colleges and extension systems, an audience to which the institutions have continued to cater by developing highly interesting and unusual courses utilizing a combination of teaching methods: study discussion, lecture-discussion, residential weekend seminars and conferences.

At one time, university adult education for the most part meant providing in the evening college a replica of the undergraduate curriculum or taking that curriculum to people everywhere in the state through the general extension system. Cooperative extension introduced the methodology of home demonstrations, specialized conferences, workshops and short courses which, excepting home demonstrations because inapplicable, were duplicated and emulated by university extension. But for a majority of institutions, adult education implied either degree work and credit courses or vocational courses in a technical or professional field. As we have said, university extension grew up, so to speak, in the philosophy of service to all the people of the state. Therefore, individuals and groups within a state looked to the university for instruction in all

Association of University Evening Colleges and the National University Extension Association to assist their members in experimenting with and expanding liberal education courses. The American Foundation for Continuing Education also worked during this same period of time with over three hundred colleges, universities and junior colleges to develop discussion groups for adults in politics, economics, cultural anthropology, the arts and science.

manner of vocational and specialized courses. Business, agricultural, trade union groups, women's organizations such as a state federation of women's clubs, and professional associations of all kinds requested and received faculty instruction and assistance in the areas of their special interests. As the population and its needs increased, the extension systems became heavily involved in meeting its requests, often using part-time or special instructors and organizing courses upon demand, perhaps in the process of running a wide-flung operation becoming somewhat detached from the central campus faculty. Where this occurred, and where university extension doubled and trebled its size, as happened often enough at the large state universities in the decade after the Second World War, a certain division and even hostility developed between academic and professional departments and the extension system. Faculty critics would characterize university adult education as an educational cafeteria, being all things to all people, essentially uncontrolled by the same standards of academic excellence which presumably governed undergraduate and graduate education.[6] At the same time, although this feeling of separation between the adult divisions and the academic departments and professional schools did exist and still exists, deans and directors of adult or continuing education have worked assiduously to cultivate close relations with all branches of the university, relying more and more on the regular faculty to teach their adult courses.

The developing concept of continuing education has in turn brought about an emphasis upon liberal education for adults, in contrast to vocational or professional training and education, which for many years comprised the standard offerings of most evening divisions. The current catalogues of the University of California, Berkeley campus, or of New York University, for example, provide a remarkable selection of liberal education courses, both credit and non-credit, as well as a large choice of vocational and technical courses. In California, during the spring or summer of 1964, one could enroll in the following special programs: The Negro Writer in the United States, a five-day residential conference; The Shakespeare Quadricentennial Lectures and a Shakespeare Weekend; Mysticism and Psychotherapy, a weekend conference; New Images, American Painting Since 1946, a series of six lectures; Wilson and Lenin, Heritage of Four Decades, a series of lectures; The Ocean, a lecture series and summer field program; J. S. Bach, The Well-Tempered Clavier, six Saturday workshops; Understanding and

Educating the Emotionally Disturbed Child, a lecture/discussion program. Or one could enroll in any of twenty new credit classes or ten non-credit classes in such diverse subjects as Introduction to General Astronomy, Elementary Latin, The British and French Legacy in Independent Africa or Issues in Municipal Administration. If one wished to enroll for credit in the department of Anthropology, one could choose from among eight courses; in Art and Architecture from among seventeen; in Psychology from among eleven. The courses offered by university extension administered from the Berkeley campus are given not only on campus or at the San Francisco center but at thirty-five locations throughout the northern half of the state, the southern half being so covered by university extension at UCLA.

At New York University in the Division of General Education and Extension Services, one finds courses during the summer session in the liberal arts, the management institute, foreign languages, college preparatory (to prepare students for college entrance, daytime or evening, in English, French, arithmetic, algebra, geometry, trigonometry, government and sociology), the American Language Institute, the Reading Institute, the Testing and Advisement Center, the Center for Safety Education and a Summer Workshop in Television and Radio. The Liberal Arts in Extension program offers study-discussion, lecture and workshop courses in all five boroughs of New York City and in Long Island, Westchester and in New Jersey in the fine arts, literature, economics and political science, psychology and religion, international affairs, investing, foreign languages and science. At the Division of General Education, in addition to liberal arts and sciences, one could study book publishing, 11 courses; advertising, 5 courses; electronic and punched-card data processing systems, 16 courses; business, including finance, purchasing, marketing, personnel management and industrial relations and advanced management programs, 34 courses. In foreign languages, a student could enroll in any one of nineteen courses, including Korean, Swahili, Indonesian, Turkish, Japanese, Chinese, Hebrew, Arabic, Urdu and Hindi in addition to European languages.

In short, at leading institutions such as the University of California and New York University, one can find an enormous range and variety of subject matter including highly specialized and even esoteric courses. But at only a dozen or two universities across the nation is such a variety offered. The rest are far more limited either because of smaller, less specialized faculties or because the adult student population cannot support a larger program.

Perhaps the most interesting development in continuing education within the past ten years has been the emergence of "special degree" programs for adults who cannot enroll in the regular day or evening college—that is, special programs for acquiring the traditional bachelor's degrees. These special degree programs differ from the traditional ones in entrance and course requirements, arrangement of subject matter and the ability of adult students to proceed at their own pace. All of them take into consideration the life experience of adults, giving credit for previous learning or experience in particular fields. Special degree programs are in operation at Brooklyn College (the oldest, having commenced in 1953), Queens and Goddard Colleges, Syracuse University, the University of Oklahoma, and Johns Hopkins; and at San Francisco Theological Seminary an in-service professional degree program has been organized for practicing ministers.[7] At all the institutions except the theological seminary, the emphasis is upon broad liberal arts courses and interdisciplinary seminars, plus a large amount of independent study. At the University of Oklahoma, a Bachelor of Liberal Studies program has been prepared which combines a high degree of individual counseling for accurate placement, independent study, discussion-seminar groups on and off campus, residential weekend conferences and seminars, auditing regular day or evening classes, correspondence study and study through educational radio or television programs.[8] This is more than a simple adaptation of undergraduate courses, and it represents a university's creative attempt to deal with a new kind of student in a new type of situation.

Although the movement in the direction of continuing liberal education has been accelerated during the past decade as university adult educators have become more responsive to the interests and needs of the large number of new students and as the national organizations provided opportunities for experimentation and innovation, the bulk of adult education has remained in traditional molds and patterns with a high concentration on credit, vocational and technical courses. Adult educators are re-evaluating their programs and methods of instruction, but perhaps not rapidly enough for the needs of the times. Given the kinds of change which have occurred in American society—the explosion of all knowledge, the increase in population, the high rate of mobility among a large and growing middle class, a shortened work week accompanied by

141

amounts of leisure time inconceivable to older generations, the revolution in industrial production achieved through automation/cybernation, the rise in expectations of Negroes and other minority groups for better jobs and living conditions, the phenomenon of urbanism or "Megalopolis" as a determinant of culture—it is necessary for university adult educators, the faculties and the senior administrative officers to reassess the role and place of adult or continuing education in their institutions. Deans and directors of continuing education must continue to ask with fresh urgency the questions of perennial interest: How extensive should extension be? What are its geographic and subject matter limits? Should courses be offered for adult students who would not, lacking previous education or achievement, normally be regarded as meeting university standards? Should the adult divisions become engaged in non-course projects such as workshops or conferences for special interest groups which might better or as easily be conducted elsewhere? Should adult students be subject to different course and degree requirements than prevail elsewhere in the university? Should the needs of society be the touchstone for organizing curricula instead of or in addition to the interests of individuals?

These questions may be broadened by asking, as many leaders in the field have asked, what is the proper role of the university in the field of continuing education for adults. What is the university equipped to accomplish that other institutions cannot accomplish? What leadership can the universities provide to the other educational instutions which are themselves grappling with difficult problems of educating the present generation of adults? What are the great and profound problems of contemporary civilization to which the university must make a special contribution through the use of its unique intellectual resources?

The Adult Student Body and the University's Responsibility for Educating It

Before considering the questions posed in the previous section, a word should be said regarding the composition and motivation of the current adult student body and the issue of defining the university's responsibility toward the education of this student body. The adult clientele for continuing education is today the largest, the wealthiest and already the best educated in our history. Estimates vary of the number of people who are returning to some form of activity broadly classified as educational from almost fifty million to just under thirty million. The NORC study[9] showed almost thirty million persons engaged in "educational pursuits," according to the classification in the following table:

Subjects	Estimated Number of Persons
1. Job-related subjects and skills	9,020,000
2. Hobbies and recreation	5,470,000
3. Religion, Morals and Ethics	3,820,000
4. General education subjects	3,500,000
5. Home and family life	3,440,000
6. Personal development	1,777,000
7. Current events, public affairs and citizenship	1,080,000
8. Agriculture	320,000
9. Miscellaneous	970,000

Of this number, we may note that 3,260,000 are attending classes in churches and synagogues, 2,640,000 are attending classes in colleges or universities and 8,000,000 are engaged in independent study.[10]

According to the NORC study, the categories of subject matter offered by the universities and colleges were divided:[11]

General Education	38%
Vocational	39%
Agriculture	1%
Hobbies/recreation	6%
Home and family life	3%
Personal development	6%
Religion	1%
Public affairs	4%
All other	2%

General education in these institutions included foreign languages, mathematics and statistics, English literature and composition (excluding speech and basic English for immigrants), history, sciences, psychology, social sciences, great books and public affairs (political education).

Regarding the motivation for adult learning, it appears that adults enroll in school or college courses because of (1) a monetary or vocational incentive, (2) a desire to remedy a lack or a gap in earlier schooling, (3) individual intellectual curiosity and (4) a wish to use new-found leisure in a meaningful way or because of the need to find recreation outside the home and ordinary, daily social relationships. The vocational incentive is the direct result of job mobility and the common desire to earn more money. Since job mobility has become a major characteristic of American business and industry, millions of adults have become involved in vocational re-education or training, and hundreds of educational institutions have seen an opportunity not only to provide a certain service to business but to earn needed income themselves. Most university institutions have made a considerable investment in vocational/ technical education in order to meet the desires of adult students for these types of courses, and there is little doubt, looking at the figures in the NORC study, that vocational education is what at least 40 per cent of the adult students who attend universities want.

It is obvious that many students enroll in extension or evening college for a combination of reasons. Intellectual curiosity and using leisure time productively are two which have become more important as more adults pass through undergraduate and graduate education, and as almost all adults gain more free time from job or home responsibilities. Perhaps not surprising but gratifying is the tendency of those who already possess good education to want more of it. This places a responsibility upon the universities for discovering and creating the kind of education which best meets both the needs of individual students and the needs of society. However, adult educators are confronted with a very difficult issue when they provide courses and instruction which attempt to do both—because, as we all know, the wants of individuals and the needs of society are not always identical.

It is evident that general education subjects, or liberal arts broadly defined, are chosen by a minority of all people in adult education and that even in the universities they are less well attended than are vocational and recreational subjects. The small number of persons in public affairs courses bears out the contention of Dr. Ralph Tyler, among others, that adults avoid the study of critical issues. Educational institutions tend to offer what the average adult student prefers—"popular" subjects often devoid of worthy intellectual content and without any true connection to the needs of society. (This may not appear evident given the examples of adult courses noted earlier, but we must remember that most institutions do not offer such a heavy concentration in the liberal arts.) There is a disparity between what adults do study and what they ought to study in view of the political-social-economic needs of their communities and of society as a whole.

To repeat, this conflict poses a very serious challenge to the administrator who wants to exercise leadership, who wants to innovate and to be imaginative, yet who must meet other educational and budgetary responsibilities in accordance with the interests of the particular student body attending his institution. One might well ask who is the university administrator that he can determine the "needs of society" as against the desires and "needs" of individuals? No sensitive administrator would wish to arrogate to himself or even to his faculty colleagues omniscience in this matter. Yet every decision to include a particular course in the university catalogue and to exclude another is a decision based on a conscious or unconscious estimate of contending factors: what the adult student wants, what the univeristy is prepared to teach, what the university ought to be doing in the translation of new knowledge produced through its faculty's research into courses of instruction for adults: in short, how to make social and scientific research meaningful to society, and how to assure sufficient income to the evening college or extension division so that it can continue. Always, the university administrator has the responsibility of making value judgments about the intellectual quality and direction of the courses offered while weighing the various factors affecting this issue. He must find his own answers to the questions his leading colleagues in the field have been asking, to which we referred earlier: what is the proper role of the institution of higher learning in the education of adults, what can the university do which other institutions cannot do or cannot do as well, and how can the university best contribute to the solution of the complex, difficult problems besetting individuals and society?

Liberal Arts and the Future of Continuing Education

Developed for the education of younger generations, the university stands today as the most important focus for the education of adults. What the university does for its undergraduates and students in its professional schools, it can also do for its adult students: provide a sound, comprehensive liberal arts and science curriculum, followed by intensive professional training for those who seek graduate studies. For the university is unique; it combines qualities and resources not found in other institutions. There are many other organizations which can provide the entertaining, recreational, hobby courses which adults want; there are other levels of the formal educational structure, such as junior colleges and technical institutes, which can offer a great deal of the technical/vocational

145

work for the improvement of skills so much in demand by adults who wish to progress in their jobs. Business and industry increasingly train their own employees, thereby reducing the necessity for higher education to undertake more work in that area. One does not demean these activities by saying that few of them belong in a university catalogue. The university has a very special function to perform: offering to adults of intellectual competence the means to increase their knowledge of truly important subjects, to study the critical problems of our time, to participate in the search for new knowledge and to develop the habit of self-education. The university should not allow itself to be diverted from what it can do best by the pressure of business, industrial and agricultural interests, or by any other group, or by the promise of earning income or by the need for good public relations.

Why is the study of the liberal arts and sciences so important in the continuing education of adults? Most thoughtful persons would agree that it is through the study of these subjects that men most nearly approach a proper understanding and appreciation of the great questions which all men in all ages have confronted. It is through the study of the liberal arts that man can understand himself, and it is through the study of the liberal arts that one develops the necessary insights into the nature of contemporary problems and issues, solutions to which we all seek, reaching toward a more perfect society and civilization. The technical questions are very important in our day: how to build a bridge or a highway system, how to develop a nuclear power system for efficient, economical civilian use, how to desalinate the oceans, how to fit an artificial valve into the human heart, how to use computers and electronic data-processing. But the nontechnical questions of purpose, of means and ends, of human aspirations, of making government responsive to the needs and desires of populations, of where to plan new cities, of social and intergroup relations, of the place of beauty and art and nature in the lives of individual men and women—these questions are no less important.

To some extent the distinction between technical and nontechnical is artificial, and adults who choose a field of endeavor in either category require from their undergraduate, professional and adult education much the same kind of knowledge and insight. In any subject, one needs to master the available information. But one needs more. As Whitehead said, "Your learning is useless to you till you have lost your textbooks, burnt your lecture notes, and for-

146

gotten the minutiae which you learnt by heart for the examination. What, in the way of detail, you continually require will stick in your memory as obvious facts like the sun and moon; and what you casually require can be looked up in any work of reference. The function of a University is to enable you to shed details in favor of principles."[12] Continuing liberal education for adults at the university level does and should fulfill that function.

In the coming years, for the university to provide a stronger and sounder liberal curriculum to adult students, a conscious act of policy will be necessary by the university's administration and faculty. Senior administrative officers and boards of trustees of the universities will need to make clear the co-equal status of the evening college or the extension division with every other department of the institution. As Dr. Ralph Tyler has pointed out, raising the status of the extension division within the university, giving it more financial support and involving the resident faculty more deeply are three critically important factors affecting the future of university adult education.[13] Two other elements are equally important, the training of teachers of adult students and research into the learning processes of adults—elements to which Professor Cyril O. Houle of the University of Chicago has given particular attention.

Research into the motivation of adult students and research on how adults at different ages and from different backgrounds learn are highly interesting questions to which adult educators are more and more devoting their time. We can visualize the useful results we may obtain from that kind of research when we recall that almost three million adult students attend at the university level, and eight million persons are engaged in self-education. How the university may serve its present constituency better and how it may develop ways of attracting to its classes some of the eight million are matters about which present research will hopefully yield new clues and insights. For example, we should understand better than we now do the psychological effects of physiological change and of aging. We should know more about the relationship of emotional stability to the constructive use of leisure and of early retirement which increasing numbers of adults are experiencing, and the effects of these factors upon the adult's ability to learn. The interconnections between occupation and leisure time, and the motivation, intellectual curiosity, temperament and age of adults comprise a whole new area for research important to the future development and direction of continuing education by the university. What we

147

do with our leisure now when most of us are fully employed is one question; what we shall do with it when all of us are underemployed by today's work standards, or when we are finished with employment and enjoying early retirement, is quite another question. We need new testing and guidance procedures in order that mature students understand themselves better and understand how to make the best use of the university's resources. Adult counseling services are currently being conducted by the leading universities. These should be expanded and extended, for it is only by acquiring knowledge of its adult student body that the university can shape its curriculum and services to meet new needs and demands.

A broad research effort is needed, then, at the university level into the nature of adults, adult learning and leisure. By strengthening the extremely useful work that has been done in the past few years, the university and its department of continuing education can take full advantage of the remarkable opportunity which will be theirs in the coming decades to educate this fast-growing, diversified, highly motivated student body of mature men and women.

In contemplating what the future directions of university adult education may be we can forecast an ever increasing student body that will continue to strain the institutions' resources. Also the demands made upon the university by a host of organizations, groups and government agencies cannot be expected to lessen. Thus the universities will probably be forced to choose among the claims for its adult and continuing education services until such time as the level of public financial support increases, enough buildings are constructed and enough teachers are available to accommodate all the demands. In making its choices, if present trends continue, university administrators will emphasize the values of the liberal curriculum in contrast to the vocational, and they will concentrate upon the advanced training needed in the older and in so many of the newer professions.

The interdisciplinary approach to learning which has characterized undergraduate education will be found increasingly in the adult curriculum. For example, several leading institutions are developing Centers for Urban Studies or Institutes of Urban Planning where adults working in the relevant fields may take advanced training in the disciplines of economics, statistics, politics, psychology, anthropology, physical geography, city planning, architecture, industrial engineering and meterology. The subject of urbanism is no doubt one to which increasing numbers of adults in various professions as well as undergraduates will be attracted. Within it are subsumed some of the most difficult and challenging problems facing our country—relations between Negroes and whites, the improvement of public education, the development of a stable tax base, the provision of city services on a metropolitan basis, increasing recreational and cultural opportunities, and re-vitalizing democratic citizenship participation. Institutions of higher education have a great role to play in this regard both in training professionals and in increasing the understanding of the general adult population. Greater emphasis upon the teaching of interna-tional affairs and world politics is also to be expected as more Americans become interested in these matters, as more citizens travel abroad for business or pleasure and as both our own and foreign governments turn to the universities for technical and pro-fessional assistance.

These are but two of the many ways in which the leading uni-versities in their adult programs are recognizing their responsibili-ties and opportunities to utilize their resources in the education of mature men and women who are concerned with social and political issues. At the same time, the university will continue to meet the intellectual and creative interests of individuals by expanding the liberal curriculum, by offering special degree programs and by giv-ing adults new opportunities to explore deeply and widely in di-verse fields of subject matter. The liberally educated man is no less a goal for adult educators than it is for those in charge of under-graduate education. The words of the report on *General Education in School and College*[14] published twelve years ago stand today, as they did then, as an expression of the hope and ideal for which educators strive in every part of the total educational system. "A liberally-educated man demands freedom. . . . We call those studies *liberal* . . . which are worthy of a free man . . . and of a free society. . . . Liberal education and the democratic ideal are related to each other in a thousand ways. It is not too much to say that they stand and fall together."

Thus the adult and continuing education departments of the universities are forming their programs on the fundamental needs of individuals and of society, needs which are becoming more congruent as their interrelation is more clearly perceived. Programs in the humanities for businessmen and scientists, in the social sci-ences for trade union leaders, in the natural sciences for nonscien-tists are signs pointing to the development of continuing education as a coherent and mature enterprise, taking the serious-minded person at whatever point he concluded his earlier formal education and giving him both the broad general knowledge and the professional training he needs to achieve his potential as a worker, parent and individual. We may anticipate a great expansion of liberal education programs for such special audiences as women graduates, teachers, people in the health professions, senior civil servants, indeed for people in many new professions or families of jobs that are yet to be created by technologies unknown at the present time. For the university recognizes society's continuing need for the liberally educated man as well as its need for the competent specialist who has mastered a complex field of knowledge. More and more, the university will try to provide both kinds of knowledge to the same individuals, the persons who by virtue of their education, talents and experience are the managers of contemporary society.

Robert Redfield once described education as exploration, conversation and creation. "Education," he said, "is of course learning something. More importantly, it is becoming something. Although knowledge is needed for education, an educated person is not the same as a man who has knowledge. If we learn things that become parts of us, if we make efforts to develop our own particular understanding of life and of the order of life's goods, it is education that we are doing. A person is something that it takes time to make; there is on everyone an invisible sign, 'Work in progress'; and the considered effort to get along with the work is education."[15]

The work in progress is what happens when an adult returns to the university. We may suppose that such a return can be and often is a critical turning point in his life. Far from treating lightly or mechanically any adult enrollment, the university faculty and administration welcomes and seizes the chance to offer our generations of adults the means for solving the great problems of our age and for attaining the highest degree of self-development of which we are capable.

REFERENCES

1. James T. Carey, *Forms and Forces in University Adult Education* (Chicago: Center for the Study of Liberal Education for Adults, 1961).

2. *Ibid.*, pp. 14–19.

3. Robert M. Roth, *A Conspectus to the Self-Study Project of University College, The University of Chicago* (Chicago: Center for the Study of Liberal Education for Adults, 1964), p. 8.

4. Paul H. Sheats, Clarence D. Jayne and Ralph B. Spence, *Adult Education* (New York: The Dryden Press, 1953), p. 176.

5. John Dyer, *Ivory Towers in the Market Place, The Evening College in American Education* (Indianapolis: The Bobbs-Merrill Company, 1956), pp. 38–39.

6. Renee Peterson and William Peterson, *University Adult Education, A Guide to Policy* (New York: Harper and Brothers, 1960), pp. 62–68.

7. A. A. Liveright and Roger DeCrow, *New Directions in Degree Programs Especially for Adults* (Chicago: Center for the Study of Liberal Education for Adults, 1963), pp. 3–4. This booklet contains a detailed description of the method of organization, requirements and course work for each of these special degree programs.

8. *Ibid.,* p. 27.

9. John W. C. Johnstone, *Volunteers for Learning: A Study of the Educational Pursuits of American Adults* (Chicago: National Opinion Research Center, University of Chicago, 1963), pp. 44–46.

10. *Ibid.,* p. 58.

11. *Ibid.,* p. 59.

12. Alfred North Whitehead, *The Aims of Education* (New York: The New American Library of World Literature, 1949), p. 38.

13. Ralph W. Tyler, *An Evaluation of General Extension Work by Land-Grant Institutions* (Proceedings of the Centennial Convocation of the American Association of Land-Grant Colleges and State Universities, November 14, 1961, Kansas City, Missouri), pp. 16–17.

14. *General Education in Schools and College. A Committee Report* by members of the faculties of Andover, Exeter, Lawrenceville, Harvard, Princeton and Yale (Cambridge: Harvard University Press, 1952), pp. 20–21.

15. Robert Redfield, *The Educational Experience* (Pasadena: The Fund for Adult Education, 1955), p. 41.

PAUL WEISS

Science in the University

"THE great tides of change which have swept over the academic world, as over all our world, have moved familiar landmarks, submerged inhabited ground, and thrown up new islands to be explored. New fields of inquiry have emerged, old fields of inquiry face new problems, vast public support is thrown behind certain lines of endeavor, and other lines receive diminished attention. It is not surprising that this continuing process of change has produced in us a habitual attitude of re-examination and re-appraisal of our goals, our assumptions, our values, and the distribution of our efforts. And, since the academic world is nothing if not articulate, this re-examination involves a great clamor of voices. Forward-looking men, who have foreseen the emerging patterns and find significance in them, welcome the changes; but at their side are the faddists and the opportunists and the unstable folk who would welcome and exploit *any* change. Sober and judicious men, who see the losses that come with tumultuous change, regret the breaks in continuity and the washing out of old landmarks; but at their side are the inert and the timid and the self-interested who would resist and condemn any changes."
Carnegie Corporation of New York, Annual Report, 1952, p. 13

"Because we are struggling to meet this multiplicity of rapidly changing aims through continual alterations in our educational system, it is perhaps not surprising that our educational world is in a continual ferment. But this ferment, though it is far-reaching, does not necessarily mean chaos. A modern and rapidly changing society inevitably must have a diverse and a rapidly changing educational system. Our society will be shocked from time to time by unexpected and startling events throughout the world. Such events may stimulate us to re-examine our educational procedures. But we cannot amend our educational system overnight, or suddenly remove our educational deficiencies. Our system must be kept on an even keel, our educational goals must be kept clear; we need to work steadily and not impulsively, constantly to improve our system and to accept change as inevitable and desirable."
Education for the Age of Science. Statement by the President's Science Advisory Committee: The White House, May 1959

152

Preamble

SCIENCE has burst upon the stage of modern life with more aplomb than foresight. The universities must face and come to terms with the precipitous changes that this so-called "scientific explosion" impresses on our culture if they wish to retain their claim to leadership in cultural evolution rather than accept the passive role of drifters in the wake of wholly extraneous trends. To examine the growing impact of science on the universities is a timely and urgent undertaking; it should, indeed, be made a continuous process. There are two sides to the problem. The university must find ways to keep accommodating the legitimate expansive claims of science, but at the same time it must protect itself against disproportionate expansion of the scientific sectors beyond the stress limit at which the very ideal of a university as a cohesive body would collapse. These matters have been and are being widely and often wisely discussed in many quarters.[1] The only possible excuse for my reverting to the subject may be that it has not before been stated in quite this same context. There is perhaps the further point that my own educational experience has been sufficiently diverse to inure me to the spirit of partisanship which often has marred the treatment of these issues. I therefore with some trepidation accepted this challenging assignment, more with the aim to state the case than to prejudge it.

From the manner in which the case of "science and the university" is often stated within and without the academic precincts, one almost gets the impression of adversaries in court or of competitors in trade, of challengers from hostile camps. And C. P. Snow's widely heralded schism between "The Two Cultures" has added its share of exacerbation to the argument. It is deplorable that so much of the debate, on which weighty decisions and actions hinge, should be carried on in a spirit of doctrinary antagonism, with myopic concentration on extreme aspects of what in truth is, or ought to be, despite diverse facets and graded scales, an integral continuum—man's quest for knowledge.

By contrast, my main object in this essay will be to expound the proposition that the issue of "science in the university," together with all its subissues, in order to be resolvable, must be removed from the area of conflicting intellectual contentions. We ought not act like umpires in a game of win or lose. The more one poses the issues in terms of mutually exclusive alternatives and looks for universal master keys to their solution, the further away one actually gets from any

153

prospect of realistic resolution. Attempts at categorical solutions—the symptoms of administrative expediency—are doomed to failure.

For instance, the question of whether the universities should expand or contract their scientific engagements cannot be resolved in simple quantitative terms. A quota system is hardly applicable to any branch of learning. The issue is complex, and the only fruitful manner of approaching it is by untangling its intricacy, bringing the full diversity of its many detailed components into view, and shaping from them, after re-evaluation, programs sufficiently elastic to meet the unprecedented opportunities for growth, as well as the resultant stresses, that lie ahead. That is what I mean by "stating the case." It is to be largely an act of anamnesis and diagnosis, to which I shall append only a brief prognosis for therapy.

Yet I must emphasize that I am speaking in a strictly personal capacity. No one scientist can any longer claim the authority to act as spokesman for the whole of science. A "scientist" today is basically a worker in some branch of science. He may be broad or narrow in outlook and experience. But unlike the days when science was the province of natural philosophers of wide perspective, the modern ascendency of technical specialists in science has given rise to such a large spectrum of sectarian opinions of what science is or ought to be that no one, however broad-minded, can any longer be acceptable as representative for all of them. So this will be my private assessment of the situation. Like everyone else, I can do nothing about my congenital blind spots. However, I shall at least try to take off those self-imposed blinders which workers in and out of science like to wear—creative minds, for better concentration and efficiency, and less creative ones, for the security of intellectual seclusion. I shall proceed by sampling a few specific issues bearing on the general topic, with no illusion or pretense that my arguments are absolutely valid. Furthermore, I would stress that I am not addressing myself to my scientific colleagues, who are familiar with the issues and who know the arguments, but rather to the academic community at large, and even more broadly to the public, which is the prime beneficiary and, in the last analysis, benefactor of academic institutions.

Quite naturally, a sampling procedure of "Science in the University" must start from a clarification of our terms of reference. Just what are we talking about when we speak of "science" and when we speak of "the university"? After all, we are to deal with real institutions, not just with ideals or allegories.

What Is "Science"?

A search of laboratories or libraries for a representative and comprehensive miniature sample of "science," true, pure, and simple, would come to naught. The term is an abstraction. It simply signifies a collective operation of mankind in which countless different efforts and aptitudes are brought to bear conjointly on those aspects of knowledge that deal with nature. Its basic motivation is man's curiosity, his wish to learn and know, accentuated by his practical experience that benefits are to be reaped from knowledge.

The quest for knowledge of itself is good, regardless of the uses men make of their knowledge, wise or foolish. Although only that part of knowledge which lends itself to verification or negation by the evidence of observation, experiment, and measurement is the legitimate province of natural science,[2] the land within those borders is so immense and variegated that no separate fraction of it can be taken to portray science truthfully. One-sided portrayals of science as either the exalted search for absolute truth or as a mundane preoccupation with practical results and products are symptoms of narrowly restricted vision, perceiving only limited absorption bands from the broad total spectrum covered by science. In consequence the man of practical affairs more often than not tends to identify science with technology, whereas the academic purist conversely prefers to exclude from his definition of science all its practical applications in agriculture, engineering, medicine, statistics, and so forth.

However uninformed and short-sighted such distinctions may seem, there is no glossing over their widespread use and uncritical acceptance. The staggering internal diversity of science is not generally appreciated. Since this is surely not the occasion to list the multitude of diverse activities included in science, let me quote a passage from an earlier attempt I made to illustrate the point for my own field of biology.

Biologists, in the sense of miniature incarnations of universal biological knowledge, no longer exist. Biological science has become a group enterprise with many servants in varied stations. . . . Anyone contributing to this collective task constructively, competently, and conscientiously, thus becomes a biologist. Consequently, it takes all kinds of biologists to make the biological world, none of them able to carry on without the others. And biology needs their full diversity.

It needs the observer, the gatherer of facts, the experimenter, the statistician, the theorist, the classifier, the technical expert, the interpreter, the critic, the teacher, the writer. It needs the student of evolutionary history as much as it does the experimental physiologist; the precise recorder of morphological data as much as the analytical biophysicist and biochemist; the investigator of molecular interactions as much as the student of supramolecular organization, of the order of events in space and time. It needs the help of all hands at all stations. They all work for a common cause and should feel above the unjustified and undignified popularity contests that center on such monomaniac questions as who is more important, the fundamental or the applied scientist; the explorer or the instructor; the technical expert or the philosopher.[3]

If it seems impossible to find a unified formula even for a section of science like biology, how much further from reality is the notion that science as a whole is uniform and can be treated as a single simple entity. The university could help to combat this notion by ceasing to lump all "science" into a membrane-bound homogenate. This, of course, might lead to an administrative monstrosity, but it would at least engender a more balanced overview of what "science" in the university really means by stressing the enormous differences in kind, composition, and maturity of the different constituents of that "scientific" compartment, as widely disparate in their requirements of aptitudes and facilities as theoretical physics and descriptive botany; on the other hand, it would also blur the demarcation line between science and the humanities by recognizing their blending in philosophy, history, and even art.

I leave for later the question of how far the university is committed and how far it can afford to go in catering to this vast array of tributaries and ramifications of science without becoming what Robert Hutchins referred to as an "academic service station." For the moment, I rather raise the sights upwards to a feature of science which deserves special emphasis in the present context. It lies in the spiritual values imparted to those who share in its pursuit. That spirit of science, more than any specific training, is a most powerful ingredient of education, if education is defined with Corner as "preparation for effective living."[4] As I once put it:

Its power stems from the strict mental discipline and critical detachment that it imparts to those who live and practice by its code. . . .
Now, just what is it that marks this spirit as superior to the mere application of logic, the Golden Rule, or just plain common sense? The answer is: the categorical demand for validation and verification of each premise, each contention, and each conclusion by the most rigorous and critical tests of evidence. Every rule and law has to be tested and enforced, and nowhere else is the penalty for error or infringement so prompt and telling. . . . Thus by reward and punishment, the scientific

156

method teaches man to discipline his thinking and his actions based on thought.

This discipline of the scientific method, broadly applied, can go far toward clearing the underbrush of superstition and prejudice that hampers civilization in its march. By its incisiveness, the scientific spirit will leave its mark wherever men strive to overcome obscurity and obscurantism.

But it has limitations. According to the code of science, no positive assertions are final. All propositions are approximations, and indeed are provisional pending conclusive proof that all alternative propositions are untenable. Viewed in this light, science is seen to advance more by denying what is wrong than by asserting what is right—and by reducing, and eventually eradicating, error, rather than by heading straight toward some preconceived final truth. . . . It is a sobering experience for the scientist thus to acknowledge the finite boundaries of his reach. It takes humility and courage to live with partial answers, and it disturbs complacency. Yet, if this critical scientific spirit can cure more men of their cocksureness that they already know the answers to questions yet unsolved, then science will have given man a new resolve to search and strive again, not just conform; to face his problems, not accept pat solutions; to exercise his ingenuity, instead of dully abdicating to authority. The scientific spirit will thus rekindle flames which one of science's products—mechanization—threatens to smother.[5]

Why then is there so little prominence given to this crucial role of science in education? Why have so few in the academic population been made aware of the broad cultural aspects of science? The failure constitutes a black mark not for science but for the faulty manner in which it is customarily taught.

While I dissent explicitly with the antithesis of "Two Cultures"— one scientific and the other humanistic—I cannot ignore the fact that party lines have been drawn along those artificial distinctions. "Liberal education" *versus* "scientific training" is turning from a slogan into a battlecry. Were both sides only to learn more about each other, the misconceptions and perverted meanings might readily subside. Of course there is a marked asymmetry to be corrected; for whereas scientists by and large respect the cultural mission of the humanities, the humanistic values and social virtues of science, in contrast to its utilitarian aspects, are rarely appreciated in the other camp. The lack of symmetry in mutual relations between scientists and non-scientists, which forms the core of C. P. Snow's argument, is an indisputable fact. As a result the profound relevance of science to education is still widely underrated. But since this is based, it seems, on sheer lack of acquaintance rather than on misjudgment, there is hope for remedial action.

It will have been plain from this discussion that I rate science, properly presented, as a major rather than an auxiliary component of "Liberal Education." Here is further supporting testimony:

No one discipline or combination of disciplines provides the unique avenue to the liberation of the mind. The natural sciences—in the first flush of enthusiasm—once thought that they had the golden key to enlightenment, but sensible scientists no longer make this assertion. On the other hand, thoughtful people will find just as ridiculous the currently fashionable characterization of the physical and biological sciences as almost the antithesis of a liberal education—fit only to produce soulless technicians, illiterate in philosophy, innocent of moral values, and strangers to the creative life of the mind and spirit. The physical and biological sciences provide as great play for the creative spirit as do the literary fields. There are as many technicians-without-values in the fine arts as in the sciences. The intellectual climate in which we live has been fashioned in no small part by the physical and biological sciences, and no educated man can ignore their contributions, nor indeed frame a philosophy without them.[6]

So much for the role of science in general education. The reciprocal contributions of a liberal education to the making of a good *scientist** have been stressed so often and so convincingly that it would seem superfluous to labor them once again. Two aspects, however, call for comment. The first is that it seems unnecessary to single out the scientist as specially benefiting from a broad liberal education, the chief aim of which is, after all, to turn out educated, responsible, and judicious citizens in general. The second aspect, which has two facets, presents greater problems. It raises the old question of the optimum ratio between the irreducible common denominator of a general education ("for effective living") for all professionals, including the prospective workers in any branch of science, and the essential requirements for professional preparation ("for greatest effectiveness in one's chosen occupation"). But it also raises the new question, emerging with the growth in volume of science, whether that optimum is alike for everyone going into science. Is it the same for those who are destined by unusual aptitude, vision, aspirations, dedication, and courage to approximate the ideal of all-around "scientists," capable of promoting knowledge by steps of telling significance, as it is for the ever growing proportion of those who neither desire nor would be qualified for such an august station, but who are content to execute competently tasks of limited

* I am using the term here in its more exalted sense, as defined, for instance, in the statement by the President's Science Advisory Committee on "Scientific Progress, the Universities, and the Federal Government" (The

scope, as partners in that campaign for human betterment that goes by the collective term of "science"?

Again we have before us a graded scale rather than sharp categories. Nevertheless, however arbitrarily the dividing line may be set, the process of differentiation of tasks in our society has reached the stage where corresponding differentiations in the schools preparing for those tasks becomes unavoidable—in the case of science, moreover, requiring further adaptation to the heterogeneity within the field itself. The voices advocating earlier specialization among science students are growing louder; but so are the counterclaims for keeping higher education unified through at least the early years of graduate school. It surely would be disastrous if one were to allow the branching points to be determined by power equilibria between vocational empiricists on the one side and academic purists on the other.

There are auspicious beginnings of a penetrating general discussion of this issue, but the deliberations seem to suffer from an unwarranted timidity. It looks as if there were no choice except to emasculate either liberal education or professional propaedeutics, whereas what is called for is not a decision in favor of one against the other, but rather a combination of both in balanced proportions. The same applies to decisions about teacher-training, technicians-training, administrative training, and other fields as well. The problems involved cannot be solved by extremists, either by ultraconservatives rockbound in status-quo positions or by ultraprogressives submitting to the momentum of political and economic pressures. Unquestionably the growing differentiation of the scientific process has created the need and explicit demands for a corresponding educational differentiation that would split the various specialized branches of the academic tree even further down into and off their common stem. However, if this process were allowed to go too far, the whole trunk would lose coherence and fall apart. And since this limit will appear different to the men living in the trunk and to those living in the branches, "science" cannot claim to enter the negotiations with a single unified voice.

The pressures for an earlier separation of the branches of profes-

---

White House, November 15, 1960), on pp. 4–5. "By the word 'scientist' we mean someone who is fit to take part in basic research, to learn without a teacher, to discover and attack significant problems not yet solved, to show the nature of this process to others—someone, in short, who is equipped to spend a lifetime in the advancement of science, to the best of his ability."

sional training from the trunk line of general education are, of course, a reflection of the progressive fragmentation of science into ever more specialized branches—a familiar subject for both complaints and justifications. The trend is here and must be faced. Its impact on the university is clear. The challenge, I believe, can be met only by better differentiation of What for Whom? Differentiation, rather than standardization, must become the key objective of the modern university. It seems to me quite feasible to resolve the conflict between the increasing clamor for *early technical specialization,* to fill the growing manpower needs of industry and government, and the equally vigorous assertion of the primacy of a *broad general education* as the sole means of salvaging that rare and precious resource of the future, the creative scientist. All that would be required would be a modulated application of both principles in different proportions of emphasis designed to fit the different types of candidates—those bent on simple training in the "tricks of the trade" at one end of the scale and those eager for a broad background of knowledge at the other.

It is worth noting that a common misconception blames the employers—industry and the professions—for the overemphasis on specialized training in universities, while my experience has been that by and large they would prefer to have academic institutions furnish them with open-minded, roundly educated people, albeit with general technical competence, rather than with indoctrinated specialist robots who would have to be retrained "on the job" anyhow. The main pressure for early specialization seems, on the contrary, to come from the prospective employees, the crowd of individuals who are heading for a limited occupational field in which to earn a living and who want to get there as directly and quickly as possible. Since this applies to large numbers of prospective physicians, chemists, veterinarians, teachers, engineers, and others, one can rightfully question whether it is justifiable to shortchange on their account the more highly motivated and qualified minority of budding genuine and creative scientists by forcing the latter to share the same pabulum with the average, who do not care for a richer diet.

Having said this, let me add, however, at once that much as I advocate discriminative treatment for different groups according to their respective aspirations and aptitudes, I still think it would be ruinous to surrender to the growing demands for almost pure professional or vocational training at the expense of breadth and flexibility, comparable to the raising of sterile workers in an ant colony. Thus, having made the case for separating, though on a graded scale,

"scientists" from specialized practitioners, I gladly associate myself
with Gerard Piel in his remarks on the education of the engineer:

> Having distinguished science from engineering by implication here,
> I should like to set that distinction aside. Such distinction always raises
> troubling metaphysical, not to mention social, questions of hierarchy and
> pecking order. Let it be said simply that understanding and control are
> inseparable. Engineering, as the closest coupling of science to society,
> is too widely celebrated for its utility and not enough for its creativity.
> What is more, engineering derives as much historical significance from
> the challenges it lays to understanding as from the applications it makes
> of understanding. . . . To careers in science, therefore, society must
> summon independent spirits. This is no work for the artisan equipped
> with slide rule and handbook, for the intellectual mercenary with his
> talents at auction. The survival and welfare of an expanding world
> population hang on the vigorous expansion of the public domain of
> science and on the efficiency and equity with which it is exploited. Men
> of science must be independent men, with the vision to comprehend the
> context of their work and the courage to assert their independence in it.[7]

After accepting such a high-principled design for socially responsive science education, how can one translate it into practice
with due regard to the growing diversity of needs, interests, talents,
and economic limitations which the university must face? Can the
university inherited from yesterday measure up to today's desid-
erata, which will be tomorrow's necessities? This, then, at last raises
the question: Who is this "University" to which we are referring in
the singular?

Who Is "the University"?

It will be noted that I have posed the question in the personified form of "Who" instead of the grammatically correct objective
"What" of current custom. The explanation is that "the University"
is indeed a personified abstraction. In a realistic view there is no
University—singular; all we have is universities—plural. Whether
there ought to be a more unified concept, and whether or not it
should then be translated into practice, are matters which have been
debated for more than a century and which other chapters of this
book will surely consider. But for the purpose of our discussion here
it seems quite evident that, just like "science," "University" remains
a generality with little definite meaning. Not even the most general
definitions will hit the mark. When John Henry Newman, the later
Cardinal, described it in 1852 as "a place of teaching universal
knowledge," but promptly added that "this implies . . . the diffusion

and extension of knowledge rather than the advancement,"[8] he certainly did not anticipate that the latter qualification would be thoroughly disavowed by the academic developments of the decades to follow with their ever greater stress on research. The point is clear: Since the category of "university," just like the category of "species," embraces a wide variety of specimens and furthermore is subject to continuous evolutionary change, any concept implying uniformity or constancy would be illusory.

Adopting this evolutionary simile, we are at once faced with the question of whether evolution is goal-directed. Organic evolution, by and large, is now considered to operate blindly, or rather by hindsight. If so, the new efficiency device it has created—the human brain with its capacity for reasoning—is radically changing evolutionary methodology in that it can replace hindsight by foresight. In other words, if universities, generated and tossed about by random currents of cultural and political history, have come to be the hodgepodge of institutions disparate in purpose, character, performances, and size which they appear to be, is it compatible with human intelligence to let their future courses continue equally capriciously and unrelatedly? Or should one try to redesign the system so as to adapt the product of the past for a more unified and concerted service to society in the future? The reason that I phrase these questions as antitheses, notwithstanding my stated aversion to such categorical distinctions, is precisely the fact that I believe them to be unanswerable in this form. And yet public pronouncements that sound like answers to them are legion. Let me paraphrase some samples of argument both for radical remodeling and for continued laissez faire; both *for* and *against* a fundamental reorientation.

Pro: The university should rise above being merely an assemblage of individuals employed for statutory service on teaching curricula or research contracts or for the privileged pursuit of their scholarly predilections. Its members should develop a strong sense of cohesion and group responsibility as a "community of scholars" with common purposes, stemming from common ideals and responsive to common needs of society.

Contra: A university should be simply a facility for able individuals to develop, display, and proffer their intellectual wares, a sort of market, like the Greek *agora*. These people need have no common collective goal or pattern so long as they do their jobs competently and honestly.

Pro: The university should not be a shelter for individuals indulging principally in tasks of no immediate and readily demonstrable

162

utility to a society ever more clamoring for practical services and concrete deliveries; one of its major aims should be to relieve the manpower shortages in the professions, particularly those which enable the population to share the benefits of scientific progress; accordingly, it should train more medical practitioners and engineers—especially the latter—even if in doing so it has to curtail more esoteric lines of traditional university interest.

Contra: Our world is already precariously close to being torn asunder by stresses engendered by unprecedented innovations too numerous, precipitous, modish, transitory, and mutually unrelated for the safe maintenance of equilibrium as our society keeps evolving; therefore, and precisely in the self-interest of society, it is imperative that at least one steady focus—the university—insure continuity of progress by asserting and strengthening its traditional role as guardian of the cohesion of knowledge, the balanced perspective, and the long-range outlook, not letting its unhurried, steady, scholarly pace be upset by fancies, fashions, or group pressures of the day.

Pro: The university should abandon its self-arrogated station as a sort of global arbiter purportedly entrusted with guardianship of the common values inherent in all human cultures; it should rather concentrate on promoting tangibly the self-interests of the particular national or group culture to which it owes allegiance, self-interests which, in a competitive scientific society, would place science and technology foremost.

Contra: The university should be dedicated broadly to the universality of truth rather than let its scope be confined and even corrupted by narrower objectives; it must retain its traditional freedom for supranational, supradoctrinal, suprapolitical thought, expression, and action. Science, by method and subject matter predisposed for such universality, must act as pacemaker for the emergence from sectarianism of all the other cultural endeavors of mankind.

This list of opposites, which could be amplified and documented by many convocation addresses, illustrates the inconsistency among the popular concepts of the essence of a university, and hence the absurdity of trying to reduce the relations between science and "the University" to a single uniform rule. Instead, the profitable course for the universities and for the scientific establishment is to accept the great multiformity of both and to try to effect *the most congruous match between their respective patterns.*

Neither pattern, of course, has to be accepted in its present form as immutable, nor need further evolution of these patterns be left to such erratic and unrelated influences as have molded them in the past. Quite to the contrary, in the evolution of human affairs deliberate reasoning must supersede the slow and painful method of organic evolution by blind trial and error. The brute decisions of organic nature, which rule in favor of the predisposedly fitter ones as against the predisposedly less fit ones in environments common to both, must now be mitigated by rational efforts at inducing the contestants to accommodate themselves to each other and to modulate their environment so as to fit them both. Of course, one must have no illusions about the limits within which opposites can be bridged and reconciled, conflicting interests harmonized, parasitism turned into symbiosis. But man has certainly not yet exploited his faculty of rational adjustment to an extent that would bring him anywhere near those limits. To exercise and to strain to their limits his powers of reasoning, foresight, and adaptive action is indeed one of man's noblest obligations, and as he goes about bringing some order into the institutions of his society, one would hope that rational powers will win out over sheer sentimental or inertial continuance of ill-matched patterns of tradition.

Both science and university are now in this phase of groping for new patterns more suited to the conditions of the present and their extrapolation into the future. In this search such one-sided dogmas as listed in the preceding pages, can serve at best, like Scylla and Charybdis, as perils to steer clear of: the safe course lies between them, the keyword being *balance*.

More specifically we are led to the following conclusions, based on the recognition that what is called "the University" is in reality a most variegated system of institutions differing individually as to objectives, methods, service, size, and rank; and what is called "science" is likewise a highly composite enterprise. So is society. Evolutionary trends, organic as well as cultural, have always been in the direction from loose aggregation of independent units toward combination into integrated higher-order systems. The change from independence to cooperative *interdependence* endows the merged constituents with heightened viability and endurance, for their very diversity gives the compound system the versatility needed to maintain its vital integrity amidst the incessant unpredictable fluctuations of the world around it. In return for submitting to some restraints on their degrees of freedom, the parts derive from their association not only the benefit of mutual support, but above all the opportunity to develop to their full potential those particular individual faculties which are most specifically their own.

Naturally the greater is the degree of diversification and the resultant specialization of parts, the greater also becomes their dependence on the system as a whole, and consequently, the task of integrative regulation; the greater, in further consequence, becomes the danger that the regulatory faculties of the system will be taxed beyond the stress limit and break down. To maintain steadiness of progress, evolution has therefore had to keep teetering between opposite pulls—balancing trends towards ever greater differentiation, which if excessive would portend eventual disintegration, against trends in the direction of ever greater uniformity, which would, as in inbreeding, lead to sterility and loss of flexibility for adapting to changing circumstances.

Evolutionary reasoning thus can condone neither anarchic individualism nor an autarchic scheme of mass conformity. Applied to the universities, this means evolutionary repudiation of both extreme indulgence in individual predilections and absolute submission to any uniform mission, that is, other than the call to serve. Universities must not renounce diversity and individual identities, but they must learn to contribute harmoniously to a *group* performance less haphazard in its total aspect than heretofore. In short, they must ascend from the state of a loose *mosaic* to that of a cohesive *system* of diverse, mutually complementary and sensitively interacting parts, or partners.

I submit that nothing short of such a collective, integrated system of plural universities with diverse functions can fulfill the ideal overall function of "the University." Any attempt to make any one existing university over into a miniature version of this total scheme is bound to end as an exemplary showcase of mediocrity and triviality, for in trying to be comprehensive a single university would have to spread itself so thin that it would lack depth and quality. The differentiation of both knowledge and its users has gone too far for any single institution to be able to attain the necessary critical mass for dealing with the total spectrum comprehensively, profoundly, and competently. Yet united in groups, universities can measure up to the requirements. They therefore should band together into integrated compounds, as in the evolution of the higher organisms single-celled precursors joined to form many-celled communities, taking advantage of the efficient principle of "division of labor." Instead of being "a community of scholars," I visualize the university of the future as being a *community of scholarly institutions.*

At present it is neither. In fact, as I have said earlier, the university—singular—does not even exist except as an allegorical abstraction. This does not mean that individual universities may not have definite general goals, as well as the will to pursue them. But one need only strip their histories of rhetorical adornments to realize how limited their power to stay on self-set courses has been. Great leaders with vision or special interest groups with more limited objectives may design blueprints for the future, but as the latter come to materialization their development is so deflected and distorted by outside influences beyond the control of the originators that the original design is largely obliterated. University histories are full of examples of how environmental factors unrelated and even inimical to good educational philosophies and practices have often defeated self-determination: political pressures and lures; manpower needs; alumni whims; deficiencies of pre-university education; fiscal stringencies as well as the temptation to accept compensatory economic bribes; excessive intrusion of unacademic managerial technicians; and at times even a fifth column of contrariness within the faculty.

Faced with such vagaries, some institutions have had the moral and financial strength to hold as firmly as possible to their self-set course, while others, lacking either clear goals or determination or resources, have kept from drowning only by riding the waves of opportunism. But here they are, these products of history, each one performing some major or minor service, useful despite their utter disparity, from the most highly principled, almost monastic centers for the search and propagation of truth at the one end to mercenary trade schools and diploma mills at the other. Confronted with the gamut of institutions, the question is not whether diversity should be renounced in favor of any one academic ideal, or not even at what point along the scale the epithet of "university" becomes inapplicable, but rather what degree of institutional diversity is essential in order to meet the enormous diversity of needs of our differentiated society and to match the wide spectrum of motivations, interests, and aptitudes of individuals to be served.

The latter point is not always taken realistically into account. It is fortunate that our society, being in need of mounting numbers of practitioners in medicine, in law, in schools, and in parishes, can count on a large quota of citizens who want, quite simply, to be just competent physicians, lawyers, teachers, priests, without aspiring to the more exalted stations of scientists, jurists, scholars, or theologians. So truly the graded scale of colleges and universities reflects the graded needs, wants, and aspirations of people. Therefore, next to the replacement of individual self-sufficiency by integrated realignment in collaborative groups the universities of the future face the added task of identifying more precisely what needs of the culture, the society, and the people they must serve and of subdividing and apportioning out among themselves their offerings accordingly. Personal preferences and predispositions for work bench over library, for theorizing over gadgeteering, for naturalist observation over dynamic analysis, for dealing with people over dealing with concepts, for professional and economic success over sheer satisfaction in self-improvement, must all be honored instead of being frustrated in a common mold purporting to serve them all—and matching none.

Unquestionably, a critical re-examination of the degree of correspondence between the current patchwork of university offerings and the pattern of needs would reveal major incongruities. Should corrective action toward higher congruance then be undertaken on the small scale of the individual campus? Hardly the right solution, for let us suppose there arose a powerful move to train, for instance, more doctors, engineers, or business administrators. Would not any given university, responding to the call by enlarging the respective schools, then have to choose between the equally undesirable alternatives of either trying to maintain its former proportionate structure by inflating the less marketable branches, or else abandoning the latter to a relative eclipse? Surely the solution would lie in recourse to the principle of the *collective system,* in which each member can choose to play, instead of an illusory *universal* role, a realistic *partial* one, thus preventing its energies from being distracted, diluted, and dissipated by ancillary commitments, historically or prestige-dictated, which no longer accord with its context; while at the same time the proportions of the whole can be preserved by other members selecting partial tasks of compensatory or complementary character.

The proposition I am here expounding is the evolutionary compromise between conservation and progress. Since no single university can encompass any longer the full scope of the ideal "universal university," it should resist the urge "to be all things to all men" and "to go it alone." Instead each one should concentrate its major energies on those selected sectors of the total field of knowledge which it is supremely qualified to investigate and teach. To some extent this practice has already come into effect as a matter, if not of principle, at least of economy. Every institution has certain areas of strength which it tends to cultivate more than others. Yet the significant distinction between this outcome of accident and necessity on the one hand, and on the other hand the orderly scheme to be envisaged for the future, is that the differentiation among universities in the past has been piecemeal and incoherent so that the various pieces do not fit together to form the harmonious whole that a university system, as here advocated, should represent.

For the formation of a truly effective and viable system, a certain minimum number—a critical mass—of institutions would have to come together, review their respective functions and capabilities, and with the least possible incursion on individuality and sovereignty work out an integrated plan so that collectively they would so supplement each other as to cover the total continuum of knowledge in all its essential scholarly and professional ramifications. Three major considerations would have to guide such integrative efforts: the filling of significant gaps, the correction of serious disproportions, and the lessening of redundancy, particularly where strength could be gained by merging separate units that had remained weak because of isolation or inadequate support. For a concerted program of this sort to succeed would, of course, presuppose, in addition to the re-allocation of educational tasks and subject matters, the harmonization of standards of performance, the free movement of students, and the facultative exchange or sharing of staff members within the association.

Without elaborating the point, it seems that efficient super-universities, "communities of scholarly institutions" of this description, could appropriately be set up by regional compacts. Each association would comprise a suitable assortment of privately endowed universities, high-grade liberal arts colleges, and professional schools. Administrative obstacles to the inclusion of state and municipal institutions and of land grant colleges might also be overcome eventually. There are signs of a growing recognition of the need for such a combining of forces and concerted programming in higher education, as for instance in a measure of program coordination among the universities of the Southern Conference; in similar arrangements among regional groups of colleges;

and in the establishment of such organizations as the Southwest Graduate Research Center, the Midwest Interuniversity Library Center, and the Brookhaven Laboratories of Associated Universities, Inc. It would seem timely to amplify and expedite similar trends wherever they appear, with the deliberate aim of furthering the emergence of the "Integrated University Compact" of the future through the linking of existing autonomous institutions of higher learning into self-regulatory networks.

In such a framework it will be easier than it is at present to satisfy the growing variety of educational needs by a corresponding variety of programs without having a rigid one-to-one connection between any given program and any given institution. By definition, the integrated group would contain collectively such a complete set of major offerings that any essential program, however broad or narrow, could be composed from them simply by combining an appropriate selection of items from that comprehensive list into program packages.

As one can readily appreciate, this scheme would be both economical and efficient; it would curtail the boundless proliferation of institutions; it would conserve and concentrate the finite resources of academic talent, funds, and facilities; it would encourage the pursuit of novel "interdisciplinary" combinations of potential "hybrid vigor"; and it would have the necessary plasticity to adapt to changing circumstances. On the other hand, it would, of course, necessitate a far greater liberalization of student transfer among institutions—a feature reminiscent of the great universities of bygone centuries—as well as greater equalization of standards at reasonably high levels. It would place greater burdens of responsibility on both administrations and students, the latter having to give up a good deal of the sense of security engendered by current lock-step tactics of indoctrination and "togetherness," in favor of a wider range of the insecure, but personality-building, freedom of choice.

Such an ideal university system of the future is both conceivable and practicable. It would achieve the restoration of the very principle of *continuity, unity, and universality of knowledge* the loss or abandonment of which our universities bemoan. The basic common trunk of the tree of knowledge, presented in the early years of study, would be allowed to branch gradually by successive dichotomies of choice from the more general to the more specific, albeit with numerous anastomoses, in the methodical

169

and consistent manner attainable solely in an integrated system; only the terminal branches would become relatively more consolidated as separate "schools," and even then not wholly single-tracked. Transition from "liberal" to "professional" education, from "undergraduate" to "graduate" preparation, from "basic" to "applied" areas, would be fluid, the terminology merely a matter of administrative convenience.

This prognostication of the emergence of harmoniously integrated university systems is based on evolutionary logic. Universities are integral parts of society. Both are in counterplay. Society is in a phase of rapid evolution. If universities were to stand still, they would be left behind to wither. Society, though suffering, would survive; universities might not. So universities must meet the changes of the social scene by corresponding adaptive alterations of their own pattern.

However, in calling on higher education to adapt itself to the evolving social environment, one must not lose sight of the reciprocity of the relation. As I have said earlier, human intelligence and foresight can improve on blind organic evolution by substituting conciliation for victory; by making adaptation a two-way proposition. In short, the social environment must in turn be receptive for adaptive claims fed back to it from the university system. Their greater service to the community would also entitle the universities to assert their leadership in intellectual matters, with full partnership in all cultural affairs, exercised most effectively through the leaders and influential members of society which they educate.

To maintain the highest possible standards of *education for responsible leadership* remains one of the prime obligations of the universities, those of the future even more so than those of the past. Of course, to strengthen and broaden *mass education* is equally vital in that it shifts the basis of public acceptance of leadership from compliance with persuasive dicta to the understanding of convincing arguments. This is indeed only repeating what has been stressed so often—but cannot be stressed too often—that while educational goals and standards must be raised on all fronts, the most important task is to give that scarce supply of individuals with superior talents, paired with responsibility, a challenge and opportunity to develop their native faculties to the maximum; this means placing quality above quantity, with a premium on excellence. Public support for this precept is one of the adaptive contributions society must make if the evolution of both universities and society is to be kept in a dynamically self-adjusting correspondence.

Science in the University

The range of inner flexibility in the integrated university system I have outlined would reduce the question of "the" place of science in a university to absurdity, for it could allow for as many different places, roles, and relations as the growing and ever more highly differentiated field of "science" can command. We read in the White House report "Education for the Age of Science":

> Science, engineering and technology have obviously been responsible for a host of conspicuous changes at all levels of our modern civilization. There is much reason to expect that such changes will continue, and will indeed accelerate. There is no way to turn back the clock or to turn off scientific advance. There will be no international moratorium on science or technology. The people of the United States, on the most practical grounds, must accept and support these propositions.

Lest this arouse the specter of scientific dominance, let me quote further from the same report:

> One of the great strengths of this nation is the diversity of its citizens. No man or council of men dictates what our people individually should do, or how they should be educated. Each of us is remarkably free to pursue that which interests or profits him personally. Out of this great diversity of individual expression comes great strength and wide capability. The diversity should be husbanded. But it cannot long be fruitful if it breaks the nation into isolated groups. Going his own way, a man must understand why other men go theirs, and must respect their right of choice.
>
> A primary objective of an improved educational system should be to bridge the gaps between important segments of the American people. There are many such gaps, even among highly educated people; between scientists and artists; between intellectuals and non-intellectuals; between scientists, humanists, and social scientists; between scholars, research workers, and teachers; between pure scientists, applied scientists, and engineers; and there are others. Such gaps inhibit the close collaboration between groups which is essential to improving the intellectual atmosphere and developing a better and stronger society.[9]

and from a later report from the same source:

> Even in the interests of science itself it is essential to give full value and support to the other great branches of man's artistic, literary, and scholarly activity. The advancement of science must not be accomplished by the impoverishment of anything else, and the life of the mind in our society has needs which are not limited by the particular concerns [i.e., scientific] which belong to this Committee and this report.[10]

In summary, the possible distortion of harmonious proportions in the pattern of education as a result of the phenomenal expansion of science is not only clearly recognized; science itself cautions against it. To maintain balance, or to compensate for disequilibrium, could be accomplished much more easily in a diversified collective system than within the rigid framework of a single institution. This applies to the correction of imbalances not only of subject matter but of functions as well. And because the issue of disproportionate attention to science in the functions of research, teaching, and public services is such a lively one, I would like now to give it special attention in the light of what I have said before.

Essentially, the major functions of a university, as I see them, are the following four:

(1) The preservation, critical interpretation, and synthesis of existing knowledge.

(2) The furtherance of the acquisition of new knowledge, and the development of the intellectual and technical tools required in this process.

(3) The training in the application of existing knowledge to the practical needs of man.

(4) The transmission and dissemination of knowledge and of its implications and applications.

Even though universities are assisted in these tasks by libraries, museums, governmental and industrial establishments, professional societies, and the like, "the university" still stands as the integrated center where all four of these functions become confluent and interact freely for the common benefit of all of them, and hence for the best utilization of knowledge for the common good. The superuniversity of the future would be in a uniquely favorable position to give balanced attention to all four aspects: to the scholarly synopsis of the accomplishments of the past and a synthesis of its lessons (1); to the discovery and formulation of new scientific principles and methods by research and the formation of theory, and to the education of scientific scholars (2); to the extraction from the store of basic knowledge of the rules and techniques leading to practical applications; and to the training of scientific specialists, practitioners, and teachers (3); and to the diffusion of scientific knowledge broadly to the populace so as to widen horizons and interests and develop maturity of judgment (4).

In each of these four categories the problem of maintaining sound proportions between the expanding scientific domain and the other academic commitments recurs. Can it be met by mutual accommodation without radical dislocations? Let us look at a few concrete examples for each of the four fundamental functions.

(1) *The preservation and synthesis of existing knowledge.* Greater concern with the history, structure, and cultural values of science has created not only an opportunity but a genuine demand for a far more active interplay between the sciences and the humanities in education. The historic and philosophic spirit in science still suffers from atrophy. Usually the fruits of science are taught without explaining the nature and roots of the tree that has borne them; preoccupation with the most recent advances is allowed to obscure the fact that they have grown steadily from an historic past. Yet it becomes increasingly important to impart a feeling for the continuity, consistency, and cohesiveness of science to the future leaders of a generation that is overly impressed by the spotlighted glitter of ephemeral novelty. There is, moreover, a goldmine of conceptual and factual material buried in the past literature of science which is practically ignored and unprocessed, bypassed in the manic rush for "doing research." Unless "doing without thinking" is to be conceded supremacy over thoughtful work or even over "thinking without doing," history and philosophy must assume a major task in science education. But they must tackle it not by the expedient of supplementary courses in "History of Science" or "Philosophy of Science," least of all of the purely chronological and anecdotal variety, but by instilling the prospective teachers and workers in science with a true appreciation of the historical and conceptual foundations of scientific thought so that they may learn to see and teach current developments as threads in an intellectual fabric extending from the past into the future.

But then, would not those same historians in the humanities profit reciprocally from closer contact with their scientific colleagues? I am not thinking of the utility of scientific techniques, such as the dating of historic documents by radio carbon, the use of pigment chemistry to check the authenticity of famous paintings, or the recourse to the statistics of cryptography in deciphering ancient tablets. These are taken for granted. But has full advantage been taken of advances in social and comparative psychology to trace the underlying motivations of major historic movements beyond the standard references to political and economic trigger actions; or of the role of modern operational physics, with its relativity and indeterminacy principles, as a possible contributor to the instability of values in our time? These are matters not just of casual interest but of broad concern for the understanding of our culture. And as he gains acquaintance with scientific principles, the humanist will also learn to appreciate better the nature of their origin from what the uninitiated often regard as trivial and redundant labor—namely, the enormous series of painstaking observations, elaborate measurements, intricate experiments and calculations—activities as germane to the purpose of "the university" as are field trips for the excavation of ancient cities or learned commentaries on literature or music. The case for harmony is further strengthened by the cross-linking between science and art through mathematics and esthetics; and there are many other illustrations of the continuity, rather than demarcation, that exists between the sciences and the humanities.

In any subject matter, whether scientific or non-scientific, there is an endless number and variety of things a person might like to do, out of curiousity or for the mere playful practice of his training. To choose among them requires a sense of direction and *relevance*. Historical and conceptual perspective helps to develop and strengthen this sense. In science it has of late shown unmistakable signs of decline.[11] It is surely imperative for the humanistic branches of a revitalized university system to take the lead in restoring it, and in the interplay strengthen their own sense of relevance as well. Such fruitful interaction is not promoted by expressions of mutual disdain, particularly in view of the fact that the purported cleavage of culture into scientific and humanistic halves, in my opinion, is a plain artifact, merely a relic of medieval divisions of knowledge.

(2) *The acquisition of new knowledge.* The criterion of relevance as guide in the self-selection of one's academic tasks applies also to one of the knottiest problems faced by the universities, namely, the disproportionate expansion of scientific research within their walls. This issue has far too many facets for me to give it here the critical evaluation which it would deserve. Instead of reiterating arguments now rather widely discussed, I shall confine myself to accentuating a few aspects that I do not find properly spotlighted in current debates.

The first pertains to the assessment of the degree and rate of expansion of the scientific domain. There is talk of a "knowledge explosion." Undeniably, the spurt of growth of science in this last century has been, as some would call it, "breathtaking." However, if it is referred to as "staggering the imagination," one wonders whether this does not mean the imagination of the unimaginative. Besides, the lack of historical knowledge and perspective deplored above has given current events an appearance of spontaneous eruption. With proper perspective, one would have recognized that this sudden explosion has really been the orderly result of a continuous evolutionary process, steadily accelerated and amplified.[12] In comparing today's picture of the universe, of matter, of life processes, and even of mind, with that of fifty years ago the progress made appears truly dramatic, but what is not usually pointed out is that in this progress we have discovered and identified more gaps of knowledge and more new problems to be solved than we had ever known existed; more even perhaps than the positive solutions we have found. Indeed our ignorance, that is our conscious realization of what we do not know, is growing so rapidly that the resulting vacuum attracts increasing numbers of curious minds. It is this suction of the void which establishes the legitimate expansive claim of science.

Yet there is another side to the coin. The vacuum is also sucking in masses of "fellow travelers" who ride the currents of prevailing fashions, neither truly conscious of the problems to be solved nor qualified to contribute to their solution except in the auxiliary services I have listed earlier. In other words, the ratio of productive over creative scientists has increased enormously by the numerical inflation of the former group. As a result, what we are facing is not a knowledge explosion but a veritable inundation of informational data finding vent in a corresponding "publication explosion."[13] Instead of problem-orientated selectivity and goal-directed uphill striving, much present research takes the downhill course of least resistance, carried forward largely by inertial forces. I have no direct substantiation for this conclusion for any of the scientific disciplines other than the life sciences; but I have been given to understand by colleagues in other fields that the situation is about the same all around.

Given this fact, the universities have an even heavier responsibility now than they have ever had before to husband the dwindling proportion, among the mounting numbers of "scientific workers," of scholarly and singularly creative individuals. These are the ones on whom society must rely for the steady and balanced continuance of scientific progress in accordance with the rigorous research discipline of the past. They are the ones whom the universities must single out, protect, promote, and provide with optimum conditions. Not only do their efforts have an infinitely higher prospective yield than do the routine operations of the average scientific workers; above all, their example resets for others the mark of morality, discretion, critical judgment, self-discipline, and dedication to that higher plane from which it has been slipping as a result of the massive influx of rote performance.

For the same reason, it is vital for the universities to resist pressures for undertaking more sharply delineated so-called "project" and "contract" research than may be useful as a training device. The project system, which allocates funds for a specific purpose, is admirably suited for developmental work, that is, for tasks that can be clearly circumscribed because we know essentially what we want to find and can spell out in detail how to get there. It likewise is suited to the testing of an existing theory, to the broadening of an existing set of data, to the improvement of an existing technique, or to the elaboration of existing doctrine. At any rate it places a premium on the continuation of existing trends rather than on the exploration of new ones; and the very source of scientific discovery, the inductive process—the prospecting of the wholly unknown—is given little of a chance.[14]

In recognition of this fact, granting agencies have come to establish a triple scale of research support as "project grants," "program grants," and "institutional grants" in ascending order of latitude and descending order of specific predelineation. In general this scale of degrees of freedom has worked well, but the pressures to narrow the range of indeterminacy and risk-taking in publicly subsidized research continue nevertheless. Their source lies in the bankruptcy of trust and in the widespread lack of comprehension of the nature and workings of the scientific process, for which the accounting system of industry and commerce is utterly unfit. Unless universities, as the last bastions of "free enterprise" in science, take a resolute stand in this matter, the efficiency coefficient of scientific yield will decline further.

One safety provision against excessive administrative intrusion into research policies lies in the fact that experienced scientists participate in policy formation and program evaluation. Although this involves a diversion of creative scientists from creative work, the use of expert consultants for evaluating scientific merit has by and large proved successful. Even if at times the rate of turnover of membership on such judicial boards and committees has exceeded the rate of maturation of sufficient people with the necessary judgment, perspective, and experience to fill the needs, the yield has still remained infinitely better than would have been possible if any of these programs had been administered by scientifically uninformed and inexperienced professional administrators. I am not saying that there is no room for improvement in current screening procedures. What I am saying is that some modicum of mature scientific counsel is a better safeguard against the waste of public funds than are incursions into the research process by legal and accounting procedures using criteria of "performance" and "productivity" which are tailored for contract work and marketing, but which are quite inapplicable, and indeed demonstrably detrimental, to scientific proficiency. Faced with the demand for tighter controls over the utilization of government funds for scientific research raised recently by the Congress, a demand which naturally has aroused anxiety and protest, the scientists themselves must share part of the blame for this retrenchment insofar as they have failed to counteract the gradual relaxation of standards of selectivity and efficiency. But the remedy must come from efforts by the universities themselves to resurrect those standards of research morality, and not from external policing.

Of course only those who do not know scientific history, or have never made an original contribution to scientific progress, can harbor the illusion that scientific discoveries can be made to order by commission and in proportion to invested funds. Those who would want to label each dollar of public funds invested in research by isotopes and trace it through to a clearly identifiable and tangible product would be disillusioned to learn that the less of the identifiable input they recover, the more the progress of science may have been furthered. I say "may" advisedly, for there is risk involved in any scientific venture. Some of the input is bound to go to waste. But no one from the outside, unfamiliar with science, can judge what is and what is not a good risk.

Free universities, standing between profit-motivated private industries and the bureaucracy of public agencies, thus have a key obligation to stand up for the principle of risk-taking by the conscientious, competent, disciplined, and dedicated investigator and to protect him against clerical shackles and importunity. But here is another side of the picture: Can universities nowadays really in clear conscience testify to the fact that most of the research within their precincts is carried out with the fullest possible measure of conscience, deliberation, responsibility, and competence? As I have said earlier,[15] there is no doubt that at least in the field of my own purview, a certain laxity of aim and effort has given rise to much shoddy, inconsequential, redundant, uncritical, and ill-conceived research, the mainsprings of which may have been nothing more than that "soft money" was available to support it. In this light, some tightening of granting policies and procedures could turn out to be a salutary stimulus to raising standards again.

This leads back to my earlier emphasis on the sense of relevance, which is so easily lost in the narrow, deep, and dark shafts of rote performance in a given specialty. Because of this, and in order that the universities may reassert their moral right to plead for freedom of research, untrammeled and uncontrolled, it is imperative that they shun any sort of investigative engagement that does not qualify on two counts: that it hold promise to contribute both to the advancement of knowledge and to the building of a person possessing knowledge and the ability to use it. The motto for scientific research in the university should become again to turn out scientific *personalities,* not scientific *products.*

Only those who have been through the process can truly understand how far superior an education is that has let the student experience the thrills as well as the disappointments of exploration, the elation of success in resourceful effort, and the disciplining power of tests of evidence which his participation in active research engender, as compared to book learning and passive submission to second-hand indoctrination. I thus conclude that *every kind* of institution in the diversified spectrum I have outlined—yes, even teacher training schools—would stand to gain from having some degree of scientific research conducted on its campus, motivated not chiefly by the need for training specialists but by the disciplining virtue of research in developing critical thinking.

These comments on research lead logically to the next point:

(3) *Teaching and training.* Research as a prominent feature of the academic scene is of relatively recent origin; witness the definition of a university by Cardinal Newman quoted earlier. In modern times, the general principle of the indissolubility of teaching from research is gradually becoming the rule. Sporadic opposition to it by educational tacticians is as one-sided as is the contrary move by technically preoccupied scientists to let handiwork in laboratory or field crowd out the cultivation and exercise of intellectual endeavor. Once again the question is one of balance—not a "Whether-or-not," but

"How much for Whom and When?" In full awareness that the student's time, resources, energies and absorptive faculties are limited, I still submit that a more sizable share than in the past can be spent on research without encroachment on the effectiveness of teaching, provided the following four premises can be fulfilled.

(a) Elementary research experience should be encouraged already on the high school level. A trend in this direction has lately made some notable gains. Its denunciation by opponents as nothing but a recruiting drive for technical professions only serves to show how little the detractors know, and partake of, the true spirit of science, and hence how important for a balanced outlook in life it is for future generations to be spared similar blind spots. On the other hand it would be ludicrous to defend some of the current high school manipulations and exercises in science as introductions to research, let alone to the spirit of science; criticism of "Science Fairs," raised in a recent exchange of communications to the journal *Science,* is quite to the point. If science is misrepresented to the young as an array of glamorous "spectaculars," the seed is sown for later anticlimactic disillusionment, perhaps even dishonesty. But trimmed of frills, some laboratory and field practice to sharpen observation, controlled analysis, and critical evaluation of the phenomena of nature cannot be started too early in life. As for the colleges and universities, such earlier initiation to research would certainly relieve some of the competitive demands of research for time that otherwise would have to be taken from teaching.

(b) Contrariwise, the teaching load in higher education can certainly stand radical curtailment. This is not the place for a philippic against the cramming of curricula with offerings from both the ultraconservative and ultraprogressive fringes of the academic scale—petrified wood at one end and excessive fertilizer, crop-destroying, at the other. But let teaching practice squeeze the water out of its own substance and revert to concentration of and on essentials, and let research likewise set an example of relevance-mindedness, and time will cease to be the limiting factor for tending the legitimate needs of both.

Implied in this proviso is that book-*learning* be made to recover from its progressive degeneration into book-*teaching*. Teaching is teacher-student-polarized; learning is bipolar interaction. A good deal of the sheer imparting of information can be relegated to automation through audio-visual aids and television with their powers of condensing instructional material into its most expert and efficient form and then disseminating the concise product. Much of the teacher's time can thus be freed for those other aspects of education in which there can be no substitution for personal effectiveness—inspiration, discussion, criticism, and interpretation. Instructors can then rise again to the role of educators, and students, from passive recipients to active acquisitors of knowledge.

(c) No rigid formula should be set for the proportion of research in teaching programs. In general the proportion should increase gradually from high school through college to graduate or professional school, but otherwise wide latitude must be left on each level for the variety of individual and institutional objectives. In this sense an integrated group of institutions, allowing among them for both maximum and minimum requirements, could meet the diversity of future needs better than any single institution pegged to a standard average.

The same argument, however, applies just as cogently to the variety of individuals within an institution, division, or department. What ratio of teaching to research is proper? There can be no universal answer. It seems essential not only for every prospective teacher to have participated in some research activity, but conversely for every professional and research man in science to have had some experience in teaching; for having to explain matters to students does more than clarify one's own thinking. Above all, it trains the faculty of articulating one's own thoughts and observations. As editor of several scientific journals, having had to face the serious deterioration which good research results suffer from inept description—and I suppose that hospitals and industries could add corroborating evidence from the transcriptions by interns or engineers of patients' histories or product tests, respectively—I am disheartened by the neglect of the art of communication in the rearing of scientists. As in the case of the history of science, I see the antidote not in remedial courses in "Science Writing," except as a stopgap measure, but in increased opportunities for the student and young instructor to express himself in public, exposed to benevolent criticism.

Having thus recommended a modicum of both research and teaching experience as beneficial for every scientist, regardless of his eventual destination, let me reiterate at once the great variety of human aptitudes and talents to be dealt with. There are first-rate investigators who are poor teachers, and there are first-rate teachers with little flair for or proficiency in research. The former gains by doing some teaching, and the latter grows by making some investigative effort of his own; but neither can be forced into a common mold by a procrustean operation. Yet this is precisely the practice of many college and university administrations, which seem to rely mechanically—the college, on a man's industriousness in teaching, the university, on the volume of his research publications—as tests of achievement and criteria for promotion. The former thereby stymie some really promising investigators, while the latter divert highly effective teachers from their true calling into "grinding out research." This pressure for mediocre research output, growing in proportion to the abundance of research grants, is doubly pernicious because not only does it add to the glut of inconsequential data; what is worse, it places resourcefulness and excellence in teaching, by implication, into a rank of inferiority. Fortunately there have been sporadic signs lately that this inequality is beginning to be redressed. One realizes that science, like music, needs not only good composers but good conductors and performers as well.

(d) No less insidious than the gauging of the creativity of an academic man by the number of published papers to his credit, at least in science, is the attempt to rate academic service and effectiveness, whether in teaching or in research, in terms of man-hours—the punch-clock mentality. What is the time scale of an idea, of a discovery, of an invention? Can accountants be persuaded that moments of deep thinking, even off-campus, or a flash of genius, even during "off-hours," can save years of expensive labor? Or are we possibly heading for a time when quantification of teaching and research performance will go even beyond the simple counting of the number of hours spent on the job and multiply it by caloric output as a measure of intensity of work?

I realize the magnitude of the problem facing many an administration in coping with vast numbers of students and faculty by other than impersonal methods. Nevertheless, save for service functions, automatic quantitative ratings will never provide a valid measure of academic performance in science. The answer may lie in giving human experience and judgment wider play. Appointments are made on a basis of faith and trust. Why then is not that spirit allowed to persevere throughout the appointive years? I have commented on a sad decline of risk-taking in research support;[16] perhaps risk-taking in individuals is likewise diminishing. At any rate there seems to be no better yardstick for judging optimum relations between research and teaching in science education than mature, sober, balanced

181

judgment, taking into account the objectives of the institution, the special functions of its subdivisions, the diverse needs of its students, the variegated complexion of its faculty, its finite means and facilities, as well as the necessary reconciliation of economy and efficiency with the principles of freedom for individual self-development and self-expression. On the point of economy, it is well to remember that, in general, it will be easier to get n% greater efficiency out of available funds, services, floorspace, and equipment than to obtain an additional n% more money, n% more manpower, n% more space, and n% more instruments.

(4) *Adult Education.* The preceding comment brings up the problem of the growing subsidy by government to the conduct of science, resulting in a concomitant increase in the awareness and concern of the public for how its funds are spent, which may portend a mounting pressure for a greater measure of control. To quote from a White House release cited earlier:

Perhaps the most important single task of the universities is to see to it that their own standards of freedom and excellence are maintained in a period of growing connection with government. While we do not share the notion that government money is necessarily subversive of university freedoms, it is obvious that large-scale Federal spending, like any other form of patronage, has its hazards.[17]

In the long run, this hazardous trend can be effectively countered only by bringing up an enlightened citizenry with comprehension of the nature and ways of science. Hopefully, as I explained earlier, the new generation now in school will already be better grounded in science than are their elders. However, in the interim till they mature and have decisive voices, there is a partial vacuum in the adult population's contact with science which in the interest of both ought to be filled. There is a patent need to introduce more science into adult education programs. Some will reply that this is already being done on an increasing scale. I disagree. With very few outstanding exceptions, what is offered in courses of "General Studies" or "Adult Education" is usually either some practically or even vocationally oriented display of "tricks of the trade" or a rather dull second-hand rendition of the elements of a specialized branch of science. Rarely is there the broad portrayal of science with its lights and shadows—its life, spirit, exhilarating adventures and satisfactions as well as its code, restraints, discipline, and frustrations; its grounding in disinterested curiosity as well as its unlimited bounty for man's self-interests; its enormous untapped potential as well as its inner limi-

182

tations. This story is seldom told to the public from the rostrums of universities.

In line with the idea of integral programs within groups of institutions, it would again be preferable perhaps to have a favorably located member of the group assume a major responsibility in this field with due assistance from the other affiliated institutions, which thereby would be relieved of some of their "extension courses." The main thing, at the present juncture, is to give wider circles of the public an appreciation not only of the fruits of science, but of the nature of the tree that bears them and of its deep rooting in our culture.

Conclusions

I have tried, in this essay, to moderate between conflicting versions of the impact of science on the university. Extreme positions commonly betray confinement in remote corners from which only a limited aspect of a field can be seen. Although one may regret that many of the discussions about "science" and "the university" nowadays bear signs of such partiality, based partly on unfamiliarity and partly on prejudice, it is far more significant to note the constructive efforts that are being made at synthesizing the separate views into a broad, well-balanced overview and presenting the total picture dispassionately in undistorted perspective. I have quoted examples from such efforts. More could be added. From their study I am encouraged to believe that the basic propositions set forth in this essay are shared by others, even though not universally. These basic tenets, in summary form, are the following:

I. Science is a major integral part of our culture, not just a service function. Its spirit is of as much concern to man as are its products.

II. The growth of science has naturally a critical impact on the future of the universities as centers of knowledge and of learning. Caution, lest growth turn into overgrowth, is indicated.

III. Harmonious growth is predicated on the reconciliation of conflicting and competing trends by mutual accommodation. Science and non-science are not opponents but partners in a common enterprise.

IV. As such, both must adjust to the emerging evolutionary change in their educational tasks by re-examining their respective roles conjointly with a deep sense of value and relevance, so as to concentrate on essentials, husband talent, and bar the infiltration of extraneous diluents. This applies to both teaching and research.

V. Both society and knowledge are in a process of progressive differentiation and particularization, which must be recognized and even assisted, but which must be kept from degenerating into tight compartmentalization and disintegration as a result of the abandonment of vital interrelations among the specialized components. The universities, as custodians of knowledge, have a solemn duty to preserve "unity amidst diversity." They must offset splintering by efforts at re-integration within their whole structure and its substructures.

VI. Differentiation has proceeded to the point where neither the diversity of objectives and fields of higher learning nor that of people's aspirations, needs, and aptitudes can any longer be served with competence within any single institution. True, schools of higher learning have also differentiated and specialized, albeit somewhat haphazardly. However, their total pattern is not sufficiently congruous with the patterns of need of either society or knowledge. Therefore, to remove present and to avert future incongruity, the universities will have to counterbalance specialization by combination into integrated groups—the only realistic method of protecting the creative potential inherent in diversity against the dulling effects of uniformity, standardization, and mediocrity. In a diversified system, science and non-science can find their proper distribution and proportions without pitting exaggerated claims of "social superiority" against an outmoded status quo doctrine of "cultural superiority."

VII. In order to achieve integration in such enormously complex systems as science and the educational continuum, it will be imperative to rise above the analytical method of singling out from an intricate problem simple component pieces for isolated solution, and to adopt the sprouting young methodology of "system thinking" appropriate to networks of intimately interdependent functions. Like other major activities of society that have already benefited from such integrative treatment, such as economics, traffic, national defense, natural resources, and others, education is such a network system and deserves like treatment, and science education cannot be viewed and dealt with rationally save in this context.

REFERENCES

1. See, for instance, three reports from the President's Science Advisory Committee: "Strengthening American Science" (The White House, December 27, 1958); "Education for the Age of Science" (The White House, May 24, 1959); "Scientific Progress, the Universities, and the Federal Government" (The White House, November 15, 1960); obtainable from the U. S. Government Printing Office, Washington, D. C. 25; and "Symposium on Science in Education," *Proceedings of the National Academy of Sciences* (U. S. A.), vol. 43, no. 7 (1957); and many others.

2. Paul Weiss, "The Message of Science," *Bulletin of Atomic Sciences,* vol. 15, no. 7 (1959), 274–277.

3. Paul Weiss, "The Challenge of Biology," *Science,* 118 (1953), 33–34.

4. G. W. Corner, in symposium on "Science in Education," *Proceedings of the National Academy of Sciences,* vol. 43, no. 7 (1957).

5. Weiss, "The Message of Science."

6. Carnegie Corporation of New York, *Annual Report* (1952).

7. *Engineering Forum,* Ford Motor Company (June 21, 1961).

8. Cited from Quincy Wright's address "What Is a University," *Bulletin of the American Association of University Professors,* vol. 30, no. 167 (1944).

9. pp. 4 and 15.

10. "Scientific Progress, the Universities, and the Federal Government," p. 3.

11. Paul Weiss, "Experience and Experiment in Biological Research." Symposium on "The Experimental Method in Biology from the Time of Antonio Vallisneri to Present," ed. U. D'Ancona, Padova, *Science,* vol. 136, no. 3515 (1962), pp. 468–471.

12. Derek J. Desolla Price, *Little Science, Big Science* (New York: Columbia University Press, 1963).

13. As regards the distinction made here between "knowledge" and "information," see "Knowledge: A Growth Process," *Science,* vol. 131, no. 3415 (1960), pp. 1716–1719.

14. Paul Weiss, "Medicine and Society; the Biological Foundations," *Journal of Mt. Sinai Hospital,* 19 (1953), 716–733.

15. Weiss, "Experience and Experiment in Biological Research."

16. Weiss, "Medicine and Society; the Biological Foundations."

17. "Scientific Progress, the Universities, and the Federal Government," p. 12.

DOUGLAS BUSH

The Humanities

SINCE "the humanities" comprise such diverse media, methods, and aims, and since I am not a universal doctor, I shall use literature as most central and representative. I shall try to deal with three main topics: the humanistic tradition of the past, its modern equivalents in scholarship, criticism, and teaching, and the general character and objects of literary study; the cultural climate outside as well as inside the university and its effect on the status and claims of the humanities, especially the powerful attractions and pressures of the modern scientific and technological revolution; and, by way of final summary, the universal, unique, and irreplaceable role of the humanities in expressing and providing experience and discipline that are both aesthetic and ethical, the communication of an individual vision of life to other individuals. If these headings are and invite clichés, an inhabitant of our world may believe that they must be continually reaffirmed. Psychologists are still illuminating the nature and destiny of man by pulling habits out of rats. Some advanced thinkers tell us that, because of scientific control of our environment and the cure of human vices by appropriate drugs, there is less and less need for the exercise of personal responsibility and for intellectual and moral struggle;[1] we are moving toward a utopia in which mankind will be a race of moral robots manipulated by social engineers. It is remarkable that well-meaning scientists can preach such a hideous gospel.

1

Since the essential aim of humanistic studies remains what it always has been, we might look briefly at the historical pattern. To go no further back than to the Renaissance humanists, who so

186

ardently revived and molded the Graeco-Roman tradition, *studia humanitatis* and similar terms comprised classical literature, history, and philosophy; these were the chief studies worthy of a free man, the kinds of liberal knowledge that nourished *homo sapiens*, that is, man as man, a human and social personality, not as a professional or technical expert. There was no modern division into humanities, social sciences, and natural sciences, since the classical writings comprised all three (and one great strength of classical education has been just that). If the early humanists, like Erasmus, were mainly indifferent to science (which had not yet become conspicuously important), some, from Rabelais to Milton, were not. But the central ideal of serious European humanists embraced intellectual cultivation and taste, rational and moral discipline, and civic responsibility—qualities which had been united in the great exemplar, Cicero, a moral teacher and magistrate as well as a model of style. The humanists looked backward in order to look forward; the classics mirrored a civilization that must be re-created as a basis for further progress toward the good life.

But the good life now included Christian faith, and many of the leading humanists, Italian as well as northern, were earnest Christians. They saw the humanities as complementary, not antagonistic, to Christianity and they carried on in more practical terms the medieval philosophic synthesis; as Cicero had said, *sapientia* is the knowledge of things human and divine. The noblest pagans had, by the light of natural reason, approached Christian ethics and faith, and the traditional alliance was unforgettably registered in Erasmus' echo of the liturgy, *Sancte Socrates, ora pro nobis*. One basic part of the synthesis was the conception of man as midway between the beasts and the angels and pulled by his animal and angelic impulses in opposed directions. If to the modern mind that idea seems quaint, it was, as an ethical and religious concept, a main source of the strength, health, and centrality of Renaissance literature, from Shakespeare down.

The primary humanistic activity was the editing, translating, interpreting, and teaching of the classics, and many men went on to application and emulation, to the writing of literature, history, and philosophy, especially for the guidance of rulers, and some were themselves engaged in public affairs. Though the division of labor was beginning, few were confined to one groove. Outside of humanism proper, the versatility of Renaissance artists has long been a byword. Within the ranks, to mention a name or two, the

187

bold philologist Lorenzo Valla wrote on ethics and on the New Testament and used philology to show that the Donation of Constantine, the document that had buttressed papal claims to temporal power, was a late forgery. Juan Luis Vives, along with writing books on classical-Christian education, was a pioneer in psychology and sociology. Copernicus got clues from ancient astronomers. But the cardinal fact is that for centuries Europe had a cultural solidarity that transcended national and religious boundaries. Indeed one object of such men as Erasmus was the abolition of war and the creation of international peace; that special effort of course failed, but Erasmus, the Christian humanist *par excellence*, had more effect on the European mind than any writer between St. Augustine and Voltaire. All or almost all the great original thinkers and writers had more or less of the same kind of classical education and read, spoke, and wrote the same language, literally or metaphorically or both—Copernicus, Kepler, and Galileo, Machiavelli, Ariosto, and Tasso, Calvin, Rabelais, and Montaigne, Erasmus, Sir Thomas More, Spenser, Shakespeare, Bacon, Milton, and a host of others. In fact, down through a good part of the nineteenth century most of the great men of Europe and America were brought up on the classics; their modern counterparts in wisdom and style are not so numerous as increases in population and enlightenment might lead us to expect.

Today, in our very different world, the natural and the social sciences are of course separate realms. The humanities have lost history to the social sciences (though some historians maintain their allegiance to Clio), and have gained music and the fine arts. Philosophy is still counted as one of the humanities although the nature of most modern philosophy would seem to place it with mathematics and science. Humanists may regard divinity as an ally or an alien. Literature, as the most direct and comprehensive expression of human concerns and the most generally accessible body of material, remains central. Along with such internal changes there is a large fact that complicates discussion: that practitioners of the humanities fall into two different groups—scholars, critics, and teachers on the one side and creative artists on the other—a much more distinct cleavage, in spite of mainly common interests, than the mere difference in intellectual power between scientific explorers and scientific teachers. In this connection we may notice a recent phenomenon most conspicuous in the United States, the inviting of creative artists for prolonged visits or life-time posts in colleges and universities. Josiah Royce observed long ago that a philosopher was expected to spiritualize the community; but now that the philosopher often limits himself to semanticizing the community, that function has fallen to the humanist, and the artist—who may or may not be scholarly—is introduced to help spiritualize the academy as well as the community. Such minds may bring provocative, unacademic freshness to the teaching of their art, and their presence is a reminder that literature, for instance, is not something always embalmed in fat anthologies but written by people who live among us and pay taxes.

Since no one, even if much more learned than I, could discuss all branches of the humanities in a few—or in many—pages, and since literature is, as I said, the most central and has the largest professional following, I shall stick mainly to it. Here a great and obvious change from the many earlier centuries must be registered at the start: that in the English-speaking world the ancient classics have been almost wholly replaced by English. The academic study of English has been a fairly recent thing; it used to be assumed that no one needed instruction in his own language and literature. Whatever the faults of traditional classical teaching (and they were often grievous), the great change—however inevitable in our changed world—has brought loss as well as gain. For one thing, it has not improved the English spoken and written by the educated; "the new illiteracy" is evident everywhere. On another level, there has been and can be no adequate substitute for authentic and active contact with the classical tradition, which has always been both a revolutionary and a steadying force.

Before we consider various modern approaches to literature it may be said that that word is not restricted to the purely imaginative, that it retains its humanistic breadth of meaning. Indeed the imaginative part of literature is perhaps smaller in bulk than the heterogeneous mass of prose, ancient and modern, which also comes under that head. Here the modern barriers that divide the humanities, the natural sciences, and the social sciences simply disappear, because works in all these areas may or must be accepted as humanistic classics if they fulfill certain conditions: they must appeal to *homo sapiens*, the general reader; that appeal must endure from age to age; and there must be special distinction of substance, form, and style—art, in short—even if the author's purpose was quite utilitarian. If such conditions sound vague, there is not much doubt in concrete cases, when time has done its sifting. But we are concerned here with imaginative writing, since that is what distinguishes literature from all other forms of thought and expression.

The study of literature has itself many areas and levels and consequently many diverse specialists. Some kinds of work carry on what was begun in antiquity and revived during the Renaissance, though their scope is now widely extended. There are many biographical and bibliographical tasks, the determination of authorship, of dates of composition, and so on. One prerequisite for serious study is the establishment of authentic texts, not merely of old writers like Shakespeare but of such moderns as Poe, Hawthorne, and Whitman. Of late years, it may be observed, the labor of collating texts has been much eased and accelerated by ingenious machines; and machines have likewise transformed the making of such useful tools as concordances. But one can only begin to suggest the variety and refinements of such primary tasks of scholarship; in themselves these may be less humanistic than scientific, though their ultimate object is not.

That ultimate object, as we all know, is to understand and interpret works of literature in their full aesthetic and substantive significance and to make them available to readers, to preserve and transmit our great heritage as a living possession. Whereas science means only the latest knowledge (unless scientists cultivate scientific history as a personal interest), great works of art are never dead or superseded; they remain not only alive but unique. The body of literature from Homer and the Bible to the present is, in the fullest humanistic sense, a timeless whole. On the other hand, the literature of Europe—not to mention the literatures of Asia and America, Australasia and Africa—comprises that of many countries, and this vast body of writing reflects the civilization, the beliefs, ideas, and manners, the language and literary modes of many times and places; and, though the very definition of a classic is that it transcends time and place, these facts of remoteness are initial barriers. The past, or rather a great many pasts, must be re-created, since, however relevant works of art may be to us in our time, they must first be understood on their own terms, as products of particular minds in particular settings. Indeed, as Lionel Trilling has emphasized, their very pastness is a part of their meaning for us. Unless we are willing to miss or misread a great deal, we have to use bifocal lenses; and such lenses mean every resource we can muster in the way of information, imagination, and disciplined intelligence.

During the several generations since professional literary scholarship began in the United States, there have been successive waves of distinct character. (Criticism in the nineteenth and the early twentieth century was largely of the impressionistic kind represented by Poe and Lowell and many others.) The first—and for a long time virtually the sole—scholarly method was derived from both the science and the literary theory of Europe and might be labeled genetic: this was the writing of literary history in terms of sources and influences, and such things were most clearly traceable in medieval and post-medieval literature. This prolonged effort accomplished much by discovering and ordering a mass of solidly factual data, but such literary history, though necessary and valuable, was more or less external and it led to revolt. The next phase, which began before 1920, was the history of ideas: religious, philosophical, ethical, social, political, scientific, aesthetic ideas. The history of literature was rewritten at a new depth, and such cultural history became an important discipline in itself; it has been still more important in enriching our comprehension of countless individual works.

But the history of ideas, like the older literary history, did not in itself carry any criteria of aesthetic value, since a mediocre author may illustrate ideologies or influences no less or better than a great one. And here the so-called "new criticism" stepped into the partial vacuum to concentrate on interpretation and evaluation of the individual work—usually though not always a short poem. This movement has done much to right the balance and keep the prime object of study before us, and it has greatly quickened insight into subtleties of texture, imagery, and tone. It has also revealed its limitations and, like the earlier approaches, it can be inadequate by itself. While these several methods have continued in operation, others have developed during the past forty years, especially through the impact of psychology and anthropology. What may be loosely termed the Freudian line needs no explanation—though its tendency to rely on formulas often needs correction. What may be loosely termed the Jungian line has been concerned with the working of archetypal myths upon the creative imagination and with the poetic language of symbols. The latest arrivals have been the structural linguists, who seem to promise much new light, though I confess that I have not encountered it—or perhaps have not sought it with proper zeal. Some other schools of thought, from the sociological to the neo-Aristotelian, must be passed by. These various approaches, or some of them, have stimulated fresh and more or less valuable kinds of perception;

they have also yielded irresponsible fancies unchecked by historical knowledge and understanding.

This brief survey covers what has happened in English (including American studies, since their rapid expansion began). Nowadays graduate teachers may not be omniscient sages, and graduate students are often deficient in breadth of reading, in writing, and in foreign languages, but the requirements and aims of graduate study have changed enormously for the better. Bibliographical training, of the kind touched on above, is available for those who want it, but it is an instrument, not an end in itself. Graduate students, as eager human beings and as prospective teachers, are in graduate courses concerned entirely or almost entirely with the fundamentals of literature and ideas, with aesthetic and philosophic criticism based on substantial historical knowledge. This is a world away from the mainly dusty grind that older generations went through decades ago. Whatever the deep personal devotion to literature of the illustrious scholars of those days, the *mystique* of graduate study seemed to start from the assumption that mature students left behind them not only hope but any humanistic concern with man, life, and the meaning of literature (I speak of the tracts of desert, not of the oases). The titles of doctoral theses now written all over the country bear concrete testimony to the great predominance of interpretative, philosophical, and aesthetic criticism. What worries graduate teachers nowadays, along with a frequent consciousness of their own shortcomings, is the frequent inadequacy of preparation and capacity in graduate students, the several kinds of deficiency mentioned above.

Today, moreover, undergraduate courses, graduate courses and seminars, and a large proportion of the books and articles written by college and university teachers are all of a piece, a coherent progression in depth. Learning and criticism are not divorced as they used to be. The various approaches to literature which I outlined are all in simultaneous operation in literary departments. In going on with an account of the humanities, therefore, I see no reason to consider "research" by the most mature scholar-critics as something remotely and austerely different from what is done in undergraduate courses. The planets are all revolving at various distances from the same sun and receive varying portions of the same light, sometimes a bit refracted.

Whatever weaknesses or excesses there have been (and the natural and social sciences have their share of these), the total accomplishment of modern scholarship and criticism has been immense. If we cannot claim such revolutionary advances as science has made, we can say that at the present time the vast and varied literature of the past is far better understood in all its aspects than it ever was before. In the nature of the case there can be no final interpretation of the more complex works of art; as the history of Shakespearian criticism makes amply clear, some ages see and emphasize some elements, other ages other elements. Still, with all the cross-currents and eddies and occasional waterfalls, there is a general movement along or toward a central channel; as Shakespeare's name again makes clear, peripheral fluctuations do not affect the stability of the general pattern. One cause for misgiving is that this modern enlightenment—and the active interest in literature of the past that kindles the enlightenment—is so largely academic. Criticism in general, in reaching new subtleties of insight, has become a specialized esoteric preserve; there are very few American critics who can be said to address and be heard by the educated community in something like the fashion of Arnold or Sainte-Beuve. But the educated public does not seem to care much about criticism of any kind; if a biography of a literary figure tries to smuggle in critical or philosophical ideas, popular reviewers brand it as highbrow and heavy.

The most cursory survey of scholarly criticism is a needless reminder that, on the higher levels, it grows out of individual knowledge, reflection, and intuition. It cannot, any more than creation, be the result of teamwork. It is obvious also that important criticism is the product of maturity, that it must grow out of experience of life and wisdom as well as out of intellectual knowledge. A commonplace fact of scientific history is that many scientists have made their chief contributions at a very early age; for the humanist a corresponding accomplishment would be next to impossible. Also, whereas under similar conditions two or more scientists may independently and simultaneously arrive at a similar idea (like Darwin and Wallace), no two artists would produce anything like similar works of art, since the scientific discovery is not a distinctively personal vision and the work of art is. And of course "discovery" is not the aim of humanistic study. There is discovery of a kind, to be sure, and reinterpretation is continually going on, but the humanist's great aim is the achieving and sharing of the experience given by works of art. And the all-important thing about that is that the experience is an individual affair. Whatever insights may be held in common, no one person can respond in exactly the same way as any other person. When a scientist has a boldly imaginative idea, that idea is made completely and uniformly intelligible to other scientists; but the intuitions of a humanist are not fully demonstrable and cannot be transferred *in toto* to other minds—as indeed the original work of art may not have completely rendered its author's conception or yielded its full import to the best of critics. The inevitable degree of imprecision in the study of literature and the other arts may to the rigorous scientific reason count as a defect in the humanities; but most of the really important things in life cannot be measured.

The ultimate and obvious aims of literary study have already been indicated, but they may be put in ampler terms, though still with pragmatic simplicity. The raw human animal, more acquisitive, aggressive, and sensual than sensitive, needs to be civilized if society and the good life are to exist. The humanities are in their very nature the chief agents of the civilizing process, since they are the distillation of universal human experience. Through the senses, the imagination (both immediate and historical), the affections, and the critical intelligence literature and the other arts enlarge and enrich the individual's very limited experience and refine and discipline his sensibility and mind and character; and there are no other agents that perform these functions on both aesthetic and ethical planes (not that we read works of art for therapeutic reasons but that full enjoyment and assimilation have therapeutic results). We might think, for instance, of what a world is added to our imaginative and moral consciousness by *Hamlet* or *King Lear*. Moreover, since traditional religion has so largely lost its power, many people, young and old, find through the humanities their chief or only understanding of man's religious quest. The greatest works of artistic creation—and the greatest are essentially religious—provide a vision of reality that nothing else provides. Of course it cannot be demonstrated with graphs that John or Betty Smith, through responding to a work of art, became a person of richer imaginative and moral insight, of finer taste and wisdom and stability; but throughout all generations that has been an experience for some people. If it had not been, our individual and communal lives would be solitary, poor, nasty, brutish, and short.

2

It may be asked why, if the humanities do all this, our world is what it is, why we are not living in a utopia of peace and culture. To repeat an answer I once gave (an answer that drew a gibe from a sociologist), the humanities have always had to contend with nothing less universal and inveterate than original sin. This comprehensive generality may be translated into more specific terms because the standing of the humanities within the university is strongly affected by the cultural climate outside. Public indifference to the humanities has always existed, even in ancient Athens and Renaissance Europe, and Gresham's law operates in the cultural as well as in the monetary sphere. In our country, in spite of occasional splashes of publicity about the newsworthy aspects of the fine arts and the performing arts, the mass of the educated public seem to have relatively little interest in literature of the past. The sale of paperbacks is a not altogether reliable index to the amount of private reading done outside of college courses, and the interest of college students often seems to end with their last examination. While the humanities, creative or critical, require mainly the time and effort of individuals and not the huge sums that go into scientific research, their unique and fundamental value does need public understanding, respect, and support. A few people, including some scientists and even members of Congress, have urged active recognition, and the newly established Commission on the Humanities and a possible National Humanities Foundation may do something to awaken proper concern.

In addition to the philistinism that thrives everywhere, a special strain runs through the American tradition. (Some of the founding fathers were cultivated intellectuals, but nowadays they might not be elected to public office.) Puritanism (which had its intellectuals but had begun its anti-humanistic campaign in England), egalitarian democracy, the spirit of the frontier, belief in practical utility, and the conviction that the business of America is business have fostered distrust or dislike of "culture," of any use of the mind for intangible ends, of being different from the crowd. Only in the last few years—and because of the Sputnik, not intellectual reasons—has there been any general revolt against the pedagogical doctrine and practice that have dominated the schools in our century: "adjustment to life" instead of education and, among other things, the conception of literature as an attractive appendage to social studies.[2] One need not cite the familiar evidence of popular taste supplied by the mass media (which are not peculiar to the United States).

If the relative lack of zeal for the humanities among us is to be attributed to the nature of our society, one large heading under that vague phrase is the many-sided pressure of science. The dazzling achievements, the prestige, the practical value, and the high rewards of scientific and technological research are more than obvious. For decades the philanthropic foundations poured out oceans of aid for the natural and social sciences and a trickle for the humanities (of late years there has been a turn for the better). Government money flows into university laboratories for research in military technology. Reaching the moon seems to be more urgent than our many social and educational needs. Every spring and summer, when college graduates enter the job market, students of the humanities are at or near the foot of the salary scale, scientists of course at the top;[3] and, while philosophic captains of industry tell Commencement throngs of the prime need for humanely educated men, their personnel officers are hiring technical experts.[4] The undergraduate as well as the graduate study of science appears to be almost wholly professional[5] and leads directly to high pay and security, while the humanities are, by mundane reckoning, quite useless.

Since the functions of the humanities were earlier summed up in simple terms, I may say briefly what I understand to be the functions of the sciences. The investigation of the terrestrial and cosmic world and the human body and mind is an essential and noble fulfillment of man's quest for knowledge; the discovery and interpretation of scientific knowledge grow out of methods that are an essential part of a liberal education; and the uses to which such knowledge has been put have enormously affected every individual by improving the conditions of life in an infinite variety of ways. This we all know and believe. The social sciences may be described in corresponding terms: their material is the social, economic, and behavioral patterns of mankind in the mass. But to say that the natural and social sciences and the humanities all look toward the benefit of man is to obscure the basic differences among these disciplines and to allow the implication that imbalance does not matter much, or that the sciences, with all their glamor of modernity, have superseded the humanities and should now take over the guidance of mankind. The last implication is a matter of course for a number of people, for example, Derek J. Price, the historian of science: "Now that science has become the chief determinant of world civilization. . . ."[6]

The academic role of the humanities cannot be understood or assessed without reference to both the rightful role of science and the claims sometimes made for it as the supreme oracle of modern man. Of course some scientists and social scientists are earnest and vocal supporters of the humanities, but there is in the air enough extravagant one-sidedness to be disturbing. To quote a casual but suggestive utterance, an eminent social scientist probably spoke for more than himself when he said to me, " I suppose poetry nowadays is on the way out." One gets the impression that humanists—the special custodians of all the great literature and art that man has produced—can now be seen as laggards behind the triumphal march, as forlorn attendants in an empty museum.

This general attitude has been recurrent ever since Bacon and Descartes excluded poetry from the world of scientific reality. I should like to cite a few heterogeneous writers on science, as representative both of scientific thought and of notions of the humanities and science that one meets in various areas and on various levels. For F. S. C. Northrop[7] modern science is the infallible lawgiver in all things, and not merely Dante (his example) but all literature that makes serious use of beliefs and ideas not now scientifically valid is dead at its center. There can be no values except those determined by science; people's emotions have long been attached to mistaken ideas and scientific reason must correct these fatal vagaries. "Without the *Weltanschauung* of modern science," says a later writer, in *Science*, "no form of thinking, feeling, or reacting has validity today."[8] Even in our ultra-scientific world are any of us, scientists or humanists, moved by scientific principles when we examine ourselves (if we do), when we fall in love or face a moral dilemma, when we feel, think, and act as citizen, friend, son, brother, husband, father—in all the situations in which man lives as man and becomes the subject of literature? To quote a historian of science (who cites Henri Poincaré to the same effect):

For neither in public nor in private life can science establish an ethic. It tells what we can do, never what we should. Its absolute incompetence in the realm of values is a necessary consequence of the objective posture.[9]

In regard to science and the nature of man one central kind of opposition is between optimists and pessimists. On the one hand, some look forward with high confidence to endless progress through endless extension of scientific knowledge. In spite of our oceans of ignorance, said Dr. Conant, "we can set no limits to the future expansion of the 'empire of the mind.' "[10] "No one," says Philippe Le-

Corbeiller, "can set limits to what science might achieve."[11] But other prophets of science tell us, with a sort of sadistic relish—one cannot say masochistic because they themselves are apparently outside the human race—that men are only lumps of impure carbon and water, links in a deterministic chain, nodes in a communication network. The first of these definitions of man is Lord Russell's old phrase; the third was used at a *Dædalus* conference in May, 1963, without, so far as I recall, any protest except from my unreconstructed self. If a man is only a node in a communication network he obviously cannot be a scientist, much less can he ordain human values and destiny—though it would appear that his mental wiring can encounter a short circuit. We might remember that Adolf Eichmann, examined by half a dozen psychiatrists, was pronounced, according to the best scientific standards, completely normal; and he was a completely efficient node. A humanist would be happier with the high than with the low view of man, though he would like some qualifications and additions.

Lord Snow's main object, humanitarian action on behalf of the hordes of people living in subhuman conditions, was more central in his second discourse[12] than in his first. But we remember his strange assertion that the second law of thermodynamics is about the scientific equivalent of a work of Shakespeare—as if the two were comparable except on the level of mere data of knowledge. A philosophic scientist, Dean Robert B. Lindsay, in *The Role of Science in Civilization* (1963), takes a broadly receptive view of the humanities, but even he can be myopic on a central point. Arguing (pp. 44 f.) that science includes value-judgments, he says that decisions have to be made among opposed scientific theories. But these are not value-judgments at all, unless the term is stretched out of recognition. They cannot be value-judgments unless the constituents of atoms and cells are moral agents whose motives and behavior are being scrutinized on moral grounds. This is the very *sine qua non* of literature, and Dean Lindsay is not the only scientist who misses the point. (What some behavioral scientists would say was partly indicated in my first paragraph.) It is often said—by Dean Lindsay and others—that scientists must be grouped with artists because both use imagination to interpret data, but such a statement merely befogs the issue. The kind of imagination that interprets the non-moral secrets of the atom or the cell is completely different from the ethical imagination that explores the workings of human nature.

Two other witnesses, on opposite sides of the fence, may be

mentioned. The late Aldous Huxley in his *Literature and Science* (1963) took a line that was very odd for the author of *Brave New World* (1932). He made a tour among the sciences in order to show the kinds of new knowledge the modern writer must assimilate and learn to use. Recalling what the nightingale's song had meant to Keats and Arnold and Eliot, he explained that the bird sings to warn other birds that it is staking out its time and territory for the consumption of caterpillars. This was not, as one might think, a spoof, but a scientific exposure of poetic fallacy—and totally irrelevant. On the other hand, Dean Barzun, in his *Science: The Glorious Entertainment* (1964), pictured modern man and civilization as thoroughly deranged by science and technology and the climate they have created. While the picture may be overdrawn, some reactions from the scientific establishment seemed to imply that the noted author was a brash schoolboy making faces at the teacher; the book shows, said one reviewer, what scientists are up against in presenting their case to the world (*New York Times Book Review*, April 5, 1964).

For a last witness on this general point we might hear a scientist of broad horizons, Loren Eiseley:

Even now in the enthusiasm for new discoveries, reported public interviews with scientists tend to run increasingly toward a future replete with more inventions, stores of energy, babies in bottles, deadlier weapons. Relatively few have spoken of values, ethics, art, religion—all those intangible aspects of life which set the tone of a civilization and determine, in the end, whether it will be cruel or humane; whether, in other words, the modern world, so far as its interior spiritual life is concerned, will be stainless steel like its exterior, or display the rich fabric of genuine human experience. The very indifference of many scientists to such matters reveals how far man has already gone toward the world of the "outside," of no memory, of contempt toward all that makes up the human tradition.[13]

One might also quote Margaret Mead's remark—made in a different context—that nowadays "students of the humanities, as they lost their hold on contemporary developments in science, began to stress their monopoly of eternal values."[14] Miss Mead perhaps overlooked our long-lived contemporary, Plato.

The fundamental differences between science and the humanities are not at all the same thing as differences between scientists and humanists, but something may be said about the latter, since the questions are often confused and especially since, at the *Dædalus* conference of May, 1963, a distinguished group of members reported their verdict that humanists are irresponsibly ignorant and neglectful of science.

To speak first of imaginative writers, if by ignorance is meant lack of technical competence in modern science, no doubt the charge is justified; but can it be wisely lodged at a time when the mathematician and the physicist, the biologist and the chemist are said to have imperfect understanding of one another? If, however, the charge means unawareness of the implications of science, its felt effects on life and thought and sensibility, it may be considered quite unjustified. One central impulse in modern American poetry and criticism has been opposition to the mechanizing and dehumanizing of man and insistence on his human individuality. Even current fiction—which, to speak with limited knowledge, may seem to have acquiesced too readily in the doctrine of the lost self—might defend its obsession with sex on similar grounds: man or woman, feeling dwarfed into nothingness by a big, mad, technological world, is moved in desperation to declare "*Amo* (or some less reputable word), *ergo sum.*" Such feelings may be exaggerated, but they cannot be dismissed as merely ignorant, stupid, or neurotic; in some degree they are quite common.

Shakespeare knew nothing of the up-to-date science of his day; he accepted as facts or as metaphors a multitude of things that were not so—and such ignorance did not matter in the least. If it is said that that may have been well enough long ago but will not do now, we might remember that Robert Frost, for instance, though perhaps not overburdened with intellectual knowledge, was well aware of science and was not crushed into surrender of individual human dignity with all its responsibilities and hazards. T. S. Eliot held religious beliefs which most intellectuals regard as obsolete, but his poetry is a very significant part of our culture; he was indeed the first or one of the first of modern writers to discern some dominant characteristics of that culture, in particular the mechanization of the human spirit. I am not pleading for ignorance or in any way disparaging science (which would be imbecile); but it seems to me deplorable and disastrous when scientific thinkers assert that there is only one kind of knowledge, one kind of truth: that of verifiable experiment and analytical reason.[15] Nearly all science of the past is now merely of historical interest; the literature of the past still speaks to us with a far more vital power than any scientific fact or idea commands. For a reminder of that obvious truth, this year 1964 is the four-hundredth anniversary of the birth of both Shakespeare and Galileo, but only one of the two is being celebrated everywhere (which is no reflection upon the greatness of Galileo).

As for the other community of humanists, the scholars, critics, and teachers, they certainly should know as much as they can absorb not only of modern science but of the whole history of science. No college teacher can deal with Donne or Milton or Pope or Shelley or Tennyson or many other poets, or with philosophers from Bacon onward, without dealing with science. In the last forty years or so literary scholarship has very fruitfully utilized—and even in many areas has written—the history of scientific ideas along with other ideas. And it is worth emphasizing that the many studies of science in relation to literature have come from literary scholars, mainly American, but not, so far as I recall, from scientists or historians of science; it seems to be assumed that the latter are either silent masters of literature or do not need to be. At any rate it is always the humanists who are charged with narrow ignorance; the charge gets its authority not from evidence but from repetition. We noted earlier the predominantly professional character of undergraduate courses in science, which are of small avail for humanistic laymen, though scientists are given to blaming young humanists for not taking more of them. College courses in the humanities could be similarly professionalized, but it is in the spirit of the humanistic tradition to keep them broadly hospitable.

3

We all agree that the humanities, the natural sciences, and the social sciences are essential elements of a liberal education, though we might not agree about respective proportions. However, it has long been recognized, not merely that the three kinds of knowledge have grown further apart from one another, but that even the internal unity of these composite disciplines has given way to heterogeneous disunity, to the multiplication of splinter groups which may be almost as much divided from one another as the original three. We may deplore this state of affairs, though there seems to be no way of replacing the innumerable tribes of specialists with a new race of polymaths. It is also fairly obvious that, while such minute specialization has greatly speeded up the advance of knowledge on all fronts, it has impoverished the individual specialists, in the humanities no less than in the other areas. The full magnitude of the price we pay appears if we look around our world. As W. H. Auden remarked a while ago, anyone is considered crazy and almost immoral if he questions the unlimited desire for knowledge. Knowledge, we know, is power, and the long history of man, viewed on its darker side, is a history of struggles for power and profit, public or private; and that is sufficient ground for affirming that the exercise of moral wisdom, which includes imagination and taste, is a function of man as man—as a human being and not as a researcher. As individuals, many natural and social scientists may have a larger portion of moral wisdom than many humanists, but in this matter disparities in individual endowment are irrelevant. The point is that the natural and social sciences in themselves are morally detached and neutral—they pride themselves on being so—and are not directly concerned with the acquisition of moral wisdom. The intellectual symbol of our time is not man thinking and feeling but a computing machine.[16] The non-moral nature of science is such that it can be and always has been used for both the benefit and the destruction of man; and in our age the destructive power has outdistanced everything else. One by-product of sociology's natural concern with averages and dominant patterns has been the translation, that is, the mistranslation—notably in pedagogical doctrine—of descriptive norms into positive ideals of uniformity and mediocrity.

Thus, as we have observed already, to many people it has appeared, with or without reason, that the sciences have tended to reduce individual man to a node or a statistical cipher, to make him feel a loss of identity. And, as we have also observed, it is in the creation of and response to literature and the arts (and in the ordinary personal relations of living) that human individuality—in the sense of total being, not merely intellect—is precious. Whatever the manifold deficiencies of humanists, the humanities in themselves are there to provide aesthetic, imaginative, and ethical experience; and the sum of individual experiences forms a large part of the more or less ordered pattern we live by, however shaken it is said to be in our time. The development of such experiences and such discipline is the whole reason for the existence of the humanities. (I am not speaking here of the varied motives of creative artists but only of their audience.)

That is why it must be insisted that the humanities are the most basic of the three great bodies of knowledge and thought. I see no use in large vague pretenses that the natural sciences, social sciences, and humanities are moving along convergent roads toward eventual unification. They are essentially different in origin, methods, and aims, and no spacious and specious generalities can gloss over the differences. In the old medical theory of the four humors, the body was healthy if the humors were in balance and unhealthy if one or other was present in excess. In our time the sickness of the cultural body has many causes, but one is surely the conspicuous excess of trust in the natural and social sciences as the sole or the main arteries of valuable truth and wisdom; and there seem to be few signs of any return to health. We may indeed reach a point in our new Dark Age—at moments one may wonder if we have not reached it already—where the literary creations of saner and nobler ages can no longer be assimilated or even dimly apprehended, where man has fulfilled his destiny as a mindless, heartless, will-less node. Meanwhile, no scientific problem is anywhere near so urgent as the preservation of individual man and his humane faculties and heritage.

I should like to end with utterances from three distinguished humanists, an architect, a scholar, and a poet. In a speech at Williams College Walter Gropius said:

The vast development of science has thrown us out of balance. Science has overshadowed other components which are indispensable to the harmony of life. This balance must be reestablished. What we obviously need is a reorientation on the cultural level. . . . This is the century of science; the artist is only a luxury member of society. True art is doomed to languish as long as science is supposed to have the only answers for our predominantly materialistic period.[17]

In a valedictory after his retirement from Harvard, Howard Mumford Jones, carrying on the Renaissance ideal of "virtue and good letters" and manfully opposing some fashionable clichés, affirmed that humane teaching must lead oncoming generations to ponder and accept "the changeless meaning of the three most powerful words in any dialect—justice, virtue, and love; concepts that arise out of history in spite of the fact that, or because, history too frequently denies them."[18] On the same occasion Archibald MacLeish, also retiring, said:

For only in literature—in the arts—in poetry—which contains the arts— only in poetry does *man* appear, man as he really is in his sordidness and his nobility. Elsewhere in the University man is a clinical specimen, or an intellectual abstraction, or a member of a mathematical equation, or a fixed point in a final dogma. Only with us is he himself—himself as Swift smelled him and as Keats saw him—himself in all his unimaginable—unimaginable if literature had not perceived them—possibilities.[19]

DOUGLAS BUSH

REFERENCES

1. B. F. Skinner, *Proceedings of the American Philosophical Society*, 108 (1964), 482–85. For a humanistic philosopher's comment on the behaviorist symposium that occupied this issue of the *Proceedings*, see Brand Blanshard, *ibid.*, 109 (1965), 22–28. Like Professor Skinner, Dr. Robert S. Morison finds that science is reducing the need for the virtues nourished by the humanities (*Dædalus*, Fall, 1964, p. 1136).

2. On the study of literature one must cite the devastating survey by James J. Lynch and Bertrand Evans, *High School English Textbooks: A Critical Examination* (Boston: Little, Brown, 1963).

3. A summary report by Fred M. Hechinger, *New York Times*, June 9, 1963.

4. Richard Schlatter, *University* (Princeton University Press), Fall 1961, No. 10.

5. Ernest Nagel, "The Place of Science in a Liberal Education," *Dædalus* (Winter, 1959), p. 63. Gerald Holton has pleaded for more and better courses in science for non-scientific students in "Science for Nonscientists," *Teachers College Record*, 64 (1963), pp. 497–508.

6. *Teachers College Record*, 64 (1963), p. 531. Some representatives of various attitudes are cited in my next few paragraphs.

7. F. S. C. Northrop, *The Logic of the Sciences and the Humanities* (New York: Macmillan Co., 1947).

8. Joseph Gallant, *Science*, 125 (1957), pp. 787–91.

9. C. C. Gillispie, *The Edge of Objectivity* (Princeton: Princeton Univ. Press, 1960), p. 154. For similar views, cf. the scientist, Hiram Bentley Glass, *Science and Liberal Education* (Baton Rouge: Louisiana State Univ. Press, 1959), pp. 84–85, and the humanist, Moody E. Prior, *Science and the Humanities* (Evanston: Northwestern Univ. Press, 1962), pp. 17–18, etc.

10. *Modern Science and Modern Man* (New York: Columbia University Press, 1952), p. 111.

11. *Dædalus* (Winter, 1959), p. 171. I make special use of this issue because its subject, "Education in the Age of Science," is highly relevant and because such a symposium is handy for readers of this journal.

12. "The Two Cultures: A Second Look" (London: *London Times Literary Supplement*), October 25, 1963.

13. "An Evolutionist Looks at Modern Man," *Saturday Evening Post* (April 26, 1958), p. 122. I must add the stirring and disturbing paper by Dr. Eiseley, "The Illusion of the Two Cultures," *The American Scholar* (Summer, 1964).

14. *Dædalus* (Winter, 1959), p. 141.

15. E.g., Ernest Nagel: "These [poetry, painting, and music] are all important and instructive forms of experience. But since nothing is stated by these objects in propositional form, in no intelligible sense can they be regarded as conveying truth or falsity. . . . In short, the contention that the humanities employ a distinctive conception of truth and represent a mode of knowledge different from scientific knowledge seems to me to be the consequence of a failure in analysis." *Dædalus* (Winter, 1959), pp. 69–70. A layman might ask how one verifies the proposition that all truth is propositional—or is it simply a dogma?

16. Cf. P. LeCorbeiller: "Advances that have taken place in the last few years in the widely differing fields of automatic computation and of biochemistry will bring as vast a social revolution as did the steam engine, and they will have a greater philosophical impact than did evolution." *Dædalus* (Winter, 1959), p. 174.

17. *New York Times* (September 23, 1963).

18. *Harvard Alumni Bulletin*, 65 (1963), p. 309.

19. *Ibid.*, p. 310.

W. MCNEIL LOWRY

The Arts

A YEAR or two ago the head of the graphic arts department at a Midwestern university asked the Ford Foundation for travel expenses to visit the Tamarind Lithography Workshop, the center of a national program which was in effect revitalizing the lithograph as an original work of art. The professor represented a growing university which, drawing upon state funds, had created the physical spaces and equipment which might be used for studio and workshop training in both the creative and the performing arts. I had had an opportunity to inspect them a few months earlier. What was lacking were the persons with standards to use the facilities in a professional way and an atmosphere which might conceivably give the students some glimmer of the creative process. Perhaps the young professor could discover something of that atmosphere at Tamarind.

Alas. The young man carried to Los Angeles all the defensiveness, the insecurity, the automatic snobbery of the academy. Tamarind had better presses than he would be able to offer his students, and that was all he could see. Some time later, the president of his university and the dean of his college asked the Ford Foundation for an enormous sum of money to bring artists to the campus and to send their students to Europe—I presume at different terms of the year.

During the same year, it should be noted, the chairmen of two other graphic arts departments, both of them professional lithographers of ability, started in conjunction with Tamarind the first systematic programs for training young artisan-printers in American higher education. The best of those screened through these programs were to receive further training at Tamarind.

This routine incident on the fringes of a minor art illustrates the

206

difficulty one has in weighing the function and role of the creative and performing arts as part of university education. Discrimination among differences is all-important, and the leaders of higher education do not commonly show the discrimination in artistic matters that they do, say, in scientific matters. Even if they are not themselves scientists, they can ask the scientists for the *facts*. But what are the *facts* in the arts? Even the question is embarrassing, making the asker feel somehow gauche or even soulless. The young Midwestern professor saw the lithographic presses; between those he could discriminate. The two professor-lithographers saw (perhaps the better word is *felt*) something else. But they, unfortunately, are in the minority. Most leaders of higher educational institutions also discriminate with confidence about the arts only in terms of the physical spaces and the rate of growth in activity.

On the campuses as well as in the cities, it is the architects and the construction companies that have reaped the first harvests of our new cultural awareness—except in those departments, or even schools, in which one or two persons with taste, professional competence, thorough grounding in the craft, or other compulsion toward discrimination have been given the liberty to concentrate and focus an artistic training program. Does participation in creation or performance deepen a student's appreciation for art? Is there any analogy between the experience gained in painting or composing and that which might be described as being produced by a certain laboratory experience in the natural sciences? It is impossible to generalize without testing the atmosphere in each department. The test, unfortunately, is not self-administering, and it is not one about which educators are very secure.

It is far safer to fall back upon tangibles—reputations of important "artists in residence"; new facilities all the way from bright new studios—the Carpenter Center or the Loeb Drama Center at Harvard—to the Hopkins Center at Dartmouth and all the larger complexes being erected with state funds; a vastly increased program of performances, both student-produced and booked from commercial managements, even to the point (for Cornell) of supporting performances at that most expensive of all locations, Lincoln Center in New York City.

This tendency to judge the arts in quantitative and physical terms is not peculiar to our educators in the United States and did not proceed from them. Indeed, most of them for a long time were perfectly willing to let their institutions continue to treat the arts in only their historical, critical, and theoretical aspects. The dominant elements in society, private and public, have also taken the materialistic view, mistaking the thing for the spirit, the setting for the act. In 1965 three important sectors of the establishment moved to perpetuate this doctrine of quantification in the arts, and two of them are likely to embed their consequences in officialdom in a way that could long prove unhelpful to our artistic development.

The least consequential, in terms of lasting effects, was the report of the Rockefeller Brothers Fund panels on the performing arts. The conclusions were simple. There ought to be more. Everyone, including the government, should therefore invest more money. A good part of the money could be spent for buildings; a good part should go to pay deficits of existing performing arts groups. More should exist, however. For example, in the category of resident professional theaters, there should be fifty, or one for every city with a population of 500,000, since the Ford Foundation had given a major grant to one theater in a city of only 400,000. There was no reference to the question whether there were as many as fifty producing directors in the United States with the peculiar concentration of temperament required to direct a resident company.

The second example came in the first official proposal of Roger L. Stevens, the President's special representative in the arts and Chairman of the new National Council of the Arts established by Act of Congress in 1963. Mr. Stevens would ask the President's aid in getting Congress to amend the Federal Home Loan and Mortgage Act so that shopping centers eligible for federal mortgage loans could include theaters. These theaters would be built to exact specifications on the assembly line in order that the same road company, with sets built in each locality to save transportation costs, could perform the same play first in one and then in another theater. If there were fifty or more such carbon-copy theaters, the Broadway producer would have the expense only of moving the actors about, and soon there might be twenty-five *Mary, Mary* companies rather than five.

The third example was President Johnson's message calling for the establishment of a National Humanities and Arts Foundation, with Mr. Stevens' National Council of the Arts and a companion National Council of the Humanities moved into it, both under another small board of government officials. Congress was asked to authorize five million dollars for the arts and an equal sum for the humanities. Since this was less than a quarter of what even one private foundation then spent in these fields, it was difficult to understand the precipitate course which the President took. The result, nevertheless, was clear: by its support of the arts the federal government achieved maximum visibility with a minimum of costs.

These examples of the "official" American attitude toward the arts—and, after eight years of intensive investigation in these fields, I believe them to be typical—make it wholly understandable that the contemporary university is not only in a stage of transition but perhaps also in a stage of confusion about the role of the creative and performing arts in higher education.

It was not so many generations ago that even the literatures written in contemporary tongues were not considered proper subjects for scholarship, particularly of the advanced sort prescribed for graduate students. Even twenty years ago I myself was a witness to a tiny change in fashion when I became the first student in a large graduate department ever to have the privilege (if that is the word) of writing a doctoral dissertation on a living author.*

In this century, university educators met no special problems from the inclusion in their curricula of musicology, theater history, the philosophy of art, the history of painting, and other such courses. The basic objective of the institution remained the liberal education of the individual undergraduate. The universities also made without difficulty another kind of accommodation with the creative and performing arts. For a long time institutions of formal education, primary, secondary, or higher, have generally afforded some opportunities for students with a taste for the arts to express this interest in peripheral or informal ways. It was only in our own century that one of these ways became the course in so-called "appreciation" of art, a curricular practice hard to defend unless such courses are taken in addition to a full and formal schedule. It has always seemed to me that the "appreciation" of literature, for example, can best come through a fairly rigorous course in literature, and similarly for the other arts. The other traditional ways—chamber music societies, the opportunity to participate in a dramatic performance without regard to courses in acting, literary clubs—all help to enrich the experience of young people living together in an educational

* For this section of his essay, and much that follows, the author is drawing upon his address before the Association of Graduate Schools, New Orleans, October 24, 1961, reprinted in *Educational Theatre Journal,* Vol. 14, No. 2 (May 1962), pp. 102–107.

community. I think this rather large and general view was what actually motivated President Pusey when he asked whether formal art history and even the existence of the Fogg Museum really gave the Harvard undergraduate all the benefits of the visual arts as a means to the liberal education of the individual.

No, the real problem came with the growth in American society of the vague idea that the arts were somehow good for people. With the idea came an expansion of the sources of money available to the arts, some of it, true, to professionals and professional companies, but most of it, and disproportionately, to the amateurs. Among the first institutions to benefit financially from the new interest in "culture" and "cultural centers" have, in fact, been the universities.

There had been little difficulty in assuming the liberal education of the individual to be the goal of undergraduate education in the humanities, and to include in that education the historical, theoretical, and critical aspects of the arts. But what was the relevance to the liberal education of the individual of training in the *techniques* of painting, acting, directing, dancing, instrumentation, musical composition, or any other branch of artistic creation or performance? Could such training, given the objectives of a university, be offered under what are known as "professional" standards? If it could not, what importance should the university attach to it? If it could, what were the problems to the university of adapting professional training in the arts to its other, more primary objectives? Could the university, in effect, have it both ways?

For the contemporary university, however, the problem does not end here. The American university has for many decades faced the difficulty of raising vastly increased funds every year. But what is sometimes forgotten is that the American university has generally been far more successful in this frustrating enterprise than have most other lay institutions in our society, including those devoted professionally to the arts. Particularly the large state universities, but also some of the larger and more energetic private institutions, have seen that even for the support of artistic performances or the acquisition of collections in the visual arts and the galleries in which to display them, they had somewhat more than an even break with private or corporate patrons of the arts. There is an inevitable trend toward a greater sharing of both university facilities and university funds by community institutions in the arts, especially and most extensively when these funds come from the taxpayers. And for many university administrators this easier access to funds for artistic performances, festivals in the arts, and physical facilities for the arts coincides also with their own concept of the public role of the university, its regional importance as a center not only of teaching and research but of culture.

It is easy, then, to see how complex are the issues facing the contemporary university in this transitional period for the arts in the United States. Both philosophically and pedagogically, the question whether exposure to the technique of creation or performance can be individually or universally rewarding to liberal education is not a simple one. For the American university in 1965 it is immediately further complicated by the question whether the ideal university should assume the task of professional training of the artist and the role of artistic entrepreneur.

For a number of years the writer was engaged in the development of a large philanthropic program in the creative and performing arts; and he has been thought by many heads of universities to be unsympathetic to their activities—training or performance—in the arts. There has really been no lack of sympathy. There has sometimes been impatience over the fact that university administrators typically have not recognized the complexities in what their art, music, and drama departments were undertaking and have appeared to move on the theory that *activity* itself would prove self-justifying—if there were only enough of it. A great university would not start off a new science laboratory in that fashion and expect the result to reflect the institution's own standards. Educational administrators may not understand every one of the scientist's requirements, but traditionally they have been accustomed to respecting him and, therefore, his requirements along with him. They must learn to respect the professional artist and artistic director, to discriminate between the professional talent and the amateur. There is no other way for the educator to overcome his insecurity, perhaps even his embarrassment, about the arts. If he accepts merely the glossy expansion of amateur activities, he betrays not only the arts but the idea of a university.

For the development of the arts at this juncture in American history, the course the university takes is in the long run important. Whatever the contemporary university's role as an artistic entrepreneur may become, it will not categorically affect the nurturing of the professional artist in the United States. But every other institution for the *training* of artists in the United States has long been financially weak, and now even new institutions—such as repertory theaters—that have come to place a premium on training programs are meeting both the age-old problem of insufficient patronage and new problems of rapidly rising costs. Though they have only begun to grapple with the issues involved, American universities are economically and socially the most favored among the institutions attempting to train young persons in artistic technique and craft.

Despite all the platitudes about a cultural "explosion" or "renaissance" in the United States since 1950, any explosion that has occurred has been largely an explosion in the size of the audience. Whence does this audience come? It is my belief that it has come largely from the increase in the proportion of our population that has been university trained. The whole phenomenon of that segment of our theater known as "off Broadway" is supported, for better or worse, by an audience that has been educated in colleges and universities. Abstract expressionism, serial or electronic music are kept alive, critically and otherwise, by allied interests. In fact there is an Alexandrianism in our interest in the arts that could not be nurtured except through the academy. But when the university, dragging onto its campus professional schools of art just as in other decades it embraced professional schools of medicine or law, purports also to train the professional artist, this same Alexandrian eclecticism produces all too often the merely imitative. Without grounding in technique, without endless time spent in apprenticeship in his craft, the student may yet produce effects which to him reflect the current vogue. There are many reasons for this result—some of them more powerful than any counter forces the university could set up—and one of them is the growth and acceleration of mass communication in American society. The mass media unchecked can make every instrument in that society, even the institution of higher education, steadily contribute to vulgarization and popularization. The artist, qua artist or qua teacher, must have a very strong idea of who he is and what he is about if he is to arrest the process even long enough for psychological or critical analysis.

My own views on the role of the arts in university education have been the subject of publications, seminars, and special conferences involving professors of music, painting, and drama over the past four years. I shall repeat them here in the form in which they were originally stated.*

* Author's address before the Association of Graduate Schools, *op. cit.*, p. 106.

One. The university has largely taken over the functions of professional training in the arts but in the main has sacrificed professional standards in doing so. The absence of discrimination has proceeded partly from the strong popularizing currents already at work in the society outside the campuses, and partly from the university's original objective, the liberal education of numerous individuals drawn from an affluent democracy.

Two. The trend is irreversible. The future of professional training in the arts depends, first, upon a radical shift in the university atmosphere surrounding students considered potential artists, and, second, upon the provision of postgraduate opportunities for professional apprenticeship removed from an academic environment.

Three. The requisite shift in the university environment for the arts will be achieved only under great difficulties, if at all. Opportunities exist for new forms of cooperation between the university and professional institutions in the arts, provided the university will regard the arts as important and give financial support to the cooperative mechanisms that must be established.

Except for the few conservatories and institutes which will survive our generation, except for a peculiar art like ballet in which the practitioners are already too old if they wait until college age, the university of the future will have the first opportunity to work with most potential artists. Therefore my question is whether the university can change the environment in one part of its campus while holding its traditional atmosphere in another. It does not help to know that this has already been done, say, in the agricultural campus or in the physical-education school. The requisite atmosphere for professional training in the arts is somewhat more subtle than that in the dairy barns or in the locker rooms.

What is that atmosphere? It is easier to describe it than to analyze it. I have met it frequently, but most often in two otherwise quite unrelated institutions—the independent school of art and the resident theater ensemble. Even at first blush, the independent art school looks different from the university art department. And the resident theater's atmosphere, contrasted to that of the academic, is not merely a product of its physical inadequacies. No, the Spartan effect one detects in professional environments in the arts is not merely physical, though that situation is general. It is also in the artist's acceptance of *concentration,* even of distortion, as a way of life, a way of life that in many ways is completely antithetical to the ideal objective of a liberal and humane education. To find a truly professional vocation, to recognize standards and have confidence in them, requires even in the young person with artistic potential, fanaticisms and abnegations.

If the university is going to allow the student's distorted concentration on craft, on apprenticeship, it cannot also require of him all the courses in the humanities, social sciences, and natural sciences that are even minimally thought to constitute a liberal education. In most universities, the answer has been to stretch out the years to be applied, as in the MFA degree. But there is a limit to that adjustment. The ballet dancer, starting at nine years to train her body as her artistic instrument, knows she must forgo the university completely, at least if the potentiality of a professional career still seems good by the time she is eighteen. There is a real question whether under professional conditions an actor, even if he spent five years in college, could leave more than two hours each weekday in those five years for anything but rehearsal or performance. It is not an accident that the university now probably does a better job in training the musician than in training other artists. Historically there have been so many branches of the musical art required of a training musician that the universities have allowed more concentration in that program. And, secondly, the most technical accomplishments of a musician are more easily tested than those of an actor, a writer, a director, or even (these days) a painter.

Another obvious implication of my general argument is that neither the professors of the creative arts nor the students can be selected for a professional curriculum and atmosphere according to the patterns now employed in universities. No one has found the litmus paper that can make a positive or a negative test for artistic talent, or even for artistic drive, which would help us almost as much in this context. But drive can be isolated for identification if certain choices are forced. Roughly eighty per cent of the university students now concentrating in one of the creative arts have chosen to major in art education; they are insuring their ability to have a second vocation if the first fails. For four-fifths of the students, then, I would be so dogmatic as to say no special atmosphere, no distorted concentration need be attempted. By all means excuse them from none of the normal requirements of a liberal education. Let them hunger for the true. Their hunger for the arts is not fanatical enough. I would recommend that the universities screen creative arts students twice: once by their own choices, as I have indicated,

and again by the choice of the individual teacher after the student
has had a term or a year of true concentration.

Selection of the directors for truly professional training in the
arts will be difficult. But, in one stroke, the university will have a
wider field of talented artists from which to choose if the reform I
have just recommended is taken and the teacher is allowed to have
his *atelier* of potential talents by his own selection. I think this principle from the training of painters and sculptors should be extended
to performing artists, to composers, and to writers, as indeed for the
last named it has already been in many universities. Another obvious
corollary is that the man who is trained to teach theater history is
not necessarily qualified to direct a play, any more than the historian
of art is qualified to teach painting or sculpture.

The concentration of courses and the selection of students and
faculty, though difficult, are probably more feasible than the creation
of that intangible atmosphere of professionalism which I mentioned
earlier. I do not want to be misunderstood; I am not suggesting that
the universities simply borrow outright the curricula and atmosphere
of independent institutes and conservatories; I am certainly not
suggesting that these independent institutions have done a perfect
job in the professional education of the artist. They have not, and
today they can not, because already they have found themselves
unable to compete with the universities in the salaries, tenure, and
fringe benefits of faculty. When I cited the atmosphere of the independent art school and the resident theater company, I was citing
an intangible spirit and not model institutions for training. How
to translate this spirit into a very different location is problematical.
Yet the spirit is undoubtedly a product of motive and procedure, to
a large extent, and the changes to which I have already alluded may
help produce it. To face the necessary distortion of the primary
objective of a university, to reflect that distortion in a highly concentrated curriculum, to open that curriculum only to the students
with the most fanatical drives, to give to the artist-professor responsibility for testing both the drives and the talents—these motives
and procedures may go part way toward producing a professional
atmosphere.

There is one other possibility, again by analogy. Wherever Spartan restrictions are logical and natural, they should be applied to
the whole enterprise of professional training in the arts. Nothing so
much as the raw need to survive pares a resident theater or other
institution in the arts to the essentials of professionalism or makes

215

it a better place for hard-nosed apprenticeship. It is fortunate that universities usually have well-equipped theater and concert halls, and fairly adequate painting and music studios. It is still possible, perhaps, to emphasize repeatedly that what goes on inside is of primary importance, and real estate of only secondary. One of the most influential of all theater departments has until now flourished for years in shockingly inadequate quarters.

None of these difficult and symptomatic efforts of the university to create an environment for professional apprenticeship in the arts may bear fruit in a generation dominated by a quantitative approach to cultural development and the acceleration of communication within the society. Fads and formulae are easily spread, and each institution must have what another has even before the first institution has met the test.

Never has there been a greater need for conscientious leadership and the willingness to respect confidence and a sense of direction, in this case in the artist and the artistic director. A host of institutions are waiting to be led, with all the challenges and all the risks consequent to that fact. But there are no more orthodox forces than those afraid of being thought so, and the great institutions of learning in the United States are by and large as insecure in their convictions about the arts as the most superficial of the newspaper critics in New York or the most ephemeral of the galleries along 57th Street.

STEPHEN ORGEL AND ALEX ZWERDLING

On Judging Faculty

THE PRESIDENT of the University of California, considering the state of the contemporary university, found it necessary to coin a new word: multiversity. The term is instructive in a number of ways, both in what it stresses and in what it ignores. Most obviously, it assumes that traditional concepts of higher education are inadequate for understanding problems that are quite new. "University" implies wholeness, many things "turning one"; in the Middle Ages the word meant simply "community." The new term emphasizes diversity, replacing the notion of wholeness with a sense of the variety of functions the new university is required to serve in modern society. But it also implies not community but fragmentation: its many things compose not one, but remain many. In certain ways the situation is deplorable, and it has been widely deplored; but the term is not to blame. In itself, it is an apt embodiment of a new set of assumptions —widely shared, though largely unacknowledged—about the university. What these assumptions and their consequent demands require of members of a university faculty is the subject of this essay. Professors, especially in the sciences and social sciences, have new and much wider fields in which to act, and the extension of academic responsibility seems to demand new standards for the selection of faculty. Modern departments constantly face the need to weigh the traditional requirements of the university—for good teachers, scholars, "pure" scientists—against what it is now expected to supply in addition—consultants, technologists, staffs primarily responsible to extra-university organizations such as government agencies or industry.

The situation is not, of course, wholly new. In fact, American universities have a distinguished history of involvement in government and industry. At the turn of the century, municipal and state governments were drawing their advisers from economists and political scientists at Johns Hopkins, the University of Wisconsin, and the University of Chicago, and the federal government began to extend the practice under Theodore Roosevelt. Franklin Roosevelt's Brain Trust and Kennedy's Harvard advisers were part of a long tradition. And industry has always supported institutions from which it could draw its scientists and technologists. But in the past twenty-five years, the demand for university professors outside the academy has vastly increased, presenting the faculty member with a wholly new set of responsibilities and temptations. These are clearest in the case of the scientist and social scientist; and, to the casual critic, the academic's willingness to spend a good part of his time away from his university serving as a consultant appears both irresponsible and basely mercenary. Defenders of the practice often implicitly endorse this view by arguing that consulting is a valid way of supplementing inadequate academic salaries. Doubtless academics are no more free of mercenary feelings than any other class of Americans, but the situation is not so simply explained. For, while consulting for large corporations can be lucrative (a fee of $500 a day is not unusual for a top-flight scientist), consulting for the government, except in extraordinary cases, is not. (The government allows $16 a day for expenses—this, of course, barely covers the cost of a Washington hotel room—and a consulting fee of $50 to $100 a day, which is paid only for the days actually spent consulting. Most scientists feel that they barely break even on trips to Washington.) A willingness to undertake such work involves not only temptations of money and prestige, but also feelings of civic responsibility and a devotion to furthering the cause of one's own science. All these must be weighed against responsibilities to the institution and its students, and as a general problem this is so new that there are no handy guides to its solution.

The problem is obviously much less severe in the humanities, but here too analogous temptations exist, and have greatly increased in the recent past. The publishing industry, for example, woos humanists and scientists alike. Publishers offer large retainers to professors who can guide them in the publication of basic texts; and, with the rapid increase in the size of freshman courses, it is well worth a publisher's while to obtain expert advice. Such consulting can involve a considerable amount of work—reading and assessing manuscripts, proposing or commenting on ideas for new textbooks— and pays commensurate rewards. A more direct sort of temptation is for the professor to write a book himself. In many cases, of course, this will be directly related to his teaching; the text will be one he can use in his own course, or will embody methods that he has developed or found effective in his work. But more and more in the past few years publishers have been encouraging the production of basic textbooks designed primarily to capture the enormous market of required freshman courses. Publishers' representatives claim that a freshman English rhetoric or reader that is adopted by only one per cent of the potential users will net the author $20,000 a year in royalties. This is not to say that such projects are necessarily undertaken cynically; but they will rarely have much relevance to the intellectual life of the author, and the rewards, in comparison with the usual academic salaries in the humanities, are so huge that the temptation to abandon more serious work in their favor is very great. Less lucrative, less useful, but also less difficult to produce are the now ubiquitous casebooks—collections of articles on particular topics, pre-selected (and in effect pre-judged) materials for student projects. These require much less time and thought to prepare than a scholarly article; they demand of the compiler primarily some bibliographical work and the effort involved in securing the rights to reprint copyright material.

Perhaps the largest class of opportunities leading professors away from teaching and a direct involvement in the life of their departments is the fellowship or foundation grant. These go begging in the social sciences; they are harder to come by in the humanities, no doubt because these fields seem less obviously useful. In general, too, except for organizations directly committed to supporting scholarly research (such as the Guggenheim Foundation and the American Council of Learned Societies), foundations seem hesitant to pay simply for time to think or write, which is what the humanist most needs. Nevertheless, even in the humanities available grants have increased greatly and can seriously deplete the teaching staff of any distinguished department. It is possible for faculty members skilled in grantsmanship to spend almost half their tenure on leave. Fellowships bring prestige to the institution as well as to the recipient, and the expanding university is a seller's market. In such a situation, it is a rare department that will be able to afford the luxury of requiring its members to remain in residence.

All these temptations are fairly overt, and come on the whole from without. But there are more complex factors leading the professor away from his students and his department, and these are

STEPHEN ORGEL AND ALEX ZWERDLING

inherent in the changing nature of the university itself. For example, many large universities administer research institutes in specific fields, for the most part in the social and applied sciences, endowed by foundations, the government, or occasionally by private corporations. Academic appointments will frequently be split between an institute and a department; in such cases, the institute pays half the professor's salary, and he teaches only half a regular load. This sort of position is, of course, extremely attractive, and such institutes allow universities to underwrite certain kinds of research on a much wider scale than would otherwise be possible. But they also put an almost intolerable strain on the inner workings of the university, requiring it either to allow gross inequities between teaching loads in the sciences and the unsubsidized humanities, or to attempt, at great expense, to support the humanities in the style to which the sciences have become accustomed.

Indeed, even in the humanities, the university's work and responsibilities have generally been directed increasingly outward since the beginning of World War II. The idea of the university has undergone a radical change. To the research scientist working on a classified government project, the student is necessarily superfluous; many universities—such as Cal Tech, Berkeley, and Harvard—will not undertake classified work, feeling that it is essentially antithetical to the proper functioning of an institution devoted to the free exchange of knowledge. A major problem in university administration, especially in state-supported institutions, is how to fulfill the university's civic responsibilities without giving in to the concept of the university as a research institute whose time may simply be bought by outside organizations with projects. For, valuable as outside support is, it necessarily fosters a dangerous disproportion between the practical and the abstract. Government and industrial contracts seldom support basic research, and so lead the professor away from pure to applied science, away from the theoretical to the utilitarian, to "development." And yet to foster basic research, pure science, theoretical thinking, has traditionally been a primary aim of the university. There is a growing awareness that this function of the university must be encouraged, and some foundation and government grants have been specifically designed to support long-range, apparently useless scholarly and scientific projects in addition to those attacking particular, practical problems. Even the step-child scholar in the humanities may someday receive government support for his research, if the bill establishing a

National Foundation on the Arts and the Humanities (modeled on the highly influential National Science Foundation) is passed.

All of these new temptations and institutions have eaten away at the traditional idea of the university as an island of contemplation. The professor's life is fragmented, and his loyalties are often sharply divided; he feels a pull to his students, to his university as an institution, but also to his discipline, to his society, to possible converts to his way of thinking beyond the borders of the academy. The modern university is a house divided, and many of its critics are not at all convinced it can stand. But the specialist in Viewing with Alarm ignores the many healthy aspects of this situation and the important ways it has changed the whole texture of American life. Obviously it is a good thing for social scientists to be directly concerned with public affairs, for federal and local governments to consult experts in the field when trying to assess the merits of a variety of possible programs in agriculture, education, economic policy, welfare, defense, public health. The plain fact of the matter is that technical advice in such fields is not only desirable but ultimately at least as important to the lives of the nation's citizens as the professor's work on the campus. To idealize the academic of twenty years ago, who had barely any time off from teaching, who spent more hours in the classroom and less thinking about his field, who breathed only the air of his particular institution, is to fashion a cult of purity and provincialism. The sheer variety of opportunity in the modern professor's life has had an extremely important effect on academic morale (a fact that is frequently ignored); and it has attracted a new sort of academic to the campus. There is no longer any reason for the professor to feel that he lives out of the world, that his own education stopped with the acquisition of the Ph.D., or that his only audience is the group of students on the other side of the desk. Whether consciously or not, the new professor is working on the assumption that a university's function is to attack ignorance wherever it is found, not merely to educate the particular students who come to any one institution. There is no doubt that such an assumption requires new ground rules, a new practice; and in a very hesitant and unmethodical way it is just such a new practice that is gradually being established in American universities. This is not to say that we must simply accept existing pressures as final, or abandon the question of the professor's duties to his particular institution. But valid answers to that question can come only after all the new conditions have been assessed not simply from the viewpoint of the university involved, but also from the perspective of the whole society of which the professor, the student and the university are only parts.

The strongest objections to the current situation come from two groups: the general, non-university public and the students themselves. The former complains that faculties do not teach enough; the latter, that the university is too impersonal, that they have too little contact with their instructors. The two objections, superficially alike, are in fact quite different. The first assumes that the university is essentially an extension of high school and that a faculty member's work is properly represented by the number of hours he spends in the classroom. The student's objection is not to the lack of formal instruction, but to the lack of informal contact with the faculty, to the university's failure to make him feel part of its intellectual life. In point of fact, the student probably gets as much faculty attention as he ever did; in this respect, it is not the university that has changed, but the student's expectations regarding it: the student too has a new idea of the university.

In financial terms, public support of higher education in America is astonishing and unparalleled: for example, the annual budget of the University of California is greater than the total endowment of Yale. This represents an enormous voluntary commitment; but popular attitudes toward the university show little real awareness of its nature and traditional responsibilities. Current claims that professors spend too little time teaching rarely involve any concern for what is taught or how one teaches: they measure quality merely by the number of hours spent in class. More complex but analogous is the notion that the faculty-member-turned-consultant does his work for the government or industry on what is essentially company time. The idea of faculties as state employees raises perplexing new problems for the university: how much of a full-time professor's day constitutes "full time"? Why should state funds be used to support research or scholarship which is not directly related to the operation of the university, but represents instead larger commitments to a whole discipline? A recent bill introduced in the California legislature would require faculty members to report to the university all income earned from outside consultation; appropriate adjustments in salary could presumably then be made. The assumption behind this is that *all* the professor's energies belong to the university—a degree of obligation elsewhere imposed only by the army and the church. (This attitude is admittedly extreme, though it has respectable antecedents. One of Robert Hutchins' abortive utopian innovations at the University of Chicago was the requirement that all royalties and consulting fees be paid not to the professor but to the university.) On the whole, the public tends to view the university in pure business terms; and the difficulty of knowing whether it is getting its money's worth is infinitely compounded by basic confusions about what, exactly, it is trying to buy.

The strongest dissatisfaction with the new university comes from the students, who feel its impersonality, its failure really to include them; they are, they feel, expected only to attend a certain number of classes and pass a certain number of exams. Behind this critique, which is often obviously valid, lie innumerable pressures and forces involving the whole of modern American culture. Students turn to the university expecting from it a new kind of care and concern; but what they are faced with, at least at large state universities, is a bureaucracy of gigantic proportions, in which the simplest processes involve endless proliferations of forms and hours of waiting in line. The nearly universal demand for a college education, which has created the enormous university and its concomitant bureaucracy, has also affected the nature of the professor's work. The fact that an extraordinary number of lower-division students are at the university for the same reason that they were in high school—because it was there—has meant that much of a professor's time is devoted to providing students with something that in the past could largely be taken for granted—a motivation for being where they are.

Just how much responsibility a first-rate institution ought to feel to such students is a complex question. In fact, however, it is not they but the serious and highly motivated students who find the greatest fault with contemporary university life. The very seriousness of their commitment makes them all the more sensitive to the large institution's tendency to treat its students impersonally. The charge that the new academy is impersonal expresses not so much a desire for more "personalized" instruction—smaller classes, more office hours (most students ignore the latter until examination time anyway)—but a feeling that they are excluded from the life of the intellectual community at large. It is informal contact with the instructor they miss—the chance not to learn his subject, but to confront him as an individual, present him with their problems, make him a part of their own lives. The idea that the university ought to provide this is very new, and reflects the growing informality of American life. Older professors tend to be slightly scandalized when

223

students call them at home: it would never have happened thirty years ago. But precisely that traditional sense of the status of the faculty, of the academy as a hierarchy, is breaking down, as it is in similar structures throughout our culture. The student naturally brings his general feelings about society to bear on the university; his feelings mirror those of his elders about the larger society in which they live, and he conceives the university as a tiny welfare state, caring for him and supporting him, but also allowing him to function within it freely as an adult.

Traditionalists may object that the idea has saturnalian implications, but in fact the pressure toward breaking down established structures in this way has good effects and comes from professional educators as well as undergraduates. Much of the formal nature of university life is under attack—the insularity of the departmental structure, the proliferation and rigidity of course requirements, the grading system itself. The general pressure behind these movements for reform is the serious student's legitimate demand to be treated as a unique person with his own requirements, interests, and worth, rather than as a familiar quantity to be effortlessly processed along the preconceived lines of the institution. Naturally, to take the individual student seriously in this way (particularly at a large university) makes heavy demands on the professor within his own institution at the very time he is being tempted by interesting, lucrative, and/or important work beyond it. But no solution to the problems which these apparently antithetical pressures create can possibly be found by denying the significance of either task or by assuming that the quality of one's performance is measured by the amount of time one devotes to each. What matters much more than time spent in these tasks is the intensity of one's commitment to them, and this, unfortunately, cannot be measured by any of the familiar methods.

The feeling that the newer temptations are not a legitimate part of the professor's work has also needlessly exaggerated the idea of their incompatibility with his more traditional tasks. There is a widespread assumption (shared by the foundations and the professors) that the best climate for scholarship or research is as far away from the student as possible, that teaching has nothing to do with the most serious aspect of a professor's life and may even be antithetical to it. This assumption is unquestioned, though largely unspoken; but, while it may be valid enough for certain kinds of research, there are alternative possibilities which have remained largely unexplored.

Instead of encouraging recipients of a fellowship to take a year off from teaching, for example, foundations might devise grants which supported an experimental course connected with a professor's research interests. Such a grant would encourage the scholar to welcome the student in the most active part of his intellectual life, the creation of his own work.

Perhaps the most damaging effect of the whole discussion of the "legitimate" work of the professor is the way it has managed to substitute simplistic formulas for a dialectical conception of the subject. The assumption that teaching and research are antithetical activities exists at every level, from the crudest to the most sophisticated, in current considerations of the problems of the university. The familiar polarities (such as "publish or perish" and "what the student needs vs. what the university expects") rest on disturbing assumptions: that the university as an institution is not seriously concerned with teaching and thus with the primary needs of its students; that its work is essentially directed outward, toward serving the community at large; that it encourages its faculty to ignore their vocation as teachers in the interests of producing a steady output of scholarship or research; that the university system is in effect founded on a set of contradictory and irreconcilable needs.

Thus far we have considered primarily factors that tend to direct the university outward, temptations and obligations that turn the professor away from his department and his students and toward concerns that are widely regarded as irrelevant. But in many respects it is the traditional responsibilities of the university, directed inward and centering on the relation between teacher and student, scholar and discipline, that cause the greatest confusions. It is in light of these responsibilities that the faculty member must be considered next. And, unlike the opportunities and temptations that urge the professor to look outward, the problems raised by the traditional academic obligations are not new. They are severe, and they have always been so; but they have never been examined seriously, and the present crisis has for the first time brought them into the realm of public discussion.

A conventional rhetoric has grown up around these problems, which obscures rather than illuminates them. Almost everything written on the subject is polemical: the rebel attacks the system, the apologist defends it. Both tend to leave their assumptions unquestioned and their terms unexamined, and neither leads to a clear understanding of the nature of the problems. To begin with, what is "good teaching"? How, if at all, is it related to research? How important is it (and to whom) that an academic publish? What does a university owe to its students on the one hand and to the various scholarly and scientific disciplines on the other? In short, by what standards can faculties be properly evaluated?

The issues are not merely abstract; they directly affect all university decisions on the hiring and promotion of professors. The question seems particularly pressing at this time because of the unprecedented expansion of American colleges and universities in the past fifteen years. This has raised special problems for the great universities and colleges, those with high intellectual standards and a real interest in maintaining and advancing the disciplines they teach. Their rapid growth, and the consequent necessity of selecting faculty quickly and in large numbers, continuously threatens to compromise their standards. In such a situation, the temptation to adopt shortcuts, to apply the principles of automation to the process of judgment, is as understandable as its implications are disturbing.

There is little real awareness of the increasing mechanization of the process of evaluating faculty, and where there is awareness there is little concern. But the decisions involved are crucial ones, affecting the vitality and growth of the university itself. This is most obviously true of the tenure decision, when a department must commit itself to keeping a relatively young man for the rest of his career. To grant tenure to someone with little intellectual vitality or potential for growth is to institutionalize mediocrity. It means thirty years of cheated students and bad research; and, when such men reach positions of power, their mediocrity is frequently perpetuated through their own decisions.

The very questions asked in evaluating faculty members, whether by students, the general public, or the department itself, reveal the mechanization of the whole process: "Is he a good teacher?" or "How important is his research?" or "What has he published?" Such questions assume that the simple answers they demand can be meaningful. And yet, do we know what we mean when we say someone is a good teacher, or how to judge the quality of his research, or what the fact that he publishes reveals about him? Moreover, even these larger questions still fragment the intellectual life of a faculty member into the two conflicting realms of teaching and research. Before we can decide how much these two commitments indeed conflict, we must understand what constitutes quality in each.

It is often assumed that the good teacher is easily recognized and that there is agreement about the nature of good teaching. But students taking the same course often disagree about its quality, and there is even wider disparity between the evaluations of a particular teacher by students at different levels and by students and faculty. Of course, some teachers have a wide appeal, but the man whose appeal is limited may be as valuable to the academic community as his more universally appreciated colleagues. To treat the question of education democratically ignores an obvious truth: students at different stages of development require different kinds of instruction. How widely a particular kind is appreciated is irrelevant to its value; its very limitations may prove its greatest strengths.

The average student comes to college without a commitment to a particular field, or even to the intellectual life itself. He is most likely to respond to an instructor who can make the work exciting; the excitement communicated is on the whole more important for him than the material taught. There are various abilities and techniques involved in such teaching. A teacher may, for example, teach primarily himself. He can project his personality, his love for the subject, his sense of what is important. Or else his talent may lie in his sensitivity to the student's unsophisticated responses, to *his* sense of what is important, and *his* personality. Such a teacher may be able to reach the student in a way that teachers who feel their first duty is to the material cannot. He takes the student seriously and can refine and direct his naïve reactions and prevent him from drifting toward apathy or alienation. Or his talent may be primarily theatrical in nature, the talent of the "dazzling" lecturer, to whom the class is an audience. Such abilities, when put at the service of educating the student, can be invaluable. But students often belatedly realize that their enthusiastic response to an introductory course was a response to the instructor rather than the subject, and they then become rightly suspicious of the purer forms of theatricalism.

It might seem that such talents and techniques appeal mainly to the uncommitted and untrained student, that the more sophisticated and advanced mind distrusts them. But such styles of teaching are essentially neutral and capable of being perverted or used to good effect at all levels of instruction. It is the faculty that most often distrusts them, fearing first that they will encourage the teacher to subordinate the material of the course to his own personality, and thus fail to equip the student to deal with the subject independently; and second, that in response to the student's naïveté or lack of commitment the material may be oversimplified or vulgarized. This is a perfectly real danger—that the teacher's talents will not be used to lead the student constantly toward an understanding of the subject. Nevertheless, teaching also requires a continual appeal to what the student, at whatever level, knows and feels and understands. In addition, education is a human activity; the teacher's values, his personal commitment to the subject, are never irrelevant. He must support the student's seriousness, direct his enthusiasm, and move him away from indifference or mechanical performance of his work.

If the uncommitted student values primarily these inspirational elements, the student who is more certain of his commitment tends to prize teaching that rigorously organizes and systematizes. Such teaching, ironically, appeals to two very different sorts of students: those who have recently become seriously interested in a field and now feel, above all, the vastness of the material to be mastered, and those who treat education as a mechanical process and use organization and "neatness" as a protection against being forced to ask the larger questions. Moreover, the examination system and, indeed, the whole idea of professionalism are geared to the more systematized kinds of learning.

Some structure is obviously necessary in any course; the problem is how much. On the one hand, the teacher has a duty to make complex and potentially confusing material readily comprehensible. Those who stress this aspect of the teacher's function tend to think of the student as an apprentice and of his mind either as *tabula rasa* or as a chaos to be ordered. The first task of the teacher, they feel, is to give the student a unified and usable approach to the subject. They tend to push into the future both the harder questions of the discipline itself and the development of the student's ability to find his own ways of organizing the material. On the other hand, this approach to teaching obviously sacrifices some of the inherent complexity of the subject and also casts the student in the passive role of a receiver of doctrine. The problem is not the value of organization itself, but how highly organized a course ought to be; and the reason it seems difficult to solve is that it assumes the possibility of a single answer for all courses. But this is to ignore the varying needs of different students at different stages of development. The whole range of courses, from the most impressionistic to the most systematic, is clearly an educational necessity.

Most limited in his appeal is the man whose teaching reflects an interest only in his own specialty. The student he attracts must already be almost an expert, since the teacher makes no effort to "inspire" the unsophisticated or uncertain. He takes the student's interest for granted, and teaches essentially his own special field. Invaluable to graduate education, he merely provokes hostility in less advanced classes. It might seem that such a man would rather not teach at all; but in fact he is often dedicated to the professional training of a few disciples, and, within the limits of his specialty, the devotion he inspires in those students is intense. In the sciences, where training is more exclusively professional, it is generally possible for him to limit himself to such advanced work; but in the humanities, where specialization tends to be treated as an extravagance, he is usually forced to teach on all levels, at least until his eminence allows him to dictate his own conditions. It is a mistake to feel that inflicting this kind of teacher on lower-level courses performs any service either for him or for the students. Conceivably, this impasse will eventually be resolved in the humanities in the way it has been in the sciences; but, until then, all students except the specialist's disciples will feel hostile or cheated, while his colleagues, aware of his contribution to graduate training and to the discipline, will be reluctant to let him go.

There is a kind of teaching which inspires even more radical disagreement. It may be called innovative, and is characterized first of all by a dissatisfaction with the traditional structures of the university—the established barriers between disciplines, the ordinary pattern of courses in a department, the accepted approaches to a subject. The innovative teacher devises courses that set new boundaries within which a subject may fruitfully be studied. His course may be interdisciplinary, or may use new methods of treating the material of a discipline or unconventional ways of organizing it. Ideally such teaching strives to make a course reflect the creative activity of the mind. The university, like all institutions, is essentially conservative; it tends to crystallize and codify the discoveries of the past, and the curriculum gives the misleading impression of a permanent and inevitable structure of knowledge. In fact, the curriculum is in constant flux; the experiments of one decade become the institutions of the next. It is the innovative teacher who keeps the university in touch with the intellectual life of its time.

Such a teacher appeals most clearly to two kinds of students: those who feel at ease with the standard approaches to a subject and are ready to participate in the work of creating new ones, and those who, impatient with all categories, are unwilling to devote themselves to mastering any of the accepted ones. He can help the former to free themselves from the relative passivity of their apprenticeship and lead their minds toward active participation in the intellectual life. On the latter he has a more detrimental effect, endorsing chaos of mind and supporting the desire to avoid real work. Though his is potentially the most creative sort of teaching, it can be very harmful to the student not yet equipped to use it—particularly one whose rebellion against the university is automatic and irrational and who uses it to confirm and harden his instinctive revolt.

The innovative teacher also inspires confusion and outright hostility. The students who dislike him most are the devotees of the rigorously organized and systematized kind of course, the recent converts to the discipline still trying to get their bearings, or the cynics concerned primarily with acquiring a degree. Some of his colleagues also distrust him; his experiments undermine the stability of their categories and structures and may threaten their sense of professional competence. They may consider him irresponsible. Any experimental teacher will be accused of irresponsibility by some, and in a sense this is accurate: he feels little responsibility to the traditional modes. But his responsibility must finally be measured by what he creates, not by what he destroys. And here he is most vulnerable to legitimate criticism. His innovations may be arbitrary or pointless, and so may either rob the student of his trust in the traditional assumptions to no useful purpose, or simply waste his time. In short, innovative teaching is both the most dangerous and the most interesting kind of instruction.

It should now be clear that the simple contrast between good and bad teaching vastly oversimplifies a complex situation. A good teacher may have various talents, and no one can possibly have them all. Each is useful at a different level and in its own way to the academic community; to eliminate any one would be crippling. This is not to say that every teacher is good "in his own way." There is an even longer list of ways in which teachers can be bad—because they are lazy, cynical, or indifferent to the material or to the problems of communicating it, or simply because they are not intelligent enough to teach well. The essential point is that a good teacher's limitations must not be confused with bad teaching.

The difficulties of judging good teaching do not end with determining its nature. There remain all the practical problems of getting and interpreting the necessary information. We ought to know how seriously the teacher takes his teaching, how he treats and organizes his material both in the individual class and in the course as a whole, at what levels of teaching he does his best work, and the whole nature of his relationship with students both in class and in conference. All of this information is extremely hard to come by. It appears first of all in the form of student gossip and reaches faculty members only in the most haphazard way. Its most tangible aspect for the faculty is found in enrollment figures, and this offers the temptation to measure the value of a course by its popularity. At several large universities, such as Harvard, Cornell, and Berkeley, student groups have attempted to codify and analyze reactions to courses as a guide for the perplexed undergraduate. Such summaries of student questionnaires, when responsibly done, can be valuable for the student. Whether they are equally valuable to the faculty member trying to judge his colleagues remains to be considered. There are also methods of gathering information initiated by the faculty. In many universities and colleges, classes are observed by an older member of the department, or younger professors are asked to give guest lectures in large lecture courses.

Each of these methods can provide some valuable information. Students are constantly exposed to a professor. Their reactions are based on a sense of the whole course, and they see the teacher at his worst as well as at his best. They can also judge aspects of a course which are not evident in classroom teaching—conferences, grading, and the usefulness and coherence of the outside work. The guide based on student questionnaires can offer a valuable analysis of student reaction; it can distinguish among diverse attitudes to a controversial professor and suggest at what levels his teaching is most appreciated. Of course, such refined discrimination depends both on wide student participation and on a sophisticated questionnaire —one that will differentiate, for example, between the responses of the outstanding and the average student. Unfortunately, these prerequisites are rarely fulfilled.

The faculty member auditing a colleague's class has a different perspective. He is less likely to be dazzled by purely theatrical talent; and he will be aware of the instructor's command of the material and thus able to judge distortions and oversimplifications. Obviously, an evaluation of a teacher that does not take into account the judgment of an intellectual peer is meaningless. Every class involves the instructor in a number of choices—of approaches to the material, of which elements to stress, of possible interpretations. Only someone aware of the variety of those choices can evaluate the ones that have been made. The faculty observer's sense, then, is different from but fully complementary to that of the student. Both, however, are in certain ways unreliable.

The ordinary student's sense of his instructor is like the response to an actor's interpretation of a role by a spectator unfamiliar with the play. If he is perceptive, he is perfectly capable of judging the actor's essential ability to perform and even the coherence of his playing of the role. But he cannot judge the intelligence, discrimination, and originality of the performance. Most students will simply not know enough about the material of a course to be aware of any but the grossest distortions. This limitation is inherent in all student evaluations and is inevitably reproduced in the student guide, however large its sampling.[1]

The limitations of the faculty observer are equally clear. Because the various teaching styles are so different and difficult to judge objectively, he may distrust methods other than his own. But, more important, he sees only a few classes out of context; he has little sense of what the whole course is like and cannot take into account the virtues of continuity and coherence. He assumes that what he sees is a true microcosm—that it corresponds exactly to the greater world of the whole course. Also, he bases his judgment exclusively on the teacher's performance in class and must ignore individual work with students, assignments, examinations, and so forth.[2]

Furthermore, the outside auditor cannot function as a neutral observer. His very presence changes the natural situation. Its effect on the teacher, aside from creating an unusual tension that is inevitably communicated to the class, is to tempt him to appeal not to the students but to the prejudices of the observer, even if only to the extent of toning down his most radical methods and observations. The class is thus turned, however subtly, into a special performance, sometimes with the complicity of the students. The presence of the observer alters the nature of the phenomenon he is attempting to observe, and the evaluation must make allowances for this fact.

Despite the undeniable limitations of student and faculty evaluations, both reveal essential aspects of a man's teaching which, when combined, can produce a valid sense of his work. Nevertheless, it is the practical difficulty of getting objective evidence of teaching ability that leads departments to place a disproportionate emphasis on research. Here, at least, the evidence is apparently tangible and readily available. It is at this point that the whole process of evaluation comes under the most bitter and violent attack. Teaching and research, it is argued, are radically different activities; ability in one does not guarantee ability in the other and, indeed, often militates against it. But the critic who emphasizes the complete disparity between the two fields is likely to be thinking of teaching only as what takes place in the classroom and, more particularly, in the lecture. Yet the classroom is not the only point of contact between student and teacher. Most obviously in advanced work in the sciences, the contact tends to be more casual and more collaborative, and thus teaching, for both the instructor and the student, clearly approaches the conditions of research. There are, moreover, excellent colleges and universities where much of the educational process goes on outside the classroom—in conferences, in tutorials, and in the sort of informal contact which implies that the university is not a set of courses but an intellectual community.

Even formal classes, however, especially in the sciences and social sciences, are frequently extensions of the professor's research interests. The sort of collaboration this involves is potentially of the greatest value for the advanced student, though the relationship can be radically abused. When the professor uses his students simply to collect his data, the experience has only minimal value for them, and they will rightly feel exploited. Research courses are less feasible in the humanities, where the tasks at every stage involve criticism and interpretation, activities which cannot be delegated. Yet, even here, the difficulty is not entirely inherent in the nature of the material, but is also the product of the tenacious parochialism and conservatism of individual departments.

Much of the creative research in all intellectual inquiry is in some sense interdisciplinary. This fact is widely recognized in the sciences and social sciences, and many of the courses given in such departments reflect it. The humanities, which deal so much more with the past and with a fixed body of knowledge, are by nature more conservative; study in these fields involves strong feelings of responsibility to the material and a relative distrust of new approaches. This means, in practice, that the kind of interdisciplinary work which interests many of the most creative members of such departments must be taught outside the department, in very specialized graduate seminars, or not at all. Few courses exist, especially at the undergraduate level, in which a professor can deal with the broad questions currently engaging his attention. Such inquiry is not necessarily more difficult or specialized than the work students

usually do, but it does require in every case an original organization of the course, to fit the particular lines of the inquiry rather
than the traditional ways of defining the material. Such courses, in
which the professor can treat the general issues that come up in his
research, should be considered essential in all departments, for it
is through them that the curriculum is kept in touch with the living
work of the discipline. For example, it should be possible in an
English department to teach a course dealing with the general question of the usefulness of linguistics as an interpretive tool in literary
analysis. The reading for such a course would be unusual: it would
include works in linguistics, philosophy, psychology, logic, even
mathematics, as well as literary works, possibly chosen without regard to period or genre. Such a course could not be a substitute for,
say, one in Shakespeare (that is, for the sort of course that offers
training in the materials or techniques of the established field). Yet
the experience of putting together a variety of disparate but related
elements, in a course dominated not by a set of works but by a set
of questions, is of tremendous potential value to both teacher and
student. Unfortunately, there is a considerable time lag between
creative thinking as it goes on in the professor's work and as it
finally becomes established in some department of the university.
And, once established, it begins to exhibit all the rigidity of the
traditional curriculum.

Such courses, which grow directly out of a scholar's intellectual
life, should not be reserved for the occasional advanced student. It
is only when students have been exposed to courses like this at
every stage of their development that they can have a sense of what
intellectual work involves. This is an essential part of their education, preparing them to deal creatively with all material and preventing them from treating knowledge as merely a fixed body of
information.

It should be clear that the endorsement and institutionalization
of the dichotomy between teaching and research is responsible for
much that is least satisfactory in the university system. This is not
to say, however, that the two realms are really "reconcilable," or
that both teacher and student do not always feel the tension between
them threatening to pull them in opposite directions. Both teaching
and research are potentially full-time activities, and the professor
will often feel a desire to devote himself fully to one or the other.
Nevertheless, the kind of faculty member who belongs to a first-
rate college or university feels a commitment to both and a desire

to pull them together; this is the only sense in which the conflict is ever "resolved." There are, naturally, certain standard courses, especially of an introductory kind, which will provide relatively few opportunities to deal with questions which actively concern a man in his research. And there will be phases of his research which will be nearly incommunicable to anyone but his fellow specialists. But these situations are the extremes, not the norms, of the work of his whole career. A much more common situation is one in which the teacher feels that what really interests him can just barely be explained to his students and the students feel that they are just barely understanding it. The idea that this tense situation should be *resolved*—when in fact it should be prized and nurtured in every possible way—is one of the saddest corollaries of the divorce between teaching and research.

Teaching and research are not related only in the classroom, however. Nearly all research, even the most specialized, is a form of teaching. Its "students" may be colleagues in a department or in other universities; the effect of a scholar's work on them is precisely analogous to the teacher's effect on his students: it extends the range of their awareness of the subject. Obviously knowledge and the communication of knowledge do not stop at the borders of a particular university, nor, indeed, at the edge of academia itself. The scholar feels a commitment to his discipline; it nourishes him just as much as his particular institution does. Teaching, even on the most elementary level, is dependent on the products of the research of many men at different institutions. Not to accept this fact is to forget that we are constantly changing the material of the university's curriculum by the work we do on it; and not to accept the scholar's commitment to this work is to doom him to intellectual parasitism and learning itself to stagnation.

In addition, it is frequently forgotten that research is a form of learning and that the professor's education should no more stop after he obtains his credentials than a student's should when he leaves the university. All the formal aspects of a student's education can be paralleled on a more informal level in the professor's research—classes are like faculty seminars and scholarly meetings; papers and examinations are like the products of the professor's scientific or scholarly investigations; both groups are attempting to master unfamiliar territory. In research the teacher is simply a student; the best teachers are always aware of the areas of their own (and human) ignorance.

235

The idea that research is an indispensable part of a professor's life assumes that his work is important to the scholarly world at large, and this brings us to the central question of how one evaluates research. In the popular mind, research is identified with publication, and all research is much the same; the only disagreement is about whether it hampers the proper functioning of the university or constitutes its greatest contribution. But though publication itself is often taken as evidence of a man's ability, the *fact* that he publishes is clearly no more illuminating about the quality of his mind (especially given the universal pressure to publish) than the *fact* that he teaches classes.

In any discipline, there is a distinction between genuinely important and misguided or relatively trivial research. Important research reinterprets or re-evaluates the basic material of the field or gathers new and significant material. Misguided research, while often not trivial, rests on anachronistic or invalid assumptions. Relatively trivial research tends to endorse and extend accepted attitudes or theories in peripheral areas and to avoid questioning any basic assumptions. It is in essence a set of footnotes appended to work already in existence, and often involves a desperate search for subject matter that has been generally ignored, assuming—often explicitly—that it is the unfamiliarity of the material which is interesting, rather than the critical intelligence focused on it. One of the most unfortunate facts of American graduate education is the prevalence of this assumption among graduate students, especially in the humanities; it is an assumption that leads to defeatism about one's own possible contribution and cynicism about the discipline itself.

"Trivial" and "important" are, of course, not absolute categories, but the extremes of a scale on which to measure creative work. The problem, then, if we are to use research as an index to the essential creativeness of a man's mind, is to decide how important a particular piece of research is. This is by no means the easy task it is often assumed to be. For one thing, the basic assumptions of a discipline, especially in this century, change very rapidly. A scholar who may have done excellent work a generation ago but who has not kept in touch with developments in his field is quite unfit to judge the importance of current contributions. Every department has its examples; it would be encouraging to think they are the exception, not the rule. Such people, moreover, are often entrusted with the task of evaluating manuscripts submitted to journals or scholarly presses. Thus, neither an unexamined "authoritative" opinion nor

236

the simple fact of publication is a guarantee of important work.

These and all the other practical difficulties of discriminating between relatively trivial and important work encourage departments to accept criteria of evaluation that are basically mechanical. In its extreme form, this attitude leads to the use of merely quantitative measures of published work. It is not uncommon for departments to require, for example, the publication of one article a year, or of a book every five years. The *value* of the research is doubtless also used as evidence; but this is not the point. To think in such quantitative terms is essentially to short-circuit the judging process. The only useful criteria are those that will reveal genuinely creative or vital thought.

This is a quality of mind which is obviously central to both research and teaching; and it can be evaluated, on the whole, more objectively in research than in teaching. The problems are essentially practical ones. Proper judging of scholarly or scientific material requires both time and special competence. Publications, manuscripts, and plans for future work must be read, not only with care, but by someone familiar with current research in the particular field. Frequently, if the field is a specialized one and the department relatively small, no such expert will be available; this necessitates soliciting outside opinions, which in turn entails further difficulties of selection and evaluation. Despite the complications of this process, the fact that research *can* be judged by objective standards, that it is at least "there" in a way that classroom work is not, is primarily responsible for the tendency to make it the sole criterion for evaluating faculty. And it is certainly true that a competent assessment of a scholar's research reveals more about his innate intellectual ability than does any other single judgment. But this information is not, unfortunately, all we need to have. We must also know how much of that ability he actually applies in his teaching. It must be more than mere potential. Thus the evaluation of research is part of the essential evidence, but it cannot be treated as if it were the whole.

The problem is complicated by the fact that the general public (and most students) cannot see the relevance of research to what they conceive as the main function of the university. Students know the professor primarily through his teaching; the faculty knows him primarily through his scholarship. This fragmentation of the data of evaluation results in the substitution of two antithetical and certainly incomplete figures for the whole man. Naturally, both camps are convinced that the figure they see is the essential one. The flaw in the theory that teachers should be evaluated simply on the basis of their teaching is that it assumes the university deals primarily in knowledge, not learning, and that what it offers is a commodity. The flaw in the argument for evaluating the man by evaluating his research is that it does not take the ways in which he communicates his knowledge seriously. Both theories reduce the dynamic process of the creation, formulation, and communication of ideas to something static or partial.

All of this should suggest that to frame the discourse in terms of teaching versus scholarship is to accept and perpetuate this fragmentation of the whole man. It is necessary for both camps to accept the existence of something they cannot directly experience. The conflict itself is not resolvable, simply because the only man who *does* experience both parts of it is the man being judged. Accepting the conflict as a given, then, it becomes essential to make use of all available evidence, however fragmentary, not simply the evidence most easily obtained. Faculty members must acknowledge that there is a fundamental aspect of their colleague's work that they cannot see when they judge only his research. This imposes on them the obligation to use the best available means for judging both a man's teaching and his scholarship and to refine those means in every possible way.

Unhappily, the current tendency is to do the exact opposite, to use shortcuts and mechanical criteria. Two of these shortcuts have already been mentioned: the practice of making research the sole criterion of excellence and, even worse, the tendency to judge that research quantitatively. A third shortcut frequently used is more universal and more subtly pernicious: it is the identification of research with publication. Since the actual process of research involves not simply writing, but reading, collecting data, thinking, teaching, talking—in fact, the whole of the intellectual life—to judge a man simply by his published work is to be concerned only with the results, again with knowledge as a product, not learning as a process. A published work is merely a temporary stopping point and represents only a part of the larger research process—and not necessarily the part which is most important for the teacher, his student, or indeed for the university as a vital community. It now becomes apparent that judging research in this larger sense can present difficulties comparable to those inherent in judging teaching. Just as it is impossible to know the quality of a course from observing a few classes, so it is impossible to judge a man's intellectual vitality from his publications alone. The publications must be viewed in context; and the context is the whole range of his intellectual response.

This is by no means to dismiss the importance of publication, which symbolizes the scholar's contribution and commitment to his discipline. It connects his work with work done beyond the borders of the university and serves thereby to make the university itself less parochial. Furthermore, since research can easily become centrifugal, the pressure to publish also comes from within and represents a desire to organize and crystallize a body of work into coherent and communicable order. But an institution that cares only about what its faculty publishes and not about the whole of the intellectual process is not providing the right encouragement and support for this sort of inner pressure; it is, on the contrary, subverting it by fostering the production of marketable items, in exchange for which the scholar receives his advancement. Such institutions have effectively replaced the promotion of research with the pressure to publish and have devalued the whole intellectual process.

It remains to be said, however, that evaluative methods such as those discussed here do not entirely describe the realities of the judging process. Only a few members of a large, democratically run department will really know anything directly about a man's teaching or research. Yet few will feel hesitant about passing judgment on him. There is nothing anomalous in this situation: the strongest sense a group of people working together have of each other is a broadly human one, rather than one arrived at in any conscious, methodical way. To dismiss the value of this intuitive sense of a man's worth is to reject the part of the judging process that we instinctively feel comes closest to judging the whole man. Any serious conversation reveals fundamental qualities of mind—originality, intellectual commitment, vitality, and responsiveness—essential to the best kind of teaching and research.

The usefulness of the intuitive judgment, then, is clear enough; its potential abuses are equally apparent. At its worst, it degenerates into a judgment of personality—of charm, cleverness, articulateness, social graces. This is inevitably the case when the only contact has been of a purely social nature. In such a case, the responsible person asked to make a judgment will disqualify himself. But even at its best, the intuitive judgment is like an aptitude test; it gives us information about a man's potentiality, but none about the quality of his actual performance. Intuition can tell us nothing about his ability to work, the connecting link between his fundamental intelligence and his successful use of it. It would be comforting to think that the ability to work (as distinguished from the mechanical performance of routine tasks) can simply be assumed in scholars. But at once the specter of George Eliot's Mr. Casaubon arises; and no one with a sense of the complicated psychological forces involved in the pursuit of fruitful research will be comforted.

Two important facts emerge. No judgment of any of a man's aspects—his teaching, his research, or his talk—can serve as the key to the man himself. And no method of judging even one of those aspects is wholly satisfactory. Furthermore, there can be few safeguards against the obvious potential abuses of the evaluative process—against judgments dictated by departmental factions, personal antipathies, or various kinds of bias. Such melancholy facts, along with the growing awareness that proper judgment demands a great deal of effort, has led many of the most able members of the academic community to respond to the whole situation with despair or, finally, with apathy. This is in ironic contrast to the storm of protest—from students, from editorial writers, from the public at large—about the university's ways of dealing with the problem. Such general dissatisfaction with the university implies general concern, and this is something new and good in American culture. But the dissatisfaction tends to be exclusive and parochial, the cry of pressure groups that their particular needs are being ignored. Like all lobbies, they press their own interests at the expense of the whole. They fail to take seriously all the faculty member's responsibilities—to students, to his discipline, to his society, and to his own intellectual development. To take all of these into account requires, first and most obviously, a strong will and considerable effort. That we are at last forced to take them seriously is in itself something to be grateful for, as it is the first step toward finding a genuine basis for judging faculty.

REFERENCES

1. Even official university-sponsored questionnaires asking students to evaluate their professors demonstrate the same impasse. The one at the University of Washington asks students to what extent their teachers can be described in the following ways: "is clear and understandable in his explanations"; "takes an active, personal interest in the progress of his class"; "is friendly and

sympathetic in manner"; "shows interest and enthusiasm in his subject"; "gets students interested in his subject." Each of these qualities describes teaching *manner;* the whole question of *what* the teacher says is left untouched. A professor could score very high in each of these categories and still be teaching his students outdated material or misguided nonsense. This is in itself enough to suggest that such questionnaires cannot *by themselves* be used as an index of a teacher's quality, since they analyze only his performance. But the teacher is not just an actor; if he is any good he also writes the script. See E. R. Guthrie, *The Evaluation of Teaching: A Progress Report* (Seattle, Wash.: University of Washington, 1954).

2. These are not insuperable problems, however. If departments really took the evaluation of teaching seriously, they could make use of much material which they now ignore—for example, course assignments, exercises, and examinations or a professor's own statement concerning the aims and methods of his course. Such information is very revealing, though of course it is subject to the faculty member's distortion. It can discriminate between fresh and routine treatment of a course and measure the imaginative effort expended in planning it. A teacher must be evaluated by others, but he should also be able to make a case for himself; there is no reason why such information should not be used in making a decision about him.

DAVID RIESMAN AND JOSEPH GUSFIELD

Styles of Teaching in Two New Public Colleges

WHILE THE ENGLISH have a very clear idea of what a university is, and even what a subject within a university is, maintained through external examiners and a fairly centralized pattern of intellectual and academic life, with us, as everyone knows, the pattern has been and remains one of profuse variety, with about two thousand institutions of higher education providing a college for nearly every purpose, pocketbook, subculture. In California and Utah we have already moved into a society in which over half the relevant age grade is enrolled in post-secondary education of some sort, and it seems quite clear that restrictionist views will no more prevail in this area than they did after World War I in the area of secondary education. Moreover, the great majority of the new entrants into higher education will be educated at public colleges and universities. The California model of co-ordinated (at least, on paper) higher education is being followed in other large states which are building or supporting community colleges for commuters, and often four-year colleges too, as well as expanding the major land-grant and other state systems.

This phenomenal growth has been accompanied by improvisation of plant and curricula and by "instant" faculties that are increasingly being recruited nationally, but so rapidly and in such great numbers as not to be inducted into any particular academic ideal relevant to the particular institution. In one of the very large state universities, 400 new faculty members may arrive on the scene annually, half of whom are replacements and half a response to growth by sheer accretion. A single department at such an institution is often larger in its budget and its student body, let alone its faculty, than many of the elite private colleges which have led the academic procession in the past.

Yet this growth has, at the same time, made possible a certain amount of innovation. Where budgets are lavish and everyone stands in line for raises and expansion, astute administrators may have more leeway in starting new programs than those where an outlook of scarcity supports an egalitarian *status quo* resting on envy. In starting new branches, the University of California has not had to be isomorphic with the existing ones. Far from undernourished, Berkeley and UCLA have imposed only the mildest of inhibitions, and, at times, generous and sympathetic support, for new ventures at Riverside, Santa Cruz, Irvine, and San Diego, each of which has proceeded along autonomous lines to create educational enterprises different from earlier branches and different from each other. At the new Florida State institution in Boca Raton, one experimental feature is that of confining admission to upper-division students, allowing transfers from junior colleges or from elsewhere to fill the new places. A second chance at innovation has also been given some state systems by the establishment of metropolitan campuses where the parent, reflecting land-grant or "down-state" origins, sets up a new urban branch, as the University of Massachusetts is now doing in Boston with a program of uncompromising liberal arts, or the University of Illinois in Chicago. Elsewhere, both in private and in public institutions, protection for experiments within the institution has been sought by developing new semi-autonomous colleges, not wholly bound to the curricular and pedagogic routines already in force. Michigan State University's Justin Morrill College, which opened in the Fall of 1965, hopefully the first of a series of such institutions, is an illustration; while its students will, of course, use the library and other central facilities of the host institution, they are independently housed and taught in a program focused on the international scene. The University of Michigan is engaged in planning a residential experiment, and the so-called Tussman College at Berkeley, which is to run for two years, is a similar example. All of these experiments have in common the double opportunity of starting with few precommitments while, at the same time, receiving backing from existing institutions. Some universities, seeking to upgrade themselves, may also make use of experimental sub-institutions as a way of doing so. Thus, Raymond College of the University of the Pacific, a private institution, has recruited faculty both from within and from outside the parent university and is designed as the first of a series which may eventually absorb a majority of the campus. At Raymond, as in the planned colleges at the University of California at Santa Cruz and Justin Morrill College at M.S.U., a recurrent theme is the effort to cope with bigness and impersonality by an enterprise of smaller scale, even though no special efforts are made to recruit a student body of higher academic or cultural aptitude than that of the sponsoring university.

No less important, the experimental colleges initiated by older institutions allow the latter to move in several directions at once. Not many American universities have the luxury, sought by purists on the faculty, to serve only a single goal, be it excellence in research as defined by the academic guilds, genteel undergraduate cultivation taken over from Oxbridge models, religious dedication, or community service in its many forms. Many state universities are committed, whether by law or by mission, to promoting equality of educational opportunity for citizens of the state—a goal that may often be at odds (as in tariffs on out-of-state students) with the actual education of the home-state students. The experimental institution within a state university may allow it at the same time to serve a large student population and also to avoid some of the side-effects of mass education in alienating students and faculty, each group being so massive as to stereotype the other group and both discovering secondary gains in a tacit treaty of limited encounter and indifference.

In a great number of the large institutions—both public and private—catering to a heterogeneous student body, honors programs have been set up so that students preselected on the basis of grades may be spared from the indifference just mentioned. They also provide the selected students with special counseling, special sections of required or large courses, and a greater measure of freedom to follow their own academic bent. Sometimes they may have seminars together or in other ways defend themselves against the widespread philistinism of the campus, while possibly intensifying these very qualities among those not selected. But these are not really very radical experiments.

Two new colleges, Hawthorne and Elmwood,[1] have taken somewhat more original approaches. They began in 1959 as satellites of major state universities in the same Midwestern state and defined themselves initially not as honors colleges for especially talented youngsters, but as commuter colleges for students eligible to attend the parent university. While the threshold for admission was not very demanding, it was raised in practice by counseling students with low test scores that they might do better at a community college or

one of the upgraded normal schools. What makes these two experimental institutions important is that their experiences may be more
generally applicable to the great wave of students who are the first
in their families to attend college and who come from the working-
class and clerical layers of an industrial city. These students will
certainly be more numerous in the future.

The goal of both new institutions was to bring an elite education
to an essentially nonselective student body. In our first contact with
the colleges, we regarded them as missions to carry the curriculum,
atmosphere, and teaching methods of Oberlin or Grinnell, the
College of Wooster or Carleton, Shimer or Chicago, to average
state-university students, all of whom commuted and the majority
of whom held part-time jobs.

Since 1959 we have systematically interviewed faculty members
and less systematically talked with students, visited classes, and
examined the available academic records. The two colleges are very
different from each other as well as from their parent universities,
but their simultaneity and physical proximity led us to study them
in a comparative way. Furthermore, both began operation with a
very strong stand against what they regarded as the evils of the big
public institutions: Big Ten frivolity, athletic overemphasis, and
glamor, on the one side, and narrow, unliberal vocationalism, on the
other. Furthermore, both colleges were designed to be relatively
small by state-university standards: Elmwood anticipated an entering class of 500 and Hawthorne, 300. Perhaps still more important,
the classes themselves were to be small although, by careful organization of the curriculum, the cost per student was not greatly to
exceed general state-university norms.

In six years of operation, there have been compromises and
adaptations of the original, often inchoate, plans. For example, Elmwood may not long remain small, nor confined to undergraduates.
But our concern in this paper is neither with original aims nor with
transformations; rather, we shall draw on our observations of classes
at both institutions to say something about styles of teaching—styles
we see as ranging from didactic to evocative. We see these styles, in
turn, bearing complex relations to the aims of faculty members
vis-à-vis students, aims which run from the desire to encourage a
youthful moratorium to an increase of pressures for adulthood and
occupational commitment. Consequently, our discussion will range
beyond the institutions in question and is not to be taken as an
adequate description of them.[2]

What we can see in observing classes is something of the concrete environment presented to students, a semblance of the aims of faculty as they emerge in demands on students for specific forms of behavior and self-presentation. In the two colleges we observed during their first two years of operation, these classroom environments were attuned to the general atmosphere of each college, an atmosphere influenced by the kinds of faculty recruited and shaped by the culture which they helped create. These observations reveal for us some of the diversities possible in developing "the college experience" and consequently the possible uses of mass colleges.

The Two Colleges

The institution we call Elmwood is the virtually autonomous off-shoot of a great land-grant university eighty miles away. It was built from scratch on what was once a large private estate, donated for this purpose, in the exurban outskirts of a great industrial city. From the very outset, its planners emphasized a post-Sputnik rigor and toughness: it was to be a no-nonsense institution, ascetically free of football, fraternities, home-coming weeks, and general social razzle-dazzle. In structure, it would follow the conventional American departmentalization. But it would be defiantly anti-vocational in postponing and muffling vocational interests. Prospective engineers would be accepted, but they would be given large doses of general science and only enough engineering to help them to get their first job. Prospective businessmen would be given economics, industrial psychology, and decision-making; prospective schoolteachers were to regard themselves as in effect applied behavioral scientists. To make clear its emphasis on the liberal arts, Elmwood, in addition to the usual requirements in English composition, required a full-year staff-taught course in Western Civilization and also a course in a non-Western culture; also, all students would have to study literature and a foreign language and choose among electives in natural science and in social science. While there was to be no graduate work to distract the faculty from their undergraduate mission, Elmwood's organization did not deviate from the conventional American academic departments, except to the degree that the Western Civilization course drew on historians, philosophers, and people in literature. It might be said that what was innovative in the conception of Elmwood was not to be found in its organization or curriculum, but in the sort of student body to which it sought to give

246

an elite education more commonly pursued by students from cultivated backgrounds who feel free to postpone full specialization to graduate or professional school.

Hawthorne College did not have to start from scratch in its physical plant, nor did it have to provide a full curriculum for its students. Physically, it consisted of two old frame houses taken over as headquarters on the amoeba-like campus of a big urban university of the sort that would once have been called a streetcar college and now might be thought of as a jalopy college. Hawthorne could use the classrooms, the libraries, the student facilities of the parent institution. It could farm its students out for specialized and upper-division work to the undergraduate professional schools and the College of Liberal Arts of the parent. Its own task, at once more modest and more ambitious than that of Elmwood, would be to provide the general-education component of a four-year program. This core consisted of three interdisciplinary staff-taught sequences: six quarters of a natural-science course (primarily history of science and logic, along with some mathematics), five quarters of a social-science course, and five quarters in the humanities. In addition, there would be a Senior Colloquium, and each student would be required to present a Senior paper. (Students taking their A.B.'s at Hawthorne rather than elsewhere in the parent university could elect courses and seminars offered optionally by Hawthorne faculty members.) In other words, Hawthorne differed not only from its parent, but from most American university-colleges in attempting to reorganize the basic divisions of subject matter and to cut the tie to graduate specialization. No innovation, of course, is wholly new, and, as already suggested, the model here could be found in the Hutchins' era College at the University of Chicago, although the actual sequences developed at Hawthorne were often original in the details of synthesis and selection.

Like Elmwood, Hawthorne College set itself in opposition to intellectual slackness and the educational complacency that came increasingly under attack in the last years of the Eisenhower administration. But it made less fanfare about this than did Elmwood. Its real attack was against departmentalism, against the efforts of proto-graduate education to recruit undergraduates into academic specialties, and against the divorce of the academic from the intellectual and the experiential. As we would expect, these differences of focus and emphasis at the two colleges showed up in differences in styles of teaching. Such differences were part of the distinctiveness of the college experience at Elmwood and Hawthorne.

Evocative and Didactic Styles

Let us begin with illustrations. At Elmwood we visited a psychology class in which the topic was "Research on Small Groups." Some thirty or thirty-five students sat in rows of separate light armchairs. (The seats were movable and could have been arranged in seminar fashion, and were so arranged on another occasion in a section meeting of the Western Civilization course.) The class began at the sound of the bell. The instructor had mimeographed a number of sociometric matrices and had put the same table on the blackboard. He then proceeded to show how Robert Bales, using such data, had derived his typology of leaders of small groups. The instructor, moving about the room, standing, and sitting on the desk, managed to convey a great deal of his own excitement about the elegance and clarity of Bales' ideas. He lectured without a break for questions or comments; the students paid attention, most of them taking notes. (On another day, the instructor set aside time for specific questions concerning materials.) About two minutes before the end of the fifty-minute class, many of the students began to put away their books. The lecture seemed extremely well organized as well as contagious in communicating the lecturer's excitement and pleasure about research on small groups. As far as we could tell, the students were diligent, although there was no way of gauging their involvement in the material.

We have termed such a style of teaching *didactic*. It was labeled a lecture rather than a discussion, although in principle there could be lectures which are more evocative and less didactic than this one, and there could be discussions that would also be didactic: oriented toward pleasing the teacher through finding the right answers. A didactic class takes for granted the instructor's greater knowledge and authority, and invites students into the material on terms set by the instructor, terms often set by his academic guild. The initiative lies entirely in the instructor's hands: the class is a production in which he is the producer, the director, the writer, while the students act at his direction and are also the ultimate audience. Even if the actors are allowed to play bit parts, this does not greatly change the mode of production.

Another class we attended was a social-science discussion section at Hawthorne in which, as it happened, small groups were also the topic. In a classroom used by the School of Education, six girls and three boys were entertaining themselves by reading the children's literature on the bookshelves while awaiting the instructor who was ten minutes late for his nine o'clock class. A group of wooden tables were arranged to form a U pattern, and the six girls all sat on one side opposite the boys. The instructor stood at the open end of the U during the entire period, sometimes walking to the blackboard and sometimes standing at the table.

He began the class by quoting from the syllabus. After reading a quotation proposing that the next logical step after studying "relations" was to study "small groups," he asked, "Why is the study of small groups the next logical step?" Variations on this question comprised the content of the period. He wrote on the blackboard the terms describing the major topics studied during this term in the social-science sequence, namely: relation, small groups, socialization, differentiation, pattern. "What we want to do is get the logical connection between 'relations' and 'small groups'."

He proceeded by asking questions and soliciting answers from the students until he received an answer he regarded as satisfying. Students also volunteered, and he called on them, at times ignoring some of the volunteers. He managed to draw out the point that moving from relation to small group was an increase in depth and a decrease in extensiveness.

The participation of the class grew as the hour went on, and most of the students volunteered at some time. The instructor's questions set up tensions of finding the "right" answer, tensions which would be dissipated when he moved on to the next point. Several times a student interrupted to make suggestions, but the instructor did not encourage him. This same student, at another time, proposed a logical but false solution to a problem; the instructor shrugged his shoulders, said "maybe," and passed on to others in his quest for the answer he wanted. Occasionally, dialogue would develop among students. The instructor would sit back and listen, and then return to the earlier point at issue. Five minutes before the hour's close, the instructor himself began to answer the major questions with which he had opened. He said that the relation among the various terms or headings was not additive. Then he stated the original question again and read the answer from the syllabus, explaining each term, such as locus and constellation.

It would seem on the surface that this second class was more evocative than the first one. Perhaps it was. Certainly it was overtly participative. Many students might well feel that they took a more active part when they raised their voices than when they were silent. But such an assumption would neglect both the vicarious evocativeness that is possible in a lecture and the over-controlled activism of a discussion where the prime task of the student is to fill in the blanks on a diagram already given. One could say that, in this second classroom, both students and teacher were subordinate to the syllabus, but the responsibility for the proper outcome remained almost entirely in the instructor's hands. The latter saw the task as getting the students to understand the syllabus, to "cover ground," or to get across a certain content. In fact, though he brought the students in as props, he conveyed somewhat less enthusiasm for his subject than did the instructor at Elmwood.

Our notes on another social-science class at Hawthorne may illuminate the differences here. This also took place in a borrowed classroom, too large for the five boys and six girls constituting the class. Here, the students clustered together at one end of a U-shaped arrangement of the tables, and the instructor sat close to the students; the effect was that of a small group huddling together in the corner of a large room. The class began with a question from one of the boys, asked just before the bell rang. Erving Goffman's article, "On Face-Work," had been assigned in the week's reading, and the student wanted to know if the article related to the concept of "patterns." The instructor responded to this as a prelude. Then he began the class by asking the group, "What impressed you most in this section?" One of the girls responded, "The article on the dyad." (She was referring to an essay by Georg Simmel on numbers and social groups which was also part of the assignment.) A boy commented, "We know these things ourselves, but we have never realized them before." A middle-aged woman asked if this article on the dyad was sociology or philosophy, and the instructor said, "Let's defer the question until we find out more about the idea of 'relation.' "

The concept of relation then occupied much of the discussion. The middle-aged woman talked of this in the light of her personal experiences, and an exchange developed between this woman and a girl sitting next to her, who disagreed with her conclusions. This exchange became heated, but the instructor did not interfere. Then he asked if a relation ends when a person dies. He mentioned a primitive tribe in which the death of a relative was followed by the adoption of a child to replace the relative. The older woman compared this to a Jewish custom, that of naming a child after a dead person. One of the students responded to this, as the instructor did also.

Only when the topic seemed to have exhausted itself did the instructor move on to something else. "What did you think of Orwell's essay, 'Shooting an Elephant'?" This elicited a few reactions, and the instructor asked if anyone could use the article to explain how a person might be led to an action violating his own ethical norms. The irrepressible woman said that one might be put into a position of feeling obligated to comply with another's demands. A boy entered the discussion in very general terms, using the word "relation" pretentiously in an apparent effort to impress the instructor. The instructor did not respond to this but sought instead to get students to talk about their own lives as a way of illustrating his questions about the Orwell essay. He asked whether any of them had ever felt themselves in a situation where, as in "Shooting an Elephant," there was only one thing to do in the light of the expectations of others.

By this time, half the class time had elapsed, and most of the eleven students had participated. The instructor tried different ways of escaping the domination of the middle-aged woman, sometimes ignoring her and sometimes encouraging others to speak in order to shunt her out of the discussion. In the remaining time, the discussion turned to dyadic and triadic relations, and students drew on their own relationships with friends and relatives for illustration. After the bell had rung, the instructor suggested they write a paper on face-work and dating behavior. Someone asked if it could be a personal experience, and the instructor said it could.

Chaotic as this class may have seemed to those accustomed to more structured classroom situations, the instructor was in charge at all times. But his effort was less to cover ground or to convey ideas than to get the students to connect what they were reading with their own experience, even at the cost of a certain fuzziness of outline. What he rewarded was never the correct answer—nor did he actually propose "correct" answers—but rather the effort by students to draw on personal observation and to gain a new purchase on it through the reading and discussion. Mere slinging of terms uncoupled with experience was negatively sanctioned. In considerable measure, what happened was not in the script. For one thing, the older, talkative woman could only barely be kept in control; she

251

was indeed meeting the payroll of personal experience, only too much of it. (In one of the classes we visited at Elmwood, just such an older woman, neither innocent nor docile, was of immense help in breaking the ice in a rather frozen discussion where that was what the instructor wanted.) At the same time, the class was not permissive or "student-centered" in the way those terms are often used, for the instructor was not seeking experience alone and uninterpreted, nor was he allowing students to assault or invade each other under the guise of candor or therapy. We could see that he must have already gone a long way toward reducing the barriers of age and rank. He appeared to use the class to evoke the experiences generated by the materials.

He did not do this in isolation, for a climate of evocativeness was consciously sought for at Hawthorne. And while it might seem that classes in the more "social" social sciences (or in some of the humanities) would lend themselves more readily to this, we found a similar climate in a class in the natural sciences.

This was a class of about half a dozen students, scheduled for eight o'clock. On the morning we visited it, the instructor arrived about eight minutes late, and the students had already begun asking each other questions about the material. The instructor came in and sat down at the head of the table; and, after the students had handed in their outlines (their reading had concerned the historical development of atomic theory), he began the discussion by asking what had led chemists (Davies and Berzelius) to propose a dualistic theory of matter. How did one of the experiments bearing on the idea of elements support the received theory as against new theory? In the state of the art at that time, molecules were thought to repel, while atoms must attract to make up a molecule. The discussion proceeded in question-and-answer fashion in an attempt to develop possible explanations or theories for the facts that were known at that time.

The instructor at one point referred to an experiment in their readings where, with electrodes and water, there was a separation of water into hydrogen at one pole and oxygen at the other. The problem then became one of developing a theory which would resolve the problem of repulsion and attraction. One of the girls made a suggestion, which the instructor restated and then diagrammed on the board. Another student criticized this. The instructor agreed with the criticism and pointed out the grounds for his view. Then the girl tried to defend her original idea against the criticism. The instructor rejected this, explaining in detail why he did so. Then he gave a hint as to how the problem had been solved historically, saying that the ideas of this girl were indeed on the right track. One had to think in terms of a "mechanical" answer (by which he meant an answer in terms of what atoms were thought to look like). Two members of the class volunteered their own ideas, and the same girl who had presented an idea earlier now proposed an ingenious model of molecules in which the atoms were arranged as on a color wheel. At one point, her model of complementary colors or atoms became complex, and the instructor said she had lost him. She then went to the board and made a diagram of it. The instructor added a new condition to the discussion to see if she could integrate this into her model. One of the boys asked if the model really did explain the facts of the experiment, and those known at the time. Much discussion then focused on the girl's model and its potential usefulness, and another student sought to add to the model. Most of the class entered in.

At this point the instructor pointed out what was unclear in the model and what it failed to take into account, and also indicated the reasons why it would have been rejected in the historical period under consideration. Another boy then suggested a new model. As the hour drew to a close, the instructor himself suggested still another model, and pointed out how the girl's model had come close to meeting the problem.

In this class, as compared with the one just described in the social sciences, the emphasis is somewhat more on readings that are to be understood than on experiences that may be shared. Even so, the instructor was not especially concerned with eliciting the correct answer, and what he rewarded in students was the contribution of something interesting, whether or not correct; the materials were a means to elicit the class, to involve it in problem-solving. To be sure, when dealing with the history of science, the instructor could count on less knowledge than when talking about dyads and human relations. But he did his best to erase differences of age and knowledge so that the students would feel free to talk and to make mistakes.[3]

One might wonder whether the examinations would provide any control over the instructor's balancing act between conveying content and creating an experience of discovery for the student. To a certain extent, the entire staff in the social sciences and the natural sciences at Hawthorne shared an ideology about their methods of teaching and the kinds of examinations they gave. These could be

answered without a premium on factual accuracy or clarity of outline. But beyond that, a certain looseness pervaded the examination
system itself, especially in the social sciences, where students were
permitted to take examinations over again and erase previous
failures and where, in any case, in the casual climate of a state
university, students did not feel that they must graduate in a four-
year lockstep.[4] Hawthorne opposed premature specialization, and,
to the degree that its students in fact wanted to prepare themselves
as undergraduates for specific careers or to acculturate themselves
in a specialty, they could do so on the larger campus outside Hawthorne. This allowed Hawthorne to maintain its sense of mission
through its tension with that larger campus. In the Hawthorne
ideology, didactic teaching was considered suitable for the development of specialists and "mere technicians," but not conducive to
meeting the kinds of intellectual and personal issues which could
prepare a student emotionally for academic life, or for comparable
professional goals.

In this ideology, in our judgment, an error is sometimes made in
seeing didactic teaching not only as authoritative, but also as
authoritarian. This psychological transposition is not automatically
justified. In our observations at Hawthorne, we saw a good many
classes in which the instructor appeared to be merely one of the
boys, sitting on the desk with his coat off, swinging his legs and
talking in hipster argot, drawing on his own experiences in order to
evoke those of the students. But such a procedure, as any student
of transference realizes, can be quite intrusive and oppressive,
stifling to a student who wants to maintain his distance and even his
individuality. Conversely, a didactic class can be conducted with
genuine warmth, simply recognizing and employing the instructor's
greater knowledge and experience.

Nevertheless, we are inclined to think that in dealing with the
sort of student body drawn to both institutions, didactic styles of
teaching have certain limitations which would perhaps be less
evident in elite colleges where the students come already conversant
with ideas and prepared to enjoy the play of the mind.

Our misgivings can be suggested by an experience on one of our
early visits to Elmwood. We had been observing classes and talking
with some faculty members about the diligence of the students, their
readiness to work extremely hard. There was some surprise at this,
for the young faculty had been recruited from leading institutions
and had come expecting to be faced with Midwestern philistinism

and a "collegiate" withdrawal of effort.[5] It appeared that the students, coming as isolated commuters, had not formed themselves into a cohesive student culture to resist faculty demands even though these were exorbitant in the light of previous high-school experience. Yet, some of the faculty were vaguely dissatisfied. They told us about what had occurred when, a few days earlier, the students in the required Western Civilization course had been asked to see a showing of *Henry V*, the Laurence Olivier film, in an effort to lend vividness and excitement to materials currently being read. To the faculty's dismay, the students had attended *Henry V* as they would have attended a lecture, with assiduity rather than delight. Anxiously and effortfully, they had sought to grasp what it was about and what they were expected to get out of it. Indeed, had the film not been required, as became evident when many other voluntary cultural events were offered at the College, the great majority of students would not have gone to the film but would have attended to their required reading, to their part-time jobs,[6] to the families with whom they lived, or to the bursts of relaxation they deemed owing to them.

Experiences of the sort typified by the showing of *Henry V* suggested to some Elmwood faculty members the limits of a didactic program even for preparing specialists. To become, for instance, a professor of English, one needs to possess more than a force-fed knowledge of Elizabethan drama, although how much more is an open question. Mere diligence is unlikely to carry a student through the rigor, boredom, and uncertainty of graduate school; some additional motivation, some at least rudimentary interest in the topic, some connection between the topic and one's inner life may also be required. To be sure, all of us know many men and women in academic life who have suffered an attrition of interest and simply go through the motions, as they might in some other bureaucratic or entrepreneurial post. But we are dealing here with students who, until they arrived at Elmwood or Hawthorne, in almost no case would have imagined becoming a professor; a schoolteacher, yes, for that was a familiar role, or an engineer, or some vaguely defined respectable white-collar job. Both colleges did, in fact, in their very first years, produce a number of converts to the academic life, who have gone on to leading graduate schools, legitimizing the possibility for later generations of students. But, when they entered as freshmen, most of them were scarcely aware of the fields of knowledge into which they are now going. A number of students we have interviewed or talked with informally have given us the impression that it was an evocative rather than a didactic type of instructor who furnished the original inspiration and impetus.

Who Is a Good Teacher?

In addition to sitting in on classes, we asked faculty members in both colleges what they considered to be a good class and what it was that made them feel they had done a good job of teaching. Here again one could see a range between the didactic and the evocative, between the communication of content and the communication of commitment or involvement. The former style is illustrated by the response of a mathematician at Elmwood to the question, "What is a good class? When do you feel you've done a good job of teaching?"

When you teach mathematics and teach something difficult and feel that the students are getting it—you can sense the reaction. A good day is when I feel I've had difficult concepts and have gotten them across.

Another Elmwood mathematician placed his emphasis less on the clarity of communication and more on the creation of an affective stance toward the subject:

I feel I've done a good job with these students in this class. Everyone distrusted mathematics when we began and dared me to get them to like it. Now they are interested. They are reading and getting together. There is a difference between active and passive students though . . . [like the active theater-goer] the active student must be part of the process . . . A good teacher is going to create this atmosphere.

An anthropologist at Hawthorne talked at length about his horror of distant and didactic teaching in large, impersonal settings. For him, a good class was one which was responsive to itself; he continued:

When no one addresses himself to anyone else's point it's a poor discussion . . . when it gets off the ground there is a certain sense of excitement, talking to each other. The instructor becomes a part of the group.

In contrast, he described a bad class:

As I was more directive, they were more silent. The class became polarized into a student-against-faculty situation . . . the students began to get the idea that they shouldn't participate, that, like high school, they should play it cool.

In this interview, nothing was said about content; and, when we observed the classes of this same instructor, it was clear that he made efforts to erase any symbols of authority that came from his knowledge and rank. For him and for others in the markedly evocative group of teachers, the ideal was a classroom in which they were, at most, first among equals, following the line of the students' own interests as brought in from outside the readings, and seeking as an outcome insight and involvement rather than skill or finesse.

Sitting in on such a classroom, the observer might suppose that no demands were being made on the students who were being encouraged or permitted to trade personal anecdotes with the instructor. Such an interpretation would overlook the demands these evocative instructors (more dominant at Hawthorne, but not wholly absent at Elmwood) made upon the students for adopting a certain style of intellectual-emotional involvement; indeed, the insistent encouragement to become an intellectual, critical of received patterns and ideas, was often extended by quite charismatic instructors who underestimated their impact, seeing themselves as only a member of the peer group. In another form of corruption, the student adopts this style of response of his instructors but not the substance of experience which the style connotes.

Adult-forming and Youth-prolonging Styles

Colleges can be seen, like other teen-age institutions, as serving simultaneously to draw young people into the adult world and to prolong their youthfulness. To the extent that colleges have become the great sorters, selectors, and gate-keepers for the academically talented, they may be thought to serve an "adult-forming" function, weeding out both the childish and the childlike and judging the young by adult standards of competent performance.[7] In this aspect of the college's function, the professors act not only as gate-keepers but also as models, however limited, of at least one possible adult role. If the student is talented and what is called motivated, the faculty member may invite him into his particular subdiscipline, exposing him to the track of his own research, and perhaps also to the intramural debates within the field. Such instructors, no matter how didactic in their style of teaching, can become dedicated to the development of students who enter their field on these adult terms.

But there is also an aspect of college which may be called "youth-prolonging." Ordinarily, we think of this aspect as extra-curricular and existing in opposition to faculty and other adult demands. But an instructor who sees himself rather less as a

257

specialist and more as a member of an intellectual subculture may value in his students precisely their youthfulness and seek to protect them against what he may regard as premature and dehydrating adult demands. To the extent that he seeks to link his students with a critical, humanistic, rational outlook on the world, it could be said that he is proposing an alternative style of adulthood rather than prolonging adolescence. Yet, it is also true that faculty members of this persuasion seek to remain young themselves, young in the sense of rebellious, open, uncommitted to specific authoritative roles. Correspondingly, they are much less eager than their more didactic colleagues to induct the student into a particular specialty; what they want of them is a greater playfulness, a release of the inhibitions imposed by the parochial past and the looming vocational future—in other words, a moratorium.[8]

Joseph Adelson describes the situation of some students who respond to the opportunity of a moratorium as follows:

. . . the student who seems untouched and untouchable is in a state of limbo . . . waiting for the proper time to commit himself. He does not feel ready to find a personal identity. . . . He is not really waiting for the right model to come along; he is waiting for something to happen inside of him. Then he will make his move.[9]

Elmwood's departmental structure and system of rigorous examinations made it difficult for faculty members, no matter how intellectual they might be as individuals, to support students in such a limbo. Furthermore, as we observed at the outset, Elmwood had begun with so vehement an attack on the low-brow collegiate culture that it may also have driven out whatever small opportunity there was for the development of a high-brow version of the collegiate: the intellectual, or Bohemian version.[10] The pressures of Elmwood itself were supported by the residual Puritanism of farmers, working-class people (in this particular area, often Fundamentalists from the South), and the ascetic patricians who, since the days of Theodore Roosevelt, have feared that Americans were going soft. Entering students at Elmwood were so clearly told that theirs was to be a no-nonsense college that they could not alter their set when exposed to an uncategorized experience such as *Henry V*. Some of the faculty concluded that, while it was possible to engender discipline in a college for students who were the first in their families to pursue higher education, only with their children could one also foster appreciation and playfulness. In the very willingness of the students to subordinate both immediate career aims and teen-age self-indulgence to the demands of the faculty, these particular mentors felt there was a certain poignancy, as if the adult-forming mission had proceeded at the expense of the youth-prolonging one.

To be sure, not all the Elmwood faculty felt this way. A history professor spoke for many when, at the end of the first year, he commented on the students and what had been accomplished with them: "On the whole, they are good. . . . We have managed to build up a reputation within the general academic world. We are tough, hard, intellectual. We mean business."[11]

What we see here is an all-too-human paradox of seeking to move in two different directions at once: on the one hand, away from an excessive task-orientation and, on the other, away from certain sorts of collegiate hedonism and laxity. This latter drive was powered, especially at Elmwood, not only by the Rickover-like post-Sputnik outlook, but also by the traditional professorial antagonism to the image of a college as a football field and parking lot surrounded by a low-paid faculty. In our own judgment, this still-prevailing picture of American anti-intellectualism is overstated and increasingly outdated.[12] But many faculty members now teaching in American colleges recall their high-school days when the football or basketball star got the pretty girls and the community's approbation while he himself, no such star, was ambivalently regarded as a grind or long-hair. Moreover, the fact that Elmwood was founded as a branch of a large state university added to the faculty's defensive insistence that their own institution should have none of the Hollywood earmarks of the collegiate big time.[13]

Simultaneously, the decline of Puritanism even in the "poor but honest" lower social strata and the reasonably full employment for the educated have made it possible for young people to be at once mobile and relaxed. In the parent state universities, students drop into and out of college with a casualness that is now also becoming the pattern in some of the elite colleges. Dropouts for nonacademic reasons are increasing as students withdraw from what they regard as the rat race in order to taste life and find a better moratorium— almost always returning to graduate eventually. In the past it has been estimated that the average student at the parent institution of Hawthorne takes eleven terms to complete an eight-term college sequence. Following Florence Kluckhohn's scheme of dominant and variant value orientations, the traditional, upwardly mobile American orientation of "doing" has been infiltrated by the variant value of "being-in-becoming"; to the extent that the adult world is seen as work-driven, "being-in-becoming" favors the youth-prolonging syndrome.[14] It becomes possible for many young people to live with a kind of double vision, at once in the youth culture with its hedonism and casualness and also in the adult-oriented future to which, in due course, they will bow. They can make a passive compromise with the minatory adults, agreeing as it were to "shape up" when the time comes.[15]

Elmwood's faculty, compared with Hawthorne's, were in the main not satisfied with this compromise, but asked of the students a more rapid "putting-away" of childish things. In winning that battle, some of the faculty, as we have seen, found that a certain dehydration had occurred; several began to ask themselves whether there were not latent values even in inter-collegiate athletics. If one could not evoke in the students excitement about a problem in calculus or in Elizabethan drama, one might at least want *some* sort of play.

In contrast, Hawthorne found itself beset with problems of a somewhat different order. For a minority of its students, the vocationalism of the commuter gave way to a willingness to try out behavior which later adult life might not permit. Some became politically active on behalf of peace or civil rights—not the student politics which is as often as not adult-oriented anticipation for the future district attorney or state legislator. Moreover, since the parent university is located in a disintegrating downtown area, a small number of students found it easy to move into flats near the campus, separating themselves in this way from parental influence and making it possible, even in the face of part-time jobs, to take part in nonacademic activities, in politics, the arts, and personal exploration.

A number of the faculty were prepared to join the students in such exploration. They would agree with Richard Hofstadter's view that to be an intellectual and not merely a mental technician requires both playfulness and piety.[16] Yet there can be a piety, even fanaticism, about playfulness, as about anything else. Some of the Hawthorne faculty rejected departmentalism and the academic disciplines so totally as to lead a small minority of their students to assume that it was sufficient to have ideas, the grander the better, the more spontaneous the better, and that this is what it means to be an intellectual. Since these faculty members were themselves the product of excellent educations, they were overly modest in assuming that their undergraduate students could reach their own level without similar preparation. And when these students pursued their more specialized courses in the parent university, they would sometimes approach them with a contempt for pedantry and for prerequisites that could alienate their non-Hawthorne instructors, setting in motion a vicious circle of mutual rebuff and distrust. Like the Bohemian graduates of some elite colleges, but with less backing either in talent or money, these students might then find themselves academically unequipped to pursue a high calling in which intellectual qualities would be valued, and emotionally unequipped to pursue a less demanding one which could not satisfy their newly discovered critical faculties. Taking the style of their instruction as its substance, they would seek to extend their moratorium indefinitely, moving on to graduate school but ever contemptuous of their specialized professors.

In saying this, we are not suggesting that education must be tailored to what the labor market and the society are at any moment prepared to accept and reward. Such a policy for education would condemn the universities to an infinite regress, and the graduates to a probable obsolescence. But we are suggesting that all education has its price, and that evocative education can overreach itself, just as didactic education can underplay the potentialities of both the student and the subject.

Nevertheless, the very fact that Hawthorne College was compelled to face these dilemmas testifies, in one aspect, to a degree of success in the experiment. All the colleges in which, according to a good many studies, a majority of the students approve and seek a nonvocational general education are elite colleges, such as Oberlin, Princeton, and Williams. Despite the pressure to enter these institutions and the competition within them for the grades that will permit later graduate specialization, it is these institutions and others like them which foster the attitude that grades are but a necessary evil, a by-product of "being-in-becoming." It is in these colleges that dropouts have increased, not for academic or financial reasons, but in pursuit of personal exploration, of meaning. In other institutions, including the great state universities, the majority of students believe themselves to be in college to learn a job or at least to learn the social skills that are marketable and desirable.[17] In these elite colleges, youth-prolonging outlooks are under pressure from adult-forming ones and, as meritocratic pressures grow, nonspecialized studies begin to seem not quite so serious as those which anticipate graduate school. At the same time, many students become anxious

261

about what their academic identity will be and seek to apprentice themselves even as undergraduates to a particular discipline in order to settle the question, or so they think, once for all. Precocious by the standards of an earlier day, such students are concerned to lose their youthfulness and to be able to say of themselves at eighteen or nineteen that they are "in" Seventeenth-Century French Literature or Plasma Physics.

As we have already noted, the dominant faculty at Elmwood had themselves studied and taught at elite institutions. Perhaps, indeed, some of them look back too nostalgically at these institutions which are changing in the ways just suggested; as a social scientist at Elmwood commented:

It's kind of hard to have an Ivy League institution without an Ivy League student body. This faculty doesn't know how to teach the students to play. I would wish that they would learn to like what they are doing. Unlike the Columbia College student, these kids don't know how to play with ideas; they are too work-oriented.

He then continued by expressing his concern about the fear students had lest they make mistakes and their inability to enjoy ideas "for their own sake." In this respect, Hawthorne was, at the outset, somewhat more successful, in part reflecting its lack of departmental structure and its cadre of faculty devoted to youth-prolonging values. Hawthorne could point in this direction because it did not have to provide the full program for its students and could rely on countervailing pressures from its parent university for those students who wanted a departmental home. Correspondingly, for a minority of its own students, Elmwood could provide a departmental identity as a new home away from home. At the same time, by building dormitories through the newly available federal loans and by recruiting residential students of higher social background than most of the commuters, Elmwood is today making possible the invention of a student culture which may eventually resist some of the faculty pressure for academic adulthood.

Both new colleges recruited faculty members who were willing to preoccupy themselves with undergraduate rather than with graduate students. Moreover, the commuter student bodies are neither impoverished and deprived enough to be "interesting," as might be the case in a small Negro college in the South, nor cultivated and brilliant enough to be attractive, as one would find at Amherst or Swarthmore. Hence, the faculty of both institutions did, in the main, possess a certain missionary spirit. Of course, as with

262

most of us, motives were mixed and considerations of career not entirely foregone. On the whole, the missions of the two institutions tended to diverge, with Elmwood faculty members more likely to be didactic and to emphasize adult-forming processes, while those at Hawthorne sought a greater evocativeness and youthfulness. But it should also be clear that both colleges possessed countervailing balances against their dominant values and that the teaching styles prevalent at each could also be found at the other. In turn, each differs decisively, even aggressively, from widely prevalent values at the parent institutions.

The newness of new institutions is itself an important asset in their success. The human experiment, as Elton Mayo observed at the Hawthorne plant of the Western Electric Company, creates in its self-generating enthusiasms the requisite dedication for its own accomplishment, no matter what other factors might be at work. Such "Hawthorne effects" minimize otherwise formidable obstacles. As we suggested at the outset, the satellite-college idea, coupled to newness, may enable a large university to liberate a newly recruited faculty from both the democratic and the authoritarian restraints on curricular innovation.[18] By the same token, it may be possible to recruit for the satellite college a faculty not only of greater dedication to undergraduate teaching, but of higher general quality than is the inherited norm at the parent institution, no matter what the latter's efforts at selective self-improvement. Even so, the half-life of innovations is seldom great since so few means for institutional self-renewal exist. With time, tenure, and tedium, once-new institutions may become adult-forming rather than youth-prolonging. When this happens, their successors will have to be found in other places under other auspices.

We are indebted to the Carnegie Corporation for support of the research and reflection reported here.

REFERENCES

1. We use pseudonyms here to protect individuals and even more to protect institutions which, because they are public and dependent on legislative and popular support, may be vulnerable.

2. For further discussion, see Gusfield and Riesman, "Faculty Culture and Academic Careers: Some Sources of Innovation in Higher Education," *Sociology of Education*, Vol. 37 (1964), pp. 281–305; also "Observations

on 'The Two Cultures' in the Context of the New State College," *School Review* (1966) forthcoming.

3. In spite of what is said here, we would certainly grant that there are many subjects that cannot be handled in a particularly evocative way: elementary language training, for example. And one of us recalls visiting a class in ancient Chinese history at a progressive girls' college, where the mandate for the instructor was to be wholly nondirective and permissive, and where only discussion, and not lecturing, gained approval. Yet even a little reading of a textbook in English gave the students hardly enough to talk about; to begin their careers by playing at being Arnold Toynbee was not sensible, and the instructor, in fact, conducted a lecturette disguised as a discussion.

4. In an unpublished doctoral dissertation, Zelda Gamson has described the ways in which the examinations were adjusted when the demands of the curriculum proved too heavy for the existing student body. We are indebted to her for many helpful suggestions concerning our own work.

5. On withdrawal of effort or restriction of output in student culture, see Howard S. Becker, Blanche Geer, Everett C. Hughes and Anselm Strauss, *Boys in White* (Chicago: University of Chicago Press, 1961), Chapters 6–8.

6. Part-time or even full-time jobs were a necessity for many of the students, but not for all. Some could have managed with loans and summer work to devote full time to being students. But in the milieu out of which they came, this would not have made sense either to them or to their families. The latter could understand that a student had to drive over to the College for Chemistry I on Monday, Wednesday, and Friday at 10:00 a.m.; they could understand that he had to take an examination. But if he were returning in the evening only for an art-cinema or a discussion of Vietnam, he might as well stay home, help fix the roof, or join the family in watching television. In any case, unsure of the future and, in the case of the girls, fearing a negative dowry, there would have been anxiety about taking a loan even when in reality it could easily have been paid off at low rates of interest.

7. Obviously, such a statement implies a rather narrow definition of adulthood. The French or American Catholic concept of "formation" is a somewhat more humane one, implying qualities beyond those necessary for upper-middle-class professional activity.

8. Erik H. Erikson, "Ego-identity and the Psychosocial Moratorium," in Helen L. Witmer and Ruth Kotinsky (eds.), *New Perspectives for Research on Juvenile Delinquency* (Washington, D.C.: U.S. Government Printing Office, 1955), p. 5.

9. Adelson, "The Teacher as a Model," in Nevitt Sanford (ed.), *The American College* (New York: John Wiley & Sons, 1962), pp. 396–417, especially 407–414.

10. For a discussion of the variants of student subcultures on American campuses, see the study of Martin Trow and Burton Clark reported in Burton Clark, *Educating the Expert Society* (San Francisco: Chandler Publishing Company, 1962), pp. 202–211.

11. It should be borne in mind that we are not describing either Elmwood or Hawthorne as they are today, but are drawing from our material certain salient themes of their first years. By the spring of 1965, Elmwood had acquired a nonconformist group of students, in some cases from outside the state, who could manage both to satisfy the (very slightly relaxed) academic demands of the institution and to provide for themselves a more intellectual, playful, and off-beat moratorium.

12. For fuller discussion, see Riesman, "The Academic Career: Notes on Recruitment and Colleagueship," *Dædalus* (Winter 1959), pp. 147–169; "The Influence of Student Culture and Faculty Values in the American College," *The Yearbook of Education, 1959* (London: Evans Brothers, Ltd., 1960).

13. Actually, as Talcott Parsons and other functionalists have pointed out, youth culture, whether in or out of college, has a latent purposiveness, notably in the opportunity it provides to cultivate expressiveness and solidarity in the face of the pressures of an increasingly meritocratic society. See Parsons and Winston White, "The Link Between Character and Society," in S. M. Lipset and Leo Lowenthal (eds.), *Culture and Social Character* (Glencoe, Ill.: The Free Press, 1961), pp. 89–135. See, for a contrasting view, Bennett Berger, "On Youthfulness," *Social Research*, Vol. 30 (1963), pp. 319–43. We are indebted to Mr. Berger for valuable suggestions concerning the role of youth culture.

14. See Kluckhohn, "Dominant and Substitute Profiles of Cultural Orientation," *Social Forces*, Vol. 28 (1950), pp. 376–93.

15. See the discussion in Matilda White Riley, John W. Riley, Jr., and Mary E. Moore, "Adolescent Values and the Riesman Typology: An Empirical Analysis," in S. M. Lipset and Leo Lowenthal (eds.), *Culture and Social Character* (Glencoe, Ill.: The Free Press, 1961), pp. 370–386.

16. See Hofstadter, *Anti-Intellectualism in American Life* (New York: A. A. Knopf, 1963), pp. 26–27.

17. Rose Goldsen, *et al.*, *What College Students Think* (New York: Van Nostrand, 1960), pp. 5–6, 208; George Stern, "Environments for Learning," in N. Sanford (ed.), *The American College* (New York: John Wiley, 1962).

18. For discussion of restraints by colleagues on pedagogic innovation, as compared with the relative freedom of innovation in research, see Christopher Jencks, "A New Breed of B.A.'s: Some Alternatives to Boredom and Unrest," *The New Republic*, Vol. 153 (October 23, 1965), pp. 17–21.

MARTIN MEYERSON

The Ethos of the American College Student:
Beyond the Protests

THE STUDENT protests at the University of California at Berkeley starting in September 1964 attracted the scrutiny of the press, magazines, and television and their audiences as well as the academics and intellectuals of the country. The Berkeley events signified to many the end of the "silent generation," the years since World War II during which college and university students presumably viewed the American scene with little, if any, critical judgment. The students of that period were thought to be silent because of the timidity created in the time of the late Senator McCarthy or because of placid acceptance of college life as a set of rites preparatory to becoming junior organization men or suburban parents. Others attributed the silence of students to their coddled and passive existence in miniature collegiate welfare states under the umbrella of the larger welfare state.

The news media, particularly sensitive to student "insurrection" because of their extended coverage of the Berkeley experience, found examples, during the following months, of student unrest at Yale, Maryland, Ohio State, Colorado, Columbia, and elsewhere. In addition, there were the campus wrangles over United States policy in Viet Nam. Many observers linked student protests to student participation in the civil rights movement, although they split on their appraisal of the linkage: some hailed the new student militant morality, implying a modern children's crusade was underway; others deplored the lack of respect for law and order, implying a dangerous political revolution was festering.

I doubt that we can appropriately label this decade's student as vocal, and last's as silent. Instead, I prefer to try to understand today's college student as a member of an egalitarian near-majority rather than of an elite minority. The major change in American higher education in the last half century is that college has shifted from being the prerogative of a few (only one in seven young people of college age went on to college as late as 1939) to being the life pattern of almost half of the young people and, in some urban areas, more than half.

With five and a half million students, a third of whom are women, American colleges and universities have a larger population than Denmark, Ireland, or any one of a majority of the independent nations in the United Nations. At such a scale, higher education increasingly contains the divergences and convergences of the larger American culture. With these vast numbers, paradoxically, even a small minority may be large. If 98 per cent of the students are "silent," and the other 2 per cent dissenting, the latter category would have over 100,000 students, a large figure for any kind of protest. (No single national group devoted to student protest is that large; for example, the Students for a Democratic Society claimed a national membership of over 3,000 in mid-1965.) However, even a relatively small number can, if concentrated at a few influential institutions, have a potent national impact.

The Berkeley protests started over political activity and speech, but then stimulated complaints about education. It is surprising to me that there is not more student debate about education; the strains within the present educational situation suggest many sources for student dissatisfaction. I do not endorse flamboyant acts like campus sit-ins any more than I endorse the Watts solution to racial tension. But I do welcome student concern about their education and hope for continued questioning and even some answers to problems of developing further the intellectual community, the preparation for jobs, and the other functions which the American campus serves.

In the shift of higher learning to a mass base of students, many strains are put on students, since they are expected to go to college if they are to share the rewards of the middle class. I shall comment on some specific complaints which students make about their life at colleges and universities. These complaints followed the free speech protests in Berkeley. They are not all new, but they have quickly become part of the current rhetoric of students seeking university reform in several parts of the country. The issue of free speech itself and the latitude for it at Berkeley have been widely discussed elsewhere, and my comments will largely be on other matters. Neither the issue nor the discussion has ended. The questions surrounding student speech and political activity must be examined in terms of the purposes of higher education for the American student, and the redefinitions of these purposes which are and should be taking place.

Education of the Majority

A century ago there were about 50,000 students enrolled for degrees in American institutions of higher education. The Morrill Act, supporting land-grant colleges, had been passed in 1862; the egalitarian principle of the frontier and its emphasis on advanced practical education as the opening to opportunity had begun to be felt. As the American dream was sketched in, the number of students enrolled for degrees rose five times to almost a quarter of a million by the turn of the century. By the end of World War I that figure had more than doubled; it doubled again by 1929 and more than doubled once more by the end of World War II and again since then.

Never in the history of the world have so many young people continued their education beyond the secondary school as in America today. Indeed, there are as many Negro students in colleges and universities in the United States as there are students in higher education in England. However, the very poor do not share America's college bounty any more than they partake of affluence in other areas.

America's colleges and universities are not limited to a social, an economic, or an intellectual elite; they are educating nearly everyone. Soon most American families will have one or more members who have had some college or university education. Today, the supermarket manager finds a job more easily if he has had some college education; at an earlier time, even doctors and lawyers could be legitimized through apprenticeship. This transformation of the college man and woman from the rarity to the commonplace is having and will have extraordinary effects upon the society—its cultural character, its labor supply and use of resources, its living and recreational preferences, its political opinions, and its levels of aspirations.

College students attend about 2100 institutions, about a third of which are under the control of state or local government (about a dozen are controlled by the federal government) and which have two-thirds of the students. There are over 100 institutions attended primarily by Negroes. In 1963, there were 57 technological schools with 133,000 students, about as many collegiate schools of art, over 200 theological schools, and 79 other separately organized professional schools. There are also about 600 junior colleges, mostly publicly controlled. (In 1917–18 there were only 46 junior colleges with an enrollment of 4,500, of which 3,600 were in privately controlled schools.)

C. R. Pace of the University of California at Los Angeles estimates that about 5 per cent of students are in prestige liberal-arts colleges such as Swarthmore, Smith, and Reed, 10 per cent in other liberal-arts colleges, 5 per cent in Roman Catholic and other strongly denominational schools, 45 to 50 per cent in universities and state colleges, 20 per cent in junior colleges, and 10 to 15 per cent in other kinds of schools, such as technological institutes. There is no formal system of American higher education as there is no national system for our elementary- and secondary-school education. With such an apparently wide range of provisions, there should be something for everyone; each student should be able to find the educational environment most suitable for developing his capabilities.

To some extent, students do sort themselves according to their images of themselves and of the colleges to which they apply; to some extent, particularly at the prestigeful private schools, the institutions mate student characteristics to institutional ones. But, to a large extent, selections are made by accidents of propinquity, pocketbook, and propaganda. Students rarely have clear notions about their alternatives.

One reason why students do not have a clear sense of alternatives is that our colleges and universities, although diverse, tend to round the edges of difference and become more like each other, as David Riesman has astutely pointed out. Student populations are becoming more heterogeneous, especially at campuses which are growing, and at the same time, when campuses are compared, the mix at each campus increasingly resembles that at many other campuses. There is a greater range of income and ethnic or religious background on many campuses than ever before. Also, there is a great range of student subcultures, as Burton Clark and Martin Trow point out. They distinguish among the collegiate students (who seek fun and games, are loyal to the symbols of the school but not its intellectual purposes), the academic (who seek traditional intellectual or scholastic goals at the school and revere the school for those qualities), the consumer-vocational (who seek a degree and thus a job opening through higher education), and the nonconformist (who seek a variety of ideas, stimulation, and creativity

269

at school and who chafe at institutional authority). Members of each of these subcultures may be found on almost all campuses, although the combinations vary.

Distinctions between private and public institutions are being blurred. Public institutions charge high fees to out-of-state students to satisfy their locally oriented legislators and citizens, and then go out of their way to attract out-of-state students to satisfy their more cosmopolitan faculties. Private institutions may give such extensive scholarship aid that an able but poor student, particularly from a distant state, can better afford to attend an Ivy League school where his living expenses as well as tuition are underwritten than to attend a public university which is "free" but where he would have to pay various fees and living expenses. Private institutions get a great deal of their support from public money, mainly from the federal government, while many public institutions receive considerable sums from outside gifts or foundations.

Colleges and universities tend to stretch themselves out of their early character: the local campuses seek students and teachers from elsewhere in the nation and the world; Catholic schools hire more lay teachers; and all compete for distinguished professors and try to make the campus attractive to these stars. Like other American enterprises, many smaller schools are trying to grow larger. The smaller schools add graduate programs if they do not already have them, claiming that they must do so to hold their faculties. To maintain a graduate program, undergraduate programs often must be expanded so that graduate students can be supported through teaching undergraduates. To keep up with the academic Joneses, colleges and universities add more and more subdivisions to older fields and encourage greater and greater specialization. It is a rare college or university which, although it may disclaim vocationalism, does not provide vocational programs. A vocationally oriented institution may seek a patina of intellectualism in the arts; one that attracts serious lower-middle-class students may want to leaven the student body with frivolous members; an institution historically aloof from local affairs may try to be of community service. Even the most sober of colleges and universities try to suggest a collegiate image (generally compounded with other images, too) in which student life is portrayed as glamorous, relaxed, and frolicsome.

Boards of trustees, administrators, and faculties at many institutions note and often emulate the developments at the pace-setting colleges and universities. Although there may be no formal system to American higher education, there is a tendency toward the mean and for extreme characteristics to atrophy, resulting in more institutional similarities. Nevertheless a crude pattern of differentiation persists. For example, twelve universities, or about one-twentieth of the number granting at least one doctorate in the ten-year period of 1953–1963, awarded 40 per cent of the total earned doctorates. About half of the remaining universities with doctorate programs graduated an average of fewer than ten per year. The same twelve universities (half of them public, half private) which award the main share of doctorates receive more than a quarter of federal monies going to colleges and universities. Another 5 per cent—about one hundred schools—get almost all the rest of federal research monies.

Endowments are also distributed unevenly. In 1960, all institutions had an endowment fund of $1,645 per student, $517 per student in publicly controlled institutions and an average of only $3,145 in privately controlled ones. This average endowment for private schools would yield a return of about $150 per student per year, suggesting that it is only in a handful of private schools with huge endowments (and annual gifts, too) that students are heavily subsidized through private funds.

Four-fifths of the institutions of higher education have under 2,500 students. These schools have only a minority of students, however.

Thus, in the seeming diversity of America's colleges and universities, perhaps a tenth of them—some very large and some very small—dominate higher education quantitatively and qualitatively. A much smaller number set the main tone for the changes which take place.

The Strain of Being Part of Neither the Elect Nor the Electorate

The status which came from college attendance has been diluted. The college student is no longer one of the happy few—he is one of the frustrated many. As higher education has become more diffused in the population, it has become, paradoxically, both more and less important to the general public and to the specific people experiencing it. The disillusionment which comes from dilution is not the simple disaffection with the familiar. It is the more complex dissatisfaction which arises out of dependence upon a relationship with little or no control over that relationship. Today's student is neither one of the elect nor part of the electorate. He no longer automatically belongs to a high-status group by going to college; too many people are going to college. Today's student cannot afford not to go to college if he has middle-class career aspirations; college is as necessary to him as secondary schooling and has not much more standing than secondary schooling had a generation ago.

Today's student is not given the privileges attached to the elect, the small group anticipated as leaders, nor have new privileges befitting membership in an electorate evolved. Most colleges are as authoritarian as high schools, and the college student is far less able to influence his relationships with teachers and administrators than he is able to retort and otherwise respond to his parents. Once the youth has made a choice of an institution of higher learning and of a field within it, he has few meaningful educational choices left. Students are on the fringe of the adult world, but not in it. They are in limbo. Many are grateful for the deferral because they can test themselves in different ways and so find their identity. Others are resentful of the deferral; they sense more keenly than they did in high school that students do not have inalienable rights or, indeed, many rights at all.

There is little in the formal life of the institution that the student can control, question publicly, or about which he can seek redress. Whether the teacher shocks him, or ignores him, or bores him, or awakens him to new vistas, or patronizes him, or argues with him, or is friendly to him, the student is dependent on the teacher's mood and interest. He is also bound by the actions of the administrators. Much of the student's extracurricular life—for example, the conduct of student residences or student activities—is controlled by the institutional administration.

If many share the station of having been to college, then mere attendance becomes less significant than marginal distinctions in the college experience. Thus, parents, the general public, and students make distinctions between private institutions and public ones, between liberal arts and professional or vocational ones, between smaller and larger ones, between those with presumed high admission standards and unselective ones, and among those with a professed character—for example, between the church-dominated school and the metropolitan school, the "grind" college or the "surfer" college, the traditional or the experimental program. Students perceive a pecking order, although they may not know its subtleties. They send half of all applications to fewer than 10 per cent of the colleges and universities.

I assume that the marginal distinctions made both by the public and by entering college students are oversimplified, and that entering college students do not match themselves correctly to their oversimplified conceptions of college. The national average of those who enter college and fail to finish is estimated at 40 per cent. The college dropout is only partly a result of faulty selection and self-selection, but misperceptions of marginal characteristics do play their part.

If education is the door to job opportunities, it is hardly surprising that as higher education becomes more a majority than a minority phenomenon, it becomes more job-oriented. When a policeman is required to have at least two years' college education, as he is in some communities, all those who aspire to jobs at this level or beyond feel more than ever compelled to go on for higher education. Most undergraduate students are in education, engineering, business, and other job-oriented programs. Even where the student is following a liberal arts program, his course choices are greatly influenced by the linkage between success in college grades and entrance into graduate school or the job market. The student is thus inclined to be purposeful, to do well in conventionally prescribed terms, and to avoid risks. When the sons of the rich dominated some of our colleges, they could afford to be academic dilettantes, to regard teachers as little better than hired hands, and to be intellectually playful, for they knew they would have no job problems after graduation. When "who one was" was the critical question for success, a Harvard or Oxford accent or a Göttingen dueling scar was the most important kind of "learning." If going to Yale would open access to the top of the social and economic ladder, a gentleman's "C" was in order. When intellectual knowledge was expected, it was of a precious nature—during two millennia, the officials of China were chosen on the basis of their knowledge of Confucian literature, just as the British civil servants were chosen on their knowledge of Homer. As Veblen liked to point out, no one could accuse such knowledge of having direct utility or of being widely held.

Today, if there is kudos for the accident of birth, it is more for talent in the genes than for the silver spoon. Also, even the rich tend to go on to graduate school and cannot afford a poor grade in a difficult subject or a record that gives the impression of academic

273

flightiness. Thus, there is much more purposefulness than before in both the job-oriented undergraduate programs and the liberal arts programs. The job focus in college, necessary as it may be, dims the light of intellectual pleasure which trial-and-error exploration can provide.

When colleges and universities were training an elite, it was easier in many ways for faculty and administrators to share their world with students. At Oxford and Cambridge, Harvard, Yale, and Princeton, the rewards of teaching included the faculty's sense— even if not articulated—that their students were the sons of the famous or were themselves apt to be famous in the future. It is more attractive for teachers to spend time with the well-prepared and potentially powerful than with the mediocre student of humble origins. The professor's frequent preference is to devote intellectual and leisure energies to colleagues or in some cases to men of affairs; he can be motivated to attention toward his students by a sense of duty, but this sense functions best when duty is reinforced by pleasure. And the pleasure the teacher gets seems to increase with the social as well as the intellectual standing of his pupils.

Thus, it may be expected that unless compensatory steps are taken, the increased democratization of the student body will elicit ideological enthusiasm from the faculty but not closer faculty-student ties.

The paradoxes, then, are many in the shift of higher education from a minority to a majority phenomenon. At the same time that college is more important to youth in the sense of being required as an opening to a career, it is less important in the sense that going to college by itself does not automatically convey high status. At the same time that knowledge about the world is vastly increasing, many students continue to view college as a purposeful path to a vocation rather than as an intellectually enrichening experience. At the same time that students need greater intellectual guidance, and perhaps moral guidance as well, from their teachers because the students are poorly prepared by previous family and school background, teachers are less attracted to spend time with the students beyond the classroom and the office hour. At the same time that there seemingly are many diverse kinds of institutions among which the applicant may choose the one that fits him best, he is constrained from a rich choice by individual circumstances (previous school record, cost, and imperfect knowledge of possible options) and by the tendency of colleges and universities to grow more like one another.

274

These paradoxes are strains superimposed upon the ordinary strains of being young, being away from home for perhaps the first prolonged time, and being from lower- or middle-class origins. (Upper-class youth often has faced some of the unsettling effects of being away from home earlier.) While the student is interacting with adults who are less accountable to him than his parents are, his parents, seeing the college experience as pivotal to later success or failure for their child, are often trying their hardest to influence his life.

The student may share the parents' view of the college as a ladder to social and economic success, but he also senses that the college years are his chance to be nonconformist. The student is peripheral to adult society, confused about sex and his identity, and also bewildered by the many course and activity and friendship offerings which are available. At a time when other students are jostling him in behavior, intellect, daring, and values, and are competing with him for prominence on campus and distinction in grades, some professors regard it as a duty to shock students into questioning their beliefs and prejudices. Even those who do not aim to reveal adult hypocrisies shake the students' accepted way of looking at the world. In all this turmoil, the student finds no unifying institutional symbolic rallying points, no clear adult models; and yet he is enjoined to have the best time of his life.

The student activism which erupted in 1964–65 at Berkeley and other schools must partially be attributed to the accumulation of student strains, particularly those of being part neither of the elect nor of the electorate, as well as to specific issues such as those of free speech. I do not wish to guess whether students will resort again to this kind of activism. I assume that only a small proportion of students on any campus are both seriously enough concerned about the conduct of educational practices, or the content of their courses, or the restrictions or requirements placed on student activities, and casual enough about their career lines to tussle with authority. But the fact remains that whether or not students actively protest the kinds of patterns they are supposed to fit on a campus, many of them are dissatisfied with these patterns. And they often have reason to be.

What then are the voiced dissatisfactions of students? Following the protest at Berkeley in 1964, some of the most articulate students focused on problems which merit fresh attention by educators, whether or not students persist in pressing for recognition of a student interest, rather than an institutional interest. The several problems which follow were prominent among student dissatisfactions at Berkeley; though not central to the main intellectual and political dissatisfactions of the students, they were closely linked with them.

In Loco Parentis

Undergraduates may jest about the college and university stance of *in loco parentis* as meaning "crazy like parents," but many of them are offended by what they see as a facade of domestic sentimentality hiding bureaucratic regulations. Residential quarters are called "houses," and some have "house mothers"; deans of men and women try to act like older brothers and sisters. But these devices do not alter the fact that administrative personnel enforce a great many rules and regulations in a manner families do not. As Edgar Friedenberg points out in *Coming of Age in America,* parents respond to children as persons, and institutions do not. Even though parents may believe their families are governed by rules, they are in fact governed by a process of mutual accommodation. Institutions can rarely respond sensitively to individual needs but can only apply general regulations as impartially as possible.

What the student quarrels with most are the rules that infringe, he thinks, upon his personal dignity. These may include rules relating to appearance; to personal behavior, including the use of liquor and drugs; to living arrangements and the access of persons of the opposite sex to them; to entertainment, including what society might consider obscene; and to political expression, including the right to listen to and advocate radical views. Certain students feel that regulations on these matters are used only to control them, and are never used for their protection; some restrictions they regard as petty and inconsequential, and therefore completely unnecessary; others they regard as infringements on their liberties, and therefore intolerable.

Some students are accustomed to much more freedom of action at home than they find at college. Others may wish to escape the supervision of the parental home. For them, the sleep-in school has a special magic. Then the student discovers that, if he lives in collegiate residence halls, the supervision he was trying to escape has followed him. Furthermore, the supervisors, using such titles as "student personnel officers," have national associations through which practices for student activities adopted at one school are quickly transmitted to others. David Boroff pointed out that at least in the 1920's at American colleges there was not such a professional fostering of the *in loco parentis* role. He said that the students' "infantilism wasn't sponsored by the administration, which these days lays down the ground rules and acts as umpire for the nursery games."

Not all students object to the restraints. Some students, particularly girls, may be grateful, for example, for parietal limits set by an outside authority on dormitory hours and visitors which relieve them from the burden of saying no. Many parents, of course, request institutional surveillance. They may demand that college regulate student life, especially for girls.

Colleges and universities would do well to offer a variety of choices to students. For minors, it might ask the parents to decide whether the school should play the *in loco parentis* role or not. Students over twenty-one might make the choice themselves. But if such a policy were followed, the institution would be well advised to caution parents that it cannot shield a young person from knowing that some students will flaunt prerogatives he does not enjoy. The university can assume responsibility for enforcing a curfew for those whose parents want them to be in their quarters at a certain time; it cannot guarantee that the other students will not carouse all night, setting a "bad example."

Living Arrangements

At Berkeley, less than 12 per cent of the seniors of either sex live in residence halls, although a majority of the freshmen live there. Of all students, graduates and undergraduates, under 15 per cent live in university residence halls (including International House) and about 15 per cent live in fraternities, sororities, approved and cooperative housing. Only 8 per cent live at home with parents (a decrease from almost 20 per cent ten years earlier) and 5 per cent live in university apartments for married students. The remaining 60 per cent live in private apartments and houses, or in rooming houses.

Most students choose not to live in university-run facilities, and the university chooses not to supply housing for most students. The goal has been to house one-quarter of the single students.

The students complained that the university was interested in equalization and standardization of living quarters, and not in meeting their diverse needs. Residence halls, they said, are built primarily for ease of maintenance and administration. If they are designed at all for the student, they are designed for one kind of student—the collegiate student who likes to socialize, who does not want to be bothered about food even to the extent of choosing a restaurant to go to, who is willing to share a room, and who is not individualistic in study habits, creative abilities, or anything else. What they would like is differentiated housing, some very minimal, for those who just want shelter and want a "home" elsewhere in the university at the library, the coffee shop, the laboratory. Others want single rooms, where they can study quietly, and intellectual and cultural facilities such as a good library and a music room on the premises, and a chance to meet with faculty members. Others seek low-cost housing for married students, claiming that these are the students most at the mercy of a harsh private-housing market, and that the university has a duty to protect its most vulnerable members. Others want facilities in which they can express themselves, by such means as painting the walls or cooking.

The students have gripes about food, lack of a quiet setting for study, curfew regulations, and so on. Many were upset about the lack of flexibility on the part of a university which has 27,000 students but offers a standardized room, a standardized price, a standardized tie-in of room with food, a standardized set of ancillary lounges and facilities. A student who is ready to sacrifice other space in order to maximize private study space does not have the choice available to him; nor does he have other options except those incidental to the fact that some buildings are newer than others.

Administrators and some faculty point out that the housing accommodations were provided in the traditional manner under the strain of rapid growth, that students are not compelled to live in university-run facilities (and Berkeley has a great diversity of other close-by living arrangements), and that some students are being satisfactorily housed. However, both faculty and administrators are becoming more sensitive to the diverse housing requirements of students.

Down with Administration

At Berkeley, one of the student dramatizations of complaints was the IBM card on which was printed, "Do not fold, spindle or mutilate," and which was worn as a badge. Students, resenting lines and forms, resenting impersonality and the frictions of a large student body, resenting rules and restrictions, resented the feeling that they were as manipulated and undistinguishable as an IBM card. Objecting to what they regarded as the machine character of universities, the students, like the Luddites in England in the early nineteenth century, wished to smash the machine. Their message, like the message of the Luddites, had an easy contagion. Also, as in the case of the Luddites, it readily resulted in countermeasures by the larger society which wished to protect its institutions.

Part of smashing the machine, to the students, meant casting out those in authority. (Another favorite badge was the button, "Abolish the Regents.") Anti-administration feeling by students is no doubt widespread at many universities and is not confined to those who vocally protest; this feeling is reinforced by faculty criticism which regards administration at best as a necessary evil, at worst as an unnecessary evil. Among epithets I have heard about academic administrators are that they are inept, inefficient paper-pushers or, in other words, weak and ineffectual; they are also accused of being autocratic, compromising hypocrites. For some, it may be the very nature of an administrator, acting as a distant but substitute parent, that has become unacceptable. To those who feel the generational conflict most ("you can't trust anyone over thirty") the words of Bob Dylan, the folk-singer, have become a theme: "Come mothers and fathers throughout the land, And don't criticize what you don't understand. Your old road is rapidly aging. Please get out of the new one if you can't lend a hand/for the times they are a-changing!"

The anti-administration bias was given intellectual muscle by what has come to be called the new student left. Maoism has some appeal—its spare and lean economic and political order attracts the daring (and a radical has to be daring, by definition) more than the soft, bourgeois, bureaucratic, old-style Russian communist. But it would be a mistake to see student protests as an instrument of Maoism or other Marxist doctrines, even though the leaders of such radical groups would like nothing better than to inflate their role. Much more important, I think, are the tactical approach and the ideological implications of the civil rights movement which probably has more in common with turn-of-the-century anarchism than with Marxist doctrine and organization.

Given the linked membership of the civil rights groups and the student protest groups at Berkeley (many of the student leaders had devoted themselves earlier to civil rights work in the South), it is not surprising that direct action was used as the means to get attention from other students, faculty, university administration, and the government of the state. The civil rights movement had had the problem of getting attention to its principles and proposals, and it had learned that ideas are not so much kept from public expression as they are drowned by competing ideas in television programs, news stories, books, and magazines. Increasingly each claimant on the public ear seeks to amplify his message. The young people who lead the civil rights movement discovered that actions—particularly disobedient ones—are an excellent means to capture the interest of their elders, although not always a sympathetic interest.

The protesting students are more sophisticated in their condemnations than in their proposals. For example, some of them discount the notion that what is public is bureaucratic and what is private is enterprising (the prevalent anti-administration attitude in America); they perceive the pernicious effects of bureaucracy even in cultural activities and in activities such as the poverty program, which, to them, conceals its failings behind a cant of welfare slogans.

Devoid of a coherent interpretation of the world, protesting students at Berkeley often form a loose coalition on specific issues. They say they reject hierarchy within their own organization and they scorn the hierarchy of other organizations. They like to think that each member is totally committed to the cause. Inside some student groups the democratic ideal of the town meeting is revered, although the behavior is often autocratic. Students sometimes refer to the work of Mary Follett, the administration specialist of a generation ago, who was deeply attached to grass-roots participation in decisions. The students distrust those in power. They feel that those in power are corrupt, and they want to confront the policy-maker with their own force of dedication and militancy.

There is a tendency to overestimate the power of the administration, to see all issues in terms of polar viewpoints, and to regard any supporter of student protest who happens to side with the administration on a particular question as a "sell-out." Even faculty and administrators who happen to be less than satisfied with the cumbersomeness of university administration, recognize, as the students do not, the efficiencies of a division of labor, the necessity of full-time devotion to specialized tasks, and other Max Weber-type characterizations of the effective bureaucratic organization. They are more eager to improve the workings of the machine than to destroy it or give it a smaller, less powerful mandate.

Sandbox Government

Student government has never amounted to very much in most American colleges and universities. American higher education in the last century grew out of a graft of the Germanic autocratic scholarly tradition (in which little provision was made for the non-academic life of students) and the English residential pattern (in which the rules of a comfortable monastery were approximated). Neither pattern was conducive to providing students with more than a feeble voice in the affairs of the university. Nevertheless, most American colleges and universities do have some kind of student government, and where they do not, the student government may have been voted out of existence by the students, as has been happening at some Eastern private institutions.

But it is also a rare college or university where students do more than hold discussion forums and publish a student newspaper or magazine. They may seem to run economic enterprises such as book stores, but these, if they are large, are in the hands of a paid staff and are subject to intervention by the administration. By and large students have little involvement in student recruitment, curriculum, grading, policies for student-teacher relations including student evaluations of teachers, and campus rules and regulations. A few colleges with clearly defined aims of student participation—Antioch is a prime example—have students take part in almost all decisions.

At Berkeley the sophisticated students have regarded student government as playful pretense—their term is "sandbox government"—for they argue that even though the student government is nominally in charge of assets worth millions of dollars and its officers have the perquisites of junior executives, including private offices and university cars, and secretaries, student government is foreclosed from any actions in areas that matter. It can only rubber-stamp administration wishes. Other students, particularly preprofessional ones, are not scornful; they simply are not interested in anything outside their own field. The academic students working for high grades begrudge time to student activities. At Berkeley and at many other large universities, it is a rare election in which more than one-quarter of the students vote. It is even tremendously difficult to find candidates to fill posts on time-consuming but interesting assignments such as the judicial committee or the newspaper, let alone to be poll-watchers.

Those who have been attracted to student government at Berke-

ley are mainly a small group of conventional students who are motivated by personal advancement and a small group of radical
students who seek ideological advancement. The latter group is not
necessarily devoid of overtones of personal advancement, but they
do stand on a platform. Two major areas that this group at Berkeley
wants removed from administrative control are the budget (for
example, they wish to switch funds from support of the band to the
student bookstore) and the right of a compulsory student government to take, and make known, stands on off-campus issues such as
the war in Viet Nam.

The most extreme proposal for self-government advocated by
students at Berkeley was the establishment of the principle of *co-
gobierno*. This principle was first exercised at the University of Cor-
doba in the Argentine, and literally means co-government, wherein
students and faculties jointly run the university. The *co-gobierno*
principle dominates Latin American universities where professors
are generally part-time, the administration is weak, and students are
almost the only full-time, strongly motivated group within the university. There was almost no faculty support at Berkeley for this
approach to governing the campus except in the area of student
conduct.

In the past, there was less friction over the role of student government. Those students who were attracted to the essentially innocent character of sandbox government voted and held office; those
who found it inconsequential, ignored it. However, because of the
open dissatisfaction of some students at Berkeley with the role of
student government, even the more usual participant in the student
government has been prodded to seek a new definition and meaning
in student government. At other campuses, too, various student
groups are asking for a greater voice in educational affairs. Though
faculty and students may find common cause on other issues, they
are likely to be divided on this one.

Attention from Teachers

In the wake of the Berkeley protest, horror stories were reported
about education amid 27,000 fellow students. A senior student, for
example, claimed he could not get into graduate school because he
could not get letters of recommendation from professors. He had
attended only large lecture classes and sections led by teaching
assistants. No professor knew him well enough to write a letter of
recommendation about him.

Some of the more articulate students complained about teaching-assistant education and pressed for small classes, with the Oxford-Cambridge tutorial system as a goal. They did so in ignorance of the fact that some Oxbridge students are weary of tutors who they claim invade the privacy of their lives under the guise of intellectual intimacy. Many Oxbridge students and teachers are dissatisfied with the educational impact of the tutorial also, wherein hard-pressed tutors are bored and exasperated with individual sessions, and wherein individual tutorials are giving way to group ones anyway.

There is no simple answer to class size. Some teachers are at their best when they are lecturing to a large audience. Other teachers do not lecture, they discourse, and need the intimate response of a small group of students. Some students respond best to the stimulus of the large class and the almost anonymous, delayed response in the written examination and paper; others are stimulated by the seminar discussion.

There is no simple answer, either, to the use and abuse of teaching assistants. The teaching assistant, closest in experience and age to the students, can be more responsive to their needs than the older professor; under ideal circumstances, the teaching assistant should himself be so recently exposed to the newest findings and undertakings in his field that he would reveal the drama of the frontiers of knowledge, rather than the dreary wastes of the backwaters. Many of the new discoveries and techniques are not in the older professor's storehouse of knowledge—they are being newly and rapidly created. The young, alert teaching assistant, under ideal circumstances, may be at least as well equipped to convey new ideas and information laterally as the established professor is able to do hierarchically.

In actual situations, teaching assistants are often given more responsibility than they are capable of handling—that is, they are regarded as inexpensive and lowly teachers but suitable enough to make up exams, grade them, direct student work on research papers, as well as to hold discussion meetings. Thus, they are overworked and undersupervised as well as underpaid; to top this, they are frequently inexperienced teachers, unmotivated to do better because they are pressed to follow their own studies.

The more I met with discontented students, the more I realized that they were not so much objecting to instruction by teaching assistants, or to the large size of classes. They were objecting to being neglected. This was true for graduates as well as undergraduates. Some felt that the teachers were devoting their main energies

283

to research, to outside commitments, to committee work, to their families, rather than to the classroom. Others felt neglected intellectually out of class; they did not have an opportunity to discuss the new ideas that were troubling them (which might, incidentally, be old ideas to their professors). Others felt neglected socially— they felt that they never got to know their teachers as persons and were not known as persons to their teachers. Interestingly enough, many of these students who objected to intercollegiate athletics were seeking the kinds of ties coaches and athletes so often have with each other.

It became fashionable at Berkeley for students to blame teacher neglect on the pressure on faculty to publish. They urged that "good" teachers be given tenure despite lack of publications, forgetting that a teacher who did not contribute to the development of his field would often have little to say in five or ten years, let alone twenty. They also blurred the designation "good"; for example, students who get high grades frequently choose different "good" teachers than students who get low grades. And the students failed to recognize that the impact a teacher makes may not be directly related to how well and widely liked he may be. There have been great physics professors, for example, who have been ignored by all but a handful of students, but those few students went on to become the great physicists of the next generation.

Many of the proposals to get teachers closer to students on American campuses have a somewhat defensive tone, as though faculty had to be led to do their duty. We might as well recognize that faculty have many pulls away from their students, but that they also have many pulls toward them or they would not have become teachers. The problem is how to appeal to these latter kinds of pulls in strengthening faculty-student ties.

For example, professors often do not enjoy going to student living quarters for purely recreational purposes; they may feel ill-at-ease, just as a student feels ill-at-ease going to the office hour of a professor without a specific question. Combining social and intellectual activities can be very fruitful. For example, many professors and students enjoy work breaks at their offices, labs, or libraries. When lounges are set up at work places and refreshments are available, faculty and students talk with each other more casually, regularly, and naturally than they do at formal departmental teas when everyone is on his good behavior.

The daily informal teas at the University of Chicago social science lounge are an excellent model for the relaxed intermingling of faculty, students, and visitors. Faculty-student lounges are splendid supplements to the usual segregated student lounges in the student union or dormitory, and the segregated faculty club. Of course, the work-place lounge serves to reinforce departmental ties rather than interdepartmental ones.

Another way to create faculty-student bonds is through experimental educational programs. When faculty members are enthusiastic about an educational experiment, their enthusiasm is contagious, and their students cannot help but share in the process as well as the product of the experiment. While I think that the Hawthorne approach (the Western Electric study which showed that production rose under difficult as well as pleasant experiences, proving that what was important was being part of an experimental group) can be abused, in most colleges and universities it suffers from underuse rather than overuse.

Student Grades and the Grading of Teachers

The students at Berkeley who complained the loudest about the indignities of students being graded were the strongest advocates of schemes in which teachers would be graded by students.

Students objected to such abuses of grading as the inequalities which spring from the different attitudes of various teachers toward grading (some easy, some hard; some with an absolute standard, others marking on a curve; some capricious, others too rigid). Students are irked by a system which equates an A in quantum physics with an A in a less complex subject. They resent knowing that at institutions with lower academic standards, students can get high grades with less effort than at an institution with more exalted academic standards. They point out that the students are not uniform, the courses are not uniform, the teachers are not uniform, and even the competitor schools and colleges are not uniform; thus, with all these unique elements of education, there cannot appropriately be a rigid, quantitative, standardized set of measures. The students did not draw the analogy of grades in the education system, as David Riesman had, to money in the marketplace, but they might have done so, for they felt that numerical weights were being placed on qualitative relationships, and often for capricious reasons, and that grades were the leveler, giving a false comparison between immeasurable experiences.

The students concerned believed that these abuses could be corrected only by abolishing grading. They claimed that marks discouraged intellectualism and encouraged grubby mediocrity, that students were coerced into learning what pleased their teachers and not what concerned and interested them. Some even asserted that the establishment funneled new members into the society through the grading system which measured how docilely students absorbed the values of the establishment. Moreover some students claimed that the necessity of putting their attention to getting good grades was so distasteful that they lost all love of the subject. Here they paraphrased Einstein's autobiographical attitude:

. . . one had to cram all this stuff into one's mind for the examinations, whether one liked it or not. This coercion had such a deterring effect that, after I had passed the final examination, I found the consideration of any scientific problems distasteful to me for an entire year. . . . It is in fact nothing short of a miracle that the modern methods of instruction have not yet entirely strangled the holy curiosity of inquiry; for this delicate little plant, aside from stimulation, stands mainly in need of freedom. . . .

Student complaints about grading are matched by those of the teachers. However, the faculty more often see grading as a necessary evil and see some compensatory advantages, which the students do not acknowledge. Professors say that students are highly competitive and despite their complaints wish to be gauged. Defenders of grades point out that no matter how they may vary from course to course or instructor to instructor they do have a logic. Moreover, grades and the examinations, laboratory work and papers on which the grades are based, are teaching instruments which help students organize material, grasp the central character of a course, and otherwise prod students to do what they might put off doing, even though their intentions are good. Grades serve as both a carrot and a stick in the educational process, and many professors feel both are necessary.

The student clamor for the grading of teachers is a bid for better teaching—the students feel that no one knows better than they who is a good teacher and who is not, and that nobody else much cares. They point to the failures of faculties to weed out poor teachers, to encourage good teaching, and even to check on teaching abilities. The students resent the fact that publication is the prime guide to hiring and retention practices.

The faculty's usual retort to this student complaint is that students are incapable of making competent judgments of teachers. They are deemed incapable because they are immature and laymen in contrast to the teacher's expertise. They are also deemed incapable because of their own highly involved relationship to teachers —students are biased in diverse ways, some wanting to be intellectually spoon-fed, some wanting to be entertained, some wanting political daring, some wanting an easy course. Teachers do not want to cater to student whims or pressures any more than they wish to cater to the whims or pressures of alumni or other groups who feel they have a claim to judge the content of courses or the quality of teaching.

Unfortunately, teachers, like many other professionals, have acquired a number of protective devices which shield them from direct evaluation of part of their professional performance. Judgment of publications and departmental, institutional, or community service is done by a faculty member's peers and by the academic hierarchy, but no one inspects classroom activities. This circumstance is exacerbated by the lack of clear definitions of the values and goals of higher education; without such clarity it is extremely difficult for anyone, including fellow members of the teaching guild, to fashion standards of judgment on teaching quality.

The Years Ahead

The issues churned in the wake of the protests at Berkeley are part of the rhetoric of university reform. Most of these issues were already part of the rhetoric of reform on various campuses around the country and were used afterwards at Berkeley to justify, and even more, to supplement the free-speech protests. I have not focused on the protests themselves, and I shall not try to forecast whether or not there will be further dramatic confrontations of authority at Berkeley or at other universities or colleges. I do caution against any glib labeling of this generation of students as vocal, committed, moral, or rebellious. I agree with Professor Joseph Katz who commented, after concluding a five-year study of students at the University of California and Stanford University, that "in spite of recent student activism, the primary need is still to wake up students, not to constrain them. They rank highest their own individual careers and future family life. Involvement in international, national or civic affairs and helping other people are ranked astonishingly low."

But the issues I have raised—and others as well—merit scrutiny and action by university faculties and administrators. The rights and responsibilities of students must be worked out afresh in light of the new mass base of students. Among the specific questions to be reviewed are the nature of due process in disciplinary action against students, what types of off-campus behavior might result in academic penalties, the kinds of contractual relations students have with an institution. There is a growing set of legal cases helping to define student rights on campus. Colleges and universities ought not, however, to wait for the courts. The great questions are not so much legal ones as intellectual and moral ones which students, faculty, and administrators should not evade.

There are many ways of coping with the particular issues raised in this paper. Not all student complaints are justified; even justified complaints cannot always be rectified. But the students ought to be essential and welcome partners of a joint endeavor and not a passive and silent part of an educational equation. In government, in industry, and in universities, we have an important tendency to believe that a change in policy requires an all-or-none approach rather than a trial or partial approach.

For example, on grading, students might be permitted to take a few courses outside their major field, without grades, as at Princeton, or new approaches to grading might be tried out with small groups of students. After some experience the new procedure should be kept, discarded, or extended. Why should the grading pattern not be evaluated, if only for the faculty's and administration's enlightenment? (When we made an audit of grades over several years at Berkeley, we were surprised to learn, for example, that one department gave 48 per cent "A's" to freshmen and sophomores while another gave only 8 per cent.)

I have suggested that student-faculty ties might be furthered through various means. Students and teachers could meet informally and as a casual extension of their shared intellectual life at workplace lounges rather than more awkwardly at an arranged tea or other social event. Also, faculty and students could jointly participate in new and relatively small educational ventures, each imbued with the enthusiasm of sharing fresh educational paths. But there are other ways, including public service tasks for the community, in which the idealism of both the young and the old may be joined to practical advantage.

Students cannot be regarded as identical and be fitted into identical living accommodations any more than they can be fitted into identical intellectual experiences. Different student subcultures have different values they wish to achieve in housing, and, as far as possible, the university ought to accommodate their desires. Some students may tolerate or even appreciate the traditional university role of *in loco parentis;* some parents may insist upon it. Other parents may not demand it, and some students may reject it. I think the time has come for some colleges and universities to relinquish much of their *in loco parentis* role.

One of the most remarkable characteristics of America is its open-endedness and its willingness to adapt to changing circumstances. We have done this in education, particularly in expanding educational opportunities to vast numbers, in a way not even hoped for in other countries in the world.

There is, however, a possibility that, as more and more people go on to education beyond high school, the offerings provided students will not reflect the different interests among them. We cater to majority tastes and choices in most fields, only reluctantly recognizing that minority tastes in films, in cars, in music, in food may represent very large groups. (An American minority may be larger than the population of France.) It is not surprising that we cater largely to majority tastes in higher education as well. Yet, if the number of students in higher education increases as rapidly as we expect, in about fifteen years the present number of students may be only half the total. With such vast numbers of college and university students, minority interests of student subcultures could fill many campuses. One of the prerequisites for high quality will be the provision of more educational diversity for these minority interests.

No doubt many colleges and universities will grow larger and many new institutions will be founded. As the number of college students rises, we must expect tremendous growth pains. We shall also have an extraordinary opportunity to conserve the most valuable aspects of present American education and to change, renew, and improve the rest.

As new schools are founded, we shall, if we exert our options, be able to develop them with new educational philosophies, or with known ones, newly clarified. We have shown relatively little innovation in recent years either in the ends or in the means of higher education. A few small liberal arts colleges, such as St. John's or Antioch, continue to be our sports. New schools such as Hampshire College, which prefaced its founding by asserting that it was concerned primarily with new means rather than ends in education,

289

may help revitalize the thinking about how new schools can create a special character.

I do not deplore the recasting which is taking place within each campus: the religious school which is growing more secular, the liberal arts school which is adding graduate and professional programs, the technological institute which is setting up humanities and social science wings. However, there is a danger that the student will find a sameness about educational institutions, that they may become as bland and uninspired as turnpike restaurants, clean and wholesome though the food may be.

Instead, internal diversification, particularly at large institutions, can provide the student with clear sets of educational choices so that he multiplies rather than reduces his possibilities for self-realization. Not only could the student choose among institutions with different educational patterns and, for that matter, different mixes of student subcultures, but he could have the opportunity for important choices within the institution as well. Thus, at a large university such as Berkeley, an undergraduate should be able to choose, as I have urged, among a St. John's at Berkeley, an Antioch at Berkeley, and many other options.

I predict that many if not most of the new colleges and universities will be in or near big urban centers. The rural bias of American culture during the periods in which the early schools and later the land-grant institutions were founded is gone. America is now largely urban in population and focus, and it is the countryside that has become a nice place to visit but not to live in. Urban areas provide the art, the music, the theater, the cultural and recreational excitement which more and more Americans seek and which students and faculty wish to be near.

Urban areas are also the locus, the laboratory, for many of the problems people at universities want to study. I recall the facetious comment of a Yale president that Harvard is so outstanding because it is in a miserable metropolitan area and thus has more delinquency for its sociologists to study, more crime for its lawyers, more disease for its medical students.

If new institutions locate in urban areas, they will not be required to install a full set of residential, eating, and social facilities and services. These can be obtained, at least in part, from the existing provisions in cities and suburbs. I make this point less because of the financial savings that may be involved and more because I believe a larger proportion of students will not want colleges and universities to interfere with their personal lives. Residence halls will not atrophy. They will be attractive to some students, especially if the halls are subsidized. And some schools will probably make new attempts to integrate teaching facilities into residence arrangements. (Extensive programs of this kind are expensive, however. For example, Harvard's undergraduate houses probably have a current replacement value of $35,000 per student.) But if urban universities do not have to depend upon building residential quarters for all their students, then some students will be freed from the restrictions that go along with university-run quarters, and many urban students will be able to attend these schools who could not afford the expense of living away from home in supervised or unsupervised quarters.

If colleges and universities seek the cosmopolitan attributes of a metropolitan location, they will also contribute to the cosmopolitan character of the community in which they locate. The life of the city and of the university will be reciprocally enriched. Some tension between the community and the university is, of course, also inevitable, and this tension is not confined to ideas.

Most of all, as the college population grows, the schools get larger, and many of them, as I suggest, start in or near metropolitan areas, the problem will be to remember that faculty and administrators should be there more for the benefit of the students rather than the other way around. A new partnership hopefully will emerge in which students and teachers will pursue broad intellectual questions as well as specialized academic and professional ones. This kind of academic community can best be achieved in an atmosphere where diverse opportunities for students flourish. A new academic *ethos* of diversity and yet community will require far more spontaneity in organization than educational institutions commonly have exhibited.

This article is reprinted from a book on *Higher Education in the United States,* edited by Robert A. Goldwin (Chicago: Rand McNally, forthcoming 1966). Copyright © 1965 by the Public Affairs Conference Center, The University of Chicago. All rights reserved.

DAVID M. GORDON

"Rebellion" in Context: A Student's View of Students

HARVARD COMMENCEMENT DAY, June 17, 1965: Trumpets, brightly
hooded robes, and dignitaries—and 1,091 of us in black cap and
gown—all gathered to celebrate our admission to the "fellowship of
educated men." The spectacle dragged on for nearly three hours,
and I spent a few of those vanishing college moments wishing that
the many commentators on "The New Student Generation"—who
emerged from the libraries following Berkeley's Free Speech Demonstrations—had been there to interpret the proceedings. I started
fancying what they might have written: "Amidst the double chins
of the Establishment's representatives," I could almost see them
saying, "a solid phalanx of determined young rebels marched out to
meet society. Expressions of disdain veiled their rejection of the
'Power Structure' and all it stood for. United at last, they rose to
receive their degrees, a new and vibrant force in America."

As the hours passed, I gradually began to wonder—much more
than I had before—how accurate all those post-Berkeley articles had
been. I glanced around at my classmates, supposedly buckling under
the burden of "alienation," and was struck not by their "radicalism,"
or by their "idealism," but by their incredible diversity, by their sheer
resistance to analysis.

And many months later, now that I look back on my years at
Harvard and at what I've read about my own student generation,
I marvel at how sloppily most analysts have plied their trade. Not
only have they misinterpreted in many cases the *nature* of student
"radicalism," but they have also much more seriously misjudged its
significance. Vietnam, the civil rights movement, and the Berkeley
demonstrations notwithstanding, our generation is simply not astir
with the whisperings of revolution. Some of us are activists, to be
sure, but some of us are also blissfully apathetic, some of us are

professional scholars already "on the make," and some of us are nothing much at all.

Many commentators, first of all, make the pardonable mistake of assuming they can pin labels to our jackets to explain the noisy phenomena they see before them. And it is not simply that most of us resent being lumped together under one generic catchall. More than that, most of us—like decades of students before us—are too impetuous, and perhaps still too young, to be consistent in our thoughts and acts. Whether in politics or in our private lives, we seem to move from day to day, reacting as our slim store of experience suggests. Ideology and its guidelines are not very important. Inconsistency, when it crops up, is greeted with a kind of lighthearted indifference. And the question at hand is always much more relevant than the dictum of last month or the contract agreement signed the year before. A SNCC worker spoke for many of our age when, addressing himself to accusations of Communist influence with the civil rights movement, he said: "I'm going head-on into this stuff. I don't care who the heck it is—if he's willing to come down on the front lines and bring his body along with me to die, then he's welcome."[1]

Second, probably too many who look at the modern student assume that elements in society—like the archaism of an older generation or the banalities of the middle-class job—are purely and simply the sources of and the targets for student protest. The problem remains, of course, that virile and verbal protest is the way of life among only a small percentage of students today—at Harvard, I would guess, certainly no more than 10 per cent. What analysts fail to explain, by looking for sources of protest in society writ large, is the "normality" of the very large majority. Nearly all of us face the same general world; only a few choose to react against it. Michael Miller, an ex-graduate student at Berkeley and someone who has lived inside a world of student protest, makes the point in confronting generational explanations of recent student behavior: "Generational conflict, however, is so ancient and archetypal a social mechanism—certainly it functions in almost every revolution, political or artistic—that it affords little insight into the campus turmoil."[2]

What needs to be done in trying to understand undergraduates, then, is to consider the entire four years of college and not merely the fleeting moments of rebellious glory, to glance around, further, at both the very visible student *and* the relatively invisible. The four-year development of most students' attitudes reveals more, certainly, than the disjointed moments of outrage among the few. In taking this glance myself, I can only underscore my embarrassment at the few generalizations which will inevitably emerge. There were times during my four years at Harvard when I was unshaven and degenerate one day, and nattily clean-cut the next. I, for one, would have resented someone's imputing the resolution of my identity crises in the meantime. And when I do seem to generalize about college students, I must add, I do so only for my own college, Harvard, for elements at Berkeley, where I was brought up, and for some students in Alabama, where I spent last summer.

Graduate School Lies Ahead

The first task in trying to understand college students is necessarily to consider the context in which they play out their undergraduate years. For Harvard students—and a good many others around the country—that context is undeniably clear. They conclude very early in college that society asks of them a fixed role in life, a career in which they will become specialists—for the whole of society appears to their newly opened eyes to be built out of small, die-cast parts. And they conclude soon thereafter that almost any career with passably attractive possibilities will require a graduate degree, in some size, shape, or form—for the chance of finding an interesting career without such credentials seems hopelessly slight. Although some students pay less attention than others to the problem of graduate-school admission, and some students resent more acidly than others the requirements of professionalization, the fact that most students *expect* to enter graduate school lingers inescapably in the background. Many come to see their four years as only a brief respite before their serious work begins. Others search frantically for that proverbial "last fling" before their "real" lives get underway. Whatever the results, the attitudes with which a student looks ahead to graduate school can have an immense impact on his attitudes as an undergraduate. It would be superficial to tackle the substance of those four years of college without some sense of the shades of student approaches to graduate school.

Statistically, the vastness of the graduate dimension to undergraduate life at Harvard seems unmistakable. Of my own class of 1965, 71 per cent entered graduate school immediately, and 85 per cent intended to enter some kind of graduate school eventually.[3] At the same time, the motivations of that 85 per cent varied widely from total commitment on one extreme to resigned submission on the other. For instance, a solid 40 per cent of those who are studying further in the arts and sciences (or 12 per cent of the entire class) have no intention of entering careers in education or research. For them especially—and for many others as well—study in graduate school represents a variety of sometimes subliminal concerns.

Undeniably, to begin with, worries about the draft affect nearly everyone; they totally dominate the lives of many. Several years ago the draft was something students could face with a touch of equanimity. But now that the prospects of induction and the chances of combat duty have escalated along with the war in Vietnam, students try to avoid the threat as if the draft notice itself were promise of certain death. When I was a senior, in the spring of 1965, the situation was sufficiently relaxed so that students could at least spice their concern about the draft with a dash of humor. There were endless hours of discussion among my classmates, many of them hoping to unwind from college by an aimless post-graduate *Wanderjahr,* all of them trading secrets on how to escape the Selective Service. For every senior who had a clever tip on how to fail the physical examination, there were two more who had discovered some royal slush fund providing a year's undisciplined study at a foreign university. And for every senior who decided to dare the draft by staying temporarily out of graduate school, there was at least one more who went straight into graduate school solely because it provided certain sanctuary from Uncle Sam's all-inclusive grasp.

Now, of course, no sanctuary is fool-proof, and those same endless discussions have taken on a new tone of urgency. Without having the statistics before me, I am sure that the percentage of students entering graduate school immediately after college has sky-rocketed far above the 71 per cent figure for my own class, just a year before.

The pervasiveness of these attitudes about the draft would seem at first sight to have two additional implications. Neither, I suspect, is quite so significant as it might appear. It must seem especially shortsighted, first of all, for students to enroll in a graduate school which will very likely determine the nature of their careers only because any school is better than the army. And yet, as I have said, most students decide quite early that they will end up going to graduate school anyway, no matter what else they do. The draft serves only to make their choice seem a bit more pressured—and a bit more bitter—than it might otherwise have been. Second, the desperate avoidance of the draft would seem to suggest a conscientiously unpatriotic pacifism among my classmates. Again, the surface belies the internal realities. Many of my friends who cared so little for the thought of fighting in Vietnam came upon their views in relatively straightforward fashion. They acquired political consciousness in a period since 1955 when the Cold War was thawing and strictly anti-communistic patriotism was not necessarily required. They had become accustomed to people speaking of the complexities of the problems of the underdeveloped world; they had always assumed that the Vietnamese situation related to these complexities more directly than to the problem of Communism. Quite naturally, I think, the notion of killing people they were previously told ought only to be pitied seemed paradoxical, to say the least. These extremely simple reactions leave little room, I would guess, for a consuming hatred of the imperialistic war-mongers.

A second, very general factor behind the "universality" of graduate school is the increasing availability of graduate-school fellowships. For those who have little idea by their senior years of their career plans, graduate school is often the easiest method of prolonging the moment of decision. One could legitimately wonder if more and more fellowships are actually available because students increasingly seek some kind of graduate education, or if students flock to graduate school simply because of the availability of fellowships—but, whatever the answer, fellowships definitely make the sometimes awesome prospect of graduate study a little less unattractive. Tales of unknown but nevertheless lucrative fellowships often lightened those macabre discussions about the draft. We often felt as if we were playing a joke on society by treating the fellowship sweepstakes so lightly. And still, for those who needed money, were worried about the draft, or had nothing else in store, playing the fellowship sweepstakes was bountiful sport indeed.

Fellowship or not, those who enter graduate school seem to divide themselves very roughly into about four "types." The most silent group includes those who are genuinely interested in the material they will be studying in graduate school—be it arts and sciences, law, medicine, or business. For these students, the larger issues of professionalization and specialization seem irrelevant. At some point either before or during college, they discover a smouldering flame of intellectual curiosity and a small area of special devotion. In many cases, graduate studies are merely an extension of work they have begun as undergraduates. In any event, such students usually display a surprisingly mature independence and resourcefulness. They have in common their intellectual engagement even though their styles are varied and their extracurricular interests bear relatively little relationship to their academic concerns. They are in no particular hurry about life, for their futures are secure from the anxieties of many who are less certainly directed. One might be tempted to say of these students that ego solidity comes for them not through objective identification with their fields of interest, but through the reassuring fact that they are actively interested in something. They derive security not by announcing to the world, "I am a specialist in early Jacksonian history," but rather by thinking, "I'll be damned, I'm actually involved in a subject." They look forward, generally, to creative scholarship and not to role-playing.

A second group of prospective graduate students falls under the general category of "model-followers." For these students, at least initially uncertain about future careers, the examples of their elders become determinant. In some cases, primarily with those who choose law and medical school, the model of their fathers is most important. (In my class, about 40 per cent of those students entering law and medicine are following in their fathers' footsteps.) Perhaps more frequently, students are caught up in the pervasive atmosphere and glamor of the academic community into which they are tossed as eager freshmen. They see around them graduate students and professors blessed with a generous sprinkling of prestige. For a student suddenly buffeted by questions about his own abilities, the spectacle of assured and authoritative scholars, reeling off generalizations without the least compunction, becomes a vision of considerable enchantment. Oh! to be an expert on something, absolutely anything! Once these students make the first step towards specialization, they usually become entrapped in academia's own mechanisms. Of these, graduate school is the final and most logical step. The student enters graduate school with bifocal vision—eyes focused half on the motivating model in the distance, half on the material immediately before him. The acquired lenses of model-following screen out the field of vision in between, which might have suggested to the student alternative career possibilities or other approaches to his own field. To those who never realize, as David Riesman once said, "that there is no automatic connection between being a professor and being genuinely interested in ideas,"[4] the path is long, narrow, and very straight. To puzzle once more with the notion of identities, one could say that security is acquired for these students by their egos' objectively identifying with a role and a style in life, and much less with the particular activities associated with that role.

Third, I think, graduate schools provide a haven for the skeptical and submissive among us. These are the students who have at some point become disenchanted with the prospects of specialization suggested to them by their own environment. They do not particularly hunger for the careers which graduate schools portend, but they see no other alternatives. For the most part, these students are a free-floating lot, able at once to do intensive work and to scoff at their activity. They shut their eyes to what they regard as the unbearable doldrums of professional training; their private lives of more wide-ranging intellectual interests become their only truly important concerns. While they can talk shop with the best of them, they care surprisingly little about the merchandise.

Finally, there are the uncertain who flock to graduate school for the variety of reasons mentioned briefly above: the draft, the luxury of fellowships, the inescapable fact that they won't be hurting their undefined futures by the acquisition of a piece of paper and a colorful robe. Among these, I can certainly count a very large number of my own friends.

And, almost parenthetically, it would be foolish not to mention those who have no intention of continuing their studies at all. Among this group, which comprised 15 per cent of my own class, one finds prospective secondary-school teachers, businessmen, public servants, journalists, creative artists, and those legendary "hangers-on," the much-publicized few whose interests and convictions lead them away from a formal choice of career.

The Initial Response

As I suggested earlier, a great deal of what students do as undergraduates serves only as frosting on the cake: the basic ingredients for post-graduate study are often mixed at an early stage of college; it's only the frosting and its decorations which color one undergraduate from another.

And to understand the choice of frosting, one must necessarily start with the very beginning of college. One must remember, for instance, that students arrive at college with a great deal of eagerness and very high expectations. They have often been preparing for college since their voices changed and they broke out with pimples —if not for longer. They have been told that they will face in college the most crucial years of their lives. They have been led to believe, in fact, that their four years in college will be worth any ten they might have spent elsewhere. And such expectations, like parents, exist only to be disappointed.

At Harvard, and at Berkeley as well, a good deal of the shattering of expectations takes place during freshman year. At Harvard especially, students learn much too quickly that they are not half so good as they thought they were. They wonder if, rather than being able to give all their talents to society, society does not simply define what it wants, taking that and no more. Suddenly little fish in a confusing sea, they search quickly for ways to salvage their disillusioned hopes. Whereas they had perhaps expected college to be a time for expansive and wide-ranging activity, they decide quite suddenly that the sheer intensity of competition demands equally intensive—and limited—specialization. For most freshmen, the activity comes to be scholarship.

And, more important, the freshmen quickly feel the need to paint their newly delimited activities in colors glaring less of failure and much more of fulfillment. Unfulfilled expectations can make one feel terribly uncomfortable and incomplete; the best solution, given the apparent impossibility of achieving those expectations, is to reduce them. Goals are down-graded, in effect, to allow their attainment. As a result, one begins to find an almost frightening homogeneity of outlooks among one's classmates as the reduced expectations converge. Styles remain disparate, for the vestiges of pre-college environment have not yet been pruned. But the goals and ideals of the *nouveaux arrivés* begin to conform to a surprising degree. A computer brought into a study of freshmen at Harvard once synthesized in an abbreviated form what freshmen hoped to become: "Stands on his own two feet. Interest in learning and likes to study. Serious, has high standards. Accessible to new ideas. Knows who he is and what he wants out of life. Productive, hard-working. Genuine and friendly."[5] (From my own conceptions of freshmen ideals, I for once find few grounds on which to disagree with the computer.) As the study which produced these results goes on to say, the freshmen with these self-ideals "live in and through their work; . . . they *are* what they *do*."[6] They subscribe, for the most part, to the good old Protestant Ethic. And this necessarily involves, I think, an acceptance of externally determined criteria of success. In their course work, the freshmen accept grades as valid measurements of their academic mettle. Socially, they rely on what they imagine the Harvard community accepts as reasonable social behavior. (This means for them that they can act with considerable abandon and "deviance," but that they should involve themselves in nothing so seriously that they change their outlooks on life or their performances in their work.) In terms of career goals, they look forward to "acceptable" careers and the standard paths to success in those careers; their exposure to intense competition among their peers has humbled them sufficiently to permit a patient endurance of the apprenticeships required. And to continue constructing an ideal type which is remotely possible *only* for freshmen, they are usually sincere and fairly restrained. Conversations in the freshman dining hall, when they wander occasionally from personal to intellectual topics, feature conclusion-oriented debates rather than idle exchanges of information. Since, to repeat, the students *are* what they *produce,* they move in their discussions resolutely from one point to the next, making sure that nothing has been left out.

This very sketchy freshman portrait has little relationship to students as they emerge from college at the end of four years. And yet it is extremely important because it is a stage through which most students pass, sooner or later. Its importance lies in its carefully constructed unity, its essential completeness. Having had their original hopes proved illusory, freshmen must improvise. They must work harder than they ever have before, and they find it personally expedient to accept an ethic of identification with their work. They must "know who they are" because their unfamiliar experiences would leave them shaky and insecure without such improvised "knowledge." Like Clark Kerr's multiversity president, they accept their new situations as ideal; they have too little time to ponder how expedient their new ideals really are.

What happens apparently is that many students begin to regard this improvised construction as relatively false. From the homogeneity of the freshman portrait, students pass on to a vast heterogeneity of caricatures. The central features of these new faces relate rather closely to what students find especially false about their freshman goals.

Essentially, as far as I can tell, students begin to reconsider the standards by which they have *been* what they *do.* As they look back over their freshman years, for instance, they tend to realize that academic course work and the grades affixed to their own work seem agonizingly artificial. The answers they put forth on exams seem falsely formal and prematurely conclusive, in part because their minds have come to understand the complexities of intellectual problems. They may also begin to sense—as is often the case—that their course grades bear surprisingly little relationship to the extent of their mastery of a subject. Intellectually, they may find that the material of their elementary courses offers them little fascination. If they are studying political theory, which young political scientists always begin with, they wonder what bearing such theory has on modern political behavior. If they plunge into preparation for careers in scientific research, as 22 per cent of my classmates did, they begin to wonder how the techniques they must first acquire actually relate to real scientific problems. Or, from the other direction, they may find movies, as an example, more vitally interesting than Greek drama. But how, they wonder, does one climb in the world if one becomes an expert on "The New Wave" in French films?

This new concern for relevance among the disillusioned comes in part from their realization that they are learning much more about themselves from their own friends than from their studies. At a time when students are undergoing the agonies of identity adjustment, people very much like themselves, with the same kinds of problems, bear much more relevance to their own personal problems than academic material does. And, especially in freshman year, contact with people outside their ring of peers is infrequent and highly formal. As a result, students begin to place personal contacts and relationships above standard academic activities. Questions begin to run rampant through their minds: If people are so vitally important, why does my course work have so little to do with them? Am I learning anything about what motivates real live human beings?

Gradually, students begin to feel that if college is to be an educative process, they must learn first about more immediately relevant things than the history books. And, in a certain sense, they feel that they have the time to disregard history texts for awhile; when they go to graduate school, they will have plenty of time to learn. Now, they want to reconstruct a less artificial set of ideals. They have come to distrust externally imposed priorities. As in freshman year, they will still *be* what they *do*, in a sense, for they have not yet acquired the maturity to cope with the unsettling gaps between expectation and performance. The essential difference from freshman year is that they want their activities to be of their own choosing, to be unique and personal domains.

This reconsideration of "The Initial Response" comes at many different points in the early years of college, and it comes, as I have said, in a wide variety of forms. And students will always realign their goals to match their activities to varying degrees. But the important thing is that the *nature* of the activity—its radicalism, immorality, or extremeness—is probably less important than the *reasons* for adopting it. The reasons, if this improbably abstracted mechanism is at all valid, are fairly short-range. Students hope to get something out of college. They have four years which are distinctly their own to play with, especially if they do not have scholarships to protect or if they worry only slightly about graduate-school admission. They can often assume they will be going to graduate school and that their experiments with "relevance" will end when graduate school begins. To return to the metaphor, the color of the frosting—while immediately important—may not assume a great deal of importance in the student's life plans. If the frosting involves some kind of political protest, for instance, it may not imply a lifetime of political protest. It may only be the student's method of making his college education more meaningful than it seemed during his artificial beginning.

The Readjustment

As a background for the forms of readjustment, first of all, the noninstitutional elements of the college community become extremely important. At a time when a good deal of personal reevaluation is taking place, the college community tends to supplant the home community as a testing ground for new ideas. Home often fades out of sight and out of mind. The friends who have meant so much during the process of personal readjustment are the reassuring shoulders on which students lean with their problems. Students come back from their summers early, for instance, often searching the streets of Cambridge for familiar faces. The first few days of the term are spent catching up on friends and their recent experiences. Conversations flow out of the dining hall and back into their rooms for late-hour sessions over cigarettes and beer. Increasingly, a spirit of community develops: students who have passed through many of the same stages together develop bonds of understanding with their peers. The outside world grows more and more remote, not necessarily because it does not understand the students' new frames of mind, but more fundamentally because it has not had a part in the evolution of those attitudes. A "We-They" relationship develops, in good part due to the feeling that the college years are the sanctuary for uniquely student concerns.*

Only within this larger context does the search for relevance, uniqueness, and personalized activity unfold. A thousand forms of activity emerge; a few should be mentioned for the similar motivations they reveal.

As a first type, one finds students who plunge into student activities in heroic fashion. They strive desperately to make these activities uniquely personal domains. They merge themselves completely with the fact of activity; many lose sight of why or what they are doing, as long as they have the satisfaction of knowing they are busy. Involvement in a student activity—however menial the task—has the apparent advantage over academic work of offering the student more tangible evidence of his own efforts. He can certainly see what he does, if not be it.

The immediate involvement in activities can also become frighteningly absolute, to the abandonment of sleep, course work, and all else. But, in many ways, the sheer abnormality of existence is again proof of the personal uniqueness of the involvement. And the abandonment usually ends in time to study for final exams, when the reality of graduate-school admission re-emerges for a short two weeks—only to return below the surface after the exams are over.

In the theater world at Harvard, for instance, a large number of stage crew-hands work not at all because they are interested in the theater but primarily because they savor the taste of exhaustion, because they long for the excitement of finishing a set bare minutes before curtain call. Often the very grubbiness of their work and the filth under their nails reassures them that they are active. At cast parties, while the publicly acclaimed dramatic figures are gracefully holding court, the crew-hands stagger forcefully into their midst— paint in their hair—as if to bludgeon the world with the importance of their own parts in the production. "They're like the unknown soldiers saving the World for Democracy," a student director said. "As long as they can keep busy, and they carry some dirt around to prove it, they stay happy with the quiet satisfaction of the martyred few."

* It is interesting how strong this feeling of home-away-from-home can become. Very large numbers of Harvard students remain in or return to Cambridge for graduate school, and not always because Harvard's departments are the best in their fields.

The stage-hand phenomenon repeats itself around the colleges. Editors of the student newspaper relish the early-morning moments when they put the paper to press. They aren't just writing for a paper and watching their copy disappear down a chute; it's their own paper, and they have ink on their fingers to prove it. Young politicians hold late-night caucuses worrying about petty organizational details. Again, the organization—say, the Young Republicans —is their own, and the triviality of their worries is fully compensated by their sheer tangibility.

Much the same kinds of phenomena are evident in Harvard's final clubs as well, those peculiar vestiges of another era at Harvard when students were gentlemen and manners, *de rigueur*. Now, no more than 10 per cent of the student body belongs to the final clubs, they are for the most part politely ignored, and it often seems to some members as if they are trying to save a dying institution. A number of them linger in their building until the last bourbon has been drunk and the morning sun appears. They somehow derive satisfaction from really "participating in club life," from heroically abandoning themselves to a student club in need of their very specific attention.

The search for personal involvement can take uniquely intellectual forms, as well, in sharp contrast to the menial involvement in the activities portrayed above. Some students begin to develop almost eccentrically intellectual whims which consume their time and passion. They too pay little attention to formal course work, for they have discovered more relevant interests; the relevance comes, I understand, from the feeling that the interests are uniquely their own. One student acquires a mastery of the fiction of Vladimir Nabokov, another chooses modern mystery novels as his personal passion, and still another pores through late twelfth-century Arabian scientific treatises. For these students, in a way, as well as for those involved in activities, their absolute abandonment in their passions can become paradoxically bothersome. Guilt over neglecting their academic work sometimes causes them moments of concern, but that same feeling of guilt seems also to assure them of the reckless vitality and personal character of their involvement.

Intellectual involvement can also be found, sometimes, in the very sort of model-following among the prospective graduate students described above. For many model-followers, admittedly, the re-evaluation of freshman perspectives never takes place. For many others, however, the "stage-hand phenomenon" is so pervasive that they tear into their subjects with new intensity. At the end of senior year, when some of us participated in the selection of 90 graduating members of Phi Beta Kappa among some 250 candidates, I was particularly struck by the quality of the candidates' specialized research—as reported by their tutors. Many had involved themselves for as long as two years in previously unexplored fields and had already done significant original work in those fields. For those whom I knew personally, the original work was often yet another way of finding "meaningful" involvement in activities of their own choosing. What separated them from students involved in less academic pursuits, quite often, was that the mechanism of climbing the academic ladder seemed to require academic concentration.

Finally, to conclude an all-too-brief sketch of the search for relevance, one finds the amorphous collection of political dissidents, drug cultists, "hipsters," and generally "alienated" students. Political dissidents constitute the largest and most important segment of this collection, but all the groups are lumped together here because their characteristics seem so strikingly similar.

Most of the collection's characteristics have been fully described elsewhere and need be summarized only briefly. Many of the students reject "standard" patterns of behavior, believe in active experience, and care little about the adverse consequences of their activities as long as they serve some fundamental cause. Many of the dissidents are essentially apolitical and anti-ideological, caught up in the romance of living before they pause to think about it. Especially in the case of the political activists, the concept of "alienation" has considerable appeal. As one member of the Students for a Democratic Society (SDS) put it, "The Marxist sense of alienation is very appropriate to our own feelings. Everywhere we look in society, we find people separated from the products of their work. Doctors work for clinics, bureaucrats work for an organization, politicians work for an amorphous power structure." For most of them, it's not what they do that's important, but how they do it; and the manner is most definitely their own. Style is important, both in dress and in thought patterns. Drugs, if used, are important for the spontaneity they produce and with which they are taken, not so much because they are outlawed by society.

What I think is most significant about this odd collection of "alienated" youth is not at all that they are rejecting the conventions of respectable society, for rejection seems to play the very slightest role in the actual development of their stances and styles. Rather, I think, these students reflect once again a search for uniquely personal and individual experience. Among political activists, the most pressing concern is for involvement in situations where they can witness the tangible impact of their involvement. Civil rights workers seem attracted by very direct field work with Negroes in very intimate surroundings. Workers in ghettos, and especially tutors, expect to see the results of their efforts much more immediately than if they petitioned the national government. And they obviously find that the success or failure of their work reveals itself much more immediately through public demonstration than through legal redress. Many of the civil rights workers I knew in the South literally wailed if they were given office jobs of unusual importance. They wanted to be "out in the field with the people," where the importance of their work could be mirrored in a new excitement written on a Negro's face. I think it significant that the most popular organization on the student left these days is Students for a Democratic Society (SDS), with its central philosophy of "participatory democracy."* Fundamental to its guidelines is the notion that people should be able to have direct impact on the decisions which affect their lives; this is, indeed, the private concern of many of the activists who have forged that philosophy. The philosophy is manifested in the tactic of community organizing, where students once again can watch the results of their own work. And it is a philosophy by which the students can get furthest away from the impersonality of the standard political organizations which in their own minds (and in reality as well) deny them personal involvement.

In the same way, those who belong to the cult of vital "experience," no matter what kind of experience, find the *personal* side of their drug-taking and love-making most satisfying. They have forged their own way of life, with their own rules, their own styles, and their own methods of piercing through the barrier of convention. Only infrequently does the pot-smoker not urgently want to share his experience with another drug aficionado, and rarely do students take marijuana and hallucinogenic drugs alone. The picture is a striking one: a small room, five or six students, marijuana smoke in the air, mouths tightly closed to hold in the fumes, nothing moving but the swaying music in the background and the students' eyes— eyes groping for a moment's empathy of a meaningful exchange, for the security of common experience.

* There are probably 75 to 100 active members at Harvard; 3,000 to 5,000 nationwide.

"Rebellion" in Context: A Student's View of Students

It is often said that student political activists of the 1960's are much more idealistic than their predecessors, that they are reacting, in fact, against the insincerity of their parents and society. Although idealism does indeed play a role in their political stances, I do not find it to be the motivating source of political activism among the students I've known. Their protest stems much more from their implacable impatience with the standard channels of time-consuming bureaucracies. Who wants to weather bureaucratic mayhem in the Office of Economic Opportunity, they say, when he can work directly with the people? Who wants to work in the State Department when he can meet the people through the Peace Corps? And who wants to bother with university committees when he can stage a sit-in inside an administration building and get the same results more quickly? It seems to me that the admittedly moralistic dogmas of contempt for society and the power structure in many cases develop only after protest gets underway. Initial contempt for completely isolated elements of "society"—like one particular foreign policy—feeds upon itself and upon the contempt of other dissidents until a widely applicable set of responses emerges.

It is also commonly said that the "alienated" students of the radical left—both politically and morally—have forged a sort of "existential" existence, borne out of blanket protest without the reassuring buttress of developed standards and mores. Again I find the contrary true. Students of the left, taken in the most general sense of the word, derive a great deal of security out of the community they've developed, out of the very strong bonds among them. Nearly everything—their attitudes, their styles—is absolute and enveloping. They are provided with a great deal of support indeed; it happens only to be a new kind of foundation. And the totality of rejection and defiance among many radicals wipes out uncertainty altogether. The student who sticks out his chin and says, "I'm going to tear this place apart—I don't care if it gets put back together," requires very little courage at all.

One final note might be made about all these forms of involvement, these searches for relevance—a note about the degree to which students depend on the involvement for their security. A quite distinct segmentation develops among students, cutting one kind of politician off from another, one form of extracurricular activity off from its analogue. At a place like Harvard, the House system of small, heterogeneously populated living units provides a mechanism for throwing students of varying interests together, of breaking down segmentation, but the system is surprisingly unsuccessful in that one respect.

House dining halls are broken into tiny eating groups, with little flow among them. Students from one activity rarely pool resources with those from another. Many of the leading lights in the Harvard drama world are basically writers, for instance. But for them momentarily to break out of the theater's confines and to publish in the campus literary magazine, I am told, would be taken as rash heresy. And the reason, apparently, is that students come to be taken for granted within an organization, come to feel secure within its structure of personal relationships. Outside, they would be judged purely on the merit of their performances. I have known many students for whom the mere prospect of such bare exposure would destroy their composure for days. To pick an almost extraneous but possibly illustrative example, The Signet Society, Harvard's closest analogue to an intellectual society, brings together many of the most prominent figures of undergraduate activities, many of substantial creative and intellectual talents. At luncheon discussions, the quest for "The Third Topic" occupies all. Each seems afraid to risk discussion of his own specialty, apparently for fear of being beaten at his own game by an amateur. Exciting conversation centers not around recent literary masterpieces, when literature students participate, but around the problems of dictatorship in Haiti or the mating characterestics of the Howler monkey.

This segmentation seems even more prevalent at Berkeley than at Harvard. Berkeley's vast impersonality makes the importance of immersion into friendly niches much greater. A principal source of the mass participation in the Berkeley demonstrations was, I felt when I went back there several weeks later, that, for the first time in their college careers, students there could feel familiar with their school-mates. A very strict "We-They" division developed, particularly because of the issues involved, and along with it grew a real sense of community. Many of the students I talked to cared little about and had scant notion of the issues involved in the demonstrations; they merely wanted to reaffirm that they had been part of this emergent community. Asked if they had been arrested in the huge sit-in at Sproul Hall, they often replied: "No, I wasn't. I kept trying to get in so I could be arrested, but they locked us out. I really wanted to take part."

Is It All So New?

Having exhausted the usefulness of purely typological description, I turn more directly to questions of significance. Why do some students happen to move in the particular directions they follow? Given their directions, what is the significance of the radicalism which many adopt?

To pursue the question of how it happens the way it does, I should restate some comments made earlier. Many of the phenomena described at such length here are very local and ephemeral. They are modes of reacting to the fact of four years in college. They are means of revamping a set of ideals and goals established somewhat artificially rather early in those four years. Initially, at least, they very often do not have more far-reaching implications.

Given that much, it is possible to isolate certain factors influencing the directions in which students turn. For a very few, first of all, extreme stances of "hippiness" are assumed out of deep personal insecurity, in many cases due to unhappy family backgrounds. One Harvard professor, who has for years been very close to students, has often found himself assuming the role of a father-substitute for some of the "hippest" among his students. They tell him, often quite frankly, that they hate their parents; he, they hope, will fill in.*

Second, and most important, students' acquaintances determine to a very large extent the scope of their readjustments. Since the search for relevance often involves a search for personal relationships as well, roommates and friends provide the most available alternatives to impersonally determined standards of priority. To pick one slightly exaggerated example of this process, a serious-minded student arrived at Harvard about six years ago with scarcely a frivolous vein in his body. He was thrown in with a highly sophisticated, highly cynical group of banjo-strumming eccentrics. After he became disillusioned with institutional Harvard, he joined in the fun. He lagged in his academic work, learned to play the mandolin, and became skeptical about nearly everything. To talk with him was to face a scornful smirk and an acid tongue. Nothing was sacred. Now, two years after his graduation, he has become an unusually dedicated and determined graduate student in economics—planning, apparently, on an academic career with emphasis on the rigidly impersonal field of econometrics. The evanescence of his "rebellion" as an undergraduate seems particularly striking in retrospect.

Third, students on the proverbial search sometimes fix their sights on a few prominent gods of the undergraduate scene, not universally

---

* In general, I would guess, contempt for parents is not very common among students. The great extent to which college serves as a home for students necessarily involves a great deal of remoteness from families, but it rarely goes much further than that.

recognized, to be sure, but extremely influential within smaller segments of the college. In most cases, the gods combine a strangely personal success with a highly personal style. The combination serves as a great lure for the disenchanted and insecure. The paragon of the god was an extremely talented leader of a leftist political group several years ago, who attracted scores of students into his organization. What sometimes happens, however, is that students stop short of total emulation of the gods. They become immersed in organizations, but they sometimes fear losing their comfortable security by the dangerous exposure involved in becoming a public figure. In fact, one rarely finds public figures at all within the undergraduate world, perhaps for this very reason. Those who do project themselves into the glare of prominent positions are quite frequently characters blessed with frankly unselfconscious brashness.

At last, to return to the question of critical importance, is any of this especially new or different? In many ways, it can be argued, it is not. I'm assured by people who have been around Harvard for awhile that students used to complain about professionalism and impersonality as much eight years ago as they do now. I'm also assured that students would have participated as actively in a civil rights movement then as they do now, if only a movement had existed. And, finally, I'm assured by students and psychologists alike that the problems of identity readjustment were as acute in previous generations as they are now. In fact, to read Sir Francis Galton, this process of goal revision was operative as long ago as 1869:

The eager boy, when he first goes to school and confronts intellectual difficulties, is astonished at his progress. He glories in his newly-developed mental grip and growing capacity for application, and, it may be, fondly believes it to be within his reach to become one of the heroes who have left their mark upon the history of the world. The years go by; he competes in the examinations of school and college, over and over again with his fellows, and soon finds his place among them. He knows he can beat such and such of his competitors; that there are some with whom he runs on equal terms, and others whose intellectual feats he cannot even approach. Probably his vanity still continues to tempt him, by whispering in a new strain. It tells him that classics, mathematics, and other subjects taught in universities, are mere scholastic specialties, and no test of the more valuable intellectual powers.[7]

In a very large sense, then, external political events like Kennedy's appeal to youth and the emergence of the civil rights movement have been the sources of political activism. Students, it seems, have been looking for unique involvement for a number of years; they have merely taken advantage of new opportunities for expressing themselves as those opportunities have arisen.

But what is new are the *extreme* forms of "involvement" that *some* students have been choosing. The reasons for this particular change, I would suggest, lie very much in the character of American society. Above all, ours is a competitive society, one which, in Riesman's terms, is excessively other-directed. We must always compare ourselves with the "neighbors," and the need for faring well in those comparisons is apparently considerable. Students become acquainted with the facts of competition quite early in their lives, and the competitive urge manifests itself strongly in the attitudes which they bring with them to college.

What happens, however, is that the ways of beating out one's classmates must become unbearably subtle. Everyone in one's own circle seems bright, and everyone seems equally able to do well in course work if he wants to. New ways of gaining the ascendancy must be acquired, for the old methods of quantitative measurement —through IQ tests, college-board scores, and course grades—no longer yield competitive advantage. Instead, for instance, students compare how little work they have put into their courses to get "A" grades. Or they subtly jockey in their tutorial sessions for the favoring nod of the professor. Or, as happens so often, they imagine themselves rising above the competition by rejecting its terms of combat.

One sees, then, a magnificent struggle to feel superior to society and one's peers. College students can no longer acquire the all-important feeling of superiority merely by getting their A.B.'s or even their Ph.D.'s, for too many others around the country are up with them. And they can rarely "ascend" by simply devouring intellectual products, for the recent marketability of good books and good records has meant that the sheer consumption of things intellectual will not distinguish the student from his society.

And it is often the most intelligent who must strive for superiority in the most extreme fashion, for they both feel more strongly the need to be recognized for their own abilities and perceive more immediately the psychological limitations of standard measurements of success. The quality of the student leaders in the Berkeley demonstrations has been adequately described. At Harvard, too, the "new radicals" are some of the most brilliant students around. Berkeley's Mario Savio once gave almost clinical evidence of this need to feel superior when he told me why he did not like the system of mass education: "College ought to be set aside for those of us who can really take advantage of it," he said. "The truly intelligent people are just having their talents wasted by having all these hacks around."

So, the ante for the student striving for a feeling of superiority has gone up. Now, he must devise new, often ingenious, always subtle means. One of the most common, apart from absolute rejection, is to participate in society, but all the while to look down on it—to go to graduate school but to remain skeptical of its value, to take exams but to do so under the sublimating influence of barbiturates. Jeremy Larner recently wrote an article about drug consumption in Westchester County high schools, in which teen-agers have already learned the subtleties of achieving superiority. Bobby, the focal point of the article, would communicate well with some of today's college students, for he is already reacting as they do:

It's hip to put up with it [society] passively, and to use one's private time in search of experience which will make one inwardly superior. . . . The big thing is to cool it—to stay cool and just look out your window at the others.[8]

In a very paradoxical sense, then, it turns out to be the rats who make the race. Student involvement and student rejection of society stem in large part from the students' own needs to feel above their surroundings, and not from society's grotesque features. And the character of society has meant that the forms of achieving this superiority must become more extreme and more personal as the quality of society improves. Students who have made it into Harvard have the world open to them; but for some of them to try to take advantage of their infinite possibilities would involve too much uncertainty, too much threat of suffering a few defeats along the way. The surest way of preserving one's ego is to resent the possibilities and rule them out as unattractive. Then, if one goes ahead and seeks a place in society, one can rest assured that unpleasantness will come as no disappointment. Clark Kerr, for all the things said about him in the Berkeley demonstrations, made a very perceptive point in the weeks following the turmoil. In disputing the students' contention that the multiversity is without meaning, Kerr said:

They are given a choice. . . . The only kind of society that has only a single meaning is an authoritarian one. It seems to me that is a place where you would really expect rebellion. Essentially, what the FSM are saying is that they are rebelling against freedom of choice. . . . In fact, there is a lot of opportunity to participate, only it takes a little longer and requires more initiative to find it. Many tend to be overwhelmed by their opportunities; there are so many lectures to choose from, so many things to do, that they tend to become lost. They are torn too many ways and wind up condemning the whole structure.[9]

The most tragic aspect of this rather general quest for superiority in a competitive world, and the aloofness that it sometimes generates, is that some of the finest students emerge from the combat with a profound sense of impotence. They go to extremes in seeking some mark of superiority—be it with drugs, attitudes of rejection, or political activism—and they begin to discover that even these extremes provide them little comfort. They begin to perceive the artificiality of their drives, and they often begin to conclude that a feeling of superiority is impossible. They feel that society regulates against an individual realizing his talents, and they reconcile themselves to careers of mediocrity. The only thing they will be able to salvage, they often feel, is their private lives at home. They resign themselves to such a degree that they no longer feel challenged by unsolved social problems, no longer feel goaded to make use of their talents constructively. If it is indeed true that their resignation stems from America's creating psychological needs to feel superior, then our frenetically competitive society is wasting the talents of more than a few of its most talented youth.

REFERENCES

1. Quoted in Howard Zinn, *SNCC, The New Abolitionists* (Boston: Beacon Press, 1965), p. 227.

2. "The Student State of Mind," an article included in Michael Miller and Susan Gilmore (eds.), *Revolution at Berkeley* (New York: Dell, 1965), p. 59.

3. Among the 71 per cent, 30 chose the arts and sciences, 16 chose law school, 13 medical school, 4 business school, 2 schools of education, 2 schools of design, 1 divinity school, and 3 miscellaneous schools. These statistics, and all such subsequently cited statistics, are taken from "The Harvard College Class of 1965: Its Composition, Performance, and Plans," a report prepared by the Harvard Office of Graduate and Career Plans, Cambridge, Mass., August 1965.

4. From a speech entitled "Developments and Trends in Higher Education," presented at the annual meeting of the Commission on Higher Education, National Council of Churches of Christ, June 10, 1964.

DAVID M. GORDON

5. From an article by David Ricks and Robert McCarley, "Identity at Harvard and Harvard's Identity," *The Harvard Review*, Vol. III, No. 1 (Winter 1965), (an issue devoted to Undergraduate Education), p. 46.

6. *Ibid.*, p. 49.

7. Sir Francis Galton, *Hereditary Genius: An Inquiry into its Laws and Consequences* (London: Macmillan & Co., 1869), pp. 15–16.

8. "The New Improved Drug Scene," *The Nation,* 100th Anniversary Issue, September 20, 1965, p. 123.

9. Quoted in an article by A. H. Raskin, "The Berkeley Affair: Mr. Kerr vs. Mr. Savio and Co.," reprinted in Miller and Gilmore, *op. cit.*, p. 87.

KENNETH KENISTON

The Faces in the Lecture Room

IT IS EASIER to describe an institution than an individual, much less a generation. For institutions like universities at least have formal organizational charts, constant aims, established traditions, continuing programs, and chronically troubled relations with state and national governments. But individuals like students are by virtue of their stage in life changeable and changing, malleable yet often intransigent. Thus, for every statement we make about "the contemporary student," there is a readily available counter-statement, often backed by imposing evidence. To emphasize the activism of some highly vocal students seems to neglect the lack of commitment of the quieter majority. And to speak of the "seriousness" of many students is to ignore the frivolity evidenced by many others.

Furthermore, characterizations of students have a special way of being self-fulfilling or self-defeating, but rarely simply apt. To write about students today is also to write *for* students; no audience of adults awaits so eagerly the latest poll, the latest analysis, or the latest description of "students today." And to write for students is to write for a group who, rather than be nothing, may all too readily accept the latest label—silent, beat, activist, rebellious, cool, explosive, committed. But, at other times, students may unpredictably react *against* a label—resisting characterization, defying pigeonholing, refusing to be what they are told they are. Indeed, one factor behind the increasingly vocal activism of some students today may be their desire to reject the epithet of "silent" bequeathed them by students in the late 1950's. The process of characterization affects the characterized; an incorrect label may be accepted slavishly; a correct description may inspire a reaction that soon invalidates it.

In a society changing at a dizzying pace, we no sooner arrive at a tentative characterization of a generation of students than we

315

become aware that our generalization is no longer valid. Since the end of World War II, at least a half-dozen "generations" have been labelled and described, only to disappear before a new and different "generation." This points to one of the crucial facts about students today: their characteristics change extremely rapidly; they are extraordinarily responsive to the fluctuating pressures of American society. To the universal fact that young adults are always capable of rapid change simply by virtue of their stage in life is added the historical fact that American students are also responding to a rapidly changing society. All of this gives today's students an unusually mercurial and Protean quality.

Areas of Ignorance

Anyone who tries to discuss American students is confronted with immense areas of ignorance. For, despite years of systematic research using students as subjects, there is astonishingly little knowledge of students as people. On the whole, American psychology and sociology have been more interested in "universal" relationships between operationally defined variables than in human lives—or even in asking whether relationships discovered among college sophomores who happen to be taking Psychology 1a are necessarily true for all mankind. Students are *used* in psychological research, but rarely studied *qua* students. Only in the past decade have longitudinal studies of students' development in relation to their educational institutions begun in earnest, and most of the results are not yet in.

The state of current knowledge about students is ably summarized in Nevitt Sanford's massive compendium, *The American College*.[1] But we may well leave this opus more confused than we began it: virtually every article tells the same story of positive findings matched by negative findings, and concludes by calling for further, more sophisticated, research. Most important, there have still been very few studies of student development and student characteristics as they relate to the university. And the few important exceptions to this generalization suffer because the colleges studied were usually small, private, and intensely academic liberal-arts colleges. Just as the first sociologists to investigate social class in America studied towns where class lines were extremely rigid, so those who have studied student development have selected small liberal-arts colleges[2] where students *do* develop. But one review of research on changing values in college[3] suggests that such colleges may be the *exception* to the general rule that most American students are manifestly unaffected by their education.

Even in the private, academic, liberal-arts college it is not clear whether the college produces change or merely happens to be the setting where it occurs, for such colleges characteristically recruit the most able freshmen, who arrive already eager to discard outworn outlooks and acquire new values. Perhaps these students are already so firmly launched on a trajectory of self-transformation that even in a nonacademic college they would have insisted upon changing. Doubtless both factors—the motivations and talents of entering freshmen *and* the characteristics of the college—cooperate to produce the senior and the adult. But of how these factors interact, and of how they should be weighed, we know very little.[4]

One fact about American students today is of course clear: there are more of them than there have ever been before in any nation of the world. Not only is the college age group larger, but every year a greater proportion of this age group attends college. Already, more than 50 per cent of high school graduates go on for higher education; and in some states this figure approaches 75 per cent. Yet the vast hordes of students attending colleges and graduate schools merely add to the difficulties in characterizing "the student." American college youth is becoming more and more synonymous with American youth in general, and the study of students as a group assumes all of the complexity of the study of national character.

Furthermore, the enormous increase in the numbers of students in college and graduate school has led to a greater variety both in the types of students attending college and in the types of colleges they attend. The influx of students also permits a kind of specialization not only among academic programs but among student bodies. At the same time that the diversity of American universities has increased, the homogeneity of students within each university has probably increased as well.

This specialization most obviously affects the "elite" colleges. One consequence of the flood of students has been an increase in the intellectual caliber of those who attend the most selective colleges. Such institutions have been unable or unwilling to expand their facilities to match the growing pressure on their admissions offices. Admissions standards have therefore become increasingly selective: each new freshman class is routinely "the best in history." And more stringent entrance requirements have widened the intellectual gap between the student bodies of selective colleges and those at the bottom of the intellectual scale.[5] Some American colleges now recruit their entire student bodies from among the most talented 5 per cent, 3 per cent, or even 1 per cent of the college age group: they are able as never before to specialize in educating only the very intelligent and well-prepared. But other, less selective colleges bear the main burden of educating that growing proportion of young Americans of average and less-than-average intellectual ability who at least begin college.

What is true of talent that can be measured by IQ tests is equally true of other talents, aptitudes, and outlooks that are harder to quantify. Students of similar personality type clearly tend to be concentrated in colleges that "specialize" in educating (or failing to educate) just that type.[6] But we know very little about how to define these types precisely—of the characteristics of those who attend the new municipal and junior colleges, or of what distinguishes students at private Protestant denominational colleges, urban Catholic universities, or major and minor technological institutes. Moreover, not all colleges and universities of the same apparent category draw the same type of student. Within a broad category like city colleges or denominational colleges, student bodies range from intense academic commitment to complete vocationalism or narrow fundamentalism. Useful ways of describing and contrasting colleges and their student bodies are only beginning to be found.[7]

Furthermore, colleges and student bodies are continually changing. The growing admissions pressure on selective colleges has generated a kind of academic fall-out on secondary schools and less selective colleges. Parents who live in suburban middle-class areas are notoriously eager to have their children admitted to "good" colleges: they exert pressure on local school boards to create more advanced programs in secondary schools. The result is paradoxical, for since more students arrive each year at college gates with advanced standing, high achievement scores, and rigorous academic training, academic gate-keepers must raise their entrance hurdles still higher, generating new pressures on secondary schools to upgrade still further, and so on.

The result—more and more students with superior secondary-school training—indirectly changes less selective and less academic colleges. Since only a few of these well-qualified students can be admitted to "elite" colleges,[8] the rest must go to institutions of second and third choice. Many a college which one generation ago had no admissions standards whatsoever now finds itself able to pick and choose among its applicants. Without any expenditure, effort, or improvement of program or faculty, thousands of highly motivated students appear on campus, well-trained and chafing at the academic bit. These students can sometimes effect a real improvement in the quality of the colleges they attend, but they have also created an unprecedented phenomenon on some American campuses—a tension between a second-rate faculty and an academically committed student body.[9]

In general, there is a considerable "match" between the characteristics of a university or college and the characteristics of its students. The "better" colleges obviously get the high-IQ, high-performance students: admissions tests alone can guarantee this. Similarly, the most academically motivated students tend to find their way to liberal-arts colleges that provide a maximum of intellectual stimulation. And high school graduates who still view college as "learning to get along with other people" usually enter institutions where fun, social life, fraternities, and sororities still dominate the campus. But precisely how and why this matching of student to college takes place remains unclear.[10] Certainly the "image" of a college has a great deal to do with the selective application of the "right" type of student. But in no college is the match between student needs and capacities and the institution's provisions and demands perfect.

Nor should a perfect match be viewed as the ideal. Education, after all, aims at inducing change in students; and some disparity between what the entering freshman is and what the college thinks he should become by graduation is necessary if college is to be more than stagnation or play. But no one really knows how to define the optimal disparity. If the gap between what the student wants and expects and what the college provides and asks is too great, then frustration, a sense of failure, or discontent is likely to result. But if what the student brings with him to college and what the college expects from him are too perfectly matched, the result is likely to be that stagnation which some observers think characteristic of student development at many major American colleges.

Furthermore, an ideal match for men students may not be at all ideal for women; yet little is known about the educational differences between the sexes. Most studies concentrate on one or the other sex, yet generalize to both. But anyone who has taught both sexes can personally document the enormous difference between their educational outlooks, concerns, and motivations. It is not yet clear, for example, to what extent student development as described in two classic studies of Bennington and Vassar[11] should be generalized to most students, most liberal-arts students, most female students, or most female liberal-arts students. Other accounts of contemporary students seem relevant primarily to men; thus, for example, very few of the "activists" in the present generation are drawn from among co-eds. Whether we consider it a result of anatomy or social conditioning, women view their educations and their lives very differently than do men.

Many discussions of contemporary students have an implicitly historical or cross-cultural perspective, comparing students today and yesterday, here and abroad. Yet our historical and cultural ignorance about students is once again more impressive than our knowledge. Today, at least, we have public opinion polls and a number of on-going studies of student development. About the past, however, we have only impressionistic and journalistic accounts. When researchers attempt to compare today's students with their forebears, they are inevitably forced to rely on studies of alumni, where the effects of aging are almost impossible to distinguish from real generational differences.[12] Cross-cultural studies, too, are in their infancy. Everyone knows that American students are different even from students in Western Europe, to say nothing of the developing nations.[13] Americans are less politicized, less ideological, and more concerned with the practical and private aspects of life. But how much of this difference is due to the different selectivity of universities abroad, how much to differences in national style and character, how much to different stages of national economic and political development, how much to specifically educational influences—all these questions remain unanswered.

Still another unanswered question concerns the role of masses and elites in the contemporary American university. Whatever the modal characteristics of any given student body as reflected in a public opinion poll,[14] every campus has its deviants, its leaders, and its subcultures. In some cases, these may be of greatest interest to the college psychiatrist.[15] But in other cases, markedly atypical students may be the leaders of their generation. In retrospect, for example, extreme left-wing students in the 1930's were clearly in a minority. But their articulateness, visibility, and energy have left their mark on the entire generation. Similarly, student activists, beatniks and voluntary dropouts constitute a minority of the more than five million students attending college today. Yet these students have a disproportionate influence, not only on the public image of students as transmitted through the mass media, but also on students' images of themselves. Even more than other age groups, students are prone to vicarious identification with others; and many an apathetic student on a vast campus where only a few dozen classmates are active in civil rights work considers himself a member of an "activist" generation.

Nor should this judgment be considered automatically invalid when it is not substantiated by a public opinion poll. Most revolutions are made by small elites that are ahead of the masses; yet revolutions do occur. The Bolsheviks were but a fringe of a faction in Russian radical thought, but they eventually dominated the Russian Revolution. In this respect, public opinion surveys can be misleading, for, in characterizing students, we need to know not only what is typical, but what is salient, visible, and prominent in students' judgments of themselves.

The next decade is likely to bring some light into these areas of ignorance. At a number of American colleges and universities, research now underway will help characterize more exactly the variety of American colleges and student bodies, helping distinguish between men and women, the past and the present, here and abroad, the typical and the salient.[16] But as of today one group of American students seems likely to remain almost completely unstudied. Most commentators on the contemporary university at least recognize that undergraduates and undergraduate education remain an "unsolved problem." But graduate students are discussed, if at all, as if theirs was but the idyllic reward for superior college performance.[17] In fact, however, the plight of graduate students is probably more dire than that of any other student group. Undergraduates may be ignored and neglected, but neglect at least gives those who desire it a certain freedom. The graduate student, in contrast, is often pressured, judged, graded, indentured, and exploited in a way that has few parallels in the annals of civilized oppression. He is, at present, the forgotten man in American education: no one is even studying him.

However we may explain it, this considerable body of ignorance about the contemporary student is symbolic of, if not a reflection of, one of the crucial facts about students today. In discussions of the university, the education of students is too often relegated to the end of the list of unsolved problems. And most American universities

321

devote vastly more attention to every conceivable research question than they do to trying to understand their own students. To be sure, everyone acknowledges that without students there can be no university; and so too, "education" is widely admitted to be one of the functions of a university. Yet the characteristics of students—the fact that they have commitments, aspirations, values, dreams, needs, psyches, and perhaps souls even *before* being admitted to college—are largely ignored in the concentration on more easily describable features of the university. To many administrators and to some faculty members, students remain a kind of unleavened lump to be molded by the university, blank cards on which education will punch imperishable information, shapeless ingots to be pressed into useful forms by "the college experience." All too often students must bring their real existence forcibly to the attention of college administrators through demonstrations, misbehavior, or vocal misery. The university remains, while student bodies change; the lecture room endures, only slowly eroded by time, whereas the faces in the lecture room change year by year and hour by hour.

Just as our attention is more readily caught by the institutions that students attend than by the students who attend them, so students themselves often feel lost in the contemporary university and in contemporary society. This fact, and all it portends about both university and society, is probably the central fact about American students today. They are embedded from kindergarten to the grave in the complex, organized, specialized, professional, bureaucratized, and impersonal institutions of American life. Whether we like it or not, we all—student and teachers alike—live in the most advanced technological nation of the world; and in such a society, as in its educational institutions, individuals tend to feel lost and to have to devise new ways to assert their individuality and justify their lives.

Even in the absence of solid information which would make a definitive portrait of American students possible, we must attempt to understand the contemporary student. For much of what goes on in a university goes on among students; and education is not merely the molding of an inert lump, but a transaction between an institution on the one hand and students on the other. In this transaction, the characteristics of students are as crucial as those of the university; only in so far as the university understands the potentials, commitments, and needs of those it teaches can it really educate them well.

In the remarks to follow, I will attempt to characterize, however impressionistically, one segment of American students—those who attend the more selective and traditionally more pace-setting colleges and universities. I will be talking largely of students at the great state universities like California and Michigan, the great private universities and university colleges on the East and West coasts, and the small private liberal-arts colleges across the nation. I will be dealing largely with the problems and outlooks of men students and will stress what seems to me characteristically different about today's student. Thus, I will be comparing the contemporary student with the student of previous generations, and not with students abroad. And I will draw not only on the research and impressions of others, but also upon my own subjective impressions.[18]

From Gentleman to Professionalist

Even within a relatively homogeneous liberal-arts college, it is impossible to speak of *the* student: we meet instead a variety of clearly distinguishable *types* of student. These can be classified in various ways, according to intelligence, field of concentration, social background, future profession, and the like. But the most useful classification, if we are interested in what is new about students today, will be historical. Any American university contains student types whose origins lie at different points in American history: there is a kind of historical stratification within American student bodies, each layer originating in a distinct historical era, having outlooks dating from that era, partaking of a different historical style of life. The past never disappears or fades away: it is merely submerged under the present. And the representatives of past ways of life continue to live in today's society, only gradually being buried under more contemporary types. Thus, a historical typology of students can serve as an introduction to the distinctly contemporary student.

Two centuries ago, advanced education was largely the prerogative of the most privileged groups in American society. Colleges like Harvard, Yale, or William and Mary existed primarily to educate the religious leaders, future merchants, and "gentlemen" of society. Education was intimately involved with the way of life embodied in the established Protestant churches, the descendants of Anglo-Saxon settlers, and the Federalist establishment. Often aping the manners of European aristocrats, this group emphasized Christianity in

323

religion, prosperity in commerce, and aristocratic disdain for the masses, tempered by commitment to social service.

Students of this era were thus largely *gentlemen-in-waiting*. Some later became parsons, other merchants, and still others scholars and teachers; but, for all, education was not so much a preparation for a specific vocation as a refinement of the gentlemanly qualities. Nor did education "make" a gentleman: to be educated at all, one had first to possess gentlemanly antecedents. But education was a finishing school, a way of acquiring polish, knowledge of the world, familiarity with the classics—all topped off with a Grand Tour. In this sense, education was dispensable: since gentlemen are born, not made, advanced schooling has never been a necessity for upper-class Americans. Striving and "achievement" motivation were largely irrelevant; going to college could not make a student into something he was not. Nor did it really provide useful vocational training for anyone but the parson-to-be. Rather, education merely confirmed a gentleman in what he already was, perhaps teaching him how to express it better.

With the extension of democratic rights in the first half of the nineteenth century and the ensuing decline of the Federalist establishment, a new conception of education began to emerge. Education was no longer a confirmation of a pre-existing status, but an instrument in the acquisition of higher status. For a new generation of upwardly mobile students, the goal of education was not to prepare them to live comfortably in the world into which they had been born, but to teach them new virtues and skills that would propel them into a different and better world. Education became training; and the student was no longer the gentleman-in-waiting, but the journeyman *apprentice* for upward mobility.

In the nineteenth century, a college education began to be seen as a way to get ahead in the world. The founding of the land-grant colleges opened the doors of higher education to poor but aspiring boys from non-Anglo-Saxon, working-class, and lower-middle-class backgrounds. The myth of the poor boy who worked his way through college to success drew millions of poor boys to the new campuses. And with this shift, education became more vocational: its object was the acquisition of practical skills and useful information. In Edgar Z. Friedenberg's metaphor, college was like the Pennsylvania Railroad Station: its function was to teach the route and timetable for the journey ahead.

For the gentleman-in-waiting, virtue consisted above all in grace and style, in doing well what was appropriate to his position; education was merely a way of acquiring polish. And vice was manifested in gracelessness, awkwardness, in behaving inappropriately, discourteously, or ostentatiously. For the apprentice, however, virtue was evidenced in success through hard work. The requisite qualities of character were not grace or style, but drive, determination, and a sharp eye for opportunity. While casual liberality and even prodigality characterized the gentleman, frugality, thrift, and self-control came to distinguish the new apprentice. And while the gentleman did not aspire to a higher station because his station was already high, the apprentice was continually becoming, striving, struggling upward. Failure for the apprentice meant standing still, not rising.

In the early twentieth century, still another type of student began to appear. As American society became more developed economically and more bureaucratized, upward mobility was no longer guaranteed by ambition, drive, and practical knowledge. In addition, those who aspired to success had to possess the ability to make friends and influence people. Mastering the human environment became more important than mastering the physical and economic environment. The function of education thus became not vocational training, but teaching the ability to be likeable and persuasive and to get along with all kinds of people. College life was increasingly seen as an informal training ground for social skills; virtue was defined as popularity; and a new type, exemplified by the *Big Man on Campus*, began to emerge.

Students who sought popularity and skill in dealing with people were naturally likely to emphasize the social rather than the academic or vocational aspects of higher education. Fraternities, student governments, even casual walks across the college campus, calling friends by name and saying "Hi" to strangers, were the new classrooms. Vocational skills became secondary—or, more precisely, the most important skills in *any* vocation were the capacity to make oneself respected, well liked, and a leader. The new sin was not gaucheness or standing still, but unpopularity. To the Big Man on Campus, academic and intellectual interests were irrelevant: whatever intelligence he possessed went into a rather calculated effort to please and impress others, win their respect, and dominate them without their knowing they were being dominated.

The emergence of the Big Man on Campus as an ideal type among American students coincided with the appearance of a distinctively nonacademic youth culture. The gentleman and the apprentice were both oriented primarily to the adult world: their most relevant models were adults—either the parental generation of gentlemen or the older generation of upwardly mobile and successful entrepreneurs. For the Big Man on Campus, however, the adult world was less immediately important. He looked mainly to his peers, for only by establishing his popularity in their eyes could he demonstrate his merit. Thus student cultures became more and more insulated both from academic culture and from adult society, developing their own rites, rituals, and traditions. The world of students became a separate world, not merely a reflection of or a preparation for adulthood. And as many observers have noted, the outlooks of this world were clearly distinguishable from the outlooks of adulthood—the student youth culture emphasized immediacy, enjoyment of the moment, popularity, attractiveness, sports, daring, and intellectual indifference. Walls, barricades, and fences of apathy, deafness and blindness were built between students and the more academic, intellectual values of their teachers. The power of these fortifications is suggested by the monotonous finding of research done before World War II that so many students were so little affected by the values their colleges sought to promote.

Since that time, yet another type of student has begun to emerge. Today, "superior academic performance" is a prerequisite for admission to any desirable college, let alone graduate school. Grace, ambition, and popularity have fallen into secondary position, for, without good grades and the ability to do well on IQ tests, the gentlemanly, ambitious, or popular student is not even considered by the admissions office.[19] From an early age, students are therefore exposed and overexposed to academic demands: they are taught from kindergarten onward that prestige and rewards are impossible without intellectual competence, cognitive efficiency, intellectual skill, and a high degree of specialization.

But these pressures within American education themselves reflect and are made weightier by comparable pressures in American society at large. The growth of the pressure for academic performance coincides with the full development of a technological society, with a new set of technological virtues. Even our new technological heroes, the astronauts, are a carefully selected and screened group of experienced professional pilots, all of whom have IQ's of 130 and over and a B.S. in engineering. And though they may be heroes in the eyes of the nation, heroism plays little part among their own motives. One study finds that "they are less concerned with abstractions and ideas as such than with the application of thought to problems solvable in terms of technical knowledge and professional experience." Even their trust in their fellow men "seems to depend largely on their sharing common standards of professional and technical competence with co-workers. It is faith in the *expertness* of the man, rather than dependence on the *man* himself, that allows them to accept interdependence without suspicion."[20]

The virtues of the astronauts are the ascendant virtues of the technological age. Our contemporary heroes are not men of mere aristocratic lineage, driving ambition, or social skill, but men of intense technical competence, high professional expertise, and careful specialization. These qualities are the prerequisites for a responsible position in adult society; and, without them, aristocrats, robber barons, or grown-up Big Men on Campus get nowhere. Although aristocratic grace, drive, and popularity naturally remain helpful, their relative importance has waned before the need for highly developed intelligence, competence, and expertise—the capacity to be "really good" in a professional field.

In our bureaucratized and organized society, it is the professional who counts. And the jobs that students at selective colleges will eventually take are almost without exception professional jobs. They will become research scientists, government administrators, accounts managers, research and development experts. They will be tomorrow's corporation lawyers, aeronautical engineers, medical specialists, and the up-and-coming professors of the "knowledge industry." For these students, "success" in the old sense is no longer an issue at all: fewer and fewer students strive to get ahead in the world, but more and more labor to become experts. And failure for today's students is not awkwardness, lack of ambition, or unpopularity; rather, the new sin is underachievement.[21] The burden of institutional sanctions falls most heavily not upon the rebellious, the mischievous, or the selfish, but upon those who "fail to live up to their potential."

The last two decades have seen a slow shift from a predominantly social view of education to an increasingly academic and pre-professional view. The major trend on most American campuses is away from the old pattern of a fun, football and fraternity student culture that subverted the intellectual efforts of the faculty, and toward student bodies that sometimes demand more intellectual challenge and individual instruction than faculties are willing or able to provide. Both students and colleges have changed in the past decades: increasingly, the new campus hero is becoming the committed *professionalist* who is "really good in his field."

Although each of these four student types originates in a different historical period, all four continue to coexist on most American campuses. Furthermore, these types are differently distributed among institutions. Today's jaded gentlemen are to be found largely in a few Ivy League colleges, often prepared at those few Eastern boarding schools that still consider it their primary function to instill Christian values and concepts of *noblesse oblige* into the children of the upper class. The Big Man on Campus today finds his most natural home in the state universities of the South, and in some fraternity subcultures of large public universities in the North. The apprentice also can be found in the large public universities and, increasingly, in municipal and technical colleges. And the new academic and professionalist student is most visible at the more selective private universities and liberal-arts colleges.

Moreover, modern society has required changes in each of these earlier types. The gentleman-in-waiting, deprived of an aristocratic society which respects his status, has increasingly been forced to emphasize the outward tokens of upper-class position: membership in the Social Register, debutante parties, belonging to exclusive clubs. At best, such students possess a lack of status anxiety that gives them great personal openness and helps them excel in the more reflective, artistic, and humanistic fields; at worst, they seem merely pretentious to their more academic contemporaries. Similarly, the apprentice who today gains admission to a selective college must inevitably display the cognitive skills and technical competence of the professionalist. But he continues to be distinguished by his drive to succeed and move up in the world, and by his view of education as a passport to social mobility. The Big Man on Campus, if he attends an academic college, increasingly construes popularity itself as the acquisition of specialized competence in interpersonal manipulation, gained through a study of the behavioral sciences, industrial administration, or "human relations." And, though he may succeed in his scientific quest for campus popularity, he often secretly fears that his less popular and more academic classmates (who refuse fraternity and football for library and laboratory) will end up better equipped for life in a technological age.

What is new about American students today, then, is the growing number of academically committed young men and women who value technical, intellectual, and professional competence above popularity, ambition, or grace. And while the transition from older student types is far from complete, it is the professionalist whom we must examine if we are to understand what is distinctive about American students today.

Profile of the Professionalist

The academically committed pre-professional student is a product of postwar American affluence. Born during or after World War II, he moves easily and familiarly in a world of communications revolutions, population explosions, thermonuclear bombs, brush-fire wars, interstate highways, and emerging nations. The era of the 1920's and '30's—when his own parents were formed, educated, married, and launched on careers—seems as remote as the medieval past. He is a distinctive creature of the longest period of uninterrupted peace and prosperity in American history.

His parents are usually professional people themselves— teachers, doctors, lawyers, administrators, officials, advertising men, or business men who have learned the hard way that a glad hand and a burning desire to succeed are no substitute for really knowing your business. Whether the business is teaching college or selling Buicks, what counts is skill, competence, and professionalization. Indeed, the fathers of today's students have sometimes found that lack of specialization, inability to keep up with "new developments," has meant frustration or inadequacy in their work. Thus, although they themselves may have neglected school work for social life or the football field, they are determined that their children will not make this mistake. While sometimes frustrated by their lack of training, these fathers are usually quite successful in their professions, earning between $10,000 and $20,000 per year, living in a pleasant suburban area, commuting every day to the office—and consistently urging their children to do well in school.

The contemporary student who is headed for a professional career is therefore inevitably faced with repeating the outward life-pattern of his parents. Unlike the apprentice or the Big Man on Campus, he is not attempting to change his station in life, but merely to up-grade his skills. The past provides today's students with little poverty to escape from, little anxiety about income, little fear of not getting a job, and little need for social mobility. In one way, the professionalist is like the gentleman-in-waiting, for he too was born into the status to which he aspires, and his public goals are only to do better the same kind of thing that his father did. To be sure, in an era of rapid technological change, no young man can hope simply to repeat the life-pattern of his father: even to keep up, skills, intellectual ability, and cognitive talent must be continually improved. But, on the whole, today's students are not characterized by a burning ambition to "succeed"; their financial and vocational goals are relatively modest; and they anticipate living the same professional, suburban lives now lived by their parents.

To achieve even this modest goal today requires continual diligence and performance in school. College therefore becomes less and less a "moratorium" on adulthood, and more and more a training ground for it. There is less energy or interest left for fraternities, hazing, and the tribal rites of the student culture; there is less room for experimentation, risk-taking, making mistakes, and taking false tacks. Only the exceptionally talented young man can excel academically without effort and be left free to use his energies as he chooses. For most students, the academic competition is too stiff; and they must work far harder in college than their parents ever thought of working.

Partly for this reason, the professionalist must devote himself with great seriousness to intellectual and academic matters. College grading is an important business; and a failed course or a bad year may mean an inferior graduate school or none at all. This academic seriousness is not the self-justifying eagerness of the "grade-hound," for good grades are but an instrumental rung on the academic ladder to graduate school, a post-doctoral fellowship, and a specialized job after graduation. Nor is it typically the seriousness of the committed intellectual, for whom the pursuit of knowledge and understanding is a goal in its own right. Indeed, students often unhappily admit to a fear of "getting too interested" in their work, because it might jeopardize the detachment they could otherwise bring to getting good grades. To their teachers, today's students appear unprecedentedly dedicated, well-trained, intelligent, and devoted; they study hard and do well; they "perform." But they are often disappointingly unwilling to become excited about ideas and, if pressed, will often admit they cannot afford the luxury of enthusiasm when the next admissions office lies only around the corner.

In all men there is a distinction between public and private life; but for today's young professionalist, the gap between public persona and private self is very great. Publicly, his goals are

330

intellectual performance, the acquisition of expertise, making the academic grade. Thus he is a serious, unfrivolous, and often quite humorless student. But privately, he is often very different. One of the peculiar characteristics of the quest for intellectual competence and professional expertise is that attaining these goals helps so little in defining the ultimate aims of existence. Being a gentleman was a way of life with a world-view attached; struggling to be successful could occupy a man's entire existence; and even the search for popularity could be integrated into an ideology of interpersonal relations. But expertise, skill, and professional competence are diffi-cult to ideologize: they are clearly instrumental goals, useful only in the service of something else, and they were never intended to answer ultimate questions about life's meaning. The student whose daily life is almost inevitably spent in the pursuit of intellectual competence must therefore elaborate a private life to justify his existence. The demanding and often tedious round of courses, examinations, and admissions committees requires compensation and a rationale.

The result is that peculiar confusion often noted among able American students and variously termed a "search for meaning," a "quest for identity," a "pursuit of significance." In only a few students does this take the form of an implicit quest for a "philosophy of life." Although most students believe at least nominally in God, and some attend church, religion plays no important role in the pro-fessionalist's attempt to "find out what really matters." Exposed from early childhood by schools and mass media to the vast variety of human conviction, such students are likely to be ethical relativists. If they think philosophically, they think in terms of "existential leaps" rather than "absolute values," prefer Tillich to St. Thomas, and read Camus for inspiration but not Marx. Unable to rationalize their convictions in ultimate metaphysical terms, they speak often of "personal commitment" and "authentic acts." And, in the end, those who arrive at an articulate philosophy of life are relatively few in number. The rest *wish* they could find some principled purpose, but accept the fact that in modern American society such purposes are hard to come by.

Most students therefore turn to private life as both compensation and justification for their public activities. In the here-and-now, some respite from the demanding round of academic work can be found through friendship, love, artistic experience, and self-expression. And, as a future goal, "the rich full life"—defined as private life—

331

promises to provide justification for the often demanding round of professional activities. To be sure, there are many students who expect to enjoy their future careers and pursue their educations precisely because they lead to these careers. But, even among future physicians, public servants, and teachers, relatively few students bring high idealism or an expectation of deep personal fulfillment to their future professions. And those few who do are usually taught during graduate and professional school that love of suffering mankind does not make a doctor, nor zeal for the commonweal a government official, nor love of teaching a professor.

The resulting privatism is therefore evident both in college life and in students' visions of their futures. In college, noncurricular activities assume a new meaning as a part of a search for self-definition and self-fulfillment. Most of the students' waking hours during the week must necessarily be spent in academic work. But in the hours that remain, on weekends and holidays, students can really be themselves—or, more precisely, search to find themselves. The vehicle for this search is inevitably personal and expressive: friendship, music, art, sports, dramatics, or even poetry. Nor are these activities enjoyed in a frivolous and light-hearted way: the most casual friendship may involve a painful search for self-definition; and reading, walking in the country, or listening to music can become part of the "quest for identity." Extracurricular activities are thus losing their traditional meaning as safety valves and outlets for the exuberance of youth: they too become more serious, more intense, more involved in the search for significance.

This same seriousness also pervades the relations between the sexes: the new professionalist takes these relations earnestly, even morally. Bravado is still sometimes apparent in his accounts of his own adventures to his cronies and competitors. But scratch the surface, and the same student usually turns out to be sincerely concerned with defining an ethic of interpersonal and sexual relations. The old question of "Whether to or not" is rapidly succumbing to a new effort to define the precise circumstances under which sexual relations are meaningful and honorable. Sex itself is rarely the main issue; instead, sex is increasingly ancillary to intimacy, understanding, communication, and mutual self-definition.

The academically committed student is therefore not a gay, frivolous, or abandoned person. His public life is regulated by the need to maintain his academic rank; his private life is an effort to discover or create some rationale for his public life; and his inner life is dominated by his attempt to create some synthesis of public and private selves. American students generally lack the levity, gaiety, wit, and whimsey that characterize their counterparts of equal academic attainment in universities abroad. Simply to acquire the necessary expertise requires great effort from all but the most brilliant; and to figure out why one is making this effort—to justify the struggle, to find something worth living for—takes the rest of the effort. There is less and less time just to have fun.

Part of the apparent desperation in this search for significance comes from ambivalence about parents and their lives. Despite their conviction that their future lives will resemble those of their parents (indeed, perhaps because of this conviction), pre-professional students are often filled with subtle unease about the world they grew up in. One reason for this is that rapid social change has widened the gap between the generations, making it more and more difficult for parents and children to understand each other. But, more important, parents often appear to their sons and daughters as frustrated and unfulfilled men and women. When students speak candidly about their mothers and fathers, they often show a surprising compassion and even pity. Despite the suburban split-level, two cars in the garage, and a respected position in the community, there is often something bleak, flat, empty, and barren about parents' lives as portrayed by their children. Some of this may be merely the perennial intolerance of youth for the staidness of middle age; and some often has to do with the idiosyncratic unhappinesses of individual parents. But much is related to the vast sameness of the American social landscape—the lack of excitement, beauty, intense feeling, high indignation, passion, or idealism in the lives of affluent American parents.

Furthermore, many American parents convey a subtly negative image of adult life and adult work to their offspring. A "Dad" whose happiest moments are those he shares with his wife and children, who frequently comments that he "feels really human" only on vacation, and who "lives for the weekend" is unwittingly engaging in social criticism, suggesting that work is something to be escaped from whenever possible. He indirectly tells his son that the work which will occupy most of his waking hours as an adult is merely a price he must pay for "really living" on weekends. Since many students already feel this about much of their academic work, it is understandable that progress to the final Commencement inspires uneasy jokes about the "rat race" beyond.

But this uneasiness does not lead most students to an overt rejection of their parents nor to an attack on middle-class professional values and outlooks. Despite their sense of distance from their parents, most students feel too much genuine sympathy for their plight to repudiate them or their world. Parents are seen as victims, not villains; and, when students dread long vacations at home, it is more often because they feel sorry for their parents than because they despise them. Furthermore, to repudiate what parents stand for would involve an ideological commitment of a sort students generically distrust. In any case, many students are not quite sure what their parents *do* stand for, such is the tentativeness and diffidence of American parents toward their children. Perhaps because the explicit values of parents have so often had to be compromised by the facts of American life, and certainly because of the fashionable distrust of ideology in modern America, most students are disinclined to grand ideas, global commitments, global repudiations, or blanket rejections of anything.

Yet the subtle disquiet is there, and it expresses itself in countless ways—in an often frantic search for meaning within the psyche, in fantasies that family, friendship, and leisure will provide all of life's meaning, in jokes about the "death" that lies beyond the last professional degree, and on the occasional winter morning when the student awakes to wonder what he is doing here, but forgets the question unanswered. A vague, inarticulate, formless discontent with the pattern of present and future life is common. But none of this means that the professionalist is in any general way opposed to American society. Indeed, his focus on *private* experience and *personal* commitment acts to divert discontent from the broader social scene. Even if the meaning of his studies and his ultimate profession is not clear, meaning can be sought in personal life. And the students who fails to find this meaning usually ends by blaming himself.

But the gap between public and private life is rarely completely closed. For the meaning found in privatism often fails to justify the public activities and plans of the student. The widespread use of the term "performance" reflects this dilemma, for a "performance" is enacted on a stage for the benefit of others, and it suggests playing an alien role that is detached from the real self. This same detachment between activity and self is suggested by many of the favorite expressions of college students—"come on like," "make like," "turn on," all of which suggest a tenuous connection between deed and inclination. And the laudatory epithet, "cool," indicates the same lack of emotional involvement in external surroundings and deeds. The problem is that the logical corollary of privatism is retirement from public life at the age of twenty, not continuing academic and professional exertion.

The student I have called the professionalist reflects many of the dilemmas of life in modern American society. Hard-working, earnest, diligent in his academic work, he is publicly committed to the acquisition of expertise in a university. But in his private search for meaning, he mirrors the problem of a society where expertise counts more than individuality, and where even the most talented may feel they are but replaceable cogs in a bureaucratic, academic, or industrial machine. Similarly, the solution of such students is the solution of most Americans: they turn their best energies away from the public world onto the private, manageable, controllable world of personal experience and individual expression. The intellectual style of such students—anti-ideological, pragmatic, empirical, and distrustful of doctrine—is, of course, the traditional style of America. And the inner tension of such students is the tension of American society itself, the problem of reconciling technological development with human fulfillment, the problem of individuality and meaning in an impersonal society.

Three Minority Views

Every generation has its innovators, its deviants, and its self-defined failures. The emergence of the professionalist has brought with it new types of student dissent, marginality, and misery. These students are not main-line professionalists, but neither are they the deviants and dissenters of earlier generations. Instead, they are those who have not been able to resolve so happily the fundamental tension of the professionalist, the schism between public performance and private meaning. All of them are in a sense professionalists *manqués*, and, although they constitute but a statistical minority of American students, it is these students who today make the headlines, dominate the popular image of the college generation, and help define students to themselves.

There are at least three new types of "deviant" students, who have appeared as recognizable groups only in the past decade or so. I shall call them the activist, the disaffiliate, and the under-achiever. The *activist* is the much-discussed student demonstrator, who protests against some segment of the university or society which seems in urgent need of reform. The *disaffiliate* is the nonpolitical but culturally alienated student who rejects totally the offerings and values of his society. The *under-achiever* is the student who accepts the values of the university and the society but, with them, his own inadequacy. Despite their important differences from the professionalist, each of these types shares the same dilemmas and many of the same characteristics.

In the late 1960's the student activist is primarily concerned with some specific issue.[22] He is emphatically not an ideologue; and herein lies the enormous difference between activism in the '60's and activism in the '30's. His commitment is not a commitment to a way of life or to a coherent set of political beliefs; rather it is "existential" in its emphasis on simple personal expressions of moral indignation. Camus and William Golding, rather than Marx or the novelist of social protest, are the spokesmen for such students. The particular issue in question is always one of apparent moral simplicity: civil rights, "free speech" on campus, the abolition of college paternalism, peace, the promotion of a devoted teacher. Moreover, the activist's initial commitment normally extends no further than a single cause. The student civil rights movement has, on the whole, steadfastly refused to take positions on other issues. The Free Speech Movement in Berkeley disbanded when the university grudgingly granted the legitimacy of its demands.

To student activists, demonstrations are usually precisely that— acts whose primary motive is to demonstrate and express where the student stands. The original impulse is to make a statement about one's convictions and one's indignation; instrumental activity follows primarily from this expression of indignation and is almost always limited to the achievement of relatively short-range objectives. To be sure, when "demonstrating" students meet strong opposition from a university administration or the "power structure," they are often forced to evolve organized plans for action. But these programs are usually *ad hoc*, short-range, pragmatic, and empirical. Once the technique of demonstration has been learned, of course, it can be used in other areas. Even more important, once the student begins to demonstrate his indignation over one issue, he may feel morally compelled to express his stand on other matters as well. Thus, students who protest campus policies or foreign policies are likely to have been "trained" in the civil rights movement. But what unites these demonstrations is not a coherent ideology of protest or reform, much less an organized political group, but a personal sense of ethical obligation to take a visible stand against injustice or oppression.

Compared to his classmates, the typical activist tends to be a better-than-average student, a committed and dedicated "intellectual," ethically or even religiously oriented, and a relatively well-balanced and well-liked person. He is rarely a "failure" in his own eyes or in the eyes of the college community. The better his grade average, the more likely that he will be involved in and/or support student activism; the less vocational his personal values, the greater his propensity for activism. Indifference and opposition to activism come primarily from students and colleges where the older success and popularity outlooks prevail. In contrast, humanists and social scientists at highly academic liberal-arts colleges and universities are those most disposed toward active expressions of dissent.

Despite much that has been written about the motivating role of student dissatisfaction with the impersonal "multiversity," few participants in campus demonstrations seem outstandingly dissatisfied with their academic experience. On the contrary, most of these better-than-average students probably find more stimulation in their academic work and closer relations with the faculty than do their nonactivist classmates. Nor is it really necessary to search for hidden motives and discontents to explain their activism: the goals of most campus demonstrations are understandable, specific, and often legitimate. Admittedly, some of the leaders of the Free Speech Movement, the Student Non-Violent Coordinating Committee, or Students for a Democratic Society occasionally issue indictments of the entire multiversity, the "power structure," or the "military-industrial complex." This handful of students of the "New Left" does have a vague ideology of dissent, based on writers like C. Wright Mills, Paul Goodman, and Michael Harrington. What Goodman calls "the Organized System" is clearly bad. But what is good, how to reform the multiversity, precisely what "far-reaching changes in the power structure" are needed—these are never made quite clear. In practice, even this small dissenting group usually spends more time and energy trying to build community organizations among Mississippi Negroes or tutoring slum children in Northern ghettos than in ideological debates.

The personal background of the rank-and-file activist is usually an ordinary, middle-class background. His activism is more often *premised* upon the liberal values of his parents and the credal values

337

of American society than *opposed* to them. Indeed, if there is any single psychological thread that runs through student activism today, it is this "identification with parental values." When parents and their activist offspring disagree, it is usually not over principle but over practice; and when these students criticize their parents, it is not for what their parents believe, but for their failure to practice the beliefs they drummed into their children's ears from an early age. Thus, "generational conflict" and "rebellion against parents" are gross oversimplifications as applied to these students: most of them get along moderately well with their parents, and most of their parents feel compelled—at least in principle—to support their children's activism. Overt conflict enters only because parents commonly feel that "discretion" might dictate a less active pursuit of the values they themselves taught their children.

There has been much misunderstanding of student activism, some of it originating with Mississippi sheriffs and Alabama mayors, some coming (less forgivably) from frightened college administrators. These students are not, with rare exceptions, Maoists or Castroites, professional rebels, beatniks, or hooligans. Nor do the self-disciplined nonviolent students in the civil rights movement in any way resemble the undisciplined student rowdies who periodically riot on resort beaches during spring vacation. Furthermore, student activists generally *are* students: the much-touted "non-students" involved usually turn out to be graduate students, plus a few students on leave of absence, ex-students, and students' wives. Whatever evidence is available—and increasing amounts are—consistently suggests that student activists are selectively drawn from among the most talented and committed students in the humanities and social sciences, that they are largely concentrated at the most academic colleges and universities, and that in most cases their professed public motives are quite adequate to explain their behavior. Perhaps the basic motive of such activists is their desire to make public their private convictions, indignations, and sense of moral outrage—and to change specific sectors of society so that they will no longer be so outrageous.

A second deviant response to the new academic climate is disaffiliation,[23] resentful withdrawal from American society, repudiation of conventional adulthood. Like activists, disaffiliates are often inconscient existentialists; but their existentialism is that of Heidegger, not Camus. Such students are too pessimistic and too firmly against the "system" to demonstrate their disaffiliation in any organized public way. Their demonstrations are private: these are the residual beatniks, the Bohemians, and the "LSD crowd" that exist on many American campuses. Often capable and imaginative, sensitive and hyper-aware, they usually manage to do passable academic work, though their hearts are in their alienation. Their real campus is the school of the absurd, and they have more affinity with existentialist ontology than with American pragmatism. When such students become involved (usually peripherally) in protest movements, their presence is disruptive, for they dislike accepting responsibility and care more about shocking authorities than about demonstrating where they stand or achieving specific reforms.

As people, disaffiliates tend to be disorganized. They generally lead unconventional lives, and are unwilling or unable to conform to conventional social expectations. In their personal lives, one sometimes finds considerable psychological disturbance; and they are vehemently at odds with the values of their parents, which are the values of conventional middle-class life. Their rejection of American society is based less upon personal idealism and outraged indignation than upon temperamental disaffinity for the requirements and rewards of American society—and for their fathers who epitomize this society to them.

On many campuses, disaffiliates constitute a kind of hidden underground into which especially disturbed, withdrawn, or creative students are drawn. Now that the bright lights of the "Beat Generation" have been dimmed by publicity and advancing age, disaffiliates increasingly turn to the "psychedelic" drugs—such as LSD, psilocybin, mescaline, and marijuana—in their search for intensification of experience. The promise of free passage through the doors of perception and the intense interpersonal cultism that surrounds the use of these drugs provide a provisional identity for many who cannot achieve one on the surface of campus life. The most striking feature of these cults is the virtually complete withdrawal of significance from public life—only intense, drug-assisted subjectivity is real; the rest is but role-playing. In this group, the schism between public and private is resolved by denying the reality of the public.

The third deviant type, the under-achiever, differs from the activist and disaffiliate in that he rejects himself rather than part or all of society. Such students often do poorly, drop out of college,[24] or see to it that they are thrown out by failing academically; but simple lack of intellectual ability will rarely suffice to explain their "failure." Indeed, excessive seriousness and desperate academic effort often block their academic success more than lack of intelligence does. They characteristically take the requirements of the academic system very earnestly; and, as a result, they find it impossible to take short-cuts, to manipulate and calculate for good grades, and to "work the system."

Of all American students, "under-achievers" find it most difficult to weld the connection between their own personal search for meaning and the continual academic pressures they face in their college lives. Often ambitious and intellectually mobile, they may be overwhelmed upon entering a college where most of their freshman class is culled, as they are, from the top 1 per cent of high-school graduates. If they do less than outstanding academic work, they begin to feel that they are failing—failing their parents, failing to live up to their potential, failing themselves. Once this feeling develops, its common consequences are depression, confusion, increasing but futile efforts to study harder, and a mounting sense of disaster which may eventually reach panic proportions. Many students who fit this type do not actually drop out of college; but, if they remain, they do so with a self-conforming suspicion that they are not so good as they had hoped, that they are not "really first-rate." They almost always blame themselves, not college or society; indeed, they generally lack enough critical detachment from the colleges they attend to be able to criticize them at all.

The background of the under-achiever, like that of the activist and the disaffiliate, tends to be staunchly middle-class. But in the under-achiever's personal history there is often especially great familial pressure to achieve, and strong parental emphasis on academic performance as an indicator not merely of intellectual competence but of moral and human worth. Far from rejecting these values, the under-achiever overaccepts them, using them as weapons against himself when his performance flags. He comes to feel that he is inadequate and intellectually incompetent, and that low grades are a sign of moral failure. Society merely confirms his self-deprecation by deeming under-achievement mistaken, cowardly, short-sighted, lazy, weak, and an insult to the national economy.

But under-achievement is often a motivated act, and, although self-deprecation and a sense of personal inadequacy predominate in consciousness, the same student is often engaged in a desperate unconscious maneuver to slough off standards of performance that remain unconnected with his private purposes. The under-achiever is thus often involved in an unconscious (and usually self-defeating) protest against parental, academic, and social pressures. When this is true, dropping out of college may be a useful act of self-assertion that allows a student to return (or not to return) on his own terms and for his own reasons. The unhappy under-achiever is, paradoxically, the student who most exaggerates the significance of the public values of intellectual achievement and is therefore unable to elaborate a valued autonomous private self. In this respect, he is the polar opposite of the disaffiliate.

In practice, of course, no individual student ever fits any type perfectly; nor are these types always clearly distinguishable from the main-line professionalist. Most professionalists, for example, at least *consider* dropping out of college; many identify with and occasionally join activists; and some are secretly fascinated by the cult of disaffiliation, perhaps to the extent of a puff of marijuana. Nor are these dissenting types always clearly distinguishable one from the other: the activist may harbor doubts about his own adequacy, and the disaffiliate is increasingly likely to become a fringe member of a protest group. Only as an oversimplification, perhaps justified as an effort to underline recurring themes and dilemmas among American students, can we speak of ideal types at all.

Students and the University

If these interpretations are correct, they suggest that the faces in the lecture room are the faces of a new generation, in many respects qualitatively different from previous student generations in America. The old faces are of course still there, scattered across the room: the gentlemen devoted to being gentlemen, the apprentices committed to making good, the Big Men on Campus who want to be popular. But increasingly they are outnumbered by serious, academically committed students who are headed for a career in the professions, and by their first cousins, the demonstrating activists, the withdrawn disaffiliates, and the self-deprecating under-achievers.

All of these new types have a great deal in common. All are non-ideological or anti-ideological; all oppose or despair about large-scale political and social planning; all distrust "politicians" and dogmatists in societal matters. Furthermore, all are essentially privatistic: they start not from a desire to reform society nor from a blueprint for the future, but from a personal or existential statement; the activist emphasizes personal demonstration, the disaffiliate emphasizes personal withdrawal, and the under-achiever emphasizes personal blame. Paradoxically, for a generation whose most publicized members are often termed "social activists," the broader social scene rarely exists as a clearly defined or sharply articulated entity. Instead, its significant existence is denied altogether by the disaffiliate, globally and unselectively overaccepted by the underachiever, forgotten by the typical activist's emphasis on a "single issue," or blurred by a few activist leaders in vague indictments of "the Organized System."

The absence of a differentiated picture of American society, coupled with a lack of overriding ideology, is important in appraising the future of American students. For without a clear specification of what is good and what is bad about American society, coupled with a coherent ideology of social reform, few individuals can sustain for long the mishaps and disappointments that inevitably plague anyone who seeks to improve society. The motive of "personal demonstration" by itself is not likely to endure: two hours a week in a slum area, two months in Mississippi during the summer, or two years in Afghanistan with the Peace Corps may serve to dissipate rather than confirm the student's "activism." Once he has demonstrated where he stands, there is little need for further involvement: the demonstration has been made, idealistic impulses have been exhausted, and he can resume his course up the academic stepladder, putting aside all thoughts of social reform in the interests of a Ph.D., a professional job, and a rich full life.

The "expressive" and anti-ideological outlook of students today suggests that those who anticipate a coming generation of adults committed to social reform are mistaken. Peace Corps graduates generally return from two years of working with deprived nations to enter graduate and professional schools where they give little thought to their own deprived status as graduate students, much less to the greater deprivations of other Americans. To be sure, a few dedicated workers in the civil rights movement, largely Negro students, have made a commitment to reform that extends far beyond a few months' work in the field. But, in general, there seems little need to worry (or rejoice) that students are becoming so involved in "causes" that they will neglect their studies or turn against their society. One socialist onlooker at the Berkeley demonstrations put it this way: "Ten years from now most of them will be rising in the world and in income, living in the suburbs from Terra Linda to Atherton, raising two or three babies, voting Democratic, and wondering what on earth they were doing in Sproul Hall—trying to remember, and failing."[25]

In the end, the vast majority of American students remains privatistic. Even for the student activist, the main tension is not the effort to realize a vision of social reform, but the tension between his private search for meaning and his public activities. To attribute this tension solely to the bureaucratization, impersonality, and bigness of the university is an oversimplification and an evasion, for the university only reflects the characteristics of American society. The divorce of public from private reflects all too faithfully the demands of a society that expects of its responsible citizens extraordinary objectivity, impersonality, competence, control, and cognitive efficiency and leaves little room in public life for private commitment, idealism, passion, zeal, indignation, and feeling. What matters to most students is not that they do not know their professors, but that they find it hard to integrate their private search for meaning with their public quest for professional competence. Even the activist, who temporarily links the two spheres of life, usually lapses back to privatism once his final examinations near—few student demonstrations take place at the end of the semester.

Yet it would seem that one of the functions of the liberal-arts college and of the university might be to help mend this schism by providing an education and an environment that encourages students to gather intellect, ethical sense, and action into one related whole. And it would also seem that graduate and professional education might assist the pre-professional to weld close connections between his inner self and the vocation that will occupy his life for the next fifty years. But this too rarely happens. Each university is a part of the educational system, and the most determined effort of any one university cannot cancel the fact that another admissions committee usually lies around the corner. Grades or no grades, tutorial or teaching by television, the student knows what graduate schools expect, and he may feel driven anyway. It takes extraordinary efforts to reduce the pressure to perform.

One reason so few universities even try, I think, is a too narrow interpretation of the functions of American universities. Everyone grants that education should ultimately serve the community, but it is widely thought that this obligation is fully discharged by producing millions of well-trained, technically competent, and professionally skilled young men and women to man the American economy. But another even more important need of American society is for men and women with a capacity for critical detachment from their communities, a sense of ethics above traditional piety, a capacity to articulate new goals, and a sustained determination to

343

work toward the realization of these goals. These qualities differ from professional skills in that a university cannot guarantee them, but can only provide a setting where they may flourish. Moreover, their development requires time, freedom from external pressure, the chance to make mistakes, and the opportunity to experiment— none of which is readily available on most American campuses. And, perhaps crucial, these qualities are controversial, impolitic, and unpopular with many state legislators and boards of trustees.

Yet there are hopeful signs. This student generation probably has a greater potential for informed detachment, a high sense of ethics, articulateness, and determination than any before it. Today's students have been exposed to ideas from kindergarten onward with an intensity that has no American precursor. Their minds are well trained; they are well informed; they deal easily with both the abstract and the concrete. They are less plagued than any previous generation by status anxiety and the dread of poverty. Most important, they are eager to find some way of reconciling their private lives with their academic activities. And some few succeed. A few activists find in social service and action an enduring and informed commitment that will not easily be dissipated. Even the voluntary dropout may be creating a new way to escape the pressures of academic routine for long enough to connect education to his life. And there are, I think, increasing numbers of students who are led so often to the trough of knowledge that they finally stay to drink— not merely for the sake of an admissions committee, but because of the heady taste of enlightenment. Once real connections between disciplined intellect, inner self, and outer activity are made, the result will likely be a determination to retain these connections throughout the rest of life. Despite the pressures of American higher education, individual students are often able to marry the parts of their lives into a lasting union.

Nor is the institutional picture completely bleak. For any system that can expose so many students so intensively to so many ideas has great potential—even though it may be dismayed when students want their universities and their society to practice ideas they teach. Furthermore, there are dozens of colleges across America that push their students not merely to perform well on examinations, but to think independently, to connect intellect with the rest of life. Such colleges—some ancient and famous, others recent and unknown— can help provide students with a respite from pressure, a chance to experiment, grow, and connect what they learn with their future

344

lives. Some few professional schools, too, contribute to real enlighten-ment even while they teach professional skills. By admitting the genuinely inquiring, by encouraging intellectual curiosity, diversity, innovation, and speculation, they create an atmosphere in which their students can link their personal goals to their professional careers. To be sure, all of this runs against the main academic tide, and it still happens rarely. But it suggests that American universities could easily do more than provide professional man-power for the economy.

In essence, I am arguing that American colleges too often simply mirror the pressures and human schisms of American society. We need to ask whether a major goal of a great university should not be to provide a countervailing center to the immediate trends of society. We need to recognize that all human development is discontinuous and that one prime function of the university is to provide for its students a moratorium from adult pressures, rather than a caricature of them. Perhaps our society's greatest long-range need is not for more skilled engineers, lawyers, scientists, and physicians, but for more whole and integrated men and women who can bring educated minds to both personal and public life. Perhaps the university serves both society and its students best when it serves neither directly, but attempts to create a friendly culture for the growth of critical intelligence, the joining of reason and action, and that detachment from the daily pressures of society which has always characterized educated men. If so, and if American universities can move toward these goals, they will find today's students more ready and able to follow them than any previous generation.

REFERENCES

1. Nevitt Sanford (ed.), *The American College* (New York: John Wiley, 1962). This work (henceforth referred to as *TAC*) provides the most use-ful introduction to and review of studies of students and colleges.

2. See T. M. Newcomb's ground-breaking study of Bennington: *Personality and Social Change: Attitude Formation in a Student Community* (New York: Dryden, 1943), and N. Sanford *et al.'s* studies of Vassar, reported in *TAC* and *Journal of Social Issues*, Vol. 12 (1956).

3. P. W. Jacob, *Changing Values in College* (New York: Harper, 1957). For critical reviews of the Jacob report see A. Barton, *College Education* (New Haven, Conn.: Hazen Foundation, 1959) and D. Riesman, *American Sociological Review*, Vol. 23 (1958), pp. 732–739.

4. Several studies concerned with the relationship of input and output in American colleges and universities conclude that the greatest part of a college's "productivity" (as measured by Ph.D.'s, distinguished scientists, and so forth) is a function of the caliber of its incoming freshmen. But the correlation is far from perfect. See T. R. McConnell and P. Heist, "The Diverse College Student Population," in *TAC*, especially p. 228.

5. For a discussion of the variety of talents present in American colleges and universities, see McConnell and Heist, *op. cit.*

6. See George S. Stern, "Environments for Learning," in *TAC*, for studies that discuss the degree of "match" between institution and student. Stern reports, for example, that although "academic" liberal arts recruit the most "academic" undergraduates, they are still far ahead of their undergraduates in their academic demands, producing a greater disparity between student needs and what Stern calls environmental "press" than is found at less academic colleges. This may explain the common observation that students change most at private and academic liberal-arts colleges.

7. See Stern, *op. cit.*, for a preliminary taxonomy of educational environments and student body characteristics. In general, Stern's work is the most promising existing approach to the development of systematic techniques for describing and comparing college environments and student bodies, and for studying the "match" between them. Many of my observations are influenced by Stern's preliminary findings.

8. Rejection rates at many selective colleges are already more than five to one, and promise to reach ten to one within the next decade. Even allowing for multiple applications, many students are rejected by all of their "first choices."

9. Similarly, the mass presence of academically committed students at paternalistic institutions may explain growing student impatience with restrictive regulations and a college definition of its role as *in loco parentis*. Stern, in "The Book on Bardot's Bottom" (mimeo, 1965), finds that entering freshmen at a great variety of colleges *expect* their colleges to be strongholds of academic freedom, but that graduating seniors at many colleges have become disillusioned in this regard. Again, the gap between student expectations, potentials, and needs, on the one hand, and the "realities" of college life, on the other, is crucial in understanding student disaffection.

10. See David Riesman and Christopher Jencks, "Patterns of Residential Education: A Case Study of Harvard," in *TAC*, for a suggestive analysis of how students select themselves and are selected for residential houses within one college. See also E. Douvan and C. Kaye, "Motivational Factors in College Entrance," in *TAC*.

11. See reference 2.

12. In studies of Vassar alumnae, the characteristic style and outlook of women as undergraduates was an excellent predictor of their later life-patterns. But it is virtually impossible to disentangle the effects of increasing age from

the effects of real generational differences in such studies. See M. B. Freedman, "Studies of College Alumni," in *TAC*.

13. See J. M. Gillespie and G. W. Allport, *Youth's Outlook on the Future* (New York: Doubleday, 1955), for a study of national differences among pre-college students. See also D. H. Funkenstein (ed.), *The Student and Mental Health. An International View* (World Federation of Mental Health, 1959), for other cross-cultural perspectives.

14. See, for example, the March 22, 1965 *Newsweek* poll, "Campus '65."

15. See B. M. Wedge, *et al.*, "Spontaneous Neurotic Clique Formation in University Students," *Psychiatric Quarterly Supplement*, Vol. 25 (1951), p. 191. On the general psychiatric problems of college students, see D. L. Farnsworth, *Mental Health in College and University* (Cambridge, Mass.: Harvard University Press, 1957); B. M. Wedge (ed.), *Psychosocial Problems of College Men* (New Haven, Conn.: Yale University Press, 1958); G. B. Blaine, Jr., and C. C. McArthur, *Emotional Problems of the Student* (New York: Appleton-Century-Crofts, 1961); *The College Experience. A Focus for Psychiatric Research*, Report No. 52, Group for the Advancement of Psychiatry, 1962.

16. Among the principal on-going studies are those of the Center for the Study of Higher Education at Berkeley, the Harvard Student Study, the Center for the Study of Human Problems at Stanford, and the comparative studies by George Stern at Syracuse.

17. There are two studies of medical students: H. S. Becker, *et al.*, *Boys in White* (Chicago: Chicago University Press, 1961), and R. K. Merton, *et al.*, *The Student-Physician* (Cambridge, Mass.: Harvard University Press, 1957). See also H. I. Lief and R. Fox, "Training for Detached Concern in Medical Students," in H. I. Lief, *et al.*, *The Psychological Basis of Medical Practice* (New York: Hoeber, 1963). But, in general, studies of how students are recruited, selected and affected by graduate and professional schools are rare.

18. Some of my observations are based on research supported by NIMH Grants M-1287 and MH-0850801. For two earlier accounts, see my "Youth and Social Change in America," in E. H. Erikson (ed.), *The Challenge of Youth* (New York: Anchor, 1965) and "American Students and the 'Political Revival,'" *The American Scholar*, Vol. 32 (1962), pp. 40–64. Donald N. Michael, *The Next Generation* (New York: Random House, 1963), especially Ch. 12 ("Values and Viewpoints"), provides an excellent analysis of the future of today's students. Stanley King's distinction between "traditional" and "emergent" types of students at Harvard has been useful in this portrait of the professionalist.

19. At colleges with five or more candidates for every available place, the typical admissions procedure is to eliminate at least half of the applicants on the basis of "low" intelligence test scores and "poor" secondary-school performance; thus, only if both are outstanding will other personal characteristics enter into the admissions judgment. In graduate departments and

professional schools where the ratio of rejections to acceptances is often more than ten to one, applicants are weeded out even more ruthlessly on the basis of college grades.

20. S. J. Korchin and G. E. Ruff, "Personality Characteristics of the Mercury Astronauts," in G. H. Grosser, *et al., The Threat of Impending Disaster* (Cambridge, Mass.: M.I.T. Press, 1964), pp. 203–204.

21. See the cited *Newsweek* poll. Asked how they felt they had let their parents down, 28 per cent of the respondents said by doing poorly in their studies, and 25 per cent by not working to potential.

22. There are already a number of excellent studies of student activists. See, for example, Howard Zinn, *SNCC, The New Abolitionists* (Boston: Beacon, 1965); John Ehle, *The Free Men* (New York: Harper and Row, 1965); Robert Coles, "Serpents and Doves: Non-violent Youth in the South," in Erikson, *op. cit.*; the 1964 issue of *Journal of Social Issues* on "Youth and Social Action." Three books have recently appeared about the Berkeley demonstrations in 1964: Hal Draper, *Berkeley: The New Student Revolt* (New York: Grove [Evergreen Black Cat], 1965), M. V. Miller and S. Gilmore (eds.), *Revolution at Berkeley* (New York: Dell, 1965) and S. M. Lipset and S. F. Wolin (eds.), *The Berkeley Student Revolt. Facts and Interpretations* (Garden City, N. Y.: Anchor, 1965). Several empirical studies support the general picture of activists I have drawn here. See R. H. Somers, "The Mainsprings of the Rebellion: A Survey of Berkeley Students in November 1964," in Lipset and Wolin, *op. cit.* Unpublished research by the Center for the Study of Higher Education at Berkeley suggests that activist students are concentrated not only among the most academic students, but at the most academic colleges. Donald Gastwirth, "Why Students Protest" (unpublished paper, 1965), independently arrived at a similar portrait of the leaders of the Yale demonstrations in the spring of 1965. Far from being anti-intellectual, activists are selectively drawn from the most intellectual groups on the most intellectual campuses. Virtually all studies also agree on the non-ideological outlook of most such students.

23. There is a large journalistic literature on disaffiliated students who were drawn into the "beat generation" in the late 1950's. See also F. J. Rigney and L. D. Smith, *The New Bohemia* (New York: Basic Books, 1961), and Lawrence Lipton, *The Holy Barbarians* (New York: Messner, 1959), for portraits of disaffected subcultures. K. Keniston, *The Uncommitted* (New York: Harcourt, Brace and World, 1965), deals explicitly with a group of disaffiliated college students.

24. On college dropouts (not all of whom are under-achievers) see J. Summerskill, "Drop-outs from College," in *TAC* and L. A. Pervin, *et al.* (eds.), *The College Drop-out and the Utilization of Talent* (Princeton, N. J., Princeton University Press, in press). One study done at Yale suggests that voluntary dropping out is an alternative to overt disaffiliation and disaffection with the college, rather than a direct expression of it. For a study of women under-achievers who were not concerned about their lack of aca-

demic performance because of their "future family orientation," see D. R. Brown, "Personality, College Environment, and Academic Productivity," in *TAC*, especially pp. 548 ff. Dean K. Whitla's studies of Harvard alumni suggest that, for men, mediocre academic standing has greater effects on self-esteem.

25. Draper, *op. cit.*, p. 169.

NOTES ON CONTRIBUTORS

DOUGLAS BUSH, born in 1896 in Morrisburg, Ontario, is Gurney Professor of English Literature at Harvard University. His extensive bibliography includes *The Renaissance and English Humanism* (1939), *English Literature in the Earlier Seventeenth Century* (Oxford History of English Literature, 1945), *Science and English Poetry . . . 1590–1950* (1950), and *Milton* (1963). The recipient of one of the first ten A.C.L.S. awards in the humanities, he is a member of the American Philosophical Society and a Fellow of the British Academy.

WILLIAM C. DEVANE, born in Savannah, Georgia, in 1898, died in 1965. He was Dean Emeritus of Yale College, where he was also Sanford Professor of English Literature. His publications include *Browning's Parleyings* (1927), *A Browning Handbook* (1935), *Tennyson* (1940), and *American Universities in the 20th Century* (1958). He was a trustee of Wells College and the Greenwood Fund and an advisor to the J. H. Whitney Foundation and to the Old Dominion Foundation.

DAVID M. GORDON, born in 1944 in Washington, D.C., is presently Research Assistant at Harvard University, where he is helping with the planning of the prospective Kennedy Institute of Politics. A former editor of the *Harvard Crimson*, he edited the issue of the *Harvard Review* on "Undergraduate Education" (Spring 1965) and was a founding member of and reporter for *The Southern Courier*, a weekly civil rights newspaper started in Alabama in 1965.

JOSEPH GUSFIELD, born in 1923 in Chicago, Illinois, is Professor of Sociology in the Department of Sociology and the Institute of Labor and Industrial Relations at the University of Illinois. His publications include *Symbolic Crusade: Status Politics and the American Temperance Movement* (1965) as well as studies on social movements, occupations, higher education, and Indian society which have appeared in academic journals.

FREDERIC HEIMBERGER, born in 1899 in Columbus, Ohio, is Dean of Faculties Emeritus and Professor of Political Science Emeritus at Ohio

State University. His services to his university include a term as President of the Ohio State University Research Foundation, 1957–1962. He has also been a member of the Board of Visitors, Air University, USAF, 1955–57, and of the Committee on Institutional Cooperation of the Big Ten and University of Chicago, 1960–1964.

KENNETH KENISTON, born in 1930 in Chicago, Illinois, is Assistant Professor of Psychology at the Yale Medical School of Yale University. His publications include *The Uncommitted. Alienated Youth in American Society* (1965) and articles in *The American Scholar, The Journal of Social Abnormal Psychology, Contemporary Psychology, Commentary,* and other professional and scholarly journals.

CLARK KERR, born in 1911 in Stony Creek, Pennsylvania, is President of the University of California. He moved to the West Coast in 1937, where, with the exception of service with the War Labor Board during World War II, his career has been based ever since. Economist, arbiter of labor disputes, educator, he joined the faculty of the University of California at Berkeley in 1945 and later served as Chancellor.

W. McNEIL LOWRY, born in 1913 in Columbus, Kansas, is Vice President of the Ford Foundation. He was the first Director of the Program in the Humanities and the Arts, which was initiated in 1957, and, since that time, his responsibilities have ranged widely across many activities in the creative and performing arts.

MARTIN MEYERSON, born in 1922 in New York City, is Dean of the College of Environmental Design at the University of California, Berkeley. He was Acting Chancellor of that campus in 1965 following the student protests there. Before going to Berkeley, he was Williams Professor of City Planning and Urban Research at Harvard University and Director of the Joint Center for Urban Studies of M.I.T. and Harvard. He is co-author of *Politics, Planning and the Public Interest* (1955), *Housing, People and Cities* (1962), *Face of the Metropolis* (1963), and *Boston: The Job Ahead* (1966). He is an advisor on urban affairs to the U.N. and to governments and private organizations in this country and abroad.

ROBERT S. MORISON, born in 1906 in Milwaukee, Wisconsin, is Director of the Division of Biological Sciences at Cornell University. Before going to Cornell, he was Director of Medical and Natural Sciences at the Rockefeller Foundation. In 1964 he published a book entitled *Scientist,* which is intended to help teenagers in search of a career. His special interests are neurophysiology and the advancement of scientific education and research, particularly in the underdeveloped countries. He is a trustee of Reed and Bennington Colleges and is a member of the National Science Board.

STEPHEN ORGEL, born in 1933 in New York City, is Assistant Professor of English at the University of California, Berkeley. His publications include *The Jonsonian Masque* (1965) and assorted studies on Shakespeare and Renaissance literature. Before going to Berkeley, he was an instructor at Harvard University.

DAVID RIESMAN, born in 1909 in Philadelphia, is Henry Ford II Professor of the Social Sciences at Harvard University. His extensive publications include *The Lonely Crowd* (1950), *Faces in the Crowd* (1952), *Thorstein Veblen* (1953), *Individualism Reconsidered* (1954), *Constraint and Variety in American Education* (1956), and *Abundance for What?* (1963). He is currently concerned with the study of higher education in America.

W. ALLEN WALLIS, born in 1912 in Philadelphia, is both President of the University of Rochester and Professor of Economics and Statistics in that institution. With Harry V. Roberts, he is the author of *Statistics: A New Approach* (1956) and *The Nature of Statistics* (1962). He is chairman of the editorial advisory board of the *New Encyclopedia of the Social Sciences* and has contributed numerous articles to various professional journals.

PAUL A. WEISS, born in 1898 in Vienna, is Dean of the Graduate School of Biomedical Sciences at the University of Texas. For the preceding ten years he was associated with the Rockefeller Institute, as member, professor, and head of its Department of Developmental Biology. His scientific work is published in three books and over two hundred original papers.

JEROME M. ZIEGLER, born in 1923 in New York City, is Central Director of the Rodman Job Corps. He was formerly Associate Director of the Chicago School Survey and President of Jerome Ziegler Associates, an educational consulting firm. While serving as President of the American Foundation for Continuing Education (1956–1962), he was concerned with establishing adult discussion seminars in economics, international affairs, the arts and sciences, and politics.

ALEX ZWERDLING, born in 1932 in Germany, is Assistant Professor of English at the University of California, Berkeley. His publications include *Yeats and the Heroic Ideal* (1965) and articles on nineteenth- and twentieth-century English literature. He was a fellow of the Center for Advanced Study in the Behavior Sciences and A.C.L.S. Study Fellow, 1964–65, and taught at Swarthmore College from 1957 to 1961.

INDEX

INDEX

Index

Index

Index

Index

Scholarly method, 190
Scholars, 110–129
Scholarship, climate for, 224
Scholarship aid, 270
Scholarships, 4, 34
  literary, 190–191
School integration, 28
Science development program, 34
Sciences:
  academic department, 42
  creativity in, 26
  and curriculum, 10
  defined, 155–157
  functions of, 196
  harmonious growth of, 183
  and humanities, fundamental differences, 199
  and nature of man, 197
  nonmoral nature, 202
  role of, in education, 158
  in the university, 152–185
Scientific studies, developing, 2
Scientific thinking, 3
Scientific training, 157
Scientific worker, 175
Scientist, creative, 103
  defined, 154
Seaborg Report, 33
Selective Service, drafting by, 294
Separation, 308
Sex behavior, study of, aid from foundations, 100, 101
  research in, 95
Sexes, relations between, 332
Significance, search for, 333
Smithson, James, 78
Snow, Charles Percy (Lord Snow of Leicester), 23, 39, 153, 157, 198
Social activist, 342
Social activities, 284
Social research, 119
  financing, 126
Social Science Research Council, 97
Social sciences:
  aid from foundations, 99–100
  developing, 3
  federal aid to, 34
  functions of, 196
  growth, 126
  and humanities, 188
  project selection, 100–101
  research centers, 112, 115–121
Society:
  involvement in life of, 27–30
  involvement and rejection, 312

Society cont'd
  pressures of, 344–345
  and university, 29
Southern states, aid to, 79, 84
Soviet Union, education in, 4
Special degree programs, 141
Specialization, 10, 39, 159–160, 317
  academic, 297–298
State universities, 17, 51–76
  academic freedom, 71
  agricultural and mechanical, 58
  aid to, 55
  as centers of power, 72–73
  curriculum, 57
  enrollment, 53
  expansion, 54
  expression, freedom of, 72
  financial support, 60–61
  growing body, 72–73
  interstate cooperation, 64
  legislature and, 57, 70–76
  legislature, freedom of, 72
  legislature, interference from, 71
  nonresidents, 63
  problems confronting, 56
  realignment, 54
  research programs, 59
  size and numbers, 66
  standards and goals, 57
  stature of, 53
  strength, 55
  student population, 52
  teaching in, 69
  tuition, 63
Status, dilution of, 271
Stevens, Roger L., 208
Student activities, 303
Student associations, 67
Student bodies, 318
Student development, 320
  research in, 316–317
Student-faculty relationships, 288
Student government, 281–283
Student lounges, 285
Student Non-Violent Coordinating Committee, 337
Student population, growth of, 52
  heterogeneity, 269
Students, 315–345
  academically committed, 332–333
  acquaintances, influence of, 309
  anti-administration feeling, 279
  anti-ideological outlook, 342
  attention to, from teacher, 282–284

362

Index